Spreading Protest

Social Movements in Times of Crisis

Edited by
Donatella della Porta and Alice Mattoni

© D. della Porta and A. Mattoni 2014

© Cover image www.occupythegame.com

First published by the ECPR Press in 2014
Paperback edition published 2015

The ECPR Press is the publishing imprint of the European Consortium for Political Research (ECPR), a scholarly association, which supports and encourages the training, research and cross-national cooperation of political scientists in institutions throughout Europe and beyond.

ECPR Press
University of Essex
Wivenhoe Park
Colchester
CO4 3SQ
UK

All rights reserved. No part of this book may be reprinted or reproduced or utilised in any form or by any electronic, mechanical, or other means, now known or hereafter invented, including photocopying and recording, or in any information storage or retrieval system, without permission in writing from the publishers.

Typeset by ECPR Press

Printed and bound by Lightning Source

British Library Cataloguing in Publication Data

A catalogue record for this book is available from the British Library

Hardback ISBN: 978-1-910259-20-7
Paperback ISBN 978-1785521-63-8
PDF ISBN: 978-1-910259-23-8
Kindle ISBN: 978-1-785520-40-2
EPUB ISBN: 978-1-785520-39-6

www.ecpr.eu/ecprpress

Series Editors:
Dario Castiglione (University of Exeter)
Peter Kennealy (European University Institute)
Alexandra Segerberg (Stockholm University)
Peter Triantafillou (Roskilde University)

ECPR – *Studies in European Political Science* is a series of high-quality edited volumes on topics at the cutting edge of current political science and political thought. All volumes are research-based offering new perspectives in the study of politics with contributions from leading scholars working in the relevant fields. Most of the volumes originate from ECPR events including the Joint Sessions of Workshops, the Research Sessions, and the General Conferences.
Books in this series:

A Political Sociology of Transnational Europe
ISBN: 9781907301346
Edited by Niilo Kauppi

Between Election Democracy
ISBN: 9781907301988
Edited by Hanne Marthe Narud and Peter Esaiasson

Deliberative Mini-Publics: Involving Citizens in the Democratic Process
ISBN: 9781907301322
Edited by Kimmo Grönlund, André Bächtiger and Maija Setälä

Europeanisation and Party Politics
ISBN: 9781907301223
Edited by Erol Külahci

Great Expectations, Slow Transformations: Incremental Change in Post-Crisis Regulation
ISBN: 9781907301544
Edited by Manuela Moschella and Eleni Tsingou

Growing into Politics
ISBN: 9781907301421
Edited by Simone Abendschön

Interactive Policy Making, Metagovernance and Democracy
ISBN: 9781907301131
Edited by Jacob Torfing and Peter Triantafillou

Matching Voters with Parties and Candidates: Voting Advice Applications in a Comparative Perspective
ISBN: 9781907301735
Edited by Diego Garzia and Stefan Marschall

New Nation States
ISBN: 9781907301360
Edited by Julien Danero Iglesias, Nenad Stojanović and Sharon Weinblum

Perceptions of Europe
ISBN: 9781907301155
Edited by Daniel Gaxie, Jay Rowell and Nicolas Hubé

Personal Representation: The Neglected Dimension of Electoral Systems
ISBN: 9781907301162
Edited by Josep Colomer

Political Participation in France and Germany
ISBN: 9781907301315
Oscar Gabriel, Silke Keil, and Eric Kerrouche

Political Trust: Why Context Matters
ISBN: 9781907301230
Edited by Sonja Zmerli and Marc Hooghe

Practices of Interparliamentary Coordination in International Politics: The European Union and Beyond
ISBN: 9781907301308
Edited by Ben Crum and John Erik Fossum

The Political Ecology of the Metropolis
ISBN: 9781907301377
Edited by Jefferey M Sellers, Daniel Kübler, R. Alan Walks and Melanie Walter-Rogg

Please visit www.ecpr.eu/ecprpress for up-to-date information about new publications.

Contents

List of Figures and Tables vii

List of Abbreviations ix

Contributors xi

Preface and Acknowledgements xvii

Part I – What Spread?

Chapter One: Patterns of Diffusion and the Transnational Dimension of Protest in the Movements of the Crisis: An Introduction 1
Donatella della Porta and Alice Mattoni

Chapter Two: Transnational Diffusion Across Time: The Adoption of the Argentinian Dirty War '*Escrache*' in the Context of Spain's Housing Crisis 19
Cristina Flesher Fominaya and Antonio Montañés Jimenéz

Chapter Three: Learning Democracy: Cross-Time Adaptation in Organisational Repertoires 43

Donatella della Porta

Chapter Four: Dramatic Diffusion and Meaning Adaptation: The Case of Neda 71
Thomas Olesen

Chapter Five: From Event to Process: The EU and the 'Arab Spring' 91
Ari-Elmeri Hyvönen

Part II – How Did It Spread?

Chapter Six: They Don't Represent Us! The Global Resonance of the Real Democracy Movement from the Indignados to Occupy 117
Jérôme E. Roos and Leonidas Oikonomakis

Chapter Seven: The Transnational Dimension of the Greek Protest Campaign Against Troika Memoranda and Austerity Policies, 2010–2012   137
Maria Kousis

Chapter Eight: Occupy London in International and Local Context   171
Nikos Sotirakopoulos and Christopher Rootes

Part III – Why Did it Spread?

Chapter Nine: Breaks and Continuities in and Between Cycles of Protest: Memories and Legacies of the Global Justice Movement in the Context of Anti-Austerity Mobilisations   193
Lorenzo Zamponi and Priska Daphi

Chapter Ten: Towards a 'Non-Global Justice Movement'? Two Paths to Re-Scaling the Left Contention in the Czech Republic   227
Jiří Navrátil and Ondřej Císař

Chapter Eleven: Flap of the Butterfly: Turkey's June Uprisings   253
Kivanc Atak

Chapter Twelve: Adapting Theories on Diffusion and Transnational Contention Through Social Movements of the Crisis: Some Concluding Remarks   277
Alice Mattoni and Donatella della Porta

Index   293

List of Figures and Tables

Figures

Figure 4.1: Dramatic cross-border diffusion and global injustice-symbol formation — 75

Figure 7.1: Total number of major protest actions and related bailout and austerity packages, Jan. 2010–Dec. 2012 — 148

Figure 7.2: Highest number of participants in main protest actions, Jan. 2010–Dec. 2012 — 151

Figure 7.3: Target groups mentioned in LPEs, Jan. 2010– Dec. 2012 — 152

Figure 7.4: Vote of the People's Assembly of Syntagma Square, 27 May — 153

Figure 7.5: Major participating groups in LPEs, Jan. 2010–Dec. 2012 — 154

Figure 7.6: Major action forms of the 32 LPEs, Jan. 2010–Jan. 2013 — 156

Figure 7.7: Total number of violent actions, number of injured protesters and number of arrests, Jan. 2010–Dec. 2012 — 157

Figure 7.8: Number of non-Greek cities participating in the 32 LPEs, Jan. 2010–Jan. 2013 — 158

Figure 10.1: Dynamics of issue and frame scales — 233

Figure 10.2: Dynamics of issue and frame scales of Czech left movements (1990–2000) — 237

Figure 10.3: Frequency of protest events by Czech radical and moderate left actors — 239

Figure 10.4: Average protest event participation — 239

Figure 10.5: Evolution of key protest issues of the radical left — 241

Figure 10.6: Evolution of key protest issues of the moderate left — 241

Figure 10.7: Evolution of the issue scale of protest events organised by the radical left — 244

Figure 10.8: Evolution of framing scale of protest events organised by the radical left — 244

Figure 10.9: Evolution of the issue scale of protest events organised by the moderate left — 246

Figure 10.10: Evolution of the framing of protest events organised by the moderate left (2000–2010, N=394) — 246

Figure 10.11: Dynamics of issue and frame scales of Czech left movements during financial crisis — 249

Figure 11.1: Temporal distribution of web searches from Turkey, using Google Trends — 271

See http://press.ecpr.eu/resources.asp for full colour figures.

Tables

Table 3.1: Dimensions of democracy: from forums to camps — 49

Table 7.1: Transnational events linked to the Greek anti-austerity campaign, Jan. 2010–Jan. 2013 — 160

Table 7.2: Names of non-Greek cities mentioned as participating in the transnational events — 161

Table 12.1: Transnational channels of diffusion — 281

Table 12.2: Paths of diffusion in the two waves of global protests — 286

List of Abbreviations

15M	15 May 2011 Protest Movement in Spain
BBC	British Broadcasting Service
CMCTU	Czech-Moravian Confederation of Trade Unions
CNA	Czech News Agency
CNN	Time Warner Transnational Media Agency
CNT	Confederación Nacional del Trabajo (National Confederation of Labour)
CONADEE	National Coordination of Ecuadorians in Spain
DG	Directorate Generale
DRY	Democracia Real YA! (Real Democracy Now)
ECB	European Central Bank
ECOFIN	Economic and Financial Affairs Council of the EU
ENP	European Neighborhood Policy
ETUC	European Trade Union Confederation
EU	European Union
EUROGROUP	Forum Of Finance Ministers of Eurozone Countries
EZLN	Zapatista Army of National Liberation
FIOM	Italian Metal-Workers Federation
G20	Group of 20 Finance Ministers and Central Bank Governors of Major Economies
G8	Group of 8 Leaders of Canada, France, Germany, Italy, Japan, Russia, The UK and the USA
GDP	Gross Domestic Product
GJM	Global Justice Movement
H.I.J.O.S.	Hijos e Hijas por la Identidad y la Justicia contra el Olvido y el Silencio (Sons and Daughters for Identity and Justice against Forgetting and Silence)
ICT	Information and Communications Technology
ICFTU	International Confederation of Free Trade Unions
ILP	Iniciativa Legislativa Popular (Popular Legislative Initiative)
IMF	International Monetary Fund
IR	International Relations
IT	Information Technology
LGBT	Lesbian, Gay, Bisexual and Transgender
LPE	Large Protest Event
LPM	Free-Pass Movement

M12M	Movimento 12 De Março De 2011 in Portugal
M15M	Movimento 15 Mayo 2011 in Spain
M15O	October 15 May 2011 in Portugal
MENA	Middle East and North Africa
MP	Members of Parliament
NAFTA	North American Free Trade Agreement
NATO	North Atlantic Treaty Organization
NGO	Non-Governmental Organization
NYGA	New York General Assembly
OECD	Organisation for Economic Co-Operation and Development
OWS	Occupy Wall Street
PAH	Platform For Those Affected By Mortgages/Platform Of Mortgage Victims
PEA	Protest Event Analysis
PCI	Italian Communist Party
PGA	People's Global Action
PP	Partido Popular (Popular Party)
PSI	Private Sector Involvement
PSOE	Partido Socialista Obrero Español (Spanish Socialist Workers Party)
RDM	Real Democracy Movement
SMO	Social Movement Organisation
SWP	Socialist Workers' Party
SYRIZA	Coalition of the Radical Left
TUC	Trades Union Congress
UfM	Union for the Mediterranean
UK	United Kingdom
US	United States
WB	World Bank
WSF	World Social Forum
WTO	World Trade Organization
ΓΣΕΕ	Confederation Of Private Sector Employees
ΑΔΕΔΥ	Confederations Of Public Sector Employees

Contributors

KIVANÇ ATAK obtained his PhD in Political and Social Sciences at the European University Institute in 2013. Currently, he is working as a research fellow for the ERC project 'Mobilizing for Democracy' run by Donatella della Porta in the Centre on Social Movement Studies (COSMOS) at the European University Institute. His research interests include the politics of the police and crime, protests and social movements and the sociology of the state.

ONDŘEJ CÍSAŘ is Associate Professor at Charles University, Prague and is also affiliated to the Institute of Sociology of the Academy of Sciences of the Czech Republic. He is editor-in-chief of the Czech edition of *Czech Sociological Review*. His research focus is on political mobilisation, social movements and political sociology. He is author or co-author of four books and numerous papers. Recent publications include: 'Promoting competition or cooperation? The impact of EU funding on Czech advocacy organizations' (with J. Navrátil, *Democratization* 2014); 'Transnational activism of social movement organizations: the effect of European Union funding on local groups in the Czech Republic' (with K. Vráblíková, *European Union Politics* 2013); 'The diffusion of public interest mobilization: a historical sociology view on the advocates without members in the post-Communist Czech Republic' (*East European Politics* 2013).

PRISKA DAPHI has an MSc in Political Sociology from the London School of Economics and Political Science and a BA *summa cum laude* from the University College Maastricht in the Netherlands. She recently finished her PhD at Humboldt University Berlin (Germany), funded by a scholarship from the German National Academic Foundation. Her research interests include collective identity, memory, transnationalisation and the culture of social movements. She is a founding member of the Institute for Protest and Social Movement Studies in Berlin. Her recent publications include: *Conceptualizing Culture in Social Movement Research* (edited with B. Baumgarten and P. Ullrich, Palgrave Macmillan 2014); 'Images of surveillance: contested visual language of anti-surveillance protests' (with A. Lê and P. Ullrich, *Research in Social Movements, Conflicts and Change* 2013); 'Collective identity across borders: bridging local and transnational memories in the Italian and German Global Justice Movement' (in L. Cox and C. Flesher Fominaya (eds).

DONATELLA DELLA PORTA is Professor of Political Science at the Istituto Italiano di Scienze Umane (on leave of absence) and Professor of Sociology in the Department of Political and Social Sciences at the European University Institute. She has directed the Demos project, devoted to the analysis of conceptions and practices of democracy in social movements in six European countries. She is now starting a major ERC project, 'Mobilizing for Democracy', on civil society participation in democratisation processes in Europe, the Middle East, Asia and Latin America. She is co-editor of the *European Political Science Review* (ECPR–Cambridge University Press). In 2011, she was the recipient of the Mattei Dogan Prize for distinguished achievements in the field of political sociology. Her main fields of research are social movements, the policing of public order, participatory democracy and political corruption. Among her very recent publications are: *Can Democracy be Saved?*(Polity Press 2013); *Blackwell Encyclopaedia of Social and Political Movements* (edited with D. Snow, B. Klandermans, and D. McAdam, Blackwell 2013); *Clandestine Political Violence* (Cambridge University Press 2013); *Mobilizing for Democracy* (Oxford University Press 2014).

CRISTINA FLESHER FOMINAYA has an MA and PhD in Sociology from the University of California, Berkeley, and a BA *summa cum laude* in International Relations from the University of Minnesota. She is currently Senior Lecturer at the University of Aberdeen. She has won numerous international awards, including the National Science Foundation Fellowship, the German Marshall Fellowship, and the Marie Curie IEF Fellowship. She has been researching and participating in European social movements since the early 1990s. Beginning in September 2013 she will be a Marie Curie Fellow at the National University of Ireland, Maynooth, for a two-year research project on anti-austerity mobilisations in Ireland and Spain. She is a founding editor of *Interface* journal, an editor of *Social Movement Studies* and founding co-chair (with Laurence Cox) of the Council for European Studies Research Network on European Social Movements. Her book *Social Movements and Globalization* will be available from Palgrave MacMillan in 2014.

ARI-ELMERI HYVÖNEN is a PhD candidate at the Department of Social Sciences and Philosophy at the University of Jyväskylä, Finland, and a researcher at the Tampere Peace Research Institute (TAPRI), Finland. He has an MSocSc from the University of Tampere (International Relations). His research interests include contemporary and twentieth-century political theory, especially the thought of Hannah Arendt, international relations, critical studies of the EU and questions of political temporalities.

MARIA KOUSIS (PhD, University of Michigan, 1984) is Professor of Sociology (Development and the Environment) at the University of Crete. She has been Chair of the Sociology Department (2002–6), Director of the MSc and PhD. programme (2004–8) and Vice-Director of the MSc in Bioethics since 2010. She was co-ordinator of the EC DGXII project 'Grassroots Environmental Action & Sustainable Development in the Southern European Union' and partner in EC projects including TEA, PAGANINI, and MEDVOICES. Recent publications include *Social Aspects of the Crisis in Greece* (co-edited with S. Zambarloukou, Pedio Press 2014, in Greek); *Contested Mediterranean Spaces* (co-edited with T. Selwyn and D. Clark, Berghahn Books 2011). Her areas of specialisation focus on social change, social movements and contentious politics, environmental politics, bioethics and society and Southern Europe. She is currently partner in the FP7, EC project LIVEWHAT (http://www.livewhat.unige.ch) and co-ordinator of the Greek team in the bi-national project 'The Greeks, the Germans and the Crisis' (ggcrisi.edu) (Freie Universität Berlin and University of Crete).

ALICE MATTONI is a research fellow in the Centre for Social Movement Studies (COSMOS) at the European University Institute, working with the Anticorrupt with Anticorrp (this is the correct name of the research project) in the Department of Sociology at the University of Pittsburgh. Alice obtained her Master of Research and PhD in Political and Social Sciences at the European University Institute. She is a co-convener of the standing group 'Participation and Mobilization' of the European Consortium of Political Research (ECPR) and an editor of *Interface: A journal for and about social movements*. Amongst her recent publications are *Research in Social Movements, Conflict and Change: Advances in the visual analysis of social movements* (co-edited with N. Doerr and S. Teune, Emerald 2013); *Mediation and Protest Movements* (co-edited with B. Cammaerts and P. McCurdy, Intellect 2013); and *Media Practices and Protest Politics: How precarious workers mobilise* (Ashgate 2012).

ANTONIO MONTAÑÉS JIMENEZ is European PhD Candidate at the University Complutense of Madrid and Pre-Doctoral Researcher (FPI Spanish National Programme). He is a member of GRESCO (Grupo de Estudios Socio-Culturales Contemporáneos-Universidad Complutense de Madrid) and has won several honourable mentions based on excellence in academics from the Autonomous Community of Madrid Higher Education Council. Likewise, he has held training internships at Spain's two leading survey and research centres, Centro de Investigaciones Sociológicas (CIS-Science Research Grant Programme) and Centro Superior de Investigaciones Científicas (CSIC-JAE-Programme). He has held an Honorary Research Assistant position within the Department of Sociology at University of Aberdeen and has been appointed to a Visiting Scholarship at National University of Ireland, Maynooth. Currently, he is developing a dissertation thesis about political-religious movements among Spanish gypsies/ Roma in the twenty-first century.

JIŘÍ NAVRÁTIL is Postdoctoral Research Fellow at the Department of Public Economics, Masaryk University in Brno, and Assistant Professor at the Department of Civil Society Studies, Charles University in Prague. His research focus is on social movements, political culture and civil society, and inter-organisational networks. He has published on the Global Justice Movement and political activism in CEE. His recent publications include 'Promoting competition or cooperation? The impact of EU funding on Czech advocacy organizations' (with O. Císař, *Democratization* 2014) and *Dreams of Civil Society Two Decades Later: Civic advocacy in the Czech Republic* (with M. Pospíšil, available from Masaryk University Press in 2014).

LEONIDAS OIKONOMAKIS is a PhD researcher at the Department of Political and Social Sciences of the European University Institute in Florence, Italy. His research focuses on the different political strategies that social movements adopt in their struggle for social change (case studies: the Zapatistas of Mexico and the Cocaleros of Bolivia). He is a member of the Greek hip-hop formation *Social Waste*, a contributing editor of *ROAR* Magazine, and was an active participant in the occupation of Syntagma Square. Throughout 2011 and 2012 he also participated in demonstrations and occupations in several other countries, including Italy, Spain, and Mexico. Together with Jerome Roos, he is co-director of *Utopia on the Horizon* (2012), a short documentary on the occupation of Syntagma Square in Greece. He writes in English and his native Greek, but his articles have also been translated into French, Urdu, Hindi, Arabic, Bahasa Indonesia, Italian, Spanish, Turkish, and Portuguese.

THOMAS OLESEN is Associate Professor at the Department of Political Science and Government, Aarhus University, Denmark. His current research focuses on activism, solidarity and symbols in global contexts. Recent publications include: 'Televised media performance for HIV/AIDS sufferers in Africa: distance reduction and national community in two Danish fundraising shows' (*Communication, Culture & Critique* 2012); 'Global injustice memories: the case of Rwanda' (*International Political Sociology* 2012); 'The transnational complexity of domestic solidarity campaigns: a cross-time comparison of Burma debates in Denmark, 1988 & 2007' (*Acta Sociologica* 2011); 'Transnational injustice symbols and communities: the case of al-Qaeda and the Guantanamo Bay detention camp' (*Current Sociology* 2011).

JEROME ROOS is a PhD researcher in International Political Economy at the European University Institute in Florence, Italy. His research focuses on the structural power of finance in sovereign debt crises and the implications for the quality of democracy. He is the founder and editor of *ROAR* Magazine – an online journal of the radical imagination providing grassroots perspectives from the frontlines of the global struggle for real democracy – and has been an organiser with *Take The Square*, the international commission of the 15-M movement in Spain. With Leonidas Oikonomakis, he is co-director of *Utopia on the Horizon* (2012), a short documentary on the occupation of Syntagma Square in Greece. Jerome has appeared on *Al Jazeera*, BBC World and RT News to comment on the global financial crisis and the social movements that have since emerged in response. His articles have been translated into dozens of languages and republished on hundreds of blogs and independent news sites.

CHRISTOPHER ROOTES is Professor of Environmental Politics and Political Sociology, and Director of the Centre for the Study of Social and Political Movements, at the University of Kent, Canterbury, UK. He is editor-in-chief of the journal *Environmental Politics*, and a member of the editorial boards of *Mobilization* and *Social Movement Studies*. As well as publishing many articles and chapters on social movement theory, student and environmental movements, protest, Green parties, the politics of climate change, and the global justice movement, he has recently edited: 'The environmental movement in Great Britain', in *Environmental Movements around the World* (T. Doyle and S. MacGregor, eds, 2014); 'Framing "the climate issue": patterns of participation and prognostic frames among climate summit protesters' (with M. Wahlström and M. Wennerhag, *Global Environmental Politics* 2013); and 'From local conflict to national issue: when and how environmental campaigns succeed in transcending the local' (*Environmental Politics* 2013).

NIKOS SOTIRAKOPOULOS is PhD candidate and Assistant Lecturer in the School of Social Policy, Sociology and Social Research at the University of Kent, Canterbury, UK. He holds a bachelor degree in European and International Studies from Panteion University of Athens and an LLB and an LLM in Environmental Law and Policy from the University of Kent. His PhD research is on the influence of lifestyle anarchism in modern social movements and, more specifically, in the case of the protest camps, such as the Camp for Climate Action and the Occupy movement. He is also interested in Marxist theory, Greek politics and the international anti-capitalist and communist movements.

LORENZO ZAMPONI is a PhD candidate in Political and Social Sciences at the European University Institute, working on a research project on the relationship between collective memories and social movements. His research interests include public memory, contentious politics, student movements, anti-austerity activism and media analysis. Among his most recent publications: '"Why don't Italians occupy?" Hypotheses on a failed mobilisation' (*Social Movement Studies* 2012); 'Protest and policing on October 15th, global day of action: the Italian case' (with D. della Porta, *Policing and Society* 2013).

Preface and Acknowledgements

This book originates from the workshop 'The Transnational Dimension of Protest: From the Arab Spring to Occupy Wall Street' that we organised at the 41st ECPR Joint Sessions in Mainz, from 11 to 16 March 2013. During that workshop we engaged in an intense week of fruitful intellectual discussions around the transnational aspects of protests that occurred, in particular in 2011: from the uprisings in the MENA region to mobilisations in the United States, passing through the anti-austerity protests in Southern Europe.

We found that the presented papers were extremely rich, not only in empirically addressing emerging protests on which little research is yet available, but also for their theoretical potential. In particular, the papers we selected for publication all address a relevant analytic issue that requires – we believe – constant attention: the changing transnationalisation of forms of contention and, related to this, the mechanisms of diffusion that were at work during this wave of mobilisation. Although literature flourished quickly on some of the countries in which massive protests occurred, during the workshop discussions it was already clear that comparative works were still to come and that a focus on the transnational dimension and the mechanisms of diffusion is a necessary starting point to understand current protests.

We hence decided to make our reflections available to a broader public of academics through a publication that was able to reflect the richness of the workshop's debates and to trigger new questions about the transnational dimension of protest and the related mechanisms of diffusion in contemporary societies.

Although some chapters in this book were drafted expressly for this volume, the majority of the contributions included in the following pages were presented in the workshop. We are grateful to the participants of the Joint Sessions for their useful comments on the first draft of the chapters and for the passionate discussions about transnational protests and mechanisms of diffusion that stimulated the writing of the Introduction and Conclusion to this volume. Besides our contributors, we are grateful to Gema Garcia Albacete, Daniel Bochsler, Tina Freyburg, Ernesto Ganuza, Paolo Gerbaudo, Emma Jorum, Eva Klambauer, Muzzamil Hussain, Gianni Piazza, Geoffrey Pleyers, and Adrien Mazieres-Vaysee.

We also wish to thank Alexandra Segerberg, the editor of this ECPR Press series, for her kind encouragement.

Donatella della Porta acknowledges the support of an Advanced Scholars' Grant from the European Research Council. Alice Mattoni acknowledges the support of the ECPR Workshop Directors Grant.

Donatella della Porta and Alice Mattoni
Berlin and Florence
August 2014

Chapter One

Patterns of Diffusion and the Transnational Dimension of Protest in the Movements of the Crisis: An Introduction[1]

Donatella della Porta and Alice Mattoni

The mobilisations that occurred in Egypt and other Middle Eastern and North African (MENA) countries, in Spain and Greece, in the United States, as well as later on in Turkey and Brazil, took place in different times and places. However, they are often grouped together in popular, journalistic and even academic discourses. Indeed, some common features seem to favour categorising all these protests as part of the same set of events. At first glance, the similarities and linkages between all these protests are quite simple to identify: they all involved massive numbers of protestors who appeared to be autonomous from the usual political actors, and including some grassroots groups active in past cycles of contention. They also all employed social-networking sites, combined with older web applications and Internet tools, in conjunction with face-to-face gatherings and the deployment of quite radical, contentious performances, amongst them the physical occupation of public spaces.

These are, perhaps, some of the most obvious similarities that recent protests share. But there are other connections as well. This volume aims at unveiling these parallels while reflecting on the very nature of the transnational dimension in current mobilisations: the relationship between current movements and those that had been active in the past decades, particularly the protests against corporate globalisation that began in the late 1990s, as we will show below; the manifold interactions, at the expressive as well as the instrumental level, that link activists belonging to different countries who acted locally, in the urban spaces of their cities, but felt nonetheless connected to other activists engaged in protests far away; and, of course, the practices and discourses, ideas and actions that travelled from one moment in history to another and from one country to another, through mechanisms of diffusion that combined many sources of inspiration and many sites

---

1. The two authors discussed and wrote collaboratively and equally the present chapter. However, Donatella della Porta is the principal author of 'Introduction' and 'Protest camps and radical democracy in the movements of the crisis' and Alice Mattoni is the principal author of the sections 'Comparing the transnational dimension' and 'This volume'. Donatella della Porta gratefully acknowledges the support of the European Research Council, advanced scholar grant on the project Mobilizing for Democracy.

of adaptation. In doing so, we explore and explain some traits of recent protests, considering them not as not as isolated instances of protest that happened to have a few characteristics in common but rather as events linked to one another as part of the wave of protest that began to develop in 2008 with the revolts in Iceland and continued with protests in Turkey and Brazil in 2013.

The many events over these five years were situated in a context of which two aspects, in particular, seem significant: that of a crisis that was not only economic but also political and which affected, to varying degrees, many countries in the world. For this reason, we group the various uprisings under the tentative label of 'movements of the crisis'. With the label 'crisis', we address at the same time the economic and political crisis from which these movements originated and at which they point, revealing the increasing inequalities even in those countries where the economic crisis seemed to have had a less intense impact – such as Brazil. This book is a first attempt to understand the many features of these 'movements of the crisis' – which are diverse, since the economic/political crisis affected different countries in different ways, but also similar, in that the crisis manifested in different regions of the world with the same seriousness, although through different specificities. Some authors have already stressed the interconnections among these different protests, considering them as part of the same 'international cycle of contention' (Tejerina et al. 2013). In this volume, we start from a similar perspective: maintaining a comparative approach among different mobilisations, we seek to discuss the diffusion of protest imageries and practices across countries. In doing so, we aim at two interrelated conceptual objectives: first, we want to understand the meaning of 'diffusion' when we consider current protests around the world; second, we want to grasp the qualities of the 'transnational' dimension in current mobilisations and the ways in which it unfolded from country to country. Both concepts – diffusion of contention and transnational protest – have quite a long tradition in social-movement studies: they became of central importance with the rise of the Global Justice Movement (GJM) in the late 1990s.

The transnational dimension in the recent wave of global protests such as the Arab Spring, the European Indignados, and Occupy Wall Street is a relevant, but largely neglected, theoretical question. In the last decade, literature on global social movements and transnational collective action has flourished, particularly with research on the Global Justice Movement (Kriesi, della Porta and Rucht 2009; Karides, Smith and Becker 2008; della Porta et al. 2006; della Porta and Tarrow 2005a; Tarrow 2005). This wave of protest acquired worldwide visibility due to demonstrations against the third World Trade Organization (WTO) summit in Seattle at the end of November 1999, developing through counter-summits and social forums that proved to be important venues in which activists from all over the world could construct a common, yet multifaceted, framework for radical criticism of corporate globalisation (della Porta 2007). Social-movement studies explained the emerging transnational social-movement organisations, global protests and cosmopolitan framing as an outcome of economic, social, political and cultural globalisation. While cross-national diffusion of movement ideas was a long-lasting phenomenon, the need to act globally – resting on the shifts of decision towards international organisations and corporations but also on the opportunities offered by new technologies – gave a new impetus to the transnational dimension of protests and movements. Upward shift from the national to the transnational level of protest seemed to be an ineluctable trend in collective action. In other words, the transnational dimension of protests seemed to be here to stay.

Although the actors, discourses and practices that developed during those transnational mobilisations did not disappear, the current global anti-austerity and pro-democracy protests require scholars to update their analytical tools, revise their research questions and look for alternative explanations related to the transnational dimension of protests. Indeed, recent protests across the world have maintained a transnational stance but national governments and policies seem to be their first target. Even though the financial crisis to which the movements react is singular, and global, its timing and dynamics varied across countries. In fact, protests followed the geography of the emergence of the economic crisis, which appeared with different strengths and at different times in different European countries.

First, between the end of 2008 and the beginning of the following year, self-convened citizens in Iceland – the first country hit by the crisis – demanded the resignation of the government and its delegates in the Central Bank and financial authority. Protests in the traditional forms of general strikes and trade-union demonstrations contesting drastic cuts to social and labour rights followed in Ireland: a country until shortly beforehand considered a showcase for the economic miracles of neo-liberal economics but which then became an exemplar of rapid economic deterioration. The Arab Spring at the beginning of 2011 – later proclaimed the year of the protester by *The Times* – targeted not only the region's authoritarian regimes but its growing poverty as well as the social and geographical inequalities introduced by various waves of neo-liberal reforms that had cut public services and subsidies and created high unemployment, especially among the young. Next, in Portugal, a demonstration arranged via Facebook in March 2011 against growing economic difficulties brought more than 200,000 young Portuguese people on to the streets. Gaining global visibility, the Indignados movement developed in Spain, a country that was quickly dropping from the eighth (or the seventh, according to some ratings) position in terms of economic development to the twentieth (according to some estimates). Beginning on 15 May, protesters occupied the Puerta del Sol in Madrid, the Placa de Catalunya in Barcelona and hundreds of other squares around the country, calling for different social and economic policies and, indeed, greater citizen-participation in their formulation and implementation. The Indignados protests, in turn, inspired similar mobilisations in Greece, where opposition to austerity measures had already been expressed in occasionally violent ways. Mobilisations then broke out in the United States in September 2011: from New York, where the first Occupy Wall Street camp was established, protests quickly spread all over the country, and beyond. Indeed, even the mobilisations that took place in Turkey, Bulgaria and Brazil, in 2013, and Bosnia in 2014, shared some aspects of those which immediately preceded them in other parts of the world.

Although protests kept a strong link to their national contexts, there is no doubt that, from the end of 2010 to 2014, mobilisations that shared some characteristics at the level of both protest visions and protest practices flourished in a number of countries. Were these actions, despite some relevant differences, just a convergence of reactions to a global economic crisis? Or are they better understood as a common struggle that unified people in a variety of countries around the world? And, if the latter was the case, were these mobilisations part of a transnational wave of contention, in which activists – but also ideas and tactics, frames and strategies – positioned themselves beyond national borders? Further, what qualities were present in the transnational dimension of recent protests that differed from previous transnational actions common in the Global Justice Movement? Within a comparative perspective, this book seeks to provide some theoretical reflection and empirical evidence about these main questions.

Together with the authors of the following chapters, we do this by exploring the mechanisms and processes of diffusion that tend to characterise transnational contention. Indeed, we consider the transnational side of current protests not as a given feature but as a problematic aspect, to be addressed by looking at which aspects of mobilisations actually spread (Part I of this volume); how protests spread not just among different countries but also across diverse social-movement cultures and waves of action (Part II); and why protests spread as well as why they did not (Part III). In this introductory chapter, we start our discussion on the transnational dimension of current protests from a preliminary comparison between the Global Justice Movement, which began to develop in the late 1990s and acquired broad visibility in the early 2000s, about a decade before the present wave, and the social movements of the global financial crisis. In the second part, we briefly present the chapters that compose the volume.

Conjuncture and disjuncture: From the Global Justice Movement to the movements of the crisis

Comparing the transnational dimension

The images of the protests against the third World Trade Organization summit, at the end of November 1999 in Seattle, travelled fast around the globe, in part due to then-emerging new channels of information and communication technologies. They quickly became symbols of something broader than a mere demonstration in North America. In fact, the three days of protest were the first visible instance of a relatively long-lasting wave of cross-border actions that further developed in macro-regional social forums and protests against international summits. About two decades after the first protests in the framework of the Global Justice Movement, another wave of global action swept the world and, in particular, the MENA region, Europe and North America. Activists in these parts of the world often shared similar concerns, shouted similar slogans and used similar organising practices. But the extent to which we can speak about a transnational wave of contention and, at the same time, how we can define today the very notion of transnational contention, are still under debate.

We argue here that a meaningful discussion about this issue should start from a comparison between the two waves of protest that, in less than three decades, have shaken many cities and countries around the globe: the anti-austerity and pro-democracy protests of the 2010s and the Global Justice Movement of the 1990s and 2000s. This comparison sounds quite obvious if we consider that many of the actors and struggles that originated in the GJM are still around today, even at the transnational level. Moreover, it is important to avoid the usual trap of seeing the novelty in social movements, when in fact previous struggles had experimented with similar discourses and practices.

But this comparison is also needed for at least two more substantial reasons. At the empirical level, the transnational protests carried on in the framework of the Global Justice Movement had already envisaged today's economic and financial crisis, proposing a critical reading of the neo-liberal globalisation that emerged from the 1970s. At the same time, they pushed forward visions linked to radical participatory democracy, conceiving deliberative and participatory democratic practices as crucial in the creation of globalisation from below (della Porta 2009a; della Porta 2009b; della Porta 2013). The two waves of protests, therefore, are, to some extent, linked by and to the economic and financial crisis, although from two mirror positions: the Global Justice Movement represented a warning that the worst was still to come for vulnerable social groups; while the present wave of protests was sustained by citizens who experienced the worst becoming reality at the peak of the economic and financial crisis that erupted in 2008.

Additionally, at the theoretical level, the Global Justice Movement became the central phenomenon through which social-movement scholars reflected on transnational activism in a globalised world. Transnational counter-summits and social forums, as venues for protests and proposals against neo-liberal globalisation respectively, provided the empirical materials for a number of scholars to elaborate further the conditions and outcomes of transnational contention that involved both professional social-movement organisations and grassroots activist groups. Since its very inception, indeed, observers and scholars of social movements have debated not only the supposed novelty of such movements but also their (sometimes contested) transnational dimension. For these two reasons, the understanding of current global mobilisations will be improved by comparing them on the transnational dimension with the GJM.

A decade ago, transnationalisation in social movements seemed to be a trend, driven by forces as diverse as cosmopolitanism and globalisation. The Global Justice Movement had been defined as the second world power: an actor capable of making powerful and secretive international organisations accountable to world citizens for their deeds and misdeeds. Transnationalisation then developed on various dimensions (della Porta 2007; 2009a; 2009b). Protests were more and more often organised at the transnational level, challenging the idea that the nation-state is the natural target of social movements. Following the shift of power from national governments to international governance, social movements took their protests to the places in which international organisations held their summits. They targeted especially those of the international financial organisations, such as the WTO, the World Bank, and the International Monetary Fund, which had played a major role in spreading neo-liberal doctrine; but the most powerful macro-regional organisation, the European Union, was also criticised for betraying its public mission of creating better conditions for citizens, instead defending the powerful (della Porta 2009b). Counter-summits were then organised, involving a complex protest repertoire that encompassed non-violent direct action in the street, but also forums devoted to the development of an alternative vision of world politics. Not only were transnational protests growing in number, they also acquired enormous value for their capacity to network activists cross-nationally, during long-lasting preparation periods and emotionally intense actions. The social-forum process was the most visible attempt to build a different knowledge from below, at the same time seeming to democratise world politics by making the decisions of international institutions more transparent to the public and denouncing their contributions to increasing inequalities.

The very conception of global justice testifies to the cognitive effects of these protests in developing cosmopolitan identities. Through the process, transnational organisations also grew – in members, in numbers and in forms. While in the past transnational social-movement organisations had been mainly formal associations, with small leaderships and strong reliance on the discrete forms of action of transnational diplomacy, the Global Justice Movement brought about a variety of horizontal groups, part local and part global, converging in common protest campaigns in which transnational ties were developed. Networking of individuals and organisations was increasingly visible in social movements' development on issues as varied as unemployment, gender rights, environmental protection and human rights. Some counter-summits – such as the contestation of the third WTO summit in Seattle in 1999 or the G8 meetings in Genoa in 2001 – were deeply transformative events that seem to have signalled a shift in the scale of contentious politics from the national to the transnational. Even when the process of social forums spread at the local level (della Porta and Mosca 2012), the global dimension still seemed to be the dominant one.

Yet, only few years later, the global crisis seems to have brought about, if not an inversion, at least a brisk halt in what seemed a trend towards the globalisation of social movements' politics. Just about ten years after the emergence of the Global Justice Movement, the new wave of protest certainly has continuities with the past; but there are also discontinuities. In particular, while both waves of protest speak a cosmopolitan language, claiming global rights and blaming global financial capital, the Global Justice Movement moved to the national (and the local) from the transnational, while the new wave took the reverse route and focused on the national level of protest.

Probably the most visible disjuncture between the two waves of protest, therefore, is indeed related to their territorial level: while the Global Justice Movement often engaged in cross-border mobilisations that moved from one country to another, the current wave of protest chose relatively stable camps, deeply inserted in the urban settings of hundreds of cities across the world, as the main venue of activism. It might be, as some scholars suggest (Sommier and Fillieule 2013), that the local dimension of the Global Justice Movement has been underestimated. For instance, participants in cross-border protests often combined a general concern about neo-liberal globalisation with grievances related to more domestic issues – as in the protests against the G8 in Genoa in 2001, in which opposition to the centre-right Italian government played a role in mobilising people (Osterweil 2013; della Porta *et al.* 2006). More importantly, the social-movement organisations and activist groups that participated in the Global Justice Movement were mostly rooted at the local level, although contributing to transnational social-movement networks and coalitions. And when cross-border protests became less central, they continued to be embedded in national and local activism (della Porta and Mosca 2012). That having been acknowledged, however, transnational activist meetings, in the form of either social forums or counter-summits, had a pivotal role in sustaining the Global Justice Movement and its worldwide imagery. While the World Social Forum continues to meet with a fluctuating level of success, and the anniversary of the European Social Forum was celebrated with the Florence 10+10 event, anti-austerity protestors of the 2010s have been only selectively present at these events. In this respect, the difference between the manifestation of the transnational dimension in the Global Justice Movement and in recent global protests is quite evident.

In the Global Justice Movement, the growing acknowledgment of the roles and responsibilities of international governmental organisations developed, together with intensified interactions, during transnational counter-summits and social forums. Activists began to present their campaigns as part of an encompassing movement calling for global justice and global democracy. Although still deeply rooted in the national political systems and corresponding movement families (della Porta 2007), cosmopolitan activists tended to bridge the local with the global and *vice versa* (della Porta and Tarrow 2005a). In doing so, they contributed to the development of a transnational political system as well as transnational identities (Tarrow 2005; della Porta and Caiani 2009). This happened only in part in the recent wave of protest, in which national pride was called for in an inclusive framing of the self by movements that claimed to represent not a network of minorities but rather the largest possible majority – the '99 per cent' against the '1 per cent'. Tunisian, Egyptian and Greek demonstrators referred to national symbols (flags and anthems) within a discourse of defence of national sovereignty against the dominance of powerful states, international organisations and big corporations. Indeed, protests address the abduction of national democracy, not only by financial powers but also by international organisations, above all the International Monetary Fund and the European Union. In Europe, for instance, pacts for the euro and stability, imposed in exchange for loans, are characterised as anti-constitutional forms of blackmail, depriving citizens of sovereignty in their countries. Moreover, given the varying timing and depth of the financial crisis, mobilisations were also more sensitive than the Global Justice Movement – then mobilised on common transnational events – to national political opportunities (or the lack thereof). In line with this, surveys carried out in various European countries indicated a growing importance given to the national level of government as target of protest (della Porta and Andretta 2013; della Porta and Reiter 2012).

Despite a substantial focus on the national level of mobilisation, however, chapters in this volume show that processes of diffusion were at work in the recent wave of protest. Indeed, research has already singled out numerous examples of cross-national diffusion of frames and repertoires of action from one country to the next. Both direct, face-to-face contacts and mediated ones have contributed to building bridges between protests in various parts of the world. Direct forms of diffusion seem to have been more relevant within some geopolitical areas: Egyptian activists learned from Tunisians, thanks also to some direct contacts. Egyptians exerted indirect influence on Spanish Indignados (Romanos 2013b), who were in turn in direct contact with Greek activists and also very relevant in steering the Occupy movement (Romanos 2013a). Across more distant areas, various means of communication facilitated rapid information-exchange and mutual learning, especially between social-movement cultures that shared some common roots (*see* Roos and Oikonomakis, Chapter Six in this volume).

Also, on some occasions, global protests certainly had a transnational flavour, as we also point out in the Conclusion to this volume. For instance, on 15 October 2011, a Global Day of Action launched by the Spanish Indignados produced demonstrations worldwide: protest events were registered in 951 cities in 82 countries (Perugorría and Tejerina 2013). However, on this and other days of global action, the degree of transnational co-ordination seemed lower than for the Global Justice Movement, for which the World Social Forums and then macro-regional social forums represented a source of inspiration and offered arenas for networking. The forms of transnational brokerage in the newest social movements emerged as, if not weaker, at least different from those of the GJM: in fact, they seem more grassroots, that is to say, less embedded in formal social-movement organisations and resting more on connections through social-networking sites, participatory web-platforms and, to some extent, micro-blogging spheres.

In line with this, in the current wave of protest, individuals without previous organisational affiliations – and sometimes even without defined political cultures – seem to take on a more central role than in the past. It is true that activists in the Global Justice Movement also joined protest activities as individuals; but the common trait was one of 'multiple belongings' (della Porta 2005) of activists, who developed inclusive and tolerant movement identities that re-combined their participation in different political and social organisations, associations and groups. The Global Justice Movement developed as a network of networks of activism, in fact often characterised as a 'movement of movements'. In contrast, the recent wave of protests mobilised a large number of 'first-comers', amongst them those who were hit hardest by austerity measures, who participated in the mobilisation as individuals without any previous political affiliations. Although social-movement organisations and groups were also present in these protests (Gerbaudo 2012), the individual level of participation of common people became a relevant trait of recent mobilisations. The logic of networking in the organisation of mobilisation, which involved intense frame-bridging activities in the Global Justice Movement, was, to some extent, overtaken by a logic of aggregation at the individual level of protest participants and promoters (Juris 2012), who recognised themselves in broad collective-action frames.

Indeed, while from the point of view of political identities (and socialisation) the movements of 2011 were even more diverse than those of the previous decade, they presented themselves through a unified conception of 'the people'. References to common feelings of indignation prevailed over any positive definition of common values, as global justice had served in the Global Justice Movement. References to 'the people' accompanied denunciation of the corruption of those in power with a radical public condemnation of the entire political class – rather than of the corruption of neo-liberal institutions and policies that had been targeted by the Global Justice Movement (della Porta forthcoming 2015). The indignation of the people was focused on the corruption of the political class, seen in both a concrete sense as bribery (engendering calls for the dismissal of corrupt people from public institutions), but also in the privileges granted to lobbies and in the common interests shared by public institutions and economic (often financial) powers. It is to *this* kind of corruption – that is, to the corruption of autocratic regimes and representative democracies – that much of the responsibility for the economic crisis, and the inability to manage it, is attributed.

Protest camps and radical democracy in the movements of the crisis

The prevalence of a national focus and the relevance of individual commitment are two traits that certainly contributed to shaping the transnational dimension in current protests. Together with other features touched upon in the following chapters, these two aspects seem to require further reflection on the quality of transnationalisation in the current economic, political, social and cultural context – a task that we tackle in the Conclusion. The cross-time comparison between the Global Justice Movement and protests in the MENA region, Europe and North America casts light on both the disjunctures and continuities that characterise the two waves of protest overall. But to deepen the understanding of the transnational dimension of such mobilisations and, in particular, the mechanisms and processes of diffusion that distinguished them, a synchronous cross-country comparison is also needed. While many chapters in this volume go in this direction, in what follows we focus on practices that developed around the protest camps – the form of protest that quickly became the common denominator in a number of countries, where visions and practices of democracy from below also developed and diffused.

The diffusion of ideas, practices and frames is a process that characterised the transnationalisation of the Global Justice Movement (della Porta and Tarrow 2005b). Diffusion also occurred in the current wave of protest, although according to different patterns from those in other movements. There is, of course, the national specificity of the crisis, which was, indeed, global but had different characteristics, timing and degree of severity in different countries. As mentioned, the protests spread with the rhythms and twists of the crisis. The camp, as a form of protest, spread from Tahrir Square in Egypt to Puerta del Sol in Madrid, and from Zuccotti Park in New York to squares and parks in many other countries of the world. In contrast to the movements of the previous decades, which had employed a varied and plural repertoire, the *acampadas* became much entrenched in the very identity of the movements – not just, as for other social movements, one action-form among others. Occupied spaces became, in fact, 'vibrant sites of human interaction that modelled alternative communities and generated intense feeling of solidarity' (Juris 2012: 268). The protest camp surely acquired different meanings and relevance according to the national context in which it was embedded: setting up a protest camp under a dictatorship in Egypt is a much more radical and dangerous act than organising such a camp in a democratic country like Spain, which tended at least to tolerate such public gatherings. Deciding to occupy a private-public park in the United States, in which the geography of the urban setting does not usually allow for spontaneous face-to-face encounters of people in the streets, also acquires a different meaning from that of organising a camp in Syntagma square in Athens, and more generally in Southern European countries, where squares in urban settings are usual spaces for politics.

Despite these obvious differences, and the consequent adaptation and translation of the camp as a form of protest, some of the visions and practices that surrounded the protest camp also diffused and became central in diverse countries. In particular, the practice of participatory democracy during informal gatherings in the squares, as well as during formal general assemblies and group meetings, combined with a strong critique of existing forms of political systems. Whether in totalitarian regimes or representative democracies, political elites in power where revolts and protests took place were always opposed to those who mobilised from below, pushing forward a different idea of politics and societies. In short, common traits of the current wave of protest are, first, the elaboration of radical imageries related to the very idea of democracy, thus effecting a semantic renovation of the terms linked to these imageries and, second, experimentation with participatory democratic practices – allowing activists and protest participants to experience, not just to imagine, different conceptions of democracy.

For this elaboration of imageries and language of democracy, protestors in Puerta del Sol in Madrid, or those in Syntagma Square in Athens and Zuccotti Park in New York, certainly went back to conceptions of participation from below: their actions resonate with the concepts and practices of deliberative democracy. Attention to deliberation, in fact, became all the more central in the most recent movements against austerity. The activists' discourse on democracy was articulate and complex, taking up some of the principal criticisms of the ever-decreasing quality of liberal democracies but also including proposals inspired by democratic qualities other than representativeness. These proposals resonate with (more traditional) participatory visions but also with new deliberative conceptions that underline the importance of creating multiple public spaces, egalitarian but plural.

But in recent mobilisation there is another vision of democracy, which normative theory has recently defined as deliberative democracy and which the Global Justice Movement has elaborated and diffused through social forums as consensus democracy. In protests against the crisis (and ineffective and unjust responses to it), protestors started to imagine and practice, in occupied public spaces, different conceptions of democracy, based on participation and deliberative values, following a vision of democracy profoundly different from that which legitimates representative democracy based on the principle of majority rule. Democratic quality here is, in fact, measured by the possibility of elaborating ideas within discursive, open and public arenas, in which citizens play an active role in identifying problems and also in elaborating possible solutions.

In the northern part of the world, as well as in the Arab countries, the elaboration of imageries linked to democracy went hand in hand with the experience of different ways of organising and taking decisions. Indeed, this conception of democracy is 'prefigured' by the democratic practices of very same protestors that occupied the squares, transforming them into public spheres made up of 'normal citizens'. It is an attempt to create high-quality discursive democracy that recognised the equal rights of all (not only delegates and experts) to speak (and be respected) in a public and plural space, open to discussion and deliberation on themes that range from situations suffered to concrete solutions to specific problems, from the elaboration of proposals on common goods to the formation of collective solidarity and emerging identities. Participatory and deliberative forms of democracy were called for and experienced during these protests. However, while the democratic concerns behind the camps spread worldwide, the specific protest performance had a selective diffusion. As some chapters in this volume discuss, while social forums and counter-summits became the characteristic global strategic innovations of the Global Justice Movement, camps developed in several countries but failed to spread in others. As we will see throughout the volume and in the Conclusion, this failure of diffusion can be explained by contextual conditions, as, for example, the camps did not spread in countries such as Germany, France, or the UK that were less severely hit by economic recession. However, this failure to spread can also be linked to the resonance, or lack of resonance, of camps as a protest-form in the specific national social-movement culture in countries, such as Portugal, Ireland and Italy, where the economic crisis hit hardest.

This volume

As mentioned above, this volume explores diffusion in the recent wave of protest as one of the processes, and theoretical perspectives, through which we can understand the transnational dimension of these mobilisations. In particular, the volume is divided into three parts, each of them addressing a specific aspect of diffusion: the what, the how and the why of diffusion.

The first part focuses on the very object of diffusion, asking what spread – in terms of discourses and practices – from one country to another, during the recent wave of protest but also from one cycle of contention to another.

In Chapter Two, Cristina Flesher Fominaya and Antonio Montañés Jimenéz investigate the diffusion of a specific contentious performance: the *escrache*, a form of citizen direct-action used primarily in Argentina to denounce unpunished criminals of the Dirty War, in which perpetrators of crimes who have not been brought to justice are publicly shamed by citizens who mark their homes or protest in front of their homes. Initiated in the 1990s, the *escrache* has become a part of the social-movement repertoire in Argentina, tied to the politics of memory but also applied to movements of swindled investors (*corralitos*). Recently, the PAH (Platform for those Affected by Mortgages) – an important precursor movement to the Indignados and one of the key participants currently active in the anti-austerity movement landscape in Spain – has decided to adopt the *escrache* to shame politicians into supporting proposed changes to the mortgage law, which, in Spain, is particularly punitive. Starting from this case study, Cristina Flesher Fominaya and Antonio Montañés Jimenéz explain what happens when a protest tactic is transferred across space and time to a very different national context, addressing the consequences of the adoption of the *escrache* tactic by the PAH. Theoretically, the authors show how the transnational adoption of tactics involves processes of cultural translation; and also how reception, contestation, and counter-contestation are dynamic processes, involving framing and counter-framing by multiple political actors but also strongly bounded by national political discursive repertoires.

In Chapter Three, Donatella della Porta looks at the spread of conceptions of democracy in the anti-austerity movements. Those who protested in Tahrir, Kasbah, Puerta del Sol, Syntagma or Zuccotti Park did not just criticise existing representative democracy as deeply corrupted; they also experimented with different models of democracy. In part, conceptions and practices of democracy were inspired by the participatory and deliberative models of previous citizens' mobilisations. In part, however, they also innovated to improve on them, in a process of collective learning from the detected weaknesses of those models in the past and adaptation to new endogenous and exogenous challenges. In all the mentioned cases, the *acampadas* – at the same time repertoire of protest and organisational form – constituted the principal democratic experiment, adopted and adapted from one context to the next. If social forums were *the* democratic invention of the Global Justice Movement of the previous decades, the *acampadas* represented in part an updating of forums but in part also a development oriented to overcome their perceived failures. Conceptions of participation from below, cherished by progressive social movements, were combined with special attention to the creation of egalitarian and inclusive public spheres. While some aspects of the *acampada* spread cross-country, there was, however, a lot of adaptation to different national opportunities and constraints, as well as to different social movements' traditions.

Thomas Olesen, in Chapter Four, adopts a macro-regional look at an important element of diffusion: images and the way in which they spread, as symbols, from one country to another at the global level. In particular, he analyses as injustice symbols representations of dead activists, which motivated and galvanised protests against the regimes held responsible for their deaths, in recent political protests in Northern Africa and the Middle East. While they are in the first instance *national* symbols, all of them have significant *global* dimensions as well: Neda

Agha Soltan has become the object of political art outside Iran; Khaled Said's face has been painted on a piece of the Berlin Wall and Mohamed Bouazizi's self-immolation in December 2010 has been credited by media around the world with more or less single-handedly initiating the Arab Spring. In discussing these injustice symbols, Thomas Olesen shows that they are part and parcel of a process of dramatic cross-border diffusion, in which a local and private event (the death of a particular individual) attains meaning for global audiences. Drawing on these and other cases, the chapter develops a theoretical and conceptual framework for analysing and understanding the role of this phenomenon in transnational activism.

Finally in Part I, Chapter Five focuses on the diffusion within the European Union of frames linked to the uprisings in the MENA region. In doing this, the author investigates a neglected, although important, area of research when it comes to global protests: the framing and reactions of transnational governmental organisations to waves of protests. In his chapter, Ari-Elmeri Hyvönen claims that the so-called Arab Spring was not only a fundamental political transformation of the MENA region: it also had transnational and global ramifications. In particular, the author employs frame analysis to understand these global repercussions, by critically examining the policy reactions of the European Union. Ari-Elmeri Hyvönen pays special attention to the ways in which the European Union as a key global actor seeks to manage the flow of external events in order to fortify its self-image and thus its power interests: the frames utilised by the EU sought to downplay the 'eventful' nature of the Arab Spring and to present those events as a continuation of a general process of transformation to liberal democracy. The protests, in other words, were normalised by equating them with other transitions, as in the so-called colour revolutions.[2]

Part II of this volume reflects on how the diffusion of discourses and practices related to protest occurred, reconstructing the mechanisms that rendered diffusion possible (or not) in the course of the recent wave of protest.

In Chapter Six, Leonidas Oikonomakis and Jérôme E. Roos consider the 2011 mobilisation against austerity and for real democracy, focusing on the organisational practices that characterised them. In particular, the authors ask how the horizontal mode of self-organisation spread so rapidly between such radically different contexts. In doing so, they argue that, to the extent that these protests can be said to have diffused from one country to another, they did so through non-relational channels and through a leaderless mode of adaptation. Through an in-depth empirical investigation of the occupations in Madrid, Athens and New York, building on extensive participant observation and interviews with key activists, the authors show how each national movement acted as both adapter and transmitter in the process of diffusion. They consider, in fact, the endogenous capacity for mobilisation that – as a result of shared structural conditions and local movement

---

2. Commentators employ the expression 'colour revolutions' to refer to a number of protest waves that occurred in several Eastern European countries – amongst them Ukraine and Georgia – during the early 2000s.

experience – was already present in each country, and was merely actualised by the inspiration provided by movements elsewhere. Rather than a contagion-effect of mindless imitation, the authors explain the spread of protest as an intensifying shock wave that resonated with shared concerns and desires, activating a latent potential for mobilisation that was lying dormant in the different national contexts.

Maria Kousis, in Chapter Seven, focuses on the Greek case, where massive protests took place from 2010 to 2013 in a complex campaign against austerity and neo-liberal restructuring imposed by transnational actors and collaborating Greek governments. Maria Kousis considers here the transnational dimension of such a campaign, focusing on three relevant processes of transnationalisation and how they developed across the years: internalisation, externalisation and diffusion. Within a Tillian perspective, she uses a data-set of the 32 largest protest events from February 2010 to January 2013. The findings illustrate the major features of an anti-austerity campaign across Greek cities, carried out in a number of parallel, significant action-forms, such as national general strikes, marches, public meetings, demonstrations, rallies and blockades. Protestors' complaints were overwhelmingly against the impact of unprecedented austerity measures, especially those concerning the economy, society, sovereignty and democracy. Moreover, the author places the Greek anti-austerity campaign within a comparative frame vis-à-vis the other South European or peripheral EU countries and discusses how the new transnational economic and political opportunities and threats affect claims-making in Southern eurozone regions as a result of the global financial crisis.

While the protests in Greece involved millions of citizens for a considerable amount of time, in other settings, actions engaged few protestors for a relatively short period. This is the case, amongst others, of Occupy London in 2011. In Chapter Eight, Chris Rootes and Nikos Sotirakopoulos investigate Occupy London and show how the Occupy Wall Street protests that originated in North America were adapted to the British context. Based on ethnographic research, open-ended interviews with more than 30 participants and a survey of more than 100 participants and supporters, the chapter points out the inspiration and influence of Occupy Wall Street and the square occupations of Madrid, Athens and the Arab Spring – but also identifies continuities with previous London protests, from anti-globalisation to the Camps for Climate Action. What needs to be explained, however, is why Occupy London attracted relatively few participants compared with its American, European or North-African precursors; why it did not last long; and why its forms of action and rhetoric were so moderate. In their chapter, Chris Rootes and Nikos Sotirakopoulos address these questions by discussing if Occupy London was a socio-political movement or, rather, a moral protest; is it is best considered as a case of failed diffusion and a weak link in the internationalisation of the 2011 protest wave? Or did it represent an innovative form of collective action, capable of reaching beyond the conscience constituencies of previous direct-action movements?

Part III of the volume goes in more depth into the geography of diffusion, considering why protests spread in certain countries but not in others and discussing what happened once protests travelled from one context to another.

In Chapter Nine, Lorenzo Zamponi and Priska Daphi focus on Italy, a country characterised by a lack of massive protests against austerity despite the occurrence of numerous minor protests. The authors consider, therefore, the relevance of the political-cultural context in a case in which protest diffusion did not seem to happen as in other countries. In particular, they investigate the role of memories and legacies for Italian activists involved in two movement gatherings that were organised in 2011 and 2012, in order to commemorate, ten years later, two key moments of the Italian Global Justice Movement: the demonstrations against the G8 summit, which shook Genoa in July 2001, and the first European Social Forum, which took place in Florence in November 2002. Interviews with activists provide insights into the peculiar lack of massive demonstrations in Italy in 2011. Focusing on Italy as a negative case of diffusion, Lorenzo Zamponi and Priska Daphi reflect on the effects that collective memory about past protests can have on the resonance of imageries related to present protests.

Another interesting case in light of the cross-border diffusion of protest is the Czech Republic, which Jiri Navrátil and Ondřej Císař address in Chapter Ten. The authors analyse the responses of Czech leftist social movements to the coming of the financial and economic crisis. Their chapter, in particular, seeks to answer two questions relevant to diffusion. The first is whether the advent of this global crisis has domestically activated some of the generally expected processes of social-movement transnationalisation, namely, externalisation and global framing. After answering this first question in the negative, the authors address the reasons why this activation has not taken place. Using protest-event analysis and frame analysis to evaluate the evolution of the framing scale and target scale of Czech leftist activism between 1998 and 2010, the authors suggest that, while the trajectories of both modes of left activism experienced dramatic shifts both upwards and downwards, there is hardly any sign of transnationalisation after the crisis hit the country in 2009. Following the analyses of institutional and discursive opportunities, the authors then show that it was the timing and way of interpretation of the financial crisis on the part of national political elites and mass media that determined the scale and intensity of political contention over its consequences.

In Chapter Eleven, Kivanc Atac enriches this section by presenting research on the Gezi protests in Turkey, which share some common traits with the other mobilisations analysed in this volume. The author, indeed, illustrates some relevant similarities at the level of contentious performances, political discourses and participation patterns. Yet he also shows that these protests demonstrate that the intertwining of transnational inspiration with local forms of diffusion helps to create an indigenous agency of mobilisation. The author then illustrates why peculiar mechanisms of diffusion occurred in Turkey, at the intra-national and transnational level, with regard to both frames and actions. Protestors in Turkey were attached to the idea of 'resistance' (*direniş*) more than to the concept of 'Occupy', particularly because of their experience with police repression. Resistance then turned into a master frame that linked protests in Istanbul and Ankara to those in Mersin, Adana and Lice in Diyarbakır through the slogan

'Resist!' (*Diren!*). Likewise, people embraced the 'looter' (*çapulcu*) as a collective identity, due to the criminalisation of protests by political authorities; and it quickly diffused through social-media channels. Therefore, the author claims that the Gezi mobilisations are not only a case of transnational influence over a predominantly nationally bounded contention but also a case of the transformative effect of local diffusion generating peculiar protest agency. In this respect, it challenges and undermines the boundaries between the transnational and the local.

In the Conclusion to this volume, we build on the findings presented in the chapters above to reflect on two crucial questions that the social movements of the financial crisis pose to scholars. In doing so, we compare further the previous wave of transnational contention, the Global Justice Movement, with the present global mobilisation. In addition, we examine more closely the quality of the transnational dimension in the latter. First, we focus on how diffusion processes and mechanisms that characterised anti-austerity and pro-democracy protests put into question more traditional models of diffusion; and we suggest some directions for future research in this area. We then consider the transnational dimension in recent mobilisations, discussing the difference between thin and thick diffusion processes, with the former being in place in present times. We also consider other processes relevant to transnational social movements: internalisation/domestication, externalisation and transnational collective action.

References

della Porta, D. (2005) 'Multiple belongings, tolerant identities, and the construction of another politics: between the European Social Forums and local social fora', in D. della Porta and S. Tarrow (eds) *Transnational Protest and Global Activism*, Lanham, MD: Rowman & Littlefield, pp. 175–202.
— (2007) *The Global Justice Movement: Cross national and transnational perspectives*, London: Paradigm Publishers.
— (2009a) *Democracy in Social Movements*, New York: Palgrave Macmillan.
— (2009b) *Another Europe*, London: Routledge.
— (2013) *Can Democracy Be Saved? Participation, deliberation and social movements*, Cambridge: Polity Press.
— (2015) *Social Movements in Times of Austerity: Bringing capitalism back in*, Cambridge: Polity Press.
della Porta, D. and Andretta, M. (2013) 'Protesting for justice and democracy: Italian Indignados?' *Contemporary Italian Politics* 5 (1): 23–37.
della Porta, D. and Caiani, M. (2009) *Social Movements and Europeanization*, Oxford: Oxford University Press.
della Porta, D. and Mosca, L. (2012) 'Global movements in local struggles: findings on the social forum process in Italy', in J. Smith, S. Byrd, E. Reese and E. Smithe (eds) *Handbook on World Social Forum Activism*, Boulder, CO: Paradigm Publishers, pp. 248–65.
della Porta, D. and Reiter, H. (2012) 'Desperately seeking politics: political attitudes of participants in three demonstrations for worker's rights in Italy', *Mobilization: An international quarterly* 17 (3): 349–61.
della Porta, D. and Tarrow, S. (2005a) *Transnational Protest and Global Activism: People, passions, and power*, Lanham, MD: Rowman & Littlefield.
— (2005b) 'Transnational protest and global activism: An introduction', in D. della Porta and S. Tarrow (eds) *Transnational Protest and Global Activism*, Lanham, MD: Rowman & Littlefield, pp. 1–20.
della Porta, D., Andretta, M., Mosca, L. and Reiter, H. (2006) *Globalization from Below: Transnational activists and protest networks*, Minneapolis, MN: University of Minnesota Press.
Gerbaudo, P. (2012) *Tweets and the Streets: Social media and contemporary activism*, London: Pluto Press.
Juris, J. S. (2012) 'Reflections on #Occupy Everywhere: social media, public space, and emerging logics of aggregation', *American Ethnologist* 39 (2): 259–79, doi:10.1111/j.1548–1425.2012.01362.x.
Karides, M., Smith, J. and Becker, M. (eds) (2008) *Global Democracy and the World Social Forums*, Boulder, CO: Paradigm Publishers.
Kriesi, H., della Porta, D. and Rucht, D. (eds) (2009) *Social Movements in a Globalizing World*, Basingstoke, Hampshire and New York: Palgrave Macmillan.

Osterweil, M. (2013) 'The Italian anomaly: place and history in the Global Justice Movement', in C. Flesher Fominaya and L. Cox (eds) *Understanding European Movements: New social movements, global justice struggles, anti-austerity protest*, Abingdon and New York: Routledge, pp. 33–46.

Perugorría, I. and Tejerina, B. (2013) 'Politics of the encounter: cognition, emotions, and networks in the Spanish 15M', *Current Sociology* 61 (4): 424–42.

Razsa, M. and Kurnik, A. (2012) 'The Occupy Movement in Žižek's hometown: direct democracy and a politics of becoming', *American Ethnologist* 39 (2): 238–58, doi:10.1111/j.1548-1425.2012.01361.x.

Romanos, E. (2013a) 'From Tahrir to Puerta Del Sol to Wall Street: a comparison of two diffusion processes within the new transnational wave of protest', paper presented to the conference Street Politics In the Age Of Austerity. From Indignados to Occupy, Université de Montréal.

— (2013b) 'From Tahrir to Puerta del Sol to Wall Street: analyzing social movement diffusion in the new transnational wave of protest', paper presented to the ECPR General Conference, University of Bordeaux.

Sommier, I. and Fillieule, O. (2013) 'The emergence and development of the No Global movement in France: a genealogical approach', in C. Flesher Fominaya and L. Cox (eds) *Understanding European Movements: New social movements, global justice struggles, anti-austerity protest*, Abingdon and New York: Routledge, pp. 47–60.

Tarrow, S. (2005) *The New Transnational Activism*, Cambridge Studies in Contentious Politics, New York: Cambridge University Press.

Tejerina, B., Perugorría, I., Benski, T. and Langman, L. (2013) 'From indignation to occupation: a new wave of global mobilization', *Current Sociology* 61 (4): 377–92, doi:10.1177/0011392113479738.

Chapter Two

Transnational Diffusion Across Time: The Adoption of the Argentinian Dirty War '*Escrache*' in the Context of Spain's Housing Crisis

Cristina Flesher Fominaya and Antonio Montañés Jimenéz

Introduction

Cross-national diffusion is not simply the spontaneous adoption by receivers of a protest idea or tactic transmitted from one protest site to another. It involves specific challenges for activists and the active and often creative cultural translation of practices from one political context to another. The effectiveness of the adoption of an idea or tactic in a new context is uncertain. Less widely studied than contemporaneous diffusion, cross-national diffusion does not only happen from one nation to the next within a single protest cycle: it can also happen across time. This historical distance combined with geo-political differences poses additional challenges for social movements engaging in cross-national diffusion.

In this chapter, we trace the dynamics and consequences of the adoption of the *escrache* from its use in Argentina in the post-dictatorial context of the latter half of the 1990s to a very different context: the Spanish anti-austerity protests following the 2008 global financial crisis and, in particular, the resurgence of the Right to Decent Housing Movement from 2011–13.

The *escrache* was originally a technique used in Argentina to denounce unpunished criminals of the Dirty War. It is a form of direct action against injustice, in which perpetrators of crimes who have not been brought to justice are nevertheless publicly shamed by citizens. It is a form of bearing witness against the accused and publicly denouncing them – a manifestation of collective ethics and social condemnation. At the same time, it is a deep critique of the injustice of the national (and international) criminal justice systems, which allow such grave crimes to go unpunished, and it highlights the disparities between justice for the powerful and injustice for the vulnerable and unprotected.

McAdam and Rucht (1993) have highlighted the crucial need for attribution of similarity across cases for transnational diffusion to take place effectively. Yet what connects a tactic used to denounce perpetrators of grave human-rights violations, such as state-sponsored torture and murder in Argentina, with the fight to change mortgage laws in Spain, following the bursting of the housing bubble in 2008? Can a tactic developed to denounce war crimes committed under a Latin American military dictatorship be effectively transferred to anti-austerity protests in a European democracy? Can tactics be translated effectively across such a different geographical, political, and historical contexts and sets of demands?

Transnational diffusion across space and time, and moral framing

There is relatively little work so far within the field of social-movement studies on transnational diffusion across time. Most work on transnational diffusion studies the phenomenon during a particular revolutionary wave or protest cycle and this has shaped the models developed to understand diffusion processes (Chabot and Duyvendak 2002). Work on contemporaneous transnational diffusion within protest waves (for example, Beissinger 2007) rarely transcends regional areas, although important research on 'global' waves has also been done (for example, Palmer 1964 [1959]). There is historical work on the adoption of previously used tactics within a particular regional or national political culture (for example, Traugott 1995) but much less often do we find clear case studies of transnational diffusion across geographical regions and across time. The most famous example would likely be the adoption of Gandhi's tactics of non-violent resistance – used against the British Raj in India (among other targets), which he began to develop in the early 1900s – by civil-rights movement activists in the United States in the 1960s (Chabot and Duyvendak 2002). But in this case, the demands for equality and rights before the law, the ability to intervene in politics through voting or self-determination, the framing of the protestors as people oppressed by a powerful white elite and even the religious and spiritual nature of the two movements' political leaderships were shared across contexts. Even in processes of contemporaneous transnational diffusion of internal movement practices – such as horizontal decision-making, for example – where there is an active and clear connection between activists across contexts and a deliberate attempt to foment certain practices via active learning or institutional channels such as NGOs, active cultural translation is necessary and these attempts are not always successful (Flesher Fominaya 2014a and b; Wood 2010). How much more difficult might be the transnational diffusion of a set of discourses, demands and claims oriented toward a heterogeneous public and divided political elites?

McAdam and Rucht (1993) argued that protestors 'do not have to reinvent the wheel at each place and in each conflict' (58). Instead, protestors can adopt tactics and ideas developed elsewhere. Diffusion processes link two people, groups, or organisations via a channel of diffusion that is either directly relational (there is direct contact between the two sites) or via an indirect channel, such as the mass media. McAdam and Rucht argued that the actors in the two sites must share 'both a structure of social relations and a system of values, or culture' (59). They develop Strang and Meyer's (1991) argument that direct relational ties are not necessary but that adopters must define themselves as 'similar to the transmitters and the idea or item in question as relevant to their situation' (60).[1] Yet, in the case of the Spanish housing crisis, it is initially difficult to see what the connection is between the housing crisis and the Argentinian Dirty War. The activists of the Platform for those Affected by Mortgages (PAH), who initiated the *escrache* campaign, had to engage in active framing work to try to make this connection clear and convincing.

In this chapter, we show the process and consequences of the adoption of the *escrache* tactic by the PAH (an important precursor movement of and actor in the 15-M/Indignados, the key actor in the current Spanish anti-austerity movement). We show how the decision to deliberately frame this tactic as an *escrache* – with its connotations of repressive dictatorships and crimes against humanity rather than simply as a direct-action tactic, had particular consequences tied closely to the Spanish political landscape, showing how transnational diffusion involves important processes of cultural translation, which may or may not be strategically successful. The *escrache* campaign formed part of a larger movement narrative formed around a powerful moral framing of the housing crisis and the immorality of the failure to address its consequences. Their endeavour to make links across the two cases contributed to a wider questioning of the legitimacy of Spanish democracy itself (Flesher Fominaya 2014b and forthcoming) in the context of widespread social contestation of the government's austerity programmes.

Moral framing is a central strategy of social movements (Jasper 1997). Jasper argues that moral protest needs to be understood as such, in other words, as being fuelled by a 'serious moral purpose' and not dismissed as a strategic ploy to serve disguised material self-interest or the pursuit of merely rational goals. We believe that the 'serious moral purpose' of the PAH is crucial to understanding their choice of the *escrache* frame over other possible ways of framing this direct-action tactic. Moral framing often involves attributing symbolic weight to a situation or event that previously was not viewed in that light, or highlighting a situation that is already defined in terms of morality or injustice and making it seem necessary to act on it, as opposed to simply lamenting it (as inevitable, unavoidable, too large to solve and so on). The adoption of the *escrache* involved considerable moral framing work on the part of the PAH to create a connection across two such different scenarios in space and time. At the same time, they behaved in highly strategic ways. Through the adoption of the *escrache* frame, the PAH initiated a framing 'war' with political elites that triggered a powerful counter-framing campaign. They were only partially successful in this, as we shall see, yet their endeavour to make links across the two cases contributed to a wider questioning of the legitimacy of Spanish democracy itself (Flesher Fominaya 2014b and forthcoming). Before turning to the particulars of the Spanish case, we will first present our methods and then explain more about the original *escraches* in the Argentinian context.

---

1. In fact, they take issue with Strang and Meyer's clear distinction between relational and non-relational diffusion, arguing that virtually all diffusion takes place via both relational and non-relational channels. However, the notion of diffusion across time throws into question the extent to which this is the case, if the time period is greater than the active period of the movements or lifespans of the participants, direct relational channels become less likely.

Methods

For our analysis of the PAH, we have collected data from the campaigns, slogans, statements to the press, news, publications and posts on the official webpage of the platform, from the period March 2009 to September 2013. In the section 'The use of the *escraches* in Spain in the context of the housing crisis', we have reconstructed a chronology of the political actions of the PAH and we have conducted a discourse analysis of all of their public statements, paying particular attention to the justifications and rhetorical strategies (such as metaphors, analogies and so on) used to legitimise the use of the practice of the *escraches* in the Spanish context as well as to the attribution of political responsibility for the solution to the problem of the evictions in Spain by the PAH. In the section 'The PAH counter strategy' we have continued our discourse analysis, to identify the principal strategies used to counteract the tactics of de-legitimation carried out by major political and media actors, especially those mobilised by the Spanish government.

For the analysis in the section 'The reaction to the *escraches* in the media and from the state' we have conducted a frame analysis of public declarations made in the political and media sphere, using Spanish newspaper sources. The frame analysis is drawn from media accounts of the *escraches* covered in four national newspapers: *El País*, *ABC*, *La Vanguardia*, and *Diagonal*, using Factiva software and the key terms '*escraches*' and 'PAH' and '*escraches*' and 'not PAH' between 24 April 2011 and 24 April 2013. In our qualitative textual content analysis we have gathered, ordered, classified and coded public statements designed to de-legitimise the PAH and the *escraches*, selecting and identifying the various master frames that structure the production of discourse against the *escraches* and the PAH.

The *escrache* in Argentina: From crimes against humanity to the financial crisis and the *corralito*

An *escrache* is a form of direct action, based on the collective, public, peaceful moral repudiation and condemnation of an individual accused of permitting, participating in or perpetrating an injustice, and which is carried out by those affected by the unjust or immoral act. The *escrache* symbolises a transformation from victim to activist and is framed within the context of a lack of access to power (a power that refuses to enact justice) and the impunity of the targeted escrachado for the crimes he or she has committed. This aspect lends the action its moral legitimacy. It involves a planned encounter with the target of the action in either home or work or a public place, in order to publicly name and shame him or her, and can include theatre, whistling, chanting, postering or graffiti.

Escraches originally evolved to denounce perpetrators of torture and assassinations during the military dictatorship in Argentina by the group H.I.J.O.S. in 1995. 'H.I.J.O.S.' stands for 'Sons and Daughters for Identity and Justice against Forgetting and Silence', a group whose goal was to recover historical memory and end the impunity of the officials who committed atrocities under the political repression of the Argentinian dictatorship of 1976–83 and who did not answer for their crimes, thanks to amnesty laws enacted between 1986 and 1990. In the slang of Rio de la Plata, *escrachar* means to publically reveal the bad intentions or actions of an individual and to damage his or her public image. H.I.J.O.S. instituted the political form of *escrache* as a last-ditch attempt to gain justice for the victims of the dictatorship. Their slogan was 'If There Is No Justice, Let There Be *Escrache*' (H.I.J.O.S. undated).

They explained their actions in terms of the impunity enjoyed by the perpetrators of crimes against humanity, who were free to resume their social lives and employment under cover of the anonymity offered by the amnesty laws. Only very few criminals of the Dirty War suffered from moral condemnation as a result of being publicly identified as criminals (H.I.J.O.S. undated). As one man explained, he decided to begin participating in *escraches* after encountering his father's torturer in a bar one day (Peregil 2013).

The *escrache* later shifted its emphasis in Argentina. In 2001, the *corralito* financial policy of President Fernando de la Rua was imposed, denying savers and investors access to their money for over a year. During this period *escraches* were carried out against politicians, banks and other companies. Since 1995, the practice has extended to Chile (where it is called *funa*, meaning 'rotten' and used against perpetrators of crimes under Pinochet) and other Latin American countries and has continued to be used in Argentina. Therefore, the *escrache* in Argentina had already undergone diffusion processes prior to its adoption in Spain, from crimes against humanity to financial crimes within Argentina and also to other Latin American countries.

The use of the *escrache* in Spain in the context of the housing crisis

The resurgence of The Right to Decent Housing movement and specifically the Platform for those Affected by Mortgages (PAH) needs to be understood against the backdrop of the great number of foreclosures and evictions in Spain, resulting from the economic crisis that began in 2008. According to the PAH, the use of the *escrache* in Spain was instituted as a last recourse after all other institutional channels for change had been exhausted. Prior to the adoption of the *escrache* campaign, the PAH had engaged in sustained mobilisation encompassing a variety of tactics, including direct action under their ongoing 'Stop Evictions!' campaign, in which they acted alongside other 15-M activists as well as their grassroots base and members of the public. Alongside direct action, however, they devoted significant efforts to pursuing institutional recourse for the hundreds of thousands of families in Spain experiencing foreclosure and eviction after the bursting of the housing bubble and the steep decline in employment following the 2008 crisis.

In Spain, the crisis was preceded by the privatisation of the housing market (and a dramatic decrease in social-housing construction), which was accompanied by an active political agenda of de-regulation and expansion of the housing market. During the boom, 70 per cent of credit was related to construction (O'Broin 2012) and housing prices increased at an annual rate of 8 per cent from 1997 to 2007, a total price increase of 288 per cent (BBVA 2010).

The profound economic crisis and high unemployment rates, combined with the legal framework that regulates most mortgages in Spain, has resulted in a catastrophic situation for hundreds of thousands of Spaniards. In Spain, the existing mortgage law has not been significantly reformed since 1909 and it does not allow (except in very exceptional circumstances, where this has been written into the mortgage contract) assets in lieu (the return of the property to the mortgage lender) to satisfy the mortgage debt (*dación en pago* in Spanish). Instead, Spanish mortgage-holders unable to meet their payments are still liable for the outstanding mortgage debt even after returning their homes to the lender and, since they are often unable to pay the mortgage because they have lost employment (Flesher Fominaya forthcoming) they face years of crippling debt and are very unlikely ever to regain financial stability. Since property values have plummeted, and many people bought at the height of the boom, the levels of debt are, indeed, very high in many cases. Bankruptcy is not an option either, as mortgage debt is specifically excluded from bankruptcy proceedings. Foreclosure proceedings incur additional court fees and, with the penalty charges imposed on defaulters, the final debt can be very great, even after returning the home to the bank or financial institution.

The PAH, therefore, has challenged the state's response to the housing crisis by appealing to the European Court of Justice (which, indeed, has determined that Spanish mortgage law contravenes EU directives on consumer protection [Council Directive 93/13/CEE]); by marching on Brussels to call attention to the housing crisis; by testifying in both the national and the European Parliament; and by collaborating closely with the UN Special Rapporteur on the Right to Housing (Flesher Fominaya forthcoming).

On the national level, in addition to numerous legal actions, PAH have concentrated their efforts on the Popular Legislative Initiative (ILP) mechanism, which allows a group or groups to submit a legal proposal for consideration for debate after satisfying a 500,000 signature requirement. Along with allied groups and unions, PAH have submitted an ILP to parliament on two separate occasions, the first to the PSOE (Partido Socialista Obrero Español) government, where it was rejected due to its alleged similarity to an already existing ILP presented by another group, the second time with nearly 1.5 million signatures to the then-governing Popular Party, who also rejected it for debate. The ILP is centred around three key demands: 1) stopping evictions; 2) retroactive implementation of the *dación en pago* or assets in lieu; and 3) the creation of new social housing. These three fundamental demands are supported by the vast majority of Spaniards (Metroscopia 2013a and b) and by high-profile judges, who have collectively spoken out against the current mortgage laws. They highlight the long-lasting high social cost caused by the 349,438 foreclosures between 2007 and 2011 and the 166,716 officially registered evictions between 2008 and 2011 (evictions reached 532 a day in the second trimester of 2012).

Although the Popular Party changed its mind and admitted the ILP for debate, it ultimately used its absolute majority vote to defeat the proposal in parliament (12 February 2013), instead, deciding to propose its own much 'weaker' law. Faced with the end of institutional possibility for influencing the law, on 13 February

2013 the PAH announced the beginning of the *escrache* campaign, which consisted of three key elements:

1. An open letter of invitation to parliamentarians to attend a PAH assembly.

2. A postering action in the neighbourhoods, leisure places and workplaces of the Popular Party, in which the demands of the ILP were reiterated and explained.

3. Visits by activists and those affected by mortgages and their families to the homes of Popular Party members of parliament's homes to 'inform and pressure' them to change their vote against the measures proposed in the ILP.

On 16 February 2013 they held another rally in support of the ILP proposals 'For the Right to Housing. Against Financial Genocide'. Throughout, the PAH legitimised their actions by framing them as expressions of popular will (as demonstrated by public-opinion polls showing high levels of support for their protests and the nearly 1.5 million signatures they gathered), to an unreceptive and inaccessible political class whose actions or inactions had resulted in violations of the human rights of the people. One slogan of the campaign was 'If Their Lordships Won't Come To the PAH, the PAH Will Come To the Homes Of Their Lordships', in reference to the invitation by the PAH for the members of parliament to come to one of their assemblies.

Through the use of the *escrache* campaign, tagged as 'Let's Put Names To The Perpetrators Of Financial Genocide', they claim a moral equivalence between the political elites (specifically PP members who voted against them) and the military dictatorship of Argentina. In this framing action, they are drawing on familiar national political cultural tropes that evoke the Popular Party as the descendants of the Franco dictatorship (the party was, indeed, founded by one of Franco's ministers, Manuel Fraga, who served in public office until 2011). At the same time they are connecting both dictatorships to the dictatorship of the markets, which subordinate human interest to financial interests, thus developing and extending a critique of the democratic deficit shared by anti-austerity and pro-democracy protestors in the global wave (Flesher Fominaya 2014b). Throughout the campaign, the PAH attempts to highlight the inaccessibility of the Popular Party, and their impunity, despite the 'crimes' they were committing by not attending to the housing needs of their citizens and instead choosing to use public money both to bail out the banks (whose holdings include most of the vacant housing property in Spain) and to benefit themselves personally. The use of the slogans 'There Are Lives At Stake and the Members Of Parliament Don't Want To See' and 'Yes It Can Be Done, But They DON'T Want To?' contest the notion of austerity as an inevitable consequence of the crisis. Other slogans include:

- #the PAH speaks: the solutions to the evictions that the PP and the PSOE ignore (PAH 2012a).

- # 'PPSOE[2] complicit in the # Financial Genocide' (PAH 2012a).

- 'They call it a crisis but it's a swindle. They call it suicide, but it's # Financial Genocide' (PAH 2012b).

Seen in this light then, we can now point to some similarities between the two cases of the use of *escrache*:

- Characterisation of politicians/public-office-holders as inaccessible and having impunity. ('If the perpetrators hide in their homes we will go to them and out them / If the politicians refuse to come to the PAH the PAH will go to the politicians.')

- Use of the home as a symbolic space of refuge.

- Targeting of elites and their juxtaposition to ordinary people directly affected by their actions.

- Public naming and shaming linked to accusations of violations of human rights.

- The notion that, in the absence of legal recourse to justice, there should be public social condemnation.

However, the adoption of the *escrache* in the Spanish housing movement context involves an active redefinition and extension of the original practice that nevertheless retains some connections to the original case:

- The moral equivalence of military/physical violence with the violence of home evictions and poverty.

- Likewise, the extension of the notion of dictatorship from the strictly political to the economic sphere (for example, dictatorship of the markets).

- Extending the notion of a lack of justice in a particular arena (housing) to a much broader critique of the democratic deficit that encompasses a vast range of social institutions and issues.

- Juxtaposing the idea of home as a space of safe refuge with the violence of having no home in which to seek refuge.

By deliberately choosing the term *escrache*, the PAH is trying to portray similarities between the military dictatorship and the dictatorship of the market and to evoke contexts in which emotional and structural comparisons can be drawn between the abandonment, anxiety and suffering the victims of both experience

---

2. This combined abbreviation PPSOE (PP plus PSOE) is widely used by autonomous Spanish activists as a means of erasing ostensible ideological differences between the two majority parties.

in a political environment that is inaccessible, complicit and therefore an active contributor to the dramatic injustice faced by those affected.

In both contexts, according to the PAH, human rights are systematically violated.

> This is the drama of thousands of people who have mortgaged themselves to gain access to a basic need and who now cannot continue to pay abusive mortgages, who have stopped eating to be able to pay their mortgages, who suffer from anxiety, who can't sleep; and who not only can be evicted from their home, but that will have to carry the burden of a lifetime of debt, condemned to civil death. This is not a drama, this is worse than any nightmare (PAH 2013a, footnote 25).

The continual allusion to human rights, financial genocide and the increasing number of eviction-related suicides are recurring elements that are used to morally condemn the government of the PP and to justify the political strategy of the *escrache*.

In stressing mortgages as a means to satisfy a basic human need (housing) the PAH is also countering a narrative heard from pundits who essentially blame the people facing eviction and foreclosure for their own plight, arguing that they have behaved irresponsibly and borrowed beyond their means. This rhetoric is often applied to society as a whole and is a common trope invoked in the face of protests against austerity measures. In this narrative, society as a whole has behaved irresponsibly, Spaniards have wanted more than they could afford, people went crazy with consumption during the boom and now the government has to pick up the pieces and make difficult decisions for the good of all. In order to counter this rhetoric, the PAH argues that 'the government obstinately persists in over protecting the interests of financial entities and in violating in a systematic way human rights in every eviction that takes place for economic reasons' (PAH 2013b).

The reaction to the *escrache* in the media and from the state

Members of parliament of both major parties (PSOE and PP) and their affiliated media responded to the *escraches* with their own counter-framing. The response was most vociferous and adamant from the PP, understandably, since they were the targets of the *escraches*, but members of the PSOE also spoke out against them. Frame analysis from the media shows that the reactions of the Popular Party to the *escraches* followed a number of discursive frames that de-legitimised these actions and the PAH, and which, in turn, link to two master frames:

1. The *escraches* are illegitimate in a democracy and, in fact, attack the very values upon which democracy is based (the sovereign will of the people as expressed through elections and representatives in Parliament).

2. The *escraches* are violent practices.

These two master frames are linked in a number of different recurrent discursive strategies:

1. *The escraches are an attack on the principle of representative democracy. They involve the use of intimidation, pressure, coercion, and fear.* The following representative quotes shows how these frames are linked: 'Violence is not a method that democracy can tolerate and even the most noble cause is prejudiced if it is defended with violence.' (PP Vice-Secretary Pons, quoted in *Europa Press*, 8 April 2013). And, also: '*Escraches* are harassment, intolerant and intolerable, directed against people who were democratically elected by the people. ... By people who were trying to coerce the free will of the members of Parliament when they go to vote.' (PP Mayor of Valencia, quoted in *ABC* 2013b).

2. *Members of Parliament and their families have the right to privacy.* Again this frame is linked to the assertion of the *escraches* as a violent form of protest: 'Scaring my family is a method of the Mafia ... This is not the way to convince me.' (PP Vice Secretary Pons, quoted in Duva 2013b).

The assertion that the *escraches* are a violent form of protest is also extended to a number of recurrent themes, like *the escraches are political strategies similar to those used by the Nazis in Germany*: 'Today they do it so that the politicians change their vote. Tomorrow they'll do it with the judges and the day after tomorrow with the journalists. This is very dangerous. They say that they are marking me out but marking people out is what the Nazis did with the Jews.' (PP Vice-Secretary Pons, quoted in Duva 2013b). And, also: 'Going to somebody's house and saying I know where you live, insulting them, harassing them – I think this is a totalitarian action comparable to those that were carried out in a certain European country in the 1930s.' (PP Secretary General Cospedal, quoted in Manetto and Fernández 2013).

The Popular Party also relied on two additional strategies often invoked to de-legitimise social movements in Spain in responding to *escraches*. The first is *to allege or infer links between the social movements and ETA, the Basque nationalist separatist terrorist group*. This discursive strategy was used repeatedly by members of the Popular Party:

There's no difference in the slogans that are shouted nor in that attitude nor in what motivates them deep down between those that come from the world of ETA to accost us and those that now come along with the excuse of mortgages to harass members of the Popular Party. To go to the door of someone's home, to threaten their family, to mark their doorway and to create difficulties in front of their neighbors is exactly how the *kale borroka* [ETA-supporting street fighters] behaves (PP President Basque Country Basagoiti, quoted in Mora 2013).

A high-profile Popular Party politician demanded that through their spokesperson Ada Colau, the PAH 'should explain why they support parties that are sympathetic to ETA and why they maintain connections with ETA sympathisers' (PP Government Delegate in Madrid Cifuentes, quoted in *ABC* 2013c).

The second discursive strategy used to de-legitimise social movements in Spain is to allege that they are, in fact, puppets being manipulated by the opposition Socialist party PSOE, or that they had partisan interests favouring the PSOE. This strategy was also repeatedly used against the PAH (Flesher Fominaya forthcoming).

The government of the Popular Party did not simply rely on discursive strategies to respond to the *escrache* campaign, however. They also used the law to criminalise the movement and to impose fines on people participating in the *escraches* (ranging from €300–€6,000, depending on whether they were classified as organisers of the *escraches* or as participants who had committed some violation of 'Law 1/92 of citizen security' (Ley Organica 1/1992) (Duva 2013a). The Ministry of the Interior issued an order that anyone involved in *escraches* should be identified in accordance with the laws of citizen security or, if they were engaged in criminal behaviour, that they should be arrested in accordance with current legislation. They also ordered that the police should protect the politicians who were being threatened or harassed by *escraches* organised by the PAH. The Ministry later stressed that the purpose of this was to identify people behaving violently and that arrests should only be made if insults, aggressive behaviour, throwing of objects or any other violence took place, as in any other protest (*ABC* 2013a).

Another police order prohibited the use of the term *escraches* in police reports, instructing police officers to instead substitute the terms 'accosting, threatening, coercion, etc.'. Interestingly, the National Police Union instructed its members to substitute for these recommended terms (all of which have violent connotations) expressions such as 'peaceful following', 'peaceful protest' instead. The National Police Union also spoke out against the Ministry of the Interior's order that people taking place in *escraches* should be asked for identification, registered and/or arrested (*La Vanguardia* 30 March 2013).

The right-wing newspaper *ABC* also ran a series of articles characterising the PAH spokesperson, Ada Colau, as having personal connections to violent militant radical organisations and offering a distorted interpretation of her political background (Flesher Fominaya forthcoming).

The response to the *escrache* campaign by the Popular Party, the PSOE and affiliated media succeeded in bringing into question the moral legitimacy of the victims of the housing crisis in Spain, hitherto widely understood to be blameless, as well as in planting doubts as to the grassroots nature of the activism and its representativeness of the needs and demands of ordinary citizens. Instead, the PAH and its supporters were characterised as professional political agitators with violent connections to terrorists and extremist ideologies, whose intent was to attack democracy and the values which support it. In so doing, political elites managed to shift the focus of social debate from the housing crisis itself to the legitimacy of the tactics of the PAH and their supporters. Despite this, public support for the *escraches* remained quite high (78 per cent) although it did drop, especially among voters of the Popular Party (decreasing 11 points in one month) (Garea 2013).

The PAH counter-strategy

In order to counter the claims made by the Popular Party and in the media against them, the PAH followed three strategies. The first was to publish an *escrache* manual, (PAH 2013d) as a means of defensively re-legitimising their choice of political action:

> ... the *escraches* are informative actions directed towards the member of Parliament and his or her neighbours. It should be done in a completely peaceful way and without bothering (the neighbours obviously). Its purpose is to gain their sympathy, to give them the opportunity to show their support for the demands of the PAH. For this reason we should inform people how to do an *escrache* in the correct manner. The *escrache* should be carried out on working days during school time to make sure that the children are not at home but at school. Children never, never!, should be involved.[3] Neither at school nor in any other place.

> ... Stickers shouldn't be placed just anywhere. The cleaning people don't have to spend all day trying to remove them. They are workers and citizens just as we are. Posters can be placed with the motto 'yes it's possible' (*Sí se puede*) with scotch tape which is easy to remove.

> ... If nobody opens the door, the postcards can be placed underneath the door. ... because it's the only way to reach them. But the area should never be left dirty and full of papers because this can cause the neighbours to become upset. People shouldn't blow whistles the whole time, only at the beginning to let them know that we are there because this can also bother the neighbours and that's not what we want. People should explain their situation without insulting or threatening, simply, narrating the drama of each case and appealing to them so that they listen to the problems of our society.

The manual goes out of its way to portray the PAH as peaceful, courteous and respectful, as a means of reclaiming the moral high ground.

The second strategy involved issuing a number of public statements to the voters of the Popular Party:

> The PAH asks the voters of the Popular Party to not believe the discrediting campaign that has been launched by the government. We are not the enemy, we are victims of the crisis and of the huge mortgage swindle that is taking place in this country as a result of the housing bubble. We are the victims who have had to organize ourselves from the grassroots to stand up against this injustice.

---

3. The original term in Spanish is *interpelado* or interpolated, meaning interacted with or spoken to or appealed to.

The PAH is a plural and transversal movement. In the PAH we have spent more than four years fighting for basic rights, overcoming factions and ideological differences and we invite everyone to show their support for the measures in the ILP by joining the Green Spring campaign (PAH 2013c).

The third strategy involved a series of provocative interviews given by charismatic PAH spokesperson Ada Colau, who also wrote an open letter to the president Mariano Rajoy, published in a book called '*Yes It's Possible! Chronicles Of A Small Great Victory*' (Colau and Alemany 2013). The letter responded to the government's discrediting campaign, reiterating the heterogeneous and grassroots nature of the PAH and stating that it was not the puppet of any party but an expression of 'the will of the people'. With specific reference to the *escraches*, she said the following:

> And finally let's talk about the *escraches*. It bothers you that we can go and protest in front of your house. I understand. I would not like it either. But if you've ever been to an eviction, you can understand that that is something infinitely more bothersome. There are thousands of people in a critical situation, in the streets and with debt, unemployed, with nothing to eat … And all this despite the fact that we live surrounded by abundance. Thousands of families living on the streets in the country in Europe that has more empty houses than any other. They're going hungry in a state that allows tons of food to be thrown away in good condition every day. And you who govern this country should therefore not be surprised when these families come knocking at your door after trying in vain to get your attention. This exemplary movement has exhausted every avenue that the insufficient Spanish democracy offers: during more than four years we have tried to negotiate with financial entities, we've spoken to the political parties, to social services, to councils … We have placed resources in the courts and we have gathered like little ants almost one and a half million signatures. But all for nothing, the Popular Party has not moved 1 millimetre and announces that it will reject the measures of the Popular Legislative Initiative. What a coincidence. Just when the PAH has more social support than ever (between 80 and 90 per cent according to all the surveys). When one and a half million signatures have already been submitted support of the ILP. When social pressure has forced you to admit for processing the ILP that you didn't even consider debating. When a European sentence has come down in favour of the people who are affected and which declares that thousands of foreclosures and evictions that have taken place over the last years in Spain are illegal. Just at this moment when it seems that nothing else can slow down this necessary legislative reform you come out with a campaign of criminalization as the only response. Instead of listening to the voice of the people you try to generate confusion by comparing our peaceful actions with the terrorism of ETA or Nazi Germany. You really must be bad people to say something like that. Remember that when we're talking about evictions the only homes that have been violated and the only death have come from

the people. Not from your Lordships who up to this moment have confined yourself to looking on from afar, and from a position of comfort, at a drama that you could have avoided if you had acted where you are supposed to act – in Parliament. Of course the people are not stupid and I have seen immediately that this criminalization campaign was nothing other than a ploy to distract attention. But it's not going to work. Reality is stubborn and thousands of people who have been swindled and evicted are not going to disappear, however much your government ignores them. Let me finish by using the parallel with Nazi Germany that you recur to with such frivolity. While the gravity of the two situations cannot be compared, in both cases we are talking about the systematic violation of human rights. Fortunately in Spain we are not facing concentration camps, deportations, or mass assassinations. But we do have violent evictions, and thousands of impoverished people who cannot meet their basic needs, condemned for life to social exclusion and to a submerged economy. And all to maintain the privileges and astronomical benefits of the financial elites. Decades after the Nazis, German society still has not forgiven itself for not having reacted in time to avoid barbarism. In Spain thousands of citizens have decided that in the future we would like to be able to look ourselves in the mirror. A democracy that permits the systematic violation of human rights and actively promotes their violation is not a democracy, however much one votes every four years. Democracy will be when the general interest is put before the dictates of the market. When nothing is more important than the life and dignity of the people. Mr President, it is never too late to change. Don't be afraid of the *escraches*, don't be afraid of the people. Come down on the street and speak to people. Do justice and stop the evictions. There are lives at stake that cannot wait any longer.

If the *escrache* manual reads as a defensive text, this letter serves as a powerful counter-offensive and a regaining of the moral high ground for the PAH and its supporters. We have reproduced it at some length here because of the many instances of moral framing it provides, invoking justice against injustice, morality/immorality, democracy/demagoguery, human rights/violation of human rights, the will of the people/the interests of the few, and the peaceful action of the exemplary movement as against the violent inaction of the political elites. This moral framing is linked to a wider social context of need and suffering in the midst of greed and abundance.

Why the *escrache*?

Our initial interest in this case came from two immediate reactions: the first was that one of the authors (Flesher Fominaya) felt the strategy would backfire in the Spanish context, shifting the debate on the urgent housing crisis to a debate about the legitimacy of the tactic itself. Although correct, I underestimated the strength of Spanish public opinion, as we found that support for the *escrache* remained quite high, despite dropping once the counter-campaign of the PP, the PSOE (to a lesser extent) and right-wing media got fully underway (Metroscopia Surveys 2013a and b, March and April). Although our focus here is on the consequences of the adoption of the *escrache*, the second immediately striking aspect was how Spanish activists looked to Argentina's past as opposed to the rest of Europe for tactical inspiration. Europe, after all is 'closer', there is established mobility across Europe through the Global Justice Movement (GJM) and squatter networks (Owens *et al.* 2013; Scholl 2013) and some members of the PAH, including their most visible spokesperson, Ada Colau, clearly had extensive experience in the GJM and the squatter movement and have made close ties with squatters in their 'Stop Evictions!' campaigns (Martinez and García 2011). Although there has been important continuity between the political culture of autonomous Spanish movements of the GJM and the 15-M /Indignados (Flesher Fominaya forthcoming), including the PAH, the *escrache* was not used by the Global Justice Movement. Why then the *escrache* as opposed to other direct-action tactics used to mobilise around housing issues in Europe? For example, during the British Anti-Roads Movement, activists also brought the housing issue home to politicians. One of the most noteworthy actions involved climbing on to the Minister of Transport's home, unfurling a massive canvas highway over it and calling the press. The symbolic impact was powerful ('How would you like it if a road went over your house?'); it highlighted the differences between the protection of the homes of the wealthy versus the working-class neighbourhoods that were being demolished, and brought the issue straight to the door of the politician responsible.

While in that case the issue was somewhat different, in that road-building schemes were forcing evictions, the loss of homes through evictions was a clear connection. It certainly seemed a much closer case than the crimes of the Argentinian dictatorship. Given the widespread use of occupation techniques in 15-M, even camping out on politicians' doorsteps as a means of highlighting the notion of 'if the politicians won't come to us we will come to the politicians' might have been a tactical extension of the technique. We simply do not have enough information about the process of adoption to answer this definitively, yet we can draw on what we know to make some informed observations. Diffusion scholarship points to the importance of relational ties and media channels in fostering diffusion processes. Even within the Global Justice Movement, Latin American movements such as the Argentinian *piqueteros* or the Mexican Zapatistas were a key source of inspiration and influence in Spain, certainly more so than British or even continental European movements, with the exception of Italy (Flesher Fominaya 2005). Shared language, political ties through exile communities and academic exchanges and ties between activists have all contributed to a strong flow between Latin American and Spanish movements, contributing to the potential for transnational diffusion of ideas, frames and repertoires. Yet the large differences in the political contexts between regions means that diffusion is far from seamless or necessarily successful.

Second, the use of the discourse of the *escrache* makes sense within Spanish political culture in a way that the more light-hearted (if serious in intent) tactics of the British Anti-Roads movement still do not. Despite a shift towards the acceptance of more use of humour (Romanos 2013), there is still a political-cultural resistance to the use of humour to treat issues that are serious and even tragic (Flesher Fominaya 2007). The cultural element is important here, because the issue of home-loss in the UK due to forced evictions was no less tragic (if not as widespread) for those affected than it was in Spain today. The British Anti-Roads protesters also made explicit links between the financial benefits accruing to political elites who supported road schemes, just as the PAH and the Indignados do for the contemporary housing crisis and the bank bailouts. It is unlikely that even had they known about the British Anti-Roads Movement's mobilisation around housing, however, that they would have opted for this more carnivalesque form of action, despite asserting in their initial campaign announcement that they wanted to work with artists to gain maximum attention and impact for the campaign. Activists in Spain, including the PAH, have reacted to eviction-related suicides by arguing that 'It's not suicide, it's homicide' or, in another version, 'austericide'. There is indeed a tragic element to the campaign despite some attempts at irony and humour. It is perhaps also for this reason that no reference whatever could be found in our searches for '*charivari*', a more geographically proximate if historically distant form of *escrache*, complete with pot-banging and whistle-blowing, involving naming and shaming popular justice, which was practised in Europe, including the Basque country, as early as the fifteenth century and is linked with carnivalesque traditions (Tilly 1976).

Nevertheless, McAdam and Rucht (1993) highlighted the crucial need for the attribution of similarity across cases for transnational diffusion to take place. In other words, the PAH needed to feel some sense of identification with the victims of the Argentinian Dirty War to adopt such a symbolically loaded form of protest. Interestingly, despite the fact that the *escrache* had already been widely used in the context of the *corralitos*, or financial crisis, in Argentina, this is not the aspect emphasised by the PAH when they launched their campaign:

> We have called this campaign '*escraches*' alluding to the protests that are carried out in Argentina (*in that country to denounce the torturers of the dictatorship*) [emphasis ours] and that take place where the person who is being denounced lives or works.

Ada Colau explained the inspiration for the campaign thus:

> What has inspired us were the campaigns that, despite differences, arose in a moment in which a situation of injustice cried out for awareness, in post dictatorial Argentina and other Latin American countries, where justice and political power did not respond to these injustices after the dictatorship ... and since there is no formal justice, a social justice is organized (França 2013).

The PAH's decision to frame the issue in terms of financial genocide is an attempt to highlight the human-rights violations that lay at the heart of the claim for legitimacy of the Movement for the Right to Decent Housing. It is this moral framing of human-rights discourse that marks out the distinctive element of the PAH campaign, one closely entwined with a wider social response to the crisis in Spain that deeply questions the democratic deficit (Flesher Fominaya 2014b). It is here that the collective identification or attribution of similarity lies for the PAH, even if this connection is less clear to the general public and opens the PAH to contestation. The *escrache* was one element of a larger campaign to reclaim the constitutional right to decent housing as a universal human right, framing the PAH's particular claims within national and global institutional frameworks. The boundary between their own collective identification with the *escrache* and its reception by the larger public outside the social-movement community highlights the conceptual usefulness of distinguishing between internal and external social-movement processes (Flesher Fominaya 2010). Successful transnational diffusion requires collective identification in both spheres and adopting activists may need to work hard to cross the bridge from one to the other.

Conclusions

Theoretically, this case illustrates that social-movement actors do not freely adopt tactics from a globally available 'toolbox'; adoption follows paths shaped by political, historical and cultural trajectories that are not always easily determined. Therefore, rather than adopt a more geographically and temporally proximate reference for their action – that of a European radical direct-action tradition unburdened by the association of dictatorial regimes – the PAH instead adopted a more geographically 'distant' (but closer to them in significant ways) frame for their action. The application of the *escrache* tactic in a very different national context shows how the adoption of transnational tactics involves active processes of cultural translation and how the reception, contestation and counter-contestation are dynamic – involving framing and counter-framing by multiple political actors – but also strongly bounded by national political discursive repertoires. The case also highlights the consequences of the specific framing of the adoption of transnational tactics for movement actors and how the framing of the tactic is not inherent to the tactic itself but is culturally constructed. While the PAH and the 15-M attempted to innovate tactically and introduce new language and associations through the *escrache*, the political elites and affiliated media relentlessly countered by trying to redefine these innovations in terms of familiar political tropes and recurrent points of reference, such as ETA terrorism, and to draw them into their partisan disputes with the PSOE, in this way attempting to deny them credibility as a grassroots non-aligned organisation. The PAH, too, drew on Spain's political history and attempted to gain political mileage from the association of the PP with the Franco dictatorship, a tactic with powerful symbolism but one that also alienated them from part of their initially sympathetic public and made accusations against them of being partisan more credible, despite their own outspoken criticism of the PSOE on numerous occasions.

This case is particularly interesting because it throws into question certain elements of dominant models of diffusion processes. As Chabot and Duyvendak

(2002: 706) have pointed out, most diffusion theorists concur that diffusion items must be clearly discernible; that they involve media and interpersonal channels of interaction; that they follow a linear and sequential temporal process; and that they spread within particular social systems, usually involving geographical proximity, especially in first instance. In contrast, they argue that diffusion may be 'dynamic, ambiguous and malleable' and that rather than simply involving emulation they can involve creative learning on the part of the 'receivers' (2002: 703). The PAH application of the *escrache* involved creative application and active framing work, first to dislocate the tactic from its known context and then to relocate it to a very different new context. Chabot and Duyvendak (2002: 706) argue that the 'key receivers' of diffusion are in fact 'critical communities', that is, 'networks of excluded citizens who identify new social problems, formulate new modes of thinking and feeling, and develop new political and cultural solutions'. The PAH and the 15-M/Indignados movement form part of this critical community. Yet, it is difficult to see the PAH as 'receivers', in that the process of adoption involved such an active resuscitation and translocation of the *escrache* tactic. The case renders problematic the language used to make distinctions between the originators of a movement practice and subsequent adopters of the practice. Distinctions between 'innovators' and 'adopters' or 'transmitters' and 'receivers', which are so often used in describing diffusion processes, fail to capture the creative and innovative activity required for adopters to translate practices across geographical, political and sometimes historical contexts. In adopting the *escrache* technique, the PAH took a gamble on their own ability to overcome the challenges posed by the 'dislocation' and 'relocation' of a foreign innovation, which was only partly successful. They combined elements of the original *escrache* with elements of its application in a financial-crisis context in a creative yet sometimes internally contradictory way. The highly moral framing of the campaign and the strong identification of the adopters with the activists of the original *escraches* perhaps helps explain this unusual cross-time, cross-national diffusion. Jasper (1997: 9) highlights the cultural creativity of moral protest and its 'vital contribution to modern societies'. The PAH directed the *escrache* campaign specifically towards targeted politicians – whose opinion leaders and affiliated media outlets reacted in predictable ways – and more generally toward the public at large. They were largely unsuccessful in changing the hearts, minds or behaviour of the former and, in fact, lost some of their initially high support among the latter. Yet, through their adoption of the *escrache*, they opened up a larger debate in Spanish society about the limits of democracy and the right to protest itself. This debate was then inserted into an even larger social debate, fostered by the many 15-M and Indignados assemblies and 'colour tides'[4] around the meaning of democracy in the context of crisis and austerity. Jasper (1997: xiii) argues that in modern society, protest movements 'are one of the few places where we can see people working out

---

4. 'Colour tides' (or *mareas cuidadanas*) are civil society protests organised around specific themes or sectors, such as health or education.

new moral, emotional and cognitive sensibilities'. The framing work done by the PAH discussed here forms part of a much wider narrative shift around the morally acceptable limits of contemporary capitalism (Flesher Fominaya 2014b). While a detailed discussion of this lies outside the scope of this chapter, it is important to situate this case of cross-national diffusion within a larger national and global process of social contestation to the notions of the 'inevitable' and 'unavoidable' negative consequences of the global financial crisis (Flesher Fominaya 2014b).

The PAH also acted as the initiators of the diffusion of the tactic to other social-movement groups and issues in Spain (such as the *escrache feminista*). The case, therefore, also highlights further the unintended and dynamic aspect of transnational diffusion, which involves not just emulation but creativity; and also shows the role of political culture in shaping its unpredictable reception in a new context. The PAH have now stopped their *escrache* campaign but don't discount using it again 'if we consider it opportune' (*El País* 2013, 'La PAH abandona los *escraches*'). Strang and Soule (1998: 278) argue that 'practices that accord with cultural understandings of appropriate and effective action tend to diffuse more quickly than those that do not.' In Spain today, the *escrache* is a highly contested practice that even practitioners seem to have some doubts about. But this is often the case with innovation. Only time will tell if the *escrache* is destined to become a durable tactical innovation in Spanish political culture and if, after its unusual and controversial leap across space and time, it will follow more habitual routes of diffusion across the European anti-austerity protest landscape, or where it might go from there.

References

ABC (2013a) 'Leopoldo Barreda recurrirá a la Justica si Stop Deshaucios le coacciona', 29 March, http://www.abc.es/espana/20130329/abci-*escrache*-leopoldo-201303282130.html (accessed 19 February 2014).

— (2013b) 'Los "antidesahucios" hacen de Valencia su base de operaciones', 6 April, http://www.abc.es/comunidad-valencia/20130406/abcp-antidesahucios-hacen-valencia-base-20130406.html (accessed 19 February 2014).

— (2013c) 'Que aclaren por qué han apoyado al entorno de ETA', 26 March, http://hemeroteca.abcdesevilla.es/nav/Navigate.exe/hemeroteca/sevilla/abc.sevilla/2013/03/26/054.html (accessed 19 February 2014).

BBVA (2010) Boletin Fundación BBVA 21, http://www.fbbva.es/TLFU/dat/Boletin_fbbva_21_pags16-17.pdf (accessed 4 March 2014).

Beissinger, M. R. (2007) 'Structure and example in modular political phenomena: the diffusion of bulldozer/rose/orange/tulip revolutions', *Perspectives on Politics* 5 (2): 259–76.

Chabot, S. and Duyvendak, J. W. (2002) 'Globalization and transnational diffusion between social movements: reconceptualizing the dissemination of the Gandhian repertoire and the "coming out" routine', *Theory and Society* 31 (6): 697–740.

Colau, A. and Alemany, A. (2013) 'Carta de Ada Colau al Presidente del Gobierno, Mariano Rajoy. *¡Sí Se Puede! Crónica de una pequeña gran victoria*', Barcelona: Destino.

Council Directive 93/13/EEC of 5 April 1993 on unfair terms in consumer contracts, http://eur-lex.europa.eu/LexUriServ/LexUriServ.do?uri=CELEX:31993L0013:en:HTML, Official Journal L 095, 21/04/1993 P. 0029 –0034 (accessed 19 February 2014).

Duva, J. (2013a) 'El Gobierno sanciona por *escrache* a 18 personas', *El País*, 11 April, http://politica.elpais.com/politica/2013/04/11/actualidad/1365680741_380337.html (accessed 4 March 2014).

— (2013b) 'La policía borra "*escrache*" del diccionario', *El País*, 23 April, http://politica.elpais.com/politica/2013/04/22/actualidad/1366630655_201564.html (accessed 19 February 2014).

El País (2013) 'La PAH abandona los *escraches*' EFE/EL PAIS, 15 June, http://politica.elpais.com/politica/2013/06/15/actualidad/1371300847_651873.html (accessed 4 March 2014).

Europa Press (2013) 'La protesta es una forma de diálogo, pero tiene un límite', afirma el PP', Agencia Europa Press, 8 April, http://www.europapress.es/nacional/noticia-pp-dice-*escraches*-protesta-puede-ser-forma-dialogo-limite-violencia-20130408172955.html (accessed 19 February 2014).

Flesher Fominaya, C. (2005) 'The Logic of Autonomy', Ph.D. Dissertation: University of California, Berkeley (Published as Cristina Flesher Eguiarte).

— (2007) 'The role of humour in the process of collective identity formation in autonomous social movement groups in contemporary Madrid', *International Review of Social History* 52: 243–58.
— (2010) 'Creating cohesion from diversity: the challenge of collective identity formation in the Global Justice Movement', *Sociological Inquiry* 80 (3): 377–404.
— (2014a) 'Movement culture as habit(us)', in B. Baumgarten, P. Daphi and P. Ullrich (eds) *Conceptualizing Culture in Social Movement Research*, London: Palgrave MacMillan.
— (2014b) *Social Movements and Globalization: How protests, occupations and uprisings are changing the world*, London: Palgrave MacMillan.
— (forthcoming) 'Debunking spontaneity: Spanish Indignados as autonomous movement', *Social Movement Studies*.
França, J. (2013) 'Nunca tiraremos la toalla porque no nos lo podemos permitir', interview with Ada Colau, El Diario.es, 15 February, http://www.eldiario.es/catalunya/entrevista-Ada_Colau-ILP-PAH-Desahucios_0_101489868.html (accessed 19 February 2014).
Garea, F. (2013) 'Mengua el fuerte apoyo inicial a los *escraches*, según Metroscopia', *El País*, 8 April, http://politica.elpais.com/politica/2013/04/07/actualidad/1365358645_241274.html (accessed 19 February 2014).
H.I.J.O.S. (undated) 'Comisión *Escrache*', http://www.hijos-capital.org.ar/index.php?option=com_content&view=section&layout=blog&id=7&Itemid=407.
Jasper, J. (1997) *The Art of Moral Protest*, Chicago, IL: Chicago University Press.
La Vanguardia (2013) 'Interior ordena a la policía identificar a los participantes en *escraches* contra políticos', 30 March.
Ley Orgánica 1/1992, de 21 de febrero, sobre Protección de la Seguridad Ciudadana, published in B.O.E., 22 February, http://noticias.juridicas.com/base_datos/Admin/lo1-1992.html (accessed 4 March 2014).
McAdam, D. and Rucht, D. (1993) 'The cross-national diffusion of movement ideas', *Annals of the American Academy of Political and Social Science*, 528 (1): 56–74.
Manetto, F. and Fernández, M. (2013) 'Cospedal advierte sobre los *escraches*: "La violencia genera violencia"', *El País*, 16 April, http://politica.elpais.com/politica/2013/04/15/actualidad/1366050042_321073.html (accessed 19 February 2014).
Martínez López, M. A. and García Bernardos, A. (2011) 'The occupation of squares and the squatting of buildings: lessons from the convergence of two social movements', http://www.miguelangelmartinez.net/IMG/pdf/articulo_Bilbao_v4_book_doc.pdf (accessed 19 February 2013).
Metroscopia Surveys (2013a) Encuesta de Metroscopia para El País, March, http://www.metroscopia.org/datos-recientes/analisis-blog/item/sentencia-*escraches*-y-burbuja (accessed 4 March 2014).
— (2013b) Encuesta de Metroscopia para El País, April, http://www.metroscopia.org/datos-recientes/analisis-blog/category/series-temporales (accessed 4 March 2014).

Mora, M. (2013) 'Rajoy tilda de antidemocrático el acoso a los políticos', *El País*, 3 March, http://politica.elpais.com/politica/2013/03/26/actualidad/1364325482_485124.html (accessed 19 February 2014).
O'Broin, M. (2012) 'PIIGS y derecho a la vivienda. Observatorio Metropolitano de Barcelona', http://stupidcity.net/articulos/piigs-y-derecho-a-la-vivienda/ (accessed 19 February 2014).
Owens, L. *et al.* (2013) 'At home on the road', in C. Flesher Fominaya and L. Cox (eds), *Understanding European Movements: New social movements, global justice struggles, anti-austerity protest*, London: Routledge.
PAH (2012a) '#HablaLaPAH: las soluciones a los desahucios que PP y PSOE ignoran. #PPSOEcómplices del #GenocidioFinanciero', 12 November, http://afectadosporlahipoteca.com/2012/11/12/hablalapah-soluciones-a-los-desahucios-ignoradas-por-pp-psoe-en-cumbre-antidesahucio/ (accessed 19 February 2014).
— (2012b) 'Lo llaman Crisis, pero es una estafa. Lo llaman Suicidio, pero es #GenocidioFinanciero', 25 October, http://afectadosporlahipoteca.com/2012/10/25/lo-llaman-crisispero-es-una-estafa-lo-llaman-suicidio-pero-es-genocidiofinanciero-la-pah-convoca/ (accessed 19 February 2014).
— (2013a) 'Campaña de envío masivo de mails a los senadores', 23 April, http://afectadosporlahipoteca.com/2013/04/23/campana-de-envio-masivo-de-mails-a-los-senadores/ (accessed 19 February 2014).
— (2013b) 'Comparecencia de la PAH en el Parlamento Europeo: La PAH denuncia en Europa la vulneración sistemática de derechos humanos', 24 April, http://afectadosporlahipoteca.com/2013/04/24/comparecencia-de-la-pah-en-el-parlamento-europeo-la-pah-denuncia-en-europa-la-vulneracion-sistematica-de-derechos-humanos (accessed 19 February 2014).
— (2013c) 'La PAH presenta: Mensaje a los votantes del PP', 5 April, http://afectadosporlahipoteca.com/2013/04/05/la-pah-presenta-mensaje-a-los-votantes-del-pp/ (accessed 19 February 2014).
— (2013d) 'Protocolos de *escrache* y acciones contra los bancos', http://*escrache*.afectadosporlahipoteca.com/wp-content/uploads/sites/2/2013/03/Protocolos-de-acciones-y-*escrache*.pdf (accessed 4 March 2014).
Palmer, R. (1959, 1964) (2 vols.) *The Age of Democratic Revolutions*, Princeton, NJ: Princeton University Press.
Peregil, F. (2013) 'Comencé a *escrachar* al encontrarme en un bar al torturador de mi padre', *El País*, 4 April, http://politica.elpais.com/politica/2013/04/12/actualidad/1365788868_011504.html (accessed 19 February 2014).
Romanos, E. (2013) 'Collective learning processes within social movements', in C. Flesher Fominaya and L. Cox (eds) *Understanding European Movements: New social movements, global justice struggles, anti-austerity protest*, New York and London: Routledge.

Scholl, C. (2013) 'Europe as contagious space: cross-border diffusion through EuroMayDay and social climate justice movements', in C. Flesher Fominaya and L. Cox (eds) *Understanding European Movements: New social movements, global justice struggles, anti-austerity protest*, New York and London: Routledge.

Strang, D. and Meyer, J. (1991) 'Institutional conditions for diffusion', paper delivered for workshop on New Institutional Theory, Ithaca, NY, cited in McAdam and Rucht 1993.

Strang, D. and Soule, S. A. (1998) 'Diffusion in organizations and social movements: from hybrid corn to poison pills', *Annual Review of Sociology* 24: 265–90.

Tejedor, E. and Reventós, L. (2013) 'Cuando la protesta llega hasta la puerta de casa', *El País*, 23 March, http://sociedad.elpais.com/sociedad/2013/03/22/actualidad/1363986241_412309.html (accessed 19 February 2014).

Tilly, C. (1976) 'Major forms of collective action in Western Europe 1500–1975', *Theory and Society* 3 (3): 365–75.

Traugott, M. (1995) 'Barricades as repertoire: continuities and discontinuities in the history of French contention', in M. Traugott (ed.) *Repertoires and Cycles of Collective Action*, Durham, NC: Duke University Press, pp. 142–73.

Wood, L. (2010) 'Horizontalist youth camps and the Bolivarian Revolution', *Journal of World System Research* 16: 48–62

Chapter Three

Learning Democracy: Cross-Time Adaptation in Organisational Repertoires

Donatella della Porta

On 25 January 2011, four meeting points for protestors are set in four areas of Cairo, including working-class neighbourhoods. Before moving towards the city centres, the marchers travel through narrow residential streets, gathering participants on their way. Marches thus create physical occasions to join, then carrying participants to their destination. As a protestor puts it, 'You're taken to Tahrir by the demonstration itself as the head of the march guides it there.' (El Chazli 2012).

On 15 May 2011, indignant citizens start a permanent occupation of Puerta del Sol in Madrid, building a tent city for hundreds of protestors, but also other infrastructures for thousands of visitors. The mobilisation quickly spreads to hundreds of Spanish cities all around the country 'as the encampments rapidly evolved into "cities within cities", governed through popular assemblies and committees' (Postill 2011).

In the summer of 2011, mobilisation against austerity grows in Greece. On 28 May, the first tents are set up on Syntagma Square, while the movement quickly spreads throughout the country. Highly choreographed protests are organised on Syntagma every day at 6 pm, but there are also daily assemblies: those who want to speak are given a number, then there is a lottery, and the numbers drawn are allowed to speak (Sergi and Vogiatzoglou 2013).

On 17 September, about a thousand protestors march on Wall Street in New York City, settling a camp in Zuccotti Park. Also there, 'from these scattered nodes in a small emergent network, a thunderous protest network grew in a matter of weeks, aided by webs of communication technologies deployed by activists and supporters who seized the political opportunities surrounding a severe economic crisis. Soon the city encampments had spread around the United States ...' (Bennett and Segerberg 2013: 180).

As emerges clearly from these short accounts, within a few months, a form of protest, the *acampada*, spread across three continents. Indeed, its relevance in the very identity-building of these mobilisations led activists and scholars alike to speak of 'square movements' (Glasius and Pleyers 2013). While Tahrir Square in Egypt is often considered the origin of the chain of diffusion, forms of *acampadas* had already developed in Latin America in the struggles against neo-liberalism in the 1990s and 2000s (Silva 2009) – although without such a strong identifying function.

While other chapters in this volume focus on the strengths and limits of cross-national spreading, linking the successful travelling of *acampadas* to the presence of some specific political and cultural resources, the aim of this chapter is to address *acampadas* as a cross-time evolution – adoption but also adaptation – of some ideas that had already emerged in the Global Justice Movement (GJM) of the beginning of the millennium. As we will see in this chapter (after reviewing some main contributions to social-movement studies on the diffusion of organisational aspects of protest), the emphasis on horizontality that characterises this anti-austerity wave of protest, much more than the previous ones, reflects not only the restatement of the role of the 'simple' citizens ('Without Us, You're Nothing') but also a search for alternatives outside hierarchical institutions. The lack of responsiveness of public institutions can explain why recent movements have emphasised the need to build such alternatives, rather than looking for party alliances (della Porta 2013c). Looking at the organisational dynamics within social movements, I shall address the search for a 'prefigurative' (Leach 2003: 1004) politics that characterised the most visible moments of the anti-austerity protest, the *acampadas* (as long-lasting protest camps in public spaces), comparing them with the most innovative organisational form of the Global Justice Movement, the forum.

This chapter aims to develop a comparison of repertoires of action, using secondary analysis of existing research on anti-austerity protests and on one of its precursors, the Global Justice Movement. This brings attention to another dimension that is rarely addressed through ideas of diffusion: the cross-time evolution of organisational repertoires. From one wave of protest to the next, ideas travel through direct channels, such as re-mobilised activists from previous generations, as well as accumulated collective memory (*see* Zamponi and Daphi, Chapter Nine in this volume). In fact, diffusion is filtered through learning processes as collective assessment of the successes and failures of previous movements in terms of organisational choices. After developing the theoretical argument, I will look at the evolution in two main organisational forms of the respective movements: the forum for the GJM and the camp for the anti-austerity protests. Next, I will propose an explanation of these changes, based on the differences in structural basis, cultural norms and resources for communication.

Theorising cross-time diffusion

Social science research on diffusion of ideas has looked especially at their spread across spaces. However, some of the findings in that literature could be paralleled in reflection on cross-time adoption and adaptation.

What facilitates cross-time diffusion?

First, physical proximity has often been considered to be a primary condition for special diffusion: research on democratisation has, for instance, evolved around specific waves in specific geopolitical areas – Southern Europe, Latin America and Eastern Europe, just to cite some examples. While geographical proximity was initially looked at especially in terms of facilitating channels of communication, important dimensions were later singled out in the contextual similarities that facilitated similar reactions, including threats or opportunities going beyond borders. So, potential access to the EU in Southern Europe in the 1970s, or changes in the Soviet Union's internal and external politics for Eastern Europe, were indeed important elements for explaining the respective waves of democratisation. Similarly, socio-economic transformations – such as neo-liberal shock therapies and their social effects – were common challenges for authoritarian regimes in Latin America as well as North Africa and the Mediterranean countries. For cross-time diffusion, this implies that ideas imported from previous movements must be adapted to contextual evolution.

Emphasis on similar conditions also helped researchers to move from an understanding of diffusion as (unreflective) imitation to a more conscious strategic choice. In other words, the spreading of ideas did not happen randomly but required, at least in order to be successful, some common facilitating circumstances. These sets of assumptions can be adapted when we think in terms of cross-time diffusion: we can indeed assume that movements will build on the ideas developed by their immediate predecessors, especially if and when their circumstances are similar to those faced by those predecessors.

This type of approach to cross-spatial diffusion accompanied conceptions of organisational choices as strategically linked to environmental conditions. In social-movement studies, the resource-mobilisation approach has long stressed the need for mobilising structures that can transform grievances into collective action. Protest is indeed not an individual act; rather, it requires planning, co-ordination and collective choices. In this perspective, research focused especially on the strategic dimension of organising: social-movement activists, like other collective actors, have had long debates (and often controversies) about the best formula to use for recruiting members, keeping commitments, influencing public opinion and reaching out to decision-makers. Social-movement organisations indeed act strategically – at least as much as other political organisations do.

This does not mean, however, that ideas coming from outside cannot also be tested under unfavourable circumstances. The importation into Europe of guerrilla models from the Cuban revolution is an extreme testimony to these failed attempts. In fact, like any organisational population, social-movement organisations are subject to environmental selection. This means that, in each wave of protest, various models are tried and tested; but only a few survive, usually transformed in order to adapt to the quick evolution (ups and downs) of the mobilisation. The context within which they interact strongly influences the range of choices available, especially the successful ones. In a cross-time perspective, we might consider previous movements as constituting organisational repertoires from which ideas are taken and tested.

In social-movement studies, some claims have indeed been made about the effects of political institutions: inclusive systems are said to allow for the development of large, unitary and moderate movement organisational structures; exclusive systems, instead, favour weak, fragmented and radical ones (for example, Kriesi 1996). Historical evolutions are relevant for cross-national diffusion, as we might expect emerging movements to adapt existing repertoires to meet the challenges of a transformed context. Reflection on globalisation processes at different levels affected reflections on cross-national development in different ways. First, technological innovations created channels of communication that could overcome boundaries easily. In parallel, transnational networks developed more and more among social-movement organisations and activists of different countries (and continents). Additionally, there was a growing recognition of common global developments having effects worldwide. Although it did not always create similar conditions, globalisation did facilitate cultural phenomena of assessment of similarities, favoured by the increasing intensity in direct and indirect channels of communication. If we adapt this way of thinking to cross-time diffusion, we can expect that this will be facilitated when there are direct and indirect channels transferring information from old movements to new. Memory can be carried on by activists who re-mobilise from one wave of protest to the next or it can be somehow embedded in various types of outlets (Zamponi and Daphi, Chapter Nine in this volume). In addition, the content of the memory of the past would affect cross-time diffusion as it filters the assessment of similarities.

While reflections on diffusion as context-bound have often been linked especially to the search for effective strategy, ideas are also transmitted on another, more normative, dimension. Movements aim at constructing organisations that are, or at least are perceived to be, at the same time efficient and just. Decision-making in social movements is not only about how to better promote protests; rather, the organisational forms it takes affects many characteristics of a movement. Research on organisational sociology stresses the positive role played by the coherence and authenticity of organisational identities and of organisational learning as knowledge-sharing (Soule 2013). In a similar direction, research on social movements has pointed at the importance of prefigurative organisational forms – prefigurative politics meaning 'a political orientation based on the premise that the ends a social movement achieves are fundamentally shaped by the means it employs, and that movements should therefore do their best to choose means that embody or "prefigure" the kind of society they want to bring about' (Leach 2013: 1004). In this sense, activists must seek to develop 'counterhegemonic institutions and modes of interactions that embody the desired transformations' (Leach 2013: 1004), in particular through consensus and participatory democracy. As Francesca Polletta has suggested, movement organisational format, even when inefficient, can be preferred by many activists for its expressive and redemptive characteristics: as 'by enacting within the movement itself values of radical equality, freedom, and community, activists have sought to bring into being a society marked by those values' (Polletta 2013: 908). As we will see, although strategic elements are certainly recognised in organisational choices, prefigurative aims are also relevant, as enacted organisational models change the relations within the movement by activating cognitive, affective and relational mechanisms. Conceptions and practices of democracy acquire central relevance in this evolution. Strategy as orientation to effective means is, therefore, only part of the story. In fact, we can expect that previously existing types of organisational structures are also relevant in cross-time diffusion: what needs to travel is not only applied knowledge but also normative concerns. In this sense, analysis of cross-time diffusion needs to include the cultural milieu in which some organisational formats and related norms can survive in the doldrums.

In sum, we can expect the cross-time learning process to be influenced by some transformations in both their contexts in general and in social-movement sectors more specifically. In particular, from one movement to the next, the social bases of mobilisation might change, together with the widespread cultures.

What travelled across time? Conceptions of democracy in social movements

The complex development of adoption and adaptation can be observed if we compare conceptions and practices of democracy in the Global Justice Movement and the anti-austerity protests. In what follows, I will discuss this perspective on cross-time diffusion by looking at the anti-austerity protests' adoption of some ideas coming from the GJM; but I will also look at the adaptation of those ideas to a changing context.

Building upon normative democratic theory, I have defined a participatory-deliberative model as made up of the following elements (della Porta 2009a and 2009b; 2013a):

- *Preference – (trans)formation*, as 'deliberative democracy requires the transformation of preferences in interaction' (Dryzek 2000: 79);

- *Orientation to the public good*, as it 'draws identities and citizens' interests in ways that contribute to public building of public good' (Cohen 1989: 18–19);

- *Rational argumentation*, as people are convinced by the force of the better argument (Habermas 1981);

- *Consensus*, as decisions must be approvable by all participants;

- *Equality*, as deliberation takes place among free and equal citizens (as 'free deliberation among equals' (Cohen 1989: 20);

- *Inclusiveness*, as all citizens with a stake in the decisions to be taken must be included in the process and able to express their views;

- *Transparency*, as a deliberative democracy is 'an association whose affairs are governed by the public deliberation of its members' (Cohen 1989: 17).

These seven elements might be distinguished in terms of conditions, means, and effects: we have participatory deliberative democracy when, under conditions of equality, inclusiveness and transparency, a communicative process based on reason (the strength of the good argument) is able to transform individual preferences and reach decisions oriented to the public good (della Porta 2009a).

I shall look at continuities and adaptation across time, moving from the Global Justice Movement to the anti-austerity protests. I will then point at learning processes as well as at to contextual adaptation as explanations for cross-time diffusion.

Adapting participatory and deliberative democracy

Those who protested in Tahrir, Kasbah, Sol, Syntagma, or Zuccotti did not just criticise existing representative democracy as deeply corrupted but also experimented with different models of democracy. In part, conceptions and practices of democracy were inspired by the participatory and deliberative models of previous citizens' mobilisations. In part, however, protestors also innovated, in a process of collective learning from detected weaknesses of those models in the past and adaptation to new endogenous and exogenous challenges.

In all of the protest waves mentioned in the Introduction, the *acampada* – at the same time repertoire of protest and organisational form – represented a major democratic experiment, adopted and adapted from one context to the next. The social forums had been the democratic invention of the Global Justice Movement of the previous decade; the *acampadas* represented, in part, an updating of those but were in part also a development oriented to overcome their perceived failures. Conceptions of participation from below, cherished by progressive social movements, are, in fact, combined with a special attention to the creation of egalitarian and inclusive public spheres.

The anti-austerity activists' discourse on democracy is articulate and complex, taking up some of the principal criticisms of the ever-decreasing quality of liberal democracies but also some proposals inspired by democratic qualities other than representation. These proposals resonate with (more traditional) participatory visions, but also with new deliberative conceptions that underline the importance of creating multiple public spaces, egalitarian but plural. To a certain extent, the *acampada* can be seen in continuity with the social-forum model, although with increased emphasis on democratic qualities of participation and deliberation.

In particular, I will point to the shifts synthesised in Table 3.1. As I will argue, while the social forums mixed both associational and assembly forms with an emphasis on consensus, the *acampadas* refused associations and privileged the participation of persons – the citizens, the members of the community. From the relational point of view, whereas the social-forum process was oriented to networking, the *acampadas* follow a more aggregative logic (Juris 2012).

From the cognitive point of view, while the forum aimed at building political alternatives, the *acampadas* were more prefigurative. In fact, referring to existing research on Tahrir Square, Puerta del Sol and Place de Cataluna, Syntagma Square and Zuccotti Park (but also to the failed *acampadas* in Italy), I will single out in what follows many similarities but also some differences. These differences are, in part, the product of learning processes, after a perceived decline in the innovative capacity of the social-forum process. However, they also reflect both adaptation to a context characterised by a legitimacy crisis of late neo-liberalism and by its social and political consequences and also to national opportunities and constraints.

Table 3.1: Dimensions of democracy: from forums to camps

	Forums	Camps
Transparency	Open meeting places	In open-air space
Equality	In associational democracy	In communitarian/direct democracy
Inclusiveness	Movement of movements	The people
Consensus	Within spokes-councils and SMOs	In assemblies, open to all
Argumentation	Rational/political	Prefigurative/emotional
Orientation to	Cognitive work towards public good	Construction of 'the common'
Preference-transformation	Within GJM	In 99 per cent

Transparency, equality and inclusivity

Transparency, equality and inclusivity are values cherished by both movements, although with some important differences. The camps are set in open-air spaces in order to enforce the public and transparent nature of the process. Meeting in public spaces also stresses the inclusiveness of the process and the refusal of delegates represents a further emphasis upon equality.

Social forums have been an innovative experiment promoted by the Global Justice Movement. Distinct from a counter-summit, which is mainly oriented towards public protest, the social forum is a space for debate among activists. The format of the social forum epitomised the cognitive processes that developed within protest events as arenas for encounters. The charter of the WSF defines it as an 'open meeting place', as participation is indeed open to all civil-society groups, with the exception of those advocating racist ideas, those using terrorist means and political parties. Its functioning involves the organisation of hundreds of workshops and dozens of conferences (with invited experts) during a very short span of time, and testifies to the importance given (at least in principle) to the production and exchange of knowledge. In fact, the WSF has been defined as 'a market place for (sometimes competing) causes and an "ideas fair" for exchanging information, ideas and experiences horizontally' (Schoenleitner 2003: 140).

Different activities converge on the aim of providing a meeting space for a huge number of loosely related groups, in order to lay the groundwork for a broader mutual understanding. Far from aiming at eliminating differences, the open debates are designed to increase awareness of each other's concerns and beliefs. The purpose of networking-through-debating was, in fact, openly stated as early as the first European Social Forum (ESF) in Florence, where the Declaration of the European Social Movements read: 'We have come together to strengthen and enlarge our alliances because the construction of another Europe and another world is now urgent ...' (*see* della Porta 2009a).

What seems to make cognitive exchanges especially relevant for the Global Justice Movement in general, and for the social forums in particular, is the positive value given to openness towards 'the others', considered in some activists' comments as a most relevant attitude in order to 'build nets from the local, to the national and the supranational' (della Porta 2009: 15). The development of inclusive arenas for the creation of knowledge emerged as a main aspiration in the social-forum process.

Diversity and transparency were highly valued but difficult to practise. Although the organisational process of social forums aimed to be open, in reality, at the global level, some main associations, as mentioned, tended to dominate decision-making. In Europe, the preparatory assemblies were open to all participants but still held in closed places. With the occupation of public squares, the Indignados movements stressed even more the open and transparent nature of their democratic model, as the very essence of parks and squares is public.

Not only are Tahrir, Kasba, Puerta del Sol and Syntagma open-air spaces but they were also most important points of encounter for the citizens. Keeping the main site of protest in the open, the movements also put a special emphasis on the inclusivity of the process, aiming at involving the entire agora. Not only parties and unions but also exclusionary associations of various types, such as racists, were indeed unwelcome.

The camps, in open air, responded to a reclaiming of public spaces by the citizens. So, in Egypt, in a society characterised by gated communities for the rich and slums for the masses of poor, the encounters at Tahrir but also the painting of murals represented a reappropriation of public space, especially after thirty years of emergency law had prevented gatherings (Winegard 2012). With the creation of a protest camp, Tahrir Square became the heart of the mobilisation in Egypt, 'participants ranging from Cairo's poor to middle and upper class people, across the political spectrum, as well as across religious divides' (Warkotsch 2012). The heterogeneity of the participants was mentioned with pride: 'people of different backgrounds, of different classes, just sitting together talking' (Gerbaudo 2012: 69). In Europe as well, the *acampadas* were intended to reconstruct a public sphere in which problems could be discussed and solutions looked for. Differently from the very temporary global convergence spaces of the social forums, *acampadas* are presented as 'rather occupation and subversion of prominent urban public spaces' (Halvorsen 2012: 431). As activists noted,

> we recovered and utilize the public space; we occupied the squares and the streets of our cities to meet and work in a collective open and visible way. We inform and invite every citizen to participate. We debate problems, look for solutions and organize actions and mobilizations. Our digital tools and networks are open: all the information is available on the Internet, in the streets, in the squares (15-M manifesto, 'How to cook a nonviolent revolution', quoted in Perugorría and Tejerina 2013: 436).

Similarly, an American activist defined Zuccotti Park as 'a sort of beautiful, exciting thing, which does not happen in public space in New York. Public space here is not really utilised in the way that it is utilised in the rest of the world.'.

If associational and participatory conceptions sometimes clashed on issues of representativeness and accountability in the forums, in the camps, participants often called for direct, unmediated democracy. In Spain, as it organised assemblies in the streets and the squares, the 15-M introduced a political logic in these spaces (Moreno Pestaña 2013), thus allowing people to learn new skills – protesting being one of them. The assemblies in the encampments were described by activists as 'primarily a massive, transparent exercise in direct democracy'. As a speaker of a commission in Sol declared: 'What unites us is a general dissatisfaction. We want a new model of society, based on the participation of all persons, an effective participatory democracy, where people can take part in decisions on the social, economic and political plans' (Nez 2012: 80). And an American activist so recounts one of the first evenings spent in Zuccotti Park:

> There were people who maybe they were there supporting like a union, or there were people who were there with signs saying they were professors ... we just stayed there and talked, it was a beautiful fall night ... and we stayed there on a ledge of the park ... and sort of just listened to other people's conversations, and there were a lot of debates. ... It was like a spirit, something that had life in it, and it was really reaffirming (Gerbaudo 2012: 122–3).

As emerges from these quotations, differently from the forums – which referred to themselves as spaces for 'the movement of movements', welcoming associations of different types (della Porta 2009a) – the camps are presented as spaces for 'the people', or the 'citizens'. The general assemblies, as main institutions of the *acampada*, testified to a broadly inclusive effort. In the social-forum process, the assemblies were important but somehow separated from the forum through the formula of the 'social-movement assemblies', usually held after the forums. The forum itself was mainly structured around workshops, in which activists exchanged information and networked rather than actually making decisions.

In the *acampadas*, the assemblies took a central role for the elaboration of strategic and tactical decisions for the movement: for the creation of a general programme, either specific as claims or at least as statements of intent but even more for the everyday management of the camps. In fact, 'the aim is to promote in all movement assemblies a transparent and horizontal way of functioning that would allow to each person to participate on an equal foot' (Nez 2011). General assemblies often broke down into committees, which then reconvened within it, the spokes of the various commissions referring to the general assemblies. Commissions on topics such as communication, mutual respect, infrastructure, laws and action co-ordinated working groups that worked through consensus. Liaison persons had to keep contacts among the various subgroups (Botella-Ordinas 2011). Thousands of propositions were thus put forward and in part approved by consensus: on politics, economy, ecology, education. On the model of the one in Puerta del Sol, all the general assemblies in Madrid neighbourhoods worked as spaces that had to be 'transparent, horizontal, where all persons can participate in an equal way' (Nez 2012: 84). In the United States, as in Spain, 'each camp quickly developed a few core institutions: if it was any size, at least there would be a free kitchen, medical tent, library, media/communication, center where activists would cluster together with laptops, and information center for visitors and new arrivals' (Graeber 2012, 240). Inclusion, absolute and of all, is a main principle of the assemblies: 'Inclusion. The strength of this movement is that we are many and different ... the spaces that make us strong, happy and active are those that everyone can perceive as her own' (toma la plaza, 12 August 2011, cited in Romanos 2011).

The more or less permanent occupations of squares were thus seen as creating a new agora in publicly owned spaces: 'Because the squares belong to us and they are locations of a new communitarian and participatory democracy' (Italian Revolution Milano 2011). Assemblies aimed at mobilising the common people, not activists but communities of persons, with personalised hand-made placards and individualised messages.

Consensual methods

Another main democratic formula, originating from the Global Justice Movement but further elaborated in the anti-austerity protests, is the consensual method. Consensual methods were adopted by several (but not all) organisations of the forum process in their internal decision-making but they were actually practised in different ways by different groups: in some cases pragmatically aiming at reaching agreements, in others with the ambition of creating a community (della Porta 2009b). In the camps, however, through inclusivity and respect for the opinions of all, a collective view was expected to emerge.

In Spain, consensual deliberative methods were proposed by young autonomous activists. While previous movements had experimented with direct democracy through consensus in spokes-councils, during the *acampadas* it was applied to the general assemblies, involving often hundreds of thousands of people. The aim was, according to a Spanish activist, to 'try to convince the other, and if the other disagree, develop the discussion in a constructive way' (della Porta 2009b). Consensual methods were similarly elaborated in the Occupy movement in the United States. A consensual, horizontal decision-making process developed based on the continuous formation of small groups, which then reconvened in the larger assembly. According to David Graeber, 'The process towards creative thinking is really the essence of the thing' (Graeber 2012: 23).

Deliberation through consensus is, in fact, seen as an instrument to prevent bureaucratisation but also as a way to prevent the assembly from becoming a matter of empty routine and to build a community. While the Global Justice Movement developed upon parties, with puppets and a carnival-like atmosphere, it was noted that 'OWS, in contrast, is not a party, it's a community' (Graeber 2012: 240).

Consensual decision-making implied some structures which were in part derived from the consensual processes devised by the horizontals in the GJM (della Porta 2009c). Building upon those experiments, the Indignados further developed those rules designed to implement equality and inclusivity. In Spain, regulations for the assemblies included limits on times for talking, hand gestures, rotating speakers and the preparation of *compte rendus* (read at the next assembly meeting). A commission on conflicts, managed by students, used techniques of psychology and group dynamics to improve participation and deliberation. Organisers also developed special techniques for assemblies; for example, participants were arranged in semi-circles and with corridors that allowed them to move around, with mediators and so on. Following horizontal practices, anyone could call for a working group; people then divided into small circles, coming back together after some time, with a speaker reporting on the debate in each group (Graeber 2012: 33). There was, moreover, the acknowledgment that the 'consensus process only works if it is combined with a principle of decentralization' (Graeber 2012: 227) and decisions are to be made 'on the smallest scale, the lowest level, possible' (Graeber 2012: 229). In the United States, instead of voting a controversial proposal up or down, groups that made decisions by consensus worked to refine it until everyone found it acceptable (Taylor *et al.* 2011: 47).

Democracy in the square was, in fact, defined as, first of all, inclusive and respectful of people's experiences. As Graeber (2012) noted about OWS,

> anyone who feels they have something relevant to say about a proposal ought to have their perspectives carefully considered. Everyone who has strong concerns or objections should have those concerns or objections taken into account and, if possible, addressed in the final form of the proposal. Anyone who feels a proposal violates a fundamental principle shared by the group should have the opportunity to veto ('block') the proposal. So, after someone made a proposal, the facilitator, after asking for clarifying questions, began to seek consensus. This process foresaw friendly amendments, temperature checks, hand signals (Graeber 2012: 214–15).

Consensus was thus assigned a deep meaning as capable of developing a truly collective view, as very different from the sum of individual ideas. The 'Fast Guide' produced by the 'Dynamisation of Assemblies' commission thus explained:

> Two people with different ideas put their energy together to construct something. It is not a question of my idea or yours. It is the two ideas together that will build something new that before neither of us knew. It is for this reason that an attentive listening, during which we are not just busy preparing our answer, is necessary. The collective thought is born when we understand that all opinions, ours and the different ones, are necessary in order to form consensus (toma la plaza, 31 May 2011, quoted in Romanos 2011).

Arguments, preference-transformation and orientation to the common

Similarly to the social forum, the *acampadas* have been sites of contention but also of exchange of information, reciprocal learning, individual socialisation and knowledge-building, in which emotions and prefiguration were given a larger role in the construction of the common. Cognitive mechanisms of frame-bridging were very important in the social-forum process. During the forums themselves but also during their preparation – sometimes up to a year long – participants prioritised the sharing of knowledge by activists from different countries, groups, ages and so on. In this process, alternative visions were built about globalisation, Europeanisation, the development of capitalism and similar concerns. Knowledge was exchanged mainly among activists and, in many cases, exchanges were facilitated by associations of various types. In the *acampadas*, the cognitive function was central but its production extended – so to speak – from the activists to the citizens. Community-building was an often-stated goal.

In Tahrir, bystanders were called to join in shouting slogans such as 'Bread, Freedom, and Dignity', as well as 'The People Want the Removal of the Regime'. Cognitive processes developed, as 'Tahrir was not all fun and festivity. The space was also infused with serious politics: fierce battles were waged against government thugs trying to break in, fiery speeches were delivered denouncing the regime, and animated discussions about Egypt's political future resounded in the night air' (Shokr 2012: 43). Similarly, interactions intensified in the many Tahrir squares that were built all over Egypt. There was an atmosphere of permanent parties ('like a night of Ramadan') but there were also political speeches.

While the forums had been described as a sort of university, where abstract knowledge was embedded in specific contexts, the *acampadas* privileged the personal knowledge of the individual participants and their direct experiences. Thus, whereas the forums privileged reason, emotions were more openly emphasised in the camps. As Postill (2012) vividly recalls, the strong sense of connection to the strangers I spoke to during that fleeting moment. ... Under normal circumstances – say, on an underground train – we would have found no reason to talk to one another, but the present situation was anything but normal. The 15-M movement had brought us together, and the sense of 'contextual fellowship' ... cutting across divides of age, class and race was very powerful.

Camps were places of talking and listening, where the building of collective identities was also sustained through the development of strong emotions. While the social-forum process was also fed by the intense moments of transnational encounters, as Naomi Klein herself observed, the stationary nature of the camps helped in building longer-lasting relations. So, the Global Justice Movement had chosen summits as targets, and 'summits are transient by their nature; they only last a week. That made us transient too. We'd appear, grab world headlines, and disappear.' (van Gelder *et al.* 2012: 46). In contrast, she noted, *acampadas* put no end to their presence and 'this is wise. Only when you stay put can you grow roots.' (van Gelder *et al.* 2012: 46).

Emotions were particularly strong in Tahrir, given the danger of the action and the dimension of the change; but they seem to have been more reflected upon in OWS, where the political culture of the activists most involved in the camp was more oriented to address individual feelings. Emotional charge was mentioned in connection with the camps in Tahrir, whose establishment on 28 January 2011 was said to represent an acceleration of history, with a cognitive shift from a language of demonstration to one of revolution (El Chazli 2012). So an activist recalled,

It was one of the most profound moments of my life. The sight of the square filled with tens of thousands heralded the long-awaited dawn. As we entered the square, the crowds installed there cheered the coming of a new battalion, greeting us with joy. I wept (quoted in El-Ghobashy 2011).

Tahrir has been described as 'the square that sings, dances, cries and hopes' (Guibal and Tangi 2011: 39), as '*Tahir vibre, Tahir exulte*' (Guibal and Tangi 2011: 40). The events were presented as part of a moment of epiphany: as a 'truly historical moment', a 'revolutionary moment' – in the words of an activist, 'everybody understood that it was, in fact, a moment' (Nigam 2012: 54).

In Spain, as elsewhere, activists talked of the joy of being together, developing a narrative of becoming (Perugorría and Tejerina 2013: 437). Open public spaces facilitated the creation of intense ties, through encounters among diverse people who suddenly felt they shared a common belonging. As Postill (2012) pointed out,

Many participants later reported a range of psychosomatic reactions such as goose bumps (*carne de gallina*) or tears of joy. I felt as if a switch had been turned on, a gestalt switch, and I had now awakened to a new political reality. I was no longer merely a participant observer of the movement, I was the movement.

In the same vein, in this Spanish activist's recollection, the encounters of so many and so different people produced an intense atmosphere of expectation:

> When I arrived to Calle de Alcalá and I saw all the people there I was very happy. And to see that there were so many people of different age, and to see that it was growing, and to see that we were a lot ... and now that I am telling you this I get goosebumps ... really I was so happy. When we arrived to Puerta del Sol, people starting sticking big posters on the buildings. People who were there were so unbelievably happy (Postill 2012).

Similarly, in the United States, the activities of Occupy Wall Street (OWS) were described as energising, inspiring, producing 'tears of inspiration. I did not know that popular power could bring with it such an overwhelming sensation. It is a chill ... a tremble that is both incredibly powerful ... and also a little scary, feeling how much power we can actually have together, side by side.' (Taylor *et al.* 2011: 31).

Both cognitive and affective mechanisms are embedded into networks of relations. Camps have at least two very relevant functions: to express protest and to prefigure new social relations.

The prefiguration of different relations was important for those who camped in Tahrir. This concern developed during the occupation, as:

> when protesters arrived at Tahrir on January 29, they did not come with the intention of creating a radical utopia. ... In many ways, Tahrir had come to represent the overall decline of public space – people could barely congregate or mingle, let alone protest – under Mubarak's thirty-year rule. The commune that Tahrir was to become was wholly improvised through the lived experience of sharing the area and protecting it from the regime encroachment. As the revolution unfolded, Tahrir was elevated from a rally site to a model for an alternative society (Shokr 2012: 42).

In Spain, Greece, and the United States, as well, in their discontent with mainstream politics, the Indignados saw the *acampadas* as experimentation with another form of democracy. As an activist wrote,

> What they want ... is to do exactly what they are doing. They want to occupy Wall Street. They have built a campsite full of life, where power is exercised according to their voices ... they are practising the politics of space, the politics of building a truly public space. ... It has become many things. Public square. Carnival. Place to get news. Daycare center. Health care center. Concert venue. Library. Performance space. School (Stoller 2011, cited in Castañeda 2012).

A discourse of management of the commons develops pragmatically around the management of the occupied spaces.

Similarly, when Occupy Wall Street started in the United States, quickly spreading to thousands of American cities, the occupations represented not only occasions to protest but also experiments with participatory and deliberative forms of democracy in the everyday life of the occupation. As an activist wrote, 'Democracy starts with people caring about one another and acting responsibly on that sense of care, taking responsibility both for oneself and for one's family, community, country, people in general and the planet' (Lakoff 2011: 1, cited in Langman 2013). In OWS, decisions about how to spend the sums donated and how to manage the camp took much time. Describing Occupy Boston, and citing an activist who talked about the 'small slice of utopia we are creating', Juris (2012: 268) singled out some tactical, incubating, and infrastructural roles of the occupied free spaces: among the first were attracting media attention and inspiring participation; among the second, 'providing a space for grassroots participatory democracy; ritual and community building, strategising and action planning, public education and prefiguring alternative worlds that embody movement visions'; among the third, networking and co-ordination.

In contrast to the movements of the previous decades, which had used a varied and plural repertoire, the *acampadas* became synonymous with the very identity of the movement, not just, as in occupations for other social movements, an action form among others. Beyond the prefiguration of a different society, which the activists already imagined, these spaces, as Razsa and Kurnik (2012) noted, were also important in the invention of alternative, but not yet imagined, futures, through what has been called a 'politics of becoming'. In the Occupy movement they studied in Slovenia, the encounters of diverse minorities transformed their respective visions. Occupied spaces have been seen, in fact, as 'vibrant sites of human interaction that modelled alternative communities and generated intense feelings of solidarity' (Juris 2012: 268). Aims included 'engaging in direct and transparent participatory democracy, exercising personal and collective responsibility ... empowering one another against all forms of oppression' (van Gelder *et al.* 2012: 25).

With more emphasis than in the social forums, what is considered most important is the process. In the United States,

> the encampments were consistently unwilling to make the effort to coalesce around what would conventionally be called demands and programs. Instead, what they seemed to relish most was themselves: their community and esprit, their direct democracy, the joy of becoming transformed into a movement, a presence, a phenomenon that was known to strangers, and discovering with delight just how much energy they had liberated. For indeed, in a matter of days, their sparks had ignited a fire (Gitlin 2012: 29).

From the forums to the camps: The learning process

While both movements stressed participation and consensus, therefore, we can see how some ideas, travelling in time, needed to be adapted in the light of what were perceived as previous mistakes. In particular, not only in the most visible peaks of protest but also in its doldrums, self-critical reflections continued to emerge on the functioning and dysfunctioning of some organisational models. Indeed, the camps grew out of a critique of the forum, which had been at the centre of the Global Justice Movement. In particular, activists built upon the strategies adopted by the GJM's horizontal wing.

The evolution of the GJM had already shown a gap between aspiration and reality, which activists critically noted. The ESF has indeed been an arena for debate and networking but also a space in which various conceptions of democracy had emerged and been developed. In addition to calls for a fluid, open and inclusive organisational structure (Andretta and della Porta 2009: 65), the internal debate between supporters of 'vertical' and 'horizontal' conceptions of democracy was already emerging at the first ESF in Florence in 2002. The representatives of local social forums called for a 'rootedness in the territory', the creation of open assemblies and a fluid structure, stressing the importance of the non-organised (Andretta and della Porta 2009: 65). By the second ESF, a main criticism addressed the role of the more 'institutional' organisations, accused of imposing a hierarchical and non-transparent structure on what was supposed to be an open and consensual process (Sommier 2005). The local social forums were particularly critical of a 'top-down' approach and those critiques were instrumental in the creation of autonomous spaces (Andretta and della Porta 2009: 65).

First and foremost, the capacity of the social forum process to overcome vertical power was thought to be limited. In the ESF assemblies, the different weight of various individuals was in fact (informally) recognised, according to their reputation within a sort of 'complex representation'. There was thus

> a process of closure due to relevance of personal networks of trust and shared experience. The EPA leadership is not inaccessible, as they welcome any help and 'expertise' to contribute to the process. But they welcome especially *new* expertise, and because of the immense experience accumulated within the leadership group, *new* expertise is difficult to find. People who can *contribute to the process* are highly valued; but what is considered as a valuable contribution is defined by those who are already there (Haug *et al.* 2009: 41).

Similarly for the WSF, the activist and sociologist Teivo Teivainen stressed that although 'it is strategically and morally desirable that movements that want to radically democratize the world apply democratic principles to themselves', 'pretending that there is no relations of power that should be made visible within the WSF process is the most harmful of these depoliticizing elements' (2004: 2–3). Although reflected in the grassroots workshop activities, the ideal of horizontality was indeed little represented in the governing body of the WSF (Pleyers 2005: 512).

As the degree of inclusiveness of the European Preparatory Assembly, which organised the various ESF editions, was often discussed, various groups preferred to organise autonomous spaces outside of the official forums. Testifying for tensions between norms and practices, the ESF organisational structure has often been reformed on such issues as the plenaries with invited speakers or the division of tasks among the national organising committees of the various ESF editions and the EPAs. Similarly, organisers have repeatedly transformed the WSF process, responding to some of the criticisms and appeals for more participatory and transparent decision-making (Teivainen 2002; Smith 2004: 417, 419; Pleyers 2007: 61). The constant restructuring of the organisational format reflects the perceived gap between norms and practices (on the ESF, *see* della Porta 2007; on the WSF, Smith *et al.* 2007).

The history of the social forums testifies, therefore, to the difficulties brought about by the implementation of deep democratic aspirations. Diversity became *per se* a source of tension. Horizontal and vertical conceptions of the movement organisation and even identity have often conflicted, bringing about several splits (della Porta 2009a). The ESF, like the WSF, emerged in fact as 'a plural and contested space' (Osterweil 2004: 187), in which different forms of power played a role in the preparatory process as well as in the days of the forum. In both, 'ideological differences were largely coded as disagreement over organisational process and form' (Juris 2005a: 264). Differences were especially visible in conceptions of democracy that contrasted horizontal versus vertical visions. If, from the normative point of view, the forum stressed 'horizontality', the organisations, as well as the activists taking part in the forum, favoured different organisational models. In various moments (especially around the third iteration of the ESF), tensions between a 'vertical' versus a 'horizontal' organisational vision indeed emerged. The same divisions have been noted in the WSF, where:

> The 'horizontals' favor more decentralized, loosely knit movement networks and organizations with flat, open, non-hierarchical, and more directly democratic decision making processes. They often are self conscious about prefiguring the type of society they want to create. However, they often lack mechanisms to ensure that those actually participating are accountable to, or represent the concerns of, constituents. The 'verticals', on the other hand, accept the need for hierarchy, institutionalism, professionalism, and representative structures. They include larger professional NGOs, trade unions, and affiliated parties. While some of these organizations, such as unions and parties, include mechanisms, such as elections or formal decision making processes, to try to keep leaders accountable to their members or constituents, larger professional NGOs often lack these mechanisms (Smith *et al.* 2007: 27–8).

These positions have been described as going beyond the preferred internal decision-making, aligning along two different registers:

> Whereas one side (the horizontals) sees culture itself as a political terrain – a site where real change is effected – the other (the verticals) believes that culture, form and structure are subservient to real politics (Osterweil 2004: 501).

Dissatisfaction with the democratic process had an effect in terms of declining mobilisation, as research on ESF participants indicated that activists' satisfaction in the GJM meetings is higher when they perceive that those who defend different and conflicting opinions treat each other as equals, and especially when the full participation of all those who are interested is promoted (Andretta and della Porta 2009: 83).

As the verticals became more and more prominent in the forum, the horizontal groups split from the forum process.

Since 2008, new waves of protest – for example, in schools and universities – were led by a new generation of activists who pushed forward new ideas that built upon, but also went beyond, the social-forum process (Zamponi 2012). At times, however, these protests lacked the capacity to expand beyond the established social movement milieu, fuelling a debate about better mobilisation strategies and practices. In addition, the dynamism of the square was counterpoised to the perceived encapsulation of cyberactivism in the digital sphere, with a statement of the importance of citizens as political protagonists: '*Sin Nosotros, No Sois Nada*' ('Without Us, They Are Nothing') (Sampedro Blanco and Sánchez Duarte 2011). The failure of previous attempts to expand protests beyond small circles of activists is stressed in Spain, as in the United States – where, Graeber noted, following 'the idea that the organizational form that an activist group takes should embody the kind of society we wish to create, the problem was breaking these ideas out of the activist ghetto and getting them in front of a wider public' (2012: 23).

In the *acampadas*, indeed, the horizontal vision prevailed, while the more associational model survived in other anti-austerity protests. A sort of learning process through movements continued within the anti-austerity protests, with self-criticism and adaptation to quickly changing conditions for mobilisation (della Porta 2015).

Organisational changes as adaptation to contextual changes

The camps reflected, therefore, a further development of the 'horizontal' vision of democracy that had been relevant, even if not dominant, in the GJM. In this section, I suggest that what made the horizontal organisation model (and conception of democracy) more successful in 2011 than in 2001 were also some contextual transformations in the potential social base, widespread norms and the available resources for protestors.

A type of constraint that social-movement studies has only sporadically addressed resides in the social characteristics of their potential basis of mobilisation, as it is affected by social structures. While researchers have established that social-movement organisations adapt to the types of networks existing in their environments (Diani 2005), stressing the need to make organisational supply and mobilising demand meet (Klandermans 2013), literature on the specific effects of activists' sociographic characteristics on social-movement organisations has been sporadic. Observing that social movements have a greater opportunity to spread in groups endowed with material resources and dense ties, new social-movement theorists have linked the decline of a hierarchical organisational model to the weakening of the reference basis of industrial workers, who had supported that model. Organisational adaptation then required a shift from hierarchy to networks. Literature on cleavages has indeed pointed to the challenges faced by traditional political parties and unions, given the numerical decline in their core constituency (Kriesi 1998). In particular, the disappearance of the ideological mass party, whose spread had been considered a victory of the labour movement, has been related to the dissolving of traditional political divisions along the left–right continuum. The attempt to expand the electoral base towards the middle class in fact brought about the (yet unsuccessful) search for new party organisational formulas. New social movements have been said to represent new social groups, which have more heterogeneous categorical tracts and are spatially less concentrated (Offe 1985). The discursive democracy of the GJM reflected, in fact, a heterogeneous social base, although the so-called 'new middle classes' were quite significantly present. In the camps, the appeal was instead to all the people affected by the austerity crisis (della Porta 2015) and to direct democracy as well as to prefiguration linked to the idea of developing a broad community oriented to a re-appropriation of the commons. Total equality and inclusivity responded, therefore, to this perception of the social basis of reference for the movement.

Beyond social structures, normative preferences also affect the choice of organisational formulas. As Elisabeth Clemens observed, an organisational model is more likely to be adopted to the extent that it 'is believed to work, involves practices and organisational relations that are already familiar, and is consonant with the organization of the rest of those individuals' social world' (1996: 154). Organisations have, in fact, been defined as arenas for conversation (Eliasoph 1998). As symbolic incentives are particularly important for activists, in order to be rewarding, participation requires social-movement organisations that embody activists' norms and values. Research on social movements has linked new organisational forms to cultural changes as well. Recent cultural transformations have been said to bring about the need to adapt mobilising strategies to multiple identities, with organisational structures that allow for multiple choices and give voices to individuals (Roggeband and Duyvendak 2013: 99). Some organisational characteristics of the camp reflect the need to attract these 'light communities', with light identities, loose ties, short-term engagement and low identification (Roggeband and Duyvendak 2013: 95). In this direction, various researchers have pointed to the 'shifting balance between organizations and individuals' (Walgrave 2013: 207), with decreasing availability to organise one's whole personal life around an activist identity. Although old types of organisations still stage protest events, the camps seems to reflect mobilisation processes in 'liquid societies' that are increasingly based on more informal co-ordination forms at the individual level. The assumption is that,

> In late modern societies, people become increasingly connected as individuals rather than as members of a community or group; they operate their own personal community networks. Traditional greedy institutions, such as trade unions and churches, which made significant demands on members' time, loyalty and energy, are replaced by light groups and associations that are loose, easy to join, and easy to leave (van Stekelenburg and Boekkooi 2013: 218).

Identities tend to be, that is, less and less pervasive (as broadly applied) and salient (Snow 2013), in a society that is more fragmented, differentiated and plural but also characterised by multiple identities. Organisational formats tend to adapt to these cultural characteristics in their strongly prefigurative functioning, as oriented to (re)build the community (and the commons).

New *technologies* have been considered not only as instruments that enhance protest ability but also as capable of shaping organisational formats, through their influence on the culture of participation. In general, social media (and new digital technologies in general) are expected to change participation in protest, as they make protesting less risky and help in forming and joining groups; but they are also less capable of producing strong bonds of solidarity (Polletta *et al.* 2013: 19). While even virtual collective identity seems able to mobilise, digital technologies facilitate especially some limited forms of commitment, such as consumption-based forms of sociability rather than more political forms of commitment (Polletta *et al.* 2013: 30). In fact, the personalisation of politics has been linked to different organisational models, in particular, through the use of digital media.

As Lance Bennett and Alexandra Segerberg (2013) have observed, personalised politics is not necessarily ineffective or disorganised but can be organised in different ways. In particular, connective action can be activated when 'interpersonal networks are enabled by technological platforms of various designs that coordinate and scale the networks' (Bennett and Segerberg 2013: 35). In fact,

> in place of content that is distributed and relationships that are brokered by hierarchical organizations, *connective action* networks involve co-production and co-distribution, revealing a different economic and psychological logic: peer production and sharing based on personalized expression (Bennett and Segerberg 2013: 35) [*author's empahsis*].

In this sense, communication not only serves to exchange information but, rather, 'communication routines can, under some conditions, create patterned relationships among people that lend organization and structure to many aspects of social life' (Bennett and Segerberg 2013: 8).

The camps were indeed closely linked to the use of new technologies. While in the past organisations had played the main role in mobilising for collective action, new forms of connective action, based on digital media, allow 'individuals to find personally comfortable ways to engage with issues on- and off-line' (Bennett and Segerberg 2013: 145). Spread through social media, personalised messages (or easily personalised ideas) emerge as easily persuasive. So the more spontaneous crowd-enabled networks, especially, are particularly efficacious in resource allocation, allowing for both short- and long-term adaptation to changing environments (Bennett and Segerberg 2013: 8). While personalised shifts have been defined as shallow and inefficient, 'personal action frames that emerge from connective networks often satisfy mass media demand for a simple angle and make it possible to intensify networking within various organizationally enabled and crowd-enabled organizations' (Bennett and Segerberg 2013: 7) – something that, indeed, worked well in the peak of mobilisation around the camps.

Learning democracy: Some conclusions

Organisational structures are, for movements, much more than instruments. Even if choices are often strategic, they are limited by a sort of inventory of available instruments that is, as an action-repertoire, built upon previous knowledge and only marginally innovatory (Clemens 1996). Not only knowledge but also norms define the realm of organisational possibilities. There is a learning process, too. Movements are, as Alberto Melucci (1989) stressed, self-reflective actors. Even from one generation to the next, the pros and cons, successes and failures of specific democratic devices are reflected upon and modified. In the short term, as well, in the intense moments of mobilisation in protest cycles or waves, movement activists develop their conceptions of democracy, introducing innovations that then travel across countries and from one movement-generation to the next. Learning processes and contextual adaptation are the main processes in this development.

As we have seen, in the *acampadas*, the principles of deliberative and participatory democracy – inherited from the previous movements – were adapted to the characteristics of a movement of 'common people' rather than activists, which privileged persons over associations (della Porta 2013b; 2013c; 2013d). Equality and inclusivity in public spaces was indeed more radical than in the Global Justice Movement, as testified by the camps' appeals to 'the 99 per cent'. To a certain extent, the emphasis on plurality as a positive value and the related need to be inclusive increased with the diversity of the citizens affected by the austerity measures. Radical inclusivity and equality were reflected in the choice of public spaces – such as parks and squares – as the pulsating heart of the movement, where there were no walls or fences to reduce the transparency and publicity of the process. The orientation to public goods to be obtained through the participation of all citizens in a high-quality discourse was embedded in the generalisation of the use of consensual methods, even for large assemblies. An alternative vision of the management of the commons was indeed prefigured in the camps.

The complex rules and norms of these horizontal conceptions of participation and deliberation were adopted from various groups, more or less embedded in national traditions, and adapted to a changing context. Spanish activists thus cited anarchism and US protesters pointed to Quakers as the progenitors of horizontalism; but also important were the ways in which the original ideas had been transformed through and by other movements, from the feminist to the anti-nuclear and the movement of autonomous squatted youth centres. In fact, the strength of these streams of national movement cultures influenced and limited the capacity of the *acampadas*, as specific democratic forms, to travel from one country to the next (Roos and Oikonomakis, Chapter Six in this volume). Moreover, it affected the adaptation of a long-lasting form of protest, the camp, as it travelled from Iceland to Egypt and then to Europe and the United States, becoming along the way more and more conceptualised by activists as a prefiguration of a different society.

Learning from previous movements does not, however, mean just adopting their forms by imitation but reflecting on their mistakes. As mentioned, even the experiences of the Global Justice Movement, the immediate progenitor, were not taken for granted but criticised because of an allegedly increasingly associational, or even hierarchical, vision of participation and deliberation that especially the new generations did not find resonant with their taste and experience. While representative democracy became increasingly affected by a deep legitimacy crisis, conceptions of direct democracy (re)emerged as more apt to organise highly critical citizens.

References

Andretta, M. and della Porta, D. (2009) 'Models of democracy: how activists see democracy', in D. della Porta (ed.) *Another Europe*, London: Routledge, pp. 65–85.

Bennett, L. and Segerberg, A. (2013) *The Logic of Connective Action: Digital media and the personalization of contentious politics*, Cambridge and New York: Cambridge University Press.

Botella-Ordinas, E. (2011) 'La démocratie directe de la Puerta del Sol', La Vie des idées, http//:www.laviedesidees.fr/La-democratie-directe-de-la-Puerta.html (accessed 24 May 2011).

Castañeda, E. (2012) 'The Indignados of Spain: a precedent to Occupy Wall Street', *Social Movement Studies* 11 (3–4): 309–19.

Clemens, E. S. (1996) 'Organizational form as frame: collective identity and political strategy in the American Labor Movement', in D. McAdam, J. McCarthy and M. N. Zald (eds) *Comparative Perspectives on Social Movements: Political opportunities, mobilizing structures, and cultural framing*, Cambridge and New York: Cambridge University Press, pp. 205–25.

Cohen, J. (1989) 'Deliberation and democratic legitimacy', in A. Hamlin and P. Pettit (eds) *The Good Polity: Normative analysis of the state*, Oxford: Basil Blackwell, pp. 17–34.

della Porta, D. (ed.) (2007) *The Global Justice Movement in Cross-National and Transnational Perspective*, Boulder, CO: Paradigm.

— (2009a) *Democracy in Social Movements*, London: Palgrave.

— (2009b) *Another Europe*, London: Routledge.

— (2009c) 'Another Europe: an introduction', in D. della Porta (ed.) *Another Europe*, London: Routledge, pp. 3–25.

— (2013a) *Can Democracy be Saved?*, Oxford: Polity Press.

— (2013b) 'Immoral neoliberalism and moral protest', keynote opening speech at the Annual Conference of the Consejo General del Trabajo Social, Malaga, November.

— (2013c) 'Bringing capitalism back in? Antiausterity protests in the crisis of late neoliberalism', paper presented at the ECPR General Conference, Bordeaux, September.

— (2013d) 'La llaman democracia y no lo es. Antiausterity protests in the legitimacy crisis of late neoliberalism', keynote opening speech at the Annual Conference of the Spanish Political Science Association, Seville, September.

— (2015) *Social Movements in Times of Austerity: Bringing capitalism back in*, Oxford: Polity Press.

Diani, M. (2005) 'Cities in the world: local civil society and global issues in Britain', in D. della Porta and S. Tarrow (eds) *Transnational Protest and Global Activism*, Lanham, MD: Rowman and Littlefield, pp. 45–67.

Dryzek, J. S. (2000) *Deliberative Democracy and Beyond*, New York: Oxford University Press.

El Chazli, Y. (2012) 'Sur les sentiers de la révolution', *Revue Française de Science Politique* 62 (5): 843–65.
El-Ghobashy, M. (2011) 'The praxis of the Egyptian revolution', *Middle East Report*, 258: 2–13.
Eliasoph, N. (1998) *Avoiding Politics: How Americans produce apathy in everyday life*, Cambridge and New York: Cambridge University Press.
Gerbaudo, P. (2012) *Tweet and the Street*, London: Pluto Press.
Gitlin, T. (2012) *Occupy Nations: The roots, the spirit, and the promise of Occupy Wall Street*, London: HarperCollins.
Glasius, M. and Pleyers, G. (2013) 'The Global Moment of 2011: democracy, social justice and dignity', *Development and Change* 44: 547–67.
Graeber, D. (2012) *The Democracy Project: A history, a crisis, a movement*, London: Allen Lane.
Guibal, C. and Tangi, S. (2011) L'Egypt de Tahrir: Anatomie d'une revolution, Paris: Seuil.
Habermas, J. (1981) *Theorie des kommunikativen Handelns*, Frankfurt-am-Main: Suhrkamp.
Halvorsen, S. (2012) 'Beyond the network? Occupy London and the Global Movement', *Social Movement Studies* 11 (3–4): 427–33.
Haug, C., Haeringer, N. and Mosca, L. (2009) 'The ESF organizing process in a diachronic perspective', in D. della Porta (ed.) *Another Europe*, London: Routledge, pp. 26–45.
Italian Revolution Milano (2011) 'Dal presidio permanente al presidio diffuso', http://italianrevolutionmilano.jimdo.com/, accessed 9 March 2014.
Juris, J. S. (2005) 'Social forums and their margins: networking logics and the cultural politics of autonomous space', *Ephemera* 5 (2): 253–72.
— (2012) 'Reflections on #Occupy Everywhere: social media, public spaces, and emerging logics of aggregation', *American Ethnologist* 39 (2): 259–79.
Klandermans, B. (2013) 'The dynamics of demand', in J. van Stekelenburg, C. Roggeband and B. Klandermans (eds) *The Future of Social Movement Research: Dynamics, mechanisms, and processes*, Minneapolis, MN: The University of Minnesota Press, pp. 3–16.
Kriesi, H. (1996) 'The organizational structure of new social movements in a political context', in D. McAdam, J. McCarthy and M. N. Zald (eds) *Comparative Perspective on Social Movements: Political opportunities, mobilizing structures, and cultural framing*, Cambridge and New York: Cambridge University Press, pp. 152–84.
— (1998) 'The transformation of cleavage politics: the 1997 Stein Rokkan lecture', *European Journal of Political Research* 33 (2):165–85.
Langman, L. (2013) 'Occupy: a new, new social movement', *Current Sociology* 61 (4): 510–24, first published on April 17.
Leach, D. K. (2013) 'Prefigurative politics', in D. Snow, D. della Porta, B. Klandermans and D. McAdam (eds) *Blackwell Encyclopedia of Social and Political Movements*, Oxford: Blackwell, pp. 1004–6.

Melucci, A. (1989) *Nomads of the Present*, London: Hutchinson Radius.
Moreno Pestaña, J. L. (2013) 'Vie et mort des assemblées', La vie des idées, www.laviedesidees.fr/Vie-et-mort-des-assemblees.html (accessed 25 March 2013).
Nez, H. (2011) 'No es un botellón, es la revolución! Le mouvement des indignés à Puerta del Sol, Madrid', *Mouvements*, /www.mouvements.info/No-es-unbotellon-es-la-revolucion.html (accessed 7 June 2011).
—— (2012) 'Délibérer au sein d'un mouvement social: ethnographie des assemblées des Indignés à Madrid', *Participations* 3: 79–101.
Nigam, A. (2012) 'The Arab upsurge and the "viral" revolutions of our times', *Interface* 4 (1): 165–77.
Offe, C. (1985) 'New social movements: changing boundaries of the political', *Social Research* 52: 817–68.
Osterweil, M. (2004) 'A cultural-political approach to reinventing the political', *International Social Science Journal* 56 (182): 495–506.
Perugorría, I. and Tejerina, B. (2013) 'Politics of the encounter: cognition, emotions, and networks in the Spanish 15M', *Current Sociology* 61 (4): 424–42, first published April 17.
Pleyers, G. (2005) 'The Social Forums as an ideal model of convergence', *International Journal of the Social Sciences* 182: 507–19.
—— (2007) *Forums Sociaux Mondiaux et défis de l'altermondialisme: De Porto Alegre à Nairobi*, Louvain-La-Neuve: Academia-Bruylant.
Polletta, F. (2013) 'Participatory democracy in social movements', in D. Snow, D. della Porta, B. Klandermans and D. McAdam (eds) *Blackwell Encyclopedia of Social and Political Movements*, Oxford: Blackwell, pp. 907–10.
Polletta, F., Chen, P. C. B., Gardner, B. G. and Motes, A. (2013) 'Is the Internet creating new reasons to protest?', in J. van Stekelenburg, C. Roggeband and B. Klandermans (eds) *The Future of Social Movement Research: Dynamics, mechanisms, and processes*, Minneapolis, MN: University of Minnesota Press, pp. 17–36.
Postill, J. (2012) 'New protest movements and viral media', *Media/anthropology*, 26 March.
Razsa, M. and Kurnik, A. (2012) 'The Occupy Movement in Žižek's hometown: direct democracy and a politics of becoming', *American Ethnologist* 39 (2): 238–58.
Roggeband, C. and Duyvendak, J. W. (2013) 'The changing supply side of mobilization: questions for discussion', in J. van Stekelenburg, C. Roggeband and B. Klandermans (eds) *The Future of Social Movement Research: Dynamics, mechanisms, and processes*, Minneapolis, MN: University of Minnesota Press, pp. 95–106.
Romanos, E. (2011) 'Les indignés et la démocrate des mouvements sociaux', La Vie des idées, /www.laviedesidees.fr/La-democratie-directe-de-la-Puerta-html (accessed 24 May 2011).

Sampedro Blanco, V. F. and Sánchez Duarte, J. M. (2011) 'La red era la plaza', www.ciberdemocracia.es/articulos/RedPlaza.pdf (accessed 3 May 2013).

Schoenleitner, G. (2003) 'World Social Forum: making another world possible?', in J. Clark (ed.) *Globalizing Civic Engagement: Civil society and transnational action*, London: Earthscan Publications Ltd., pp. 127–49.

Sergi, V. and Vogiatzoglou, M. (2013) 'Think globally, act locally? Symbolic memory and global repertoires in the Tunisian uprising and the Greek anti-austerity mobilization', in L. Cox and C. Flesher Fominaya (eds) *Understanding European Movements*, London: Routledge pp. 220–35.

Shokr, A. (2012) 'The Eighteen Days of Tahrir', in J. Sowers and C. Toensing (eds) *The Journey to Tahrir: Revolution, protest, and social change in Egypt*, London: Verso, pp. 41–6.

Silva, E. (2009) *Challenging Neoliberalism in Latin America*, Cambridge and New York: Cambridge University Press.

Smith, J. (2004) 'The World Social Forum and the challenges of global democracy', *Global Networks* 4 (4): 413–21.

Smith, J. et al. (2007) *Global democracy and the World Social Forum*, Boulder, CO: Paradigm.

Snow, D. A. (2013) 'Identity dilemmas, discursive fields, identity work and mobilization: clarifying the identity-movement nexus', in J. van Stekelenburg, C. Roggeband and B. Klandermans (eds) *The Future of Social Movement Research: Dynamics, mechanisms, and processes*, Minneapolis, MN: University of Minnesota Press, pp. 263–80.

Sommier, I. (2005) 'Produire l'événement: logique de cooperation et conflict feutrés', in I. Sommier and E. Agrikoliansky (eds) *Radiographie du mouvement altermondialiste*, Paris: La dispute, pp. 19–43.

Soule, S. A. (2013) 'Bringing organizational studies back into social movement scholarship', in J. van Stekelenburg, C. Roggeband, and B. Klandermans (eds) *The Future of Social Movement Research: Dynamics, mechanisms, and processes*, Minneapolis: The University of Minnesota Press, pp. 107–23.

Taylor, A. et al. (eds) (2011) *Occupy!: Scenes from Occupied America*, London: Verso.

Teivainen, T. (2002) 'The World Social Forum and global democratisation: learning from Porto Alegre', *Third World Quarterly*, 23 (4): 621–32.

van Gelder, S. and the staff of YES! Magazine (eds) (2012) *This Changes Everything: Occupy Wall Street and the 99 per cent movement*, San Francisco: Berrett-Koehler Publisher.

van Stekelenburg, J. and Boekkooi, M. (2013) 'Mobilizing for change in changing societies', in J. van Stekelenburg, C. Roggeband, and B. Klandermans (eds) *The Future of Social Movement Research: Dynamics, mechanisms, and processes*, Minneapolis: The University of Minnesota Press, pp. 217–43.

Walgrave, S. (2013) 'Changing mobilization of individual activists?', in J. van Stekelenburg, C. Roggeband, and B. Klandermans (eds) *The Future of Social Movement Research: Dynamics, mechanisms, and processes*, Minneapolis, MN: University of Minnesota Press, pp. 205–16.

Warkotsch, J. (2012) *Bread, Freedom, Human Dignity: Tales of an unfinished revolution in Egypt*, http://cosmos.eui.eu/Documents/Publications/WorkingPapers/2012WP14COSMOS.pdf (accessed 5 May 2013).

Winegard, J. (2012) 'Taking out the trash: youth clean up Egypt after Mubarak', in J. Sowers and C. Toensing (eds) *The Journey to Tahrir: Revolution, protest, and social change in Egypt*, London: Verso, pp. 64–9.

Zamponi, L. (2012) 'Why don't Italians Occupy? Hypotheses on a failed mobilization', *Social Movement Studies* 11 (3–4): 416–26.

Chapter Four

Dramatic Diffusion and Meaning Adaptation: The Case of Neda[1]

Thomas Olesen

Introduction

In recent years the unjust suffering or death of specific individuals, referred to here as violent person-events, has been at the centre of political protest in several countries: such as the case of Neda Agha Soltan, shot and killed by a regime-related militiaman during protests against the fraudulent presidential election in Iran in 2009; Mohamed Bouazizi, who set himself on fire in a protest against local authorities in Tunisia in 2010; Malala Yousafzai, shot and severely injured by the Taliban because of her advocacy for girls' right to education in Pakistan in 2012; and Joyti Singh, who died after being raped by several men on a Delhi bus in 2012. While these individuals and the circumstances surrounding their fates differ wildly, they all have become central injustice-symbols in their respective countries, motivating and galvanising political protest and activism. Yet from the perspective of global political sociology it is equally notable how the symbolic meaning of these events has been extended well beyond their national context. They have, in other words, been involved in a process of dramatic cross-border diffusion in which local/national events attain universalised (Alexander 2006, 2007) meanings for audiences in a global public sphere.

This scale-shift (Tarrow 2005) is a complex ideational process involving significant *meaning adaptation*. The latter term indicates how local/national events *change* meaning as they are disembedded (Giddens 1991). This chapter's main ambition is to theoretically outline and empirically analyse key patterns in the process of symbolic formation and meaning adaptation. It does so based on the case of Neda Agha Soltan and her visually documented and globally publicised death during protests in Iran in 2009. Existing research on Neda has so far been conducted from outside social-movements studies and political sociology (*see*, for example, Andén-Papadopoulos 2013; Assmann and Assmann 2010; Mortensen 2011; Naghibi 2011; Stage 2011). These studies offer crucial insights and inform

---

1. The chapter is a revised version of a paper presented at the ECPR joint sessions workshop, Mainz, 11–16 March 2013. I am profoundly grateful to the participants in the workshop for their numerous insightful comments on the paper.

this chapter in important ways. Yet, at an empirical level, the aim of the chapter is to locate and explore the case of Neda within a global political sociology framework and to demonstrate its relevance for students of global activism. In exploring the Neda case from a symbolic perspective, the chapter provides a novel perspective on the otherwise extensive literature on global activism.[2] In fact, it might be argued that the strand of social-movement theory least well adapted to a global level of analysis is the emotional and cultural turn of the last 10–15 years within social-movement studies (*see*, for example, Alexander 2006; Flam and King 2005; Goodwin *et al.* 2001; Jasper 1997, 2009; Johnston 2009; Williams 2004). The formation of injustice-symbols in the global public sphere has a significant dramatic and emotional character that is under-theorised in the extant literature. At a disciplinary level, the chapter's ambition is to activate such an agenda and give it some theoretical shape.[3]

The Neda case is relevant for the present volume in several respects. The Iranian protests in 2009 were an important, if often overlooked, forerunner of protests during the so-called Arab Spring in 2011. On a general level, even if the immediate motivation was fraudulent elections, Iranian protestors in 2009 voiced a growing dissatisfaction with authoritarian rule that would surface at a more systematic level across the Middle Eastern and North African (MENA) region only a few years later (*see* della Porta and Mattoni, Chapter One in this volume). On a more specific level, the protests and the death of Neda demonstrated the increasing power of new media technologies (especially, cell phone documentation and social media) for political activism and cross-border diffusion. An important element

---

2. The relevance of the Neda case for social-movement studies is in fact twofold: on the one hand, because the violent person-event in question was closely related to protest and activism at the national level; and, on the other, because the subsequent formation of the Neda symbol involved political activism at a global level. However, in continuation of the second point, the chapter does not restrict itself to analysing the activities of political activists in the formation of the Neda symbol. Rather, it views this process as a multi-actor process involving activists, politicians, political parties, media and networked citizens in a broadly conceived global pro-Neda movement. This is obviously also a methodological point as it orients the choice of sources and the collection of data (*see also* the section 'Analysis', below).

3. While the concept of diffusion figures centrally in the chapter, the approach taken here differs quite significantly from the existing literature on movement-related cross-border diffusion (e.g. Beissinger 2007; Chabot 2010; Chabot and Duyvendak 2002; McAdam and Rucht 1993; Snow and Benford 1999; Tarrow 2005). The issue of adaptation is also a staple in the existing literature on cross-border movement diffusion. Snow and Benford (1999: 30), for example, define it as 'the strategic appropriation of specific foreign elements that adopting agents modify, for their own purposes, in a fashion congruent with the host culture's values, beliefs, and practices'. The existing literature, as exemplified in the quote, thus typically works with a clearly defined and strategically oriented sender-recipient relationship and with concrete 'items' being diffused across space. The dramatic cross-border diffusion perspective differs in at least two ways: First, the 'item' diffused in dramatic cross-border diffusion is not a social movement slogan, repertoire, or tactic, a focus predominant throughout the existing literature (e.g. Beissinger 2007; Chabot and Duyvendak 2002), but rather a violent person-event; second, the recipient in diffusion processes is typically a social movement. In the case of dramatic cross-border diffusion, the recipient aspect is more complex. Those actors who 'receive' or engage with violent person-events may, of course, include social movements and activists, but also the media, politicians and political parties, institutions and citizens (*see also* footnote 2).

in this power is the ability of new-media technologies to rapidly and efficiently disseminate visual memes such as, for example, injustice-symbols, both within and across borders. This pattern has been visible throughout a number of countries during the Arab Spring: for example, Khaled Said in Egypt (Olesen 2013a); Mohamed Bouazizi in Tunisia (Olesen 2013b); and Hamza al-Khateeb in Syria.

While the chapter thus points to intensification in both the potential and reality of cross-border diffusion, it also attempts to provide an antidote to the 'loose' cosmopolitanism that characterised the first phase in the study of globalisation and activism (*see* della Porta and Mattoni, in Chapter One of this volume). It does so by arguing that meaning-adaptation and global symbol-formation occurs through existing dominant *interpretive packages* (Gamson and Lasch 1983; Gamson and Modigliani 1989) available in the global public sphere. This is a dialectical process. On the one hand, as the term adaptation indicates, local/national violent person-events are shaped to resonate with existing interpretive packages. On the other, interpretive packages are not static but develop in constant interaction with the empirical phenomena they provide meaning to. In the present chapter this argument is employed to shed analytical and critical light on the political-cultural interchange between the 'North' and 'South'. It is thus notable that most violent person-events attaining global resonance originate in the South. Yet their passage into the global public sphere and their transformation into global injustice-symbols are often premised on some degree of adaptation to Western-based interpretive packages. While this observation constitutes a significant line of analysis in the chapter, adaptation is not simply seen as a question of meaning reduction and of non-Western violent person-events being forced into a Western mould (for example, Said 1978; Spivak 1988). Western conceptions about the non-West are also, at least potentially, challenged, nuanced and expanded (Chabot and Duyvendak 2002; Olesen 2005). In highlighting how the production of injustice-symbols takes place in a global public sphere traversed by ideational power structures in a constant process of negotiation, the chapter offers new insights into the political-cultural dimension of contemporary globalisation (Alexander 2007; Olesen 2005; Thörn 2006) in general and into the study of global activism and cross-border diffusion in particular.

Theoretical outline

The following offers a theoretical discussion of the core concepts of the chapter. The first section defines the concept of injustice-symbol on a general level. The second section adds a global dimension by theorising the process of dramatic cross-border diffusion of injustice-symbols and with a focus on meaning adaptation.

Injustice-symbols

A symbol, in the words of Elder and Cobb (1983, 28–9), is 'any object used by human beings to index meanings that are not inherent in, nor discernible from, the object itself'. What Elder and Cobb's definition precisely outlines is that a symbol always in some sense points beyond itself; that the particularity of the background object has acquired a surplus of meaning and undergone a process of socialisation and universalisation. Based on this general definition of symbols an injustice-symbol may be defined as formed on the basis of 'objects' (such as empirical events/situations and individuals) that involve human suffering and violence and, over time (in both the short and the long term), are infused with wider injustice meanings. The focus in this chapter is on individual injustice-symbols (for example, Olesen 2013a, 2013b; for other applications of the injustice-symbol concept, see Olesen 2011, forthcoming). Violence against individuals considered innocent, decent and thus undeserving of violence is at the root of all individual injustice-symbols. Individual injustice-symbols thus consists of two basic elements: a specific individual (object) and the violence that this individual has suffered (event). The sum of these parts is referred to here as a violent person-event. A violent person-event does not automatically become an injustice-symbol but only constitutes its 'material' basis, as will be elaborated below.

Violent person-events have the potential to arouse *moral shock* (Jasper 1997; Jasper and Poulsen 1995) in an audience. Moral shock can have various sources: for example, it can derive from violence against individuals with pronounced innocence status (such as children; Sznaider 2001); from graphic visual documentation of violence (Hariman and Lucaites 2007); and from the character of the violence (such as torture and mutilation). Often, violence is committed by state authorities such as military or police but perpetrators may also be non-state actors (as in the case of Malala Yousafzai in Pakistan, 2012), fellow citizens (as in the case of Joytin Singh in India, 2012) and even the individual him or herself (the practice of self-immolation, such as the case of Mohamed Bouazizi in Tunisia, 2010). What is decisive, then, for injustice-symbol-formation is not the perpetrator but rather whether the violent person-event has 'universalising' potential (Alexander 2006), that is, whether it can be linked to a social, cultural and/or political problematic with structural roots. In this sense, injustice-symbols are always shaped in interaction with existing *injustice frames* (Gamson et al. 1982) in society (this argument is further developed and expanded to a global context below).

As indicated above, however, these qualities and characteristics only create a *potential* for injustice-symbol-formation. Countless violent person-events meet these criteria without becoming injustice-symbols. The formation of injustice-symbols requires *agency*. As a result we cannot expect to explain the formation of injustice-symbols only by pointing to the intrinsic 'qualities' of the event. The main agents in the formation of injustice-symbols are political activists and the media. While driven by different logics (Gamson and Wolfsfeld 1993; Ruchi 2004), media and activists often interact, if rarely intentionally or by design, in the production of injustice-symbols (Greer and McLaughlin 2010). For political activists, acts of violence against innocent individuals offer important opportunities to dramatise and publicly expose issues already on their agenda. For the media, violence corresponds with established news criteria, such as conflict, drama and personalisation (for example, Bennett 2005[1983]). Agency of this kind may, in some cases, occur in a paradoxical interaction with perpetrators or actors considered directly or indirectly responsible for the violence. A key dynamic in this relationship is what Hess and Martin (2006) refer to as *backfire*. In other words, injustice-symbol-formation may be facilitated by responsible actors' attempt to de-symbolise violent person-events by denying, concealing or manipulating the event.

Dramatic cross-border diffusion and meaning adaptation

Violent person-events are always local/national and particular. Yet in the contemporary political world, local/national events are increasingly disembedded (Giddens 1991) and involved in processes of scale-shift (Olesen 2005; Tarrow 2005). It is when such scale-shift happens on the basis of violent person-events that the term dramatic cross-border diffusion becomes relevant. This process is referred to as 'dramatic' because it is driven, as previously discussed, by a combination of moral-political indignation/shock on the part of activists and audiences and by the media's concern with drama, conflict and violence.

Inspired by Koopmans (2004), the concept of dramatic cross-border diffusion can be analytically broken down into two phases: *diffusion* of a violent protest-event and injustice-symbol-*formation*. According to Koopmans, a movement's message can achieve public visibility through media attention. Visibility, however, does not guarantee resonance, that is, that other actors react to the message. This terminology may be applied to the present purpose as follows: cross-border diffusion of a violent person-event primarily involves the creation of global *visibility*, that is, making the event known to audiences outside its original spatial context. Yet global injustice-symbol-formation only occurs if morally and politically indignant actors outside this context adopt and critically engage with the diffused event, to generate *resonance*. The basic argument of the chapter, as outlined in the introduction, is that *adaptation* is a central element of resonance. The first part of the following discussion focuses on how diffusion occurs; the second on adaptation and global injustice-symbol-formation. Figure 4.1 condenses the theoretical argument and main conceptual elements.

Figure 4.1: Dramatic cross-border diffusion and global injustice-symbol formation

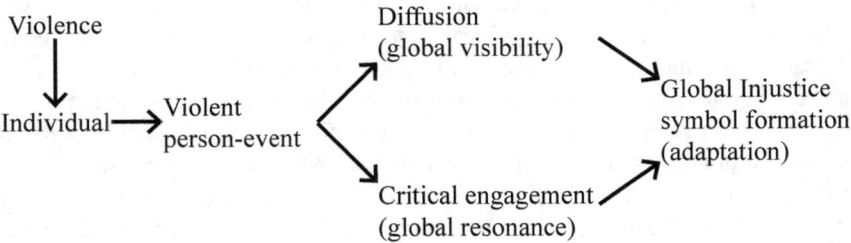

How diffusion occurs

Dramatic cross-border diffusion generally follows one of two ideal-typical trajectories. In the first, the violent person-event has already, wholly or partly, attained injustice-symbolic status at the local/national level. In other cases, diffusion circumvents the local/national level, feeding more or less directly into the global public sphere (this, as we shall see shortly, characterises the case of Neda Agha Soltan). Activists and activist organisations play central roles as diffusers in dramatic cross-border diffusion. These may usefully be divided into two categories:

1. In a dynamic resembling the so-called 'boomerang pattern' (Keck and Sikkink 1998), local/national movements may seek to 'promote' the violent person-event globally in order to activate pressure on local and national authorities (*see also* Bob 2005).

2. Movements and activists from outside the local/national context who have an interest in the relevant country and/or the issue represented by the violent person-event may use it to promote their agenda in their own national setting or at the global level (addressing, for example, international institutions).

Yet activist efforts are typically part of a complex process in which the media are also active and sometimes decisive. In continuation of the first trajectory outlined above, media-driven diffusion is often inspired by local/national protests (category 1 above); but it may also be motivated by activists in category 2. This observation mainly aims at media such as newspapers and TV channels. 'New' social media (such as Facebook, Twitter, YouTube) may also play significant roles in dramatic cross-border diffusion but predominantly as communicative *tools* utilised by networked citizens and activists (Bennett and Segerberg 2012) seeking to diffuse violent person-events. Because social media create huge communicative interfaces between the local/national and global (Castells 2012), they enable the second trajectory.

Adaptation and global symbol-formation

As noted earlier, resonance and symbolic formation occurs when actors outside the original spatial context adopt and critically engage with the violent person-event (such actors may include activists, the media, politicians and political parties and institutions). Adoption and critical engagement always involves a degree of adaptation, in which the adopter construes the issue according to their world view and belief system. In this way, global injustice-symbols not only point to the victim and his/her context but are also used to say something important about the adopter and their moral and political self-understanding. What is of interest, then, is the meaning process through which an empirical violent person-event is transformed into a symbolic end 'product' (*see* Figure 4.1). The argument advanced here is that this process occurs in and through interpretive packages (Gamson and Lasch 1983; Gamson and Modigliani 1989) available in the global public sphere. An interpretive package offers a schema that provides meaning to and orients the understanding of empirical events. The packages employed in the formation of global injustice-symbols are always critical in the sense that they contain and point to purported conditions of injustice. Interpretive packages are not static but 'ebb and flow in prominence and are constantly revised and updated to accommodate new events' (Gamson and Modigliani 1989: 2). While the symbolisation of violent person-events is a process shaped by existing ideational structures, it does not necessarily imply reduction in a negative sense (the scope and character of adaptation can only be empirically and not theoretically answered). Through the process of adaptation the event and the symbolic outcome becomes integrated in, and thus potentially changes, the interpretive package.

Analysis

The following presents an analysis of the case of Neda Agha Soltan from a dramatic diffusion perspective and with a focus on the adaptation dynamic. Methodologically, it makes use of a broad selection of empirical data sources. Given the theoretical focus on resonance, attention is primarily on the way Neda's death has been discursively infused with meaning by non-Iranian actors: these include, primarily, politicians, media, activists and networked citizens. Media sources play a central role and are used in a dual manner: on the one hand, media were among the main actors in the formation of the Neda injustice-symbol; second, journalistic work serves as a crucial source for factual information about Neda, her life and the circumstances of her death. Meaning infusion is analysed against what is labelled the Iran interpretive package. Since this package is at least partly constituted by the actions of Iranian authorities, their interventions in the aftermath of Neda's death constitute a crucial element in parts of the analysis. Temporally, the analysis focuses on roughly the first six months following Neda's death on 20 June 2009.[4] The analysis consists of three overall elements: First, a factual background section is provided; second, core elements in the Iran interpretive package are outlined; third, these provide a backdrop for an extended analysis of the formation of the Neda injustice-symbol.

Background

On 20 June 2009 in Tehran, Neda Agha Soltan, a 26-year-old woman, joined thousands of others in protests (also referred to as the Green Revolution) following the 12 June Iranian presidential elections (considered by many to have

---

4. The focus on the period immediately following Neda's death excludes a number of potentially interesting research questions. In a slightly longer time frame it can be seen how Neda has become the centre of a kind of political-cultural industry, which involves the creation of artwork (including the 2012 short film, *I Am Neda*) and political merchandise (Naghibi 2011; Stage 2011).

been fraudulent). Neda did not have a history as an activist but took part in the post-election protests as a morally outraged citizen (BBC 2009; HBO 2010). The 20 June events had been preceded by several days of protest but were widely perceived to be the most dangerous since the elections. In his Friday prayer remarks the day before, supreme leader Ayatollah Ali Khamenei had thus issued a stern warning that protestors faced potential consequences if demonstrations persisted (BBC 2009). During the protests on 20 June, her music teacher, Hamid Panahi, accompanied Neda. The two were heading back to their car as Neda fell to the ground from a gunshot. A 48-seconds-long cell-phone video recorded by a bystander shows the collapsed Neda being attended to by her music teacher and a doctor, Arash Hejazi, a fellow protestor and, later, a key witness and source in journalistic accounts of the event. In the chaotic and low-quality footage, Panahi is heard screaming 'Neda, stay with me'. A few minutes later Neda died at the scene (Assmann and Assmann 2010). Fellow protesters immediately identified a Basij militiaman as the shooter and dragged him from his motorcycle. In the chaos of the event, he was eventually released by the crowd (BBC 2009; HBO 2010) (no charges have ever been pressed by authorities against this or any other individual).[5] The (apparent) identification of the shooter immediately established a clear link between the Iranian regime and Neda's death. The 48-second video was uploaded to YouTube and Facebook by an Iranian asylum-seeker in Holland, who was contacted by a friend in Iran who had accidentally recorded Neda's death (Tait and Weaver 2009) and inadvertently become a citizen journalist (Andén-Papadopoulos 2013; Mortensen 2011). Another, shorter video recorded by an anonymous person zooms in on Neda's face and shows profuse bleeding from her nose and mouth, covering her face. Within hours, the videos were circulating the globe via YouTube, Facebook and Twitter (Assmann and Assmann 2010). From the social networks, they rapidly made their way into the mainstream media (Mortensen 2011: 7). The Neda story was confined to the networks of global communication for only a short while. Soon people all over the world took to the streets with images of Neda and messages such as 'We Are All Neda' and 'I Am Neda'.

The Iran interpretive package

The dominant interpretive package available for Neda's death has deep roots in recent global history and the continuing conflict between Iran and the West since the Iranian Revolution in 1979. What follows is obviously a simplification, in that it condenses almost 35 years of history into a few paragraphs. The goal here is thus not to offer a full account of the relationship between Iran and the West but to point to some of the defining moments in that history and outline the major political and cultural themes in this conflict.

---

5. The Basij is a paramilitary unit working with the Iranian regime and the Revolutionary Guard. During suppression of the 2009 protests, Basij members on motorbikes played a key role in the violence and in intimidation of protestors.

Since the 1979 ousting of Shah Mohammad Reza Pahlavi in the Iranian Islamic Revolution led by Ayatollah Ruhollah Khomeini, Iran has been a consistent target for activists, politicians, and states in the West. The enmity between Iran and, especially, the United States came into full global view at the time of the Iranian Revolution. In November 1979, a group associated with and backed by the new regime, took fifty-two Americans hostage inside the American Embassy (the hostage crisis ended with a negotiated release after 444 days) (Houghton 2001). The crisis was a major global news story for its duration. In a famous speech in late 1979 that set the tone for the fractious relationship and acquired significant global resonance, Khomeini referred to the United States as 'the great Satan': a label empirically founded mainly in the United States' long-standing support for Israel and for the Iranian monarchy under Shah Pahlavi (1941–79). In 1989, the relationship between Iran and the West came under new strain when Ayatollah Khomeini issued a *fatwa* (a legal judgment made by senior Muslim cleric) for Salman Rushdie's novel *The Satanic Verses* (published 1988). The *fatwa* explicitly called for Rushdie to be killed for blasphemy. The *fatwa* was followed by protests and attacks in several countries around the world (including in the West) and led to a severing of diplomatic ties between Iran and number of Western countries (Pipes 2003). The *fatwa* has been reaffirmed on several occasions since Khomeini's death in 1989 and even in recent years (Tait 2012).

During the last decades, the relationship between Iran and the West has been dominated by the issue of nuclear power and weapons. A string of reports from the International Atomic Energy Agency (IAEA) purports to document that Iran is progressing toward the development of nuclear weapons. The issue of nuclear energy and weapons remains an obstacle to the normalisation of political relations between Iran and the West (Baghat 2006). Another thorny issue, exacerbated since 9/11, has been Iran's continued support for organisations considered by the West to be terrorist organisations (Baghat 2003; Byman 2008) and its related anti-semitism (expressed, *inter alia*, in President Mahmoud Ahmadinejad's highly publicised and widely criticised denials of the Holocaust). The combination of nuclear politics and terrorist support famously led United States President George W. Bush, in his 2002 State of the Union Address, to locate Iran within a global 'axis of evil'. While these incidents and problems are clearly related to international relations, Iran has also been a repeated focal point for human-rights activists. Reports from Amnesty International (2013) and Human Rights Watch (2013) have for several decades pointed to consistent and serious human-rights violations in Iran. A significant element in this criticism pertains to women's rights and repression under Islamic law.

Symbolic formation

The interpretive package globally available for Iran thus builds on a number of dichotomies and major political-cultural themes that cast Iran as representing everything that we in the West are not: religious-secular; oppression/control-freedom; democratic-non-democratic; rational-irrational, etcetera. The themes are clearly linked. For example, the religious basis of Iranian politics and society is viewed as incompatible with democracy and women's rights in a Western conception. The guiding argument to be pursued in the following is that the formation of the global Neda injustice-symbol has drawn significantly from elements in this overall interpretive package. This is identified at four different levels: in the attempts to place Neda in a global history of struggles for freedom and democracy; in the regime's attempt to de-symbolise her; in the infusion of certain character traits; and in the visual and emotional drama of her death (the latter two points are treated together below).

From national to global history

The videos of Neda's death almost instantly drew reactions from the highest political level. This was especially the case in the United States where, for historical reasons outlined above (and also reflecting a politically vociferous Iranian community in the United States), Iran has consistently been a central concern in foreign policy. In a 23 June press conference, President Barack Obama famously referred to the videos as 'heart-breaking', going on to say that, 'anybody who sees it knows that there's something fundamentally unjust about that' (quoted in Kennedy 2009). While Obama's remarks did not clearly confer specific meanings and values on Neda, such infusion was made strongly on the same day from the Senate floor, by an emotional John McCain (Republican-Arizona) (2009): 'So, Mr President, a debate has been going on as to how much the United States of America ... should speak out in favor, and support, of these brave Iranians ... in their quest for the fundamentals of freedom and democracy that we have enjoyed for more than a couple of centuries.' In the speech, McCain links these general observations directly to the case of Neda: 'So, Mr President, today, I and all America, pay tribute to a brave young woman who was trying to exercise her fundamental human rights and was killed on the streets of Tehran.' (McCain 2009). In the speech, McCain anchors the protests in Iran in general and Neda's death in particular in a predominantly Western experience of struggling for and obtaining democratic and human rights. Despite the fact that little was known about Neda and her background at this point (see below), McCain unequivocally interprets her death as an individual sacrifice in the larger historic struggle for democracy: a global struggle in which Iran (as per the interpretive package outlined above) is evidently on the wrong side (and the West, of course, on the right side).

The sacrificial theme was invoked in several early media accounts and postings on social media in which Neda was referred to as Iran's Joan of Arc (*see*, for example, Putz 2009; this interpretation is repeated in McCain's speech).[6] It was also confirmed by people close to Neda. According to Caspian Makan (Neda's

---

6. The basis of this widespread comparison is somewhat unclear as Joan of Arc was not involved in a democratic struggle *per se*. It thus seems to refer, in a more general sense, to the fact that Joan of Arc died as a result of her refusal to compromise her fundamental (religious) beliefs.

boyfriend), who tried to persuade her to stay away from the street protests as they got increasingly violent, she responded by saying that 'If I get shot in the heart or arrested, it's not important because we are all responsible for our future' (quoted in Athanasiadis 2009). Neda, as a result, is portrayed as a fearless woman ready to sacrifice her life for the greater cause of freedom and democracy (*see also* the section on character and visuals below for an extension of this argument).[7] This portrayal in a sense disembeds her from national history and places her in a global history of iconic figures who have risked or sacrificed their lives for the common and collective goods of freedom and democracy (such as Gandhi, Martin Luther King and Nelson Mandela). Only after this disembedding exercise could she be 'returned', as it were, to the Iranian context; now equipped with new meanings accessible and intelligible for a Western audience.

The overall thrust and consequence of these interpretations was in a sense to 'erase' the accidental nature of Neda's death (this has reached a climax in the 2012 short film, *I Am Neda*, in which her death is overloaded with almost prophetic meaning). In fact, however, there is little empirical support to warrant such an understanding. First, the killing of Neda appears to have been random or even accidental. There is no evident reason that we know of why Neda should have been singled out by the shooter from the large number of demonstrators (some, however, link her death to her beauty and the fact that Iranian militia and security forces tend to single out beautiful women for aggression; *see* HBO 2010; *see also* discussions in the section on character and visuals). Second, and in continuation of the above point, Neda was not at the forefront of protest but participated mainly as one concerned individual among many. This is not to say that she was in the street on 20 June out of curiosity or by chance. Accounts suggest that she had been to several protest events since the elections on 12 June (BBC 2009), actively participating and shouting (HBO 2010; her behaviour in this regard is described by Arash Hejazi, the doctor and protestor present when she died) and that she harboured deep grievances about the Iranian regime. Yet it is quite evident that she did not belong to the organisational core of protestors but acted mainly on an individual basis.[8] It might, of course, be said that the degree of injustice is not dependent on whether the death was accidental or premeditated. This is only partly true, however. As noted in the theoretical section, it is not the injustice of a violent person-event that turns it into an injustice-symbol. The injustice must be seen to represent a wider problematic (that is, it must be linkable to existing injustice frames). This would in some ways have been 'easier' if Neda had verifiably been a

---

7. This understanding is also conveyed in the countless Neda tributes posted to YouTube in the period after her death. These often individual interventions by networked citizens are a core element of the pro-Neda global movement (*see* footnote 2).

8. This observation is, however, partly contradicted (but not verified by other sources consulted during the research) by Caspian Makan, Neda's boyfriend, who has noted: 'She was a natural leader and attracted many [protestors] to her side. I think that is why she was shot. The Iranian state and its security officials did not want her, they wanted to extinguish her.' (quoted in Athanasiadis 2009).

leading protestor. Had that been the case, it could have been claimed that she was killed in precisely that capacity. In the absence of such an anchor, adopters were required to engage more actively in meaning-infusion to provide her death with symbolic, and thus universalising, potential.

De-symbolisation

Paradoxically, the Iranian regime itself contributed strongly to the formation of the Neda injustice-symbol. Paradoxically, because it could have played the 'one bad apple' card and claimed the shooting to have been an accident. As shown at the end of the preceding section, such an account would have had some empirical credibility. Had the regime employed a combination of taking general responsibility for the event and individualising the immediate cause of her death (that is, identifying and penalising the shooter), it might have taken at least some of the political impetus out of the emotionally and morally charged attempts to link Neda's death with struggles for freedom and democracy. The power of such a strategy would have resided in its ability to 'disturb' the Iran interpretive package.

As noted in the theoretical section, states and other perpetrators of violence considered unjust by others often engage in *de-symbolisation*. Only few days after Neda's death, in a 26 June Friday sermon, leading Iranian cleric Ayatollah Ahmed Khatami accused the protestors of staging Neda's death: 'The proof and evidence shows that they have done it themselves and have raised propaganda against the system' (quoted in Gorman 2009). And on 25 June the Iranian Ambassador to Mexico, Mohammad Hassan Ghadiri, in an interview with Wolf Blitzer of CNN, pointed to possible CIA involvement: 'If the CIA wants to kill some people and attribute that to the elements of the government, and then choosing a girl, would be something good for them because it would have much higher impact.' (quoted in Malcolm 2009). Later, in a CNN interview with Larry King on 25 September, Iranian President Mahmoud Ahmadinejad took denial to the highest political level, suggesting that the incident had been fabricated to cast a negative global light on the regime (CNN 2009). And in January 2010, Iranian state television broadcast a documentary claiming that 'forensic evidence and statements by security officials show Neda was not killed in the way shown by Western media. Neda was in fact killed after playing the role in a plot whose fake pictures were shown over and over again' (quoted in Mackey 2010). These blatant attempts to deflect the accusations, disregard facts, and displace guilt only served to strengthen the formation of the Neda global injustice-symbol. It did so because it exposed and reaffirmed central themes in the Iran interpretive package. In particular, it tapped into the rational–irrational theme empirically anchored, *inter alia*, in President Ahmadinejad's public denials of the Holocaust. The paradoxical effect was that by trying to avoid blame the regime seemed to only confirm and even widen the moral distance between itself and Neda. This is a reverse proportional dynamic, in which the victim's innocence and purity increases as the direct or indirect perpetrator's moral position worsens (*see* Olesen 2013a for a related point in the context of the Egyptian Revolution in 2011). The perception of the moral-political corruption of the Iranian regime was further strengthened as it became known how Neda's family had been pressured by authorities not to mourn her publicly and denied a traditional funeral service (HBO 2010; Naghibi 2011: 65).

Character and visuals

As already briefly shown, personal character traits (some of them powerfully supported by photographs) have played a central role in the formation of the Neda injustice-symbol. A key element in this process has been a kind of political de-politicisation of Neda. What this seemingly self-contradictory term suggests is how, in most accounts, Neda was not associated with any specific ideological or party-political affiliation but cast as an individual striving for freedom and democracy in a relatively generalised sense. In a 2010 HBO documentary directed by Antony Thomas, Neda's family thus describes her as a 'rebel' since her early years. As a young and a grown woman, they recount, she felt uncomfortable submitting to the standards of behaviour and appearance set by the religious authorities. The image that transpires of Neda is that of an innocent and delicate bird in a cage (a portrait underlined by the repeatedly reported fact that one of Neda's main passions was travelling): 'Neda, outspoken, brave, clashing with authority almost from the start, a free spirit confined by a regime that does not value these qualities in a woman' (HBO 2010: 1:45–2:00) (as mentioned in footnote 7, understandings of this kind are also encountered in many of the Neda tributes posted to YouTube). In the last part of the voiceover, Neda's life and death is clearly associated with the struggle for women's rights in Islamic Iran (according to Naghibi 2011: 64, this line of interpretation was also dominant among diasporic Iranians in the United States). As argued earlier, the issue of women's rights is a core element in the oppression/control-freedom and religious-secular themes in the Iran interpretive package. The point here is obviously not to deny the relevance of this issue. Rather, what is notable is how Neda's death and its immediate context did not have a women's rights dimension per se. The demonstrations where she died were, as already mentioned, motivated by the fraudulent presidential election in Iran on 12 June and, in a wider sense, by a general dissatisfaction with the regime in broad circles of the Iranian population and not by women's rights as such. While certain observations pertaining to Neda's life definitely warrant a women's rights angle, the very direct link created in the aftermath is clearly, to some extent at least, a projection anchored in the Iran interpretive package.

The image of a determined and rebellious woman is contrasted with the description of Neda as a joyful, positive, pure and almost ephemeral person. In an early and widely circulated quote, Hamid Panahi (the music teacher who accompanied Neda on 20 June) called her 'a person full of joy' and 'a beam of light' (quoted in Daragahi 2009). And according to her sister, she never stopped smiling (HBO 2010). This combination of determination and kindness, of strength and frailty, is a central character trait in several global icons of the kind referred to earlier (for example, Mandela and Aung Sun Suu Kyi). In the case of Neda such accounts were lent powerful visual support by the set of pre-death images circulated after 20 June. Two of the best-known show Neda looking directly at us, smiling beautifully, in one of them with her hand under her cheek and in the other with her head slightly bowed to one side. In these images she is in a sense universalised; she could be a citizen of any country (Naghibi 2011: 66). (Neda's universality is also underlined by references to her aforementioned passion for travelling; and in the HBO documentary we are told how her book collection was globally oriented, with Persian-language copies of Emily Bronte's *Wuthering Heights* and Herman Hesse's *Siddhartha*.)[9]

Neda's young, vibrant, beautiful, smiling face furthermore offered a powerful contrast to the visual dimension of the Iran interpretive package. Visually, this package is associated with veiled women and the serious-looking and bearded faces of Iran's male-only politicians and clerics. Neda's beauty attained an additional layer of meaning through the above-mentioned allegations that she was targeted precisely because of her beauty and un-Islamic appearance. There is no hard evidence supporting this interpretation in the case of Neda. Yet the claim makes intuitive sense because beauty can be readily contrasted with the attempt to control women's bodies and appearances in Iran. Beauty, within this interpretive package, thus acquired a potentially political meaning. The photographs of Neda not only contrasted with certain dominant themes in the interpretive package but also, in a simpler and emotional manner, with the images of her death. What is particularly powerful about the 20 June videos is their extreme intimacy, zooming in on Neda's face as blood streams out from her mouth and nose, creating a chaotic pattern across her face. The emotional and moral distance between the smiling Neda and the dying Neda is immense and unbearable and constitutes a moral shock for the viewer (*see* Olesen 2013a for a related observation in relation to Khaled Said in Egypt).

Conclusion

Through the graphic and immediately circulated images of her death, Neda reached the global public sphere in a more or less unfiltered, sudden and raw form. The analysis demonstrates how this 'material' was transformed into a global injustice-symbol through a globally available Iran interpretive package. The Iran package is constituted by a number of dichotomous core themes: religious-secular; oppression/control-freedom; democratic-non-democratic; rational-irrational. The operation of the themes is visible on at least four levels: first, Neda and her death was placed in a wider historic and global struggle for democracy and human rights in which Iran was cast as a negative 'other'; second, the themes in the package were confirmed, as it were, by the Iranian regime itself because it denied any responsibility for Neda's death and even tried to blame it on non-Iranian actors

---

9. Universalisation was expressed, for example, in an initiative by Iranian photographer Reza Deghati, in which protestors in cities around the world held up placards with Neda's face on over their own (*see* Iran Freedom Caravans 2009), symbolically assuming her identity (Andén-Papadopoulos 2013: 10).

such as the CIA and Western journalists; third, certain character traits and previous behaviour were highlighted to portray Neda as innocent and as a victim of Islamic Iran (this involved emphasising her relevance for women's rights); fourth, these traits were supported by the circulation of pre-death photographs (showing a beautiful, young, smiling Neda) that provided a contrast to the visual dimension of the Iran interpretive package (male, old, sombre, dark). In sum, the symbolic interaction between Neda and the Iran package gave her an ideological and visual accessibility that significantly facilitated global resonance.

In the introduction, it was argued that such meaning-adaptation can be viewed from various angles. On the one hand, it is evident that the formation of injustice-symbols like Neda reflects the dominant ideational structures of the global public sphere. What is claimed here is obviously not that the Neda symbol was manufactured and manipulated (that is, not anchored in observable facts). Rather, some of these facts have been *amplified* because they resonated particularly well with core themes in the existing Iran interpretive package. This is the essence of *meaning-adaptation*. On the other hand, the very formation of the Neda injustice-symbol potentially impacts the Iran package. As noted in the theoretical section, interpretive packages are not static but constantly modified through, in particular, new empirical events. It could thus be argued that the Neda event has 'disturbed' and perhaps 'relaxed' the Iran package. Neda, and the Green Movement protests in 2009, have added a new dimension to the image of a secure and monolithic regime and a more or less subdued civil society. The 2009 protests, which were symbolised and given permanent global status through Neda's death, demonstrated that protest and activism occurs even under extremely curtailed political opportunities. As such, the Neda symbol facilitated an image of Iran that is more complex than the dominant Iran interpretive package allows for.

The overall thrust of the chapter's analysis has been to demonstrate how the global public sphere is an ideationally structured space and, thus, a space traversed by power. Yet it is also a plural space in which several and sometimes competing packages are available. And it is a constantly changing space as packages develop, expand, or lose relevance. Theorising the global public sphere as a plural and unstable ideational power field is relevant to and presently underdeveloped within the study of global activism. Activists are key players in constituting and developing this space (as argued in the theoretical section and shown in the analysis, however, their efforts typically occur in combination with that of other actors such as politicians, media, institutions, and citizens; *see also* below). First, their framing efforts actively draw on existing interpretive packages as they attempt to promote their causes before national and/or global audiences; and, second, they are not only 'users', but also 'producers' of the ideational structure of the global public sphere as their activities add new elements to existing interpretive packages. The chapter thus hopes to have accomplished two things: to have demonstrated the relevance of a symbolic, dramatic, and political-cultural approach to activism and globalisation *and* to have shown how symbolic formation is a process occurring in an ideationally structured space.

The argument advanced in the chapter is not that dramatic cross-border diffusion of injustice-symbols as such is a new phenomenon. The struggle against Apartheid, for example, produced several well known injustice-symbols, such as Steven Biko, a South African anti-Apartheid activist killed in police custody in 1977, and Hector Pieterson, a young student killed during the Soweto uprising in 1976. Yet, taking up a thread laid out in the introduction, the formation and circulation of injustice-symbols and other kinds of memes are significantly facilitated in the contemporary era by two types of media technology: portable devices with visual documentation functions (smartphones and tablets) and social media that enable rapid dissemination via vast interpersonal networks. This is not a technologically determinist call for researchers to focus solely or even primarily on the social media as we advance our understanding of cross-border diffusion. In fact, as has been shown in the chapter, contemporary cross-border diffusion seems to often result from a combination of actors and agendas. Entangling this complexity and moving beyond movement-centrism is a pertinent task for future research on the new wave of activism.

A concluding comment is that there are reasons to be sceptical about injustice-symbols. At a philosophical/critical level, it might be argued that the formation of individual injustice-symbols is problematic. The fact that global attention is nurtured by dramatic and often visually powerful instances of violence against individuals inadvertently points out the many (daily) injustices that do not garner attention in the same way. It demonstrates how global attention to suffering and injustice is often emotionally rather than philosophically and politically driven and, as a result, unsystematic and unequal. From a more theoretical perspective, this begs the question why some violent person-events attain symbolic status while others do not. Pursuing such an agenda will require two things: developing a finer typology able to distinguish between different types of injustice-symbols and a comparative approach able to uncover general patterns in injustice-symbol-formation.

References

Amnesty International (2013) http://www.amnesty.org/en/region/iran (accessed 24 May 2013).

Alexander, J. C. (2006) *The Civil Sphere*, Oxford: Oxford University Press.

— (2007) '"Globalization" as collective representation: the new dream of a cosmopolitan civil sphere', in I. Rossi (ed.) *Frontiers of Globalization Research: Theoretical and methodological approaches*, New York: Springer, pp. 271–82.

Andén-Papadopoulos, K. (2013) 'Citizen camera-witnessing: embodied political dissent in the age of "mediated mass self-communication"', *New Media and Society* (published online before print).

Assmann, A. and Assmann, C. (2010) 'Neda: The career of a global icon', in A. Assmann and S. Conrad (eds) *Memory in a Global Age: Discourses, practices, and trajectories*, Houndmills: Palgrave Macmillan, pp. 225–42.

Athanasiadis, I. (2009) 'Exclusive: Boyfriend speaks of his love for Neda Agha Soltan, murdered Iranian protester', *The Observer*, 15 November, http://www.guardian.co.uk/world/2009/nov/15/neda-agha-soltan (accessed 3 June 2013).

Baghat, G. (2003) 'Iran, the United States, and the War on Terrorism', *Studies in Conflict & Terrorism* 26 (2): 93–104.

— (2006) 'Nuclear proliferation: the Islamic Republic of Iran', *Iranian Studies* 39 (3): 307–27.

BBC (2009) 'Neda: an Iranian martyr' (documentary), http://www.youtube.com/watch?v=C4-iLG6FwRc (accessed 14 June 2013).

Beissinger, M. R. (2007) 'Structure and example in modular political phenomena: the diffusion of Bulldozer/Rose/Orange/Tulip Revolutions', *Perspectives on Politics* 5: 259–76.

Bennett, W. L. (2005[1983]) *News: The politics of illusion*, New York: Longman.

Bennett, W. L. and Segerberg, A. (2012) 'The logic of connective action: digital media and the personalization of contentious politics', *Information, Communication and Society* 15 (5): 739–68.

Bob, C. (2005) *The Marketing of Rebellion: Insurgents, media, and international activism*, Cambridge: Cambridge University Press.

Byman, D. (2008) 'Iran, terrorism, and weapons of mass destruction', *Studies in Conflict & Terrorism* 31 (3): 169–81.

Castells, M. (2009) *Communication Power*, Oxford: Oxford University Press.

— (2012) *Networks of Outrage and Hope: Social movements in the Internet age*, Oxford: Polity Press.

Chabot, S. (2010) 'Dialogue matters: beyond the transmission model of transnational diffusion between movements', in R. K. Givan, K. M. Roberts and S. A. Soule (2010), *The Diffusion of Social Movements: Actors, mechanisms, and political effects*, Cambridge: Cambridge University Press, pp. 99–124.

Chabot, S. and Duyvendak, J. W. (2002) 'Globalization and transnational diffusion between social movements: reconceptualizing the dissemination of the Gandhian Repertoire and the "coming out" routine', *Theory and Society* 31 (6): 697–740.

CNN (2009) 'CNN Larry King Live: Interview with Iranian President Mahmoud Ahmadinejad' (transcript), http://transcripts.cnn.com/TRANSCRIPTS/0909/25/lkl.01.html (accessed 2 June 2103).

Daragahi, B. (2009) 'Family, friends mourn "Neda", Iranian woman who died on video', *Los Angeles Times*, 23 June, http://www.latimes.com/news/nationworld/world/la-fg-iran-neda23-2009jun23,0,366975,full.story (accessed 8 June 2013).

Elder, C. D. and Cobb, R. W. (1983) *The Political Uses of Symbols*, New York and London: Longman.

Flam, H. and King, D. (2005) (eds) *Emotions and Social Movements*, London and New York: Routledge..

Gamson, W. A. and Lasch, K. E. (1983) 'The political culture of social welfare policy', in S. E. Spiro and E. Yuchtman-Yaar (eds), *Evaluating the Welfare State: Social and political perspectives*, New York: Academic Press, pp. 397–415.

Gamson, W. A., Lasch, K. E and Modigliani, A. (1989) 'Media discourse and public opinion on nuclear power: a constructionist approach', *American Journal of Sociology* 95 (1): 1–37.

Gamson, W. A. and Wolfsfeld, G. (1993) 'Movements and media as interacting systems', *Annals of the American Academy of Political and Social Science* 528: 114–25.

Gamson, W. A., Fireman, B. and Rytina, S. (1982) *Encounters with Unjust Authority*, Chicago, IL: Dorsey Press.

Giddens, A. (1991) *Modernity and Self-Identity*, Cambridge: Polity Press.

Goodwin, J., Jasper, J. M. and Polletta, F. (2001) (eds) *Passionate Politics: Emotions and social movements*, Chicago, IL: University of Chicago Press.

Gorman, G. (2009) 'Iranian leaders blaming CIA, protestors, for killing Neda', ABC News, 26 June, http://abcnews.go.com/blogs/politics/2009/06/iranian-leaders-blaming-cia-protestors-for-killing-neda (accessed 10 June 2013).

Greer, C. and McLaughlin, E. (2010) 'We predict a riot? Public order policing, new media environments and the rise of the citizen journalist', *British Journal of Criminology* 50 (6): 1041–59.

Hariman, R. and Lucaites, J. L. (2007) *No Caption Needed: Iconic photographs, public culture, and liberal democracy*, Chicago, IL: University of Chicago Press.

HBO (2010) 'For Neda', http://www.openculture.com/2010/06/for_neda_a_new_hbo_ documentary.html (accessed 29 May 2013).

Hess, D. and Martin, B. (2006) 'Repression, backfire, and the theory of transformative events', *Mobilization* 11 (2): 249–67.

Houghton, D. P. (2001) *US Foreign Policy and the Iran Hostage Crisis*, Cambridge: Cambridge University Press.

Human Rights Watch (2013) http://www.hrw.org/middle-eastn-africa/iran (accessed 24 May 2013).
Iran Freedom Caravans (2009) http://iranfreedomcaravans.wordpress.com (accessed 8 June 2013).
Jasper, J. M. (1997) *The Art of Moral Protest*, Chicago, IL: University of Chicago Press.
— (2009) 'Cultural approaches in the sociology of social movements', in B. Klandermans and C. Roggeband (eds) *Handbook of Social Movements Across Disciplines*, New York: Springer, pp. 59–109.
Jasper, J. M. and Poulsen, J. D. (1995) 'Recruiting strangers and friends: moral shocks and social networks in animal rights and anti-nuclear protests', *Social Problems* 42 (4): 493–512.
Johnston, H. (ed.) (2009) *Culture, Social Movements, and Protest*, Farnham: Ashgate.
Keck, M. E. and Sikkink, K. (1998) *Activists beyond Borders: Advocacy networks in international politics*, Ithaca, NY: Cornell University Press.
Kennedy, H. (2009) 'President Obama calls Iranian martyr Neda's death "heartbreaking"', *Daily News*, 23 June.
Koopmans, R. (2004) 'Movements and media: selection processes and evolutionary dynamics in the public sphere', *Theory and Society* 33 (3–4): 367–91.
Mackey, R. (2010). 'Iranian TV sees conspiracy in Neda video', *New York Times*, 7 January, http://thelede.blogs.nytimes.com/2010/01/07/iranian-tv-sees-conspiracy-in-neda-video/?_r=0 (accessed 2 June 2013).
Malcolm, A. (2009) 'Iran ambassador suggests CIA could have killed Neda Agha-Soltan', *Los Angeles Times*, 25 June, http://latimesblogs.latimes.com/washington/2009/06/neda-cia-cnn-killing.html#more (accessed 2 June 2013).
McAdam, D. and Rucht, D. (1993) 'The cross-national diffusion of movement ideas', *Annals of the American Academy of Political and Social Science*, 528: 56–74.
McCain, J. (2009) 'John McCain tribute to Neda on the Senate floor', http://www.youtube.com/watch?v=lp5ApDTfsTM (accessed 31 May 2013).
Mortensen, M. (2011) 'When citizen photojournalism sets the news agenda: Neda Agha Soltan as a Web 2.0 icon of post-election unrest in Iran', *Global Media and Communication* 7 (1): 4–16.
Naghibi, N. (2011) 'Diasporic disclosures: social networking, Neda, and the 2009 Iranian presidential elections', *Biography* 34 (1): 56–69.
Olesen, T. (2005) *International Zapatismo: The construction of solidarity in the age of globalization*, London: Zed Books.
— (2011) 'Transnational injustice-symbols and communities: the case of al-Qaeda and the Guantanamo Bay Detention Camp', *Current Sociology* 59 (6): 717–34.
— (2013a) '"We Are All Khaled Said": on visual injustice-symbols', *Research in Social Movements, Conflicts, and Change* 35: 3–25.
— (2013b) 'Dramatic diffusion and injustice-symbols: the case of Mohamed Bouazizi and the Tunisian Revolution, 2010–2011', paper presented at the ECPR joint sessions workshop, Mainz, 11–16 March 2013.

— (forthcoming) 'From national event to transnational injustice-symbol: the three phases of the Muhammad cartoons controversy', in L. Bosi, C. Demetriou and S. Malthaner (eds) *Dynamics of Political Violence*, Farnham: Ashgate.

Pipes, D. (2003) *The Rushdie Affair: The novel, the Ayatollah, and the West* (2nd edn), New Brunswick, NJ: Transaction Publishers.

Putz, U. (2009) 'Neda, is she Iran's Joan of Arc?', *ABC News*, 22 June, online at: http://abcnews. go.com/International/story?id=7897043&page=1 (accessed 1 June 2013).

Rucht, D. (2004) 'The quadruple "A": Media strategies of protest movements since the 1960s', in W. van de Bonk, B. D. Loader, P. G. Nixon and D. Rucht (eds), *Cyber Protest: New media, citizens, and social movements*, London: Routledge, pp. 29–56.

Said, E. W. (1978) *Orientalism*, New York: Vintage Books..

Snow, D. A. and Benford, R. D. (1999) 'Alternative types of cross-national diffusion in the social movement arena', in D. della Porta, H. Kriesi and D. Rucht (eds), *Social Movements in a Globalizing World*, Houndmills: Macmillan, pp. 23–39.

Spivak, G. (1988) 'Can the subaltern speak?', in C. Nelson and L. Grossberg (eds) *Marxism and the Interpretation of Culture*, Chicago, IL: University of Illinois Press, pp. 271–313.

Stage, C. (2011) 'Thingifying Neda: the construction of commemorative and affective thingifications of Neda Agda Soltan', *Culture Unbound* 3: 419–38.

Sznaider, N. (2001) *The Compassionate Temperament: Care and cruelty in modern society*, Lanham, MD: Rowman & Littlefield.

Tait, R. (2012) 'Iran resurrects Salman Rushdie threat', *Telegraph*, 16 September, http://www.telegraph.co.uk/news/worldnews/ middleeast/iran/ 9546513/ Iran-resurrects-Salman-Rushdie-threat.html (accessed 12 June 2013).

Tait, R. and Weaver, M. (2009) 'The accidental martyr', *Guardian*, 23 June.

Tarrow, S. (2005) *The New Transnational Activism*, Cambridge: Cambridge University Press.

Thörn, H. (2006) *Anti-Apartheid and the Emergence of a Global Civil Society*, Basingstoke: Palgrave Macmillan.

Williams, R. H. (2004) 'The cultural context of collective action: constraints, opportunities, and the symbolic life of social movements', in D. A. Snow, S. A. Soule and H. Kriesi (eds) *The Blackwell Companion to Social Movements*, Oxford: Blackwell, pp. 91–115.

Chapter Five

From Event to Process: The EU and the 'Arab Spring'

Ari-Elmeri Hyvönen

Introduction

The diffusion phenomenon of the 2011 protests examined throughout the present volume opens up a space of transnational political struggle and contention. If the protests, as della Porta and Mattoni argue in Chapter One of this volume, constitute a 'transnational wave of contention', this wave inexorably has political ramifications, regionally and globally. The purpose of this chapter is to analyse the world political-power dynamics against the background of the diffusion of ideas, tactics, frames and strategies that flow across national borders. In particular, I will analyse how the European Union (EU), as a key global power, formulated its own policies and provided interpretative frames vis-à-vis external protest events (the 'Arab Spring') in the context of the diffusion dynamics. The theme of framing and counter-framing (cf., for example, Chapter Two of this volume, by Cristina Flesher Fominaya and Antonio Montañés Jimenéz) is thus addressed here from a different perspective.

In the early months of 2011, the European Commission quickly acknowledged that 'the events unfolding in our southern neighbourhood are of historic proportions ... and will have lasting consequences not only for the people and countries of the region but also for the rest of the world and the EU in particular' (ECHR 2011a: 1). In the past two years, the major significance of the 'Arab Spring' has been firmly established both on the political level and in academic research. The protests and what some see as their global repercussions (such as the Occupy movement; *see*, for example, Vasconcelos 2012: 17; Shihade, Flesher Fominaya and Cox 2012: 5, 8) have already engendered a vast body of policy reviews, articles, books and special journal issues. The emerging literature on the effects of the 'Arab Spring' on Euro-Mediterranean relations is unanimous on the 'universal', 'global', or 'international' significance of the events (Achcar 2012; Behr 2011; Challand 2011; Hollis 2012; Jahshan 2011; Schumacher 2011; Vasconcelos 2012: 20). Arguably, the 'Arab Spring' has gained the status of the most momentous global occurrence since the attacks of 9/11.

The Arab uprisings can be seen as a part of the wider global wave of protests. For instance, as Olesen argues in Chapter Four of this volume, symbols originating from the 'Arab Spring' quickly gained a global meaning. Trans-border diffusion of this and other kinds is one of the key factors making all revolutions by nature 'international'. Revolutions also always occur in a particular global order and have remarkable implications for the wider international system. Immanuel Kant famously argued that it is the onlookers, the spectators, who can perceive the true meaning of a revolution. The international audience, for him, was better able than the actors were to conceive their universal implications (Kant 2006: 155).[1] Today, perhaps more than in Kant's time, each genuine revolution is a properly world-political event that radiates rays of inspiration, hope and also concern, throughout the globe.[2] In the revolutions of the past few decades, the 'international' has played a more significant role than ever before (*see* Lawson 2005 and Kumar 1992). Often the international environment plays a regulating role, tending to produce what Lawson (2005) has called 'negotiated revolutions'. This tendency is also perceivable in the 'Arab Spring' case, when the EU emphasised that it 'must not be a passive spectator' (ECHR 2011a: 1). However, in the scholarly research and media reports, the external and international dimensions – for instance, the role of the EU – of the events have been largely neglected (Schumacher 2011: 108; Perthes 2011: 74). Thus, 'it is ... important to set the record straight, to locate the events of 2011 in the totality of the global situation' (Žižek 2012: 1).[3]

From the EU's perspective, it was particularly crucial that the continuities between the Arab and the European protests challenged the policies of the Union. Neo-liberal policies and the 'democracy of experts' as practised by EU institutions were among the targets of the protests on both sides of the Mediterranean. It was therefore easy to see the European and US protests as a part of the same wave of contention as the 'Arab Spring'. This reading was actively promoted by the Occupy and Indignados movements. It was, therefore, in the interest of the EU to produce an alternative interpretation of the Arab protests that set them apart from the broader, transnational, set of protests. As will be established below, one method used for avoiding this association was to tie the Arab protests to past uprisings striving for Western-type democracy. Hence, the EU and the protestors provided two different readings of the events taking place in North Africa. This all comes down to the question of change – one of the key concepts for the study of the consequences of social movements (Earl 2004: 508). What kind of change did the Arab protests indicate? It will be argued below that, in the EU's framing, the changes taking place in its Southern neighbourhood were presented as local and contained.

---

1. Of course, Kant's remark is not a generalisation about revolutions. Moreover, even though it is about the French Revolution, his interest is not focused on the *revolutionary* aspect but rather on the natural rights implied by the event.
2. Throughout the chapter, 'world politics' is used as an almost synonymous term with global politics – covering a multiplicity of political phenomena on the transnational, international and global levels – instead of the more traditional sense, which refers to great-power politics.
3. *See also* Teti *et al.* (2013: 62), who argue that 'there is a notable paucity of attention to the conceptual construction and framing of policy'.

From the perspective of social-movement studies, the present chapter is a tentative step towards filling a more general research gap. In recent years, increasing attention has been paid to the outcomes and consequences of social movements (*see*, for example, Amenta and Caren 2004; Earl 2004; Kolb 2007; Dür 2008; Bosi and Uba 2009). Specifically, the focus has been on the *intended* effects (outcomes), on the one hand, and on impacts on the level of *national* legislation, on the other (*see*, for example, Giugni 1998: 374, 385). Intended outcomes and national policy, however, cover only partly the area of consequences and impacts. As Tilly (1998) has pointed out, the effects of social movements go well beyond the explicit demands made by the activists. Social movements, protest events and, particularly, revolutions have impacts well beyond their immediate scope or objectives. A particular kind of indirect impact is the transnational ramifications of the protests, increasingly in the contemporary period characterised by the transnationalisation of political relationships (della Porta and Diani 2006: 43; Imig and Tarrow 2001). While transnational social movements and networks have been widely studied, there is a deficit of research on the impacts of social movements on the level of the global 'polity' – the key global players and organisations. We do not know enough of the transnational aspects of protest events of such scale that seemingly external global actors feel compelled to react. In short, the discursive outcomes or reactions on the side of transnational bodies have been mostly neglected.

Taking its cues mainly from the discipline of International Relations (IR), the present chapter is a first step in disclosing the dynamics of external/global/transnational discursive reactions to major protest events.[4] If the events, as the Commission stated, are of historic proportions and have *lasting* consequences for the whole world, their transnational context should also be closely scrutinised. The EU's significance is remarkable, both in the Mediterranean region and globally, and hence the EU plays a defining role in the context in which the revolutions occurred and in which they will potentially bear fruit. The reactions of the EU were thus far from an indifferent matter for the protestors of the Middle East and North Africa (MENA) region. My focus is on the ways in which the EU utilises external events in building its self-image and in legitimising the political order it represents. In this sense, the chapter is a contribution to the body of literature that aims at 'challenging how events in the Arab world have been explained and represented' (Shihade, Flesher Fominaya and Cox 2012).

---

4. The present chapter can also be read as a contribution to a broader discussion. In the discipline of IR, recent years have witnessed a growing interest in events as a unit of analysis, particularly in the subfield of critical IR theory. It has been argued that 'the event' has recently emerged as a dominant imaginary of global politics, with immense 'implications for how we conceive of time, space, ethics, and political possibility' (Brassett and Clarke 2012: 18). Relatedly, some scholars have emphasised the often unexplored international character of revolutionary events (Lawson 2005). Most emphasis thus far, however, has been put on traumatic events (Brassett and Clarke 2012; Brassett and Vaughan-Williams 2012; Lundborg 2012). The present chapter will provide a different perspective on the problem of events. As we will see, the political dynamics of events are highly context-specific. From an empirical perspective, the ways and degrees in which different phenomena are framed as events or not vary from case to case.

The guiding questions of my analysis are the following: what means did the EU utilise in its responses to the 'Arab Spring' in order to legitimise itself as a global and regional actor? How did the EU's reactions relate to the dynamics of diffusion and commonalities between the 'Arab Spring' and the contemporaneous movements in Europe and the United States? What aspects of the events did the EU seek to accentuate; were the revolutions portrayed as being meaningful as individual events or were they seen as a part of a wider process? What kinds of trajectories were anticipated for the transformations? These questions will be addressed by providing a frame-analytic reading of the relevant documents produced by the EU bodies. Particular attention will be paid to two Joint Communications addressing the EU neighbourhood policy towards the Southern Mediterranean (ECHR 2011a and ECHR 2011b).[5] Apart from this, Declarations of the European Council and speeches by the President and the High Representative directly addressing the Southern Neighbourhood since the beginning of 2011 are analysed. The focus is on the commonalities of the frames used by EU agencies. Hence, differences between the EU bodies are largely disregarded. Since the trajectory of the Syrian case has been different from the rest of the region, it has been excluded from the analysis.[6]

The analytic approach

The literature on the EU as an 'ethical' or 'normative' power is an important point of reference for the present chapter. The general traits of the discussion of the EU as an actor will be expanded by analysing its agency in the context of a specific event and, further, by taking a more critical stance towards the analysis of power than is usually done. The chapter borrows from critical – mainly Foucauldian – analyses of the EU's policies and utilises an eclectic set of conceptual tools derived from Hannah Arendt (the distinction between events and processes), Roland Barthes and James Ferguson (depoliticisation/the 'anti-politics machine').

First and foremost, however, the examination builds on a frame-analytic methodology, paying attention to the ways in which key actors (in this case, the EU) seek to manage the flow of (external) events in order to fortify their self-

---

5. For a detailed analysis of the two documents, *see* Teti 2012 and Teti *et al.* 2013. The latter also compares the documents with earlier EU democracy-assistance and European Neighbourhood Policy (ENP) documents.

6. *In toto*, I have analysed ten documents, representing the immediate responses of the EU to the events of 2011: two communications by the Commission; one Commission Press release; three Declarations by the European Council or Extraordinary European Council; four speeches by the High Representatives; and a press release by the European Bank for Reconstruction and Development. I have also read a larger set of documents by the aforementioned bodies up to May 2013, to see if there are any remarkable changes in the discourse. Since no substantial changes were perceivable, I have mainly limited myself here to the immediate responses.

images and thus their power-interests.[7] Framing, broadly speaking, is a way of organising experience.[8] By selecting certain aspects of political occurrences and experiences, and by presenting them in a certain light, actors seek to mould the meanings attached to events and, at the same time, to 'conjure up a desired self-image' (Fine and Manning 2003: 46; Snow 2004: 384). Frame analysis proceeds from the notion that, in most situations, many different things are happening simultaneously yet actors usually seek to provide a clear answer to the question 'what *is* it that's going on here?', thereby biasing matters 'in the direction of unitary exposition and simplicity' (Goffman 1986, 9). Frames also define certain events as problems or challenges, providing a moral ground for political judgments and hence presenting certain solutions as self-evident or inevitable (Aaltola 2008; Entman 1993: 52). Frame analysis thus enables us to illuminate aspects usually left in the background, even by critical approaches. Above all, the focus on the EU's use of certain frames as a practice of building a self-image provides a fresh perspective, not only to the EU's world political agency but also to the ways in which protests and uprisings become sucked into the wider context of global politics.

When approaching major events such as the 'Arab Spring' from the frame-analytic perspective, we should pay attention to the ways in which already-familiar frames are invoked by relevant actors in order to steer attention to certain aspects of the events, to give them a specific interpretation (and thus to simplify) and to articulate their own positions. Indeed, a crucial method for political actors is to create the right kind of resonance between past, present and anticipated occurrences, in order to fortify their policy frames. More precisely, frame analysis focuses attention on the ways political speech persuades, not only through argumentation but also (perhaps even primarily) indirectly, through images, perceptions, associations, emotions and so forth.[9] The framing approach allows us to focus on issues such as the underlying logics of actions, world-views, political imaginaries and the intertwining of power, interest and the self-images of actors (*see*, for example, Haukkala 2010: 56). Particularly relevant from the perspective of this chapter is the attention paid by frame analysts to the ways in which different actors seek to manage the flow of (external) events and occurrences for their own benefit. The focus on framing thus allows us to analyse the politics of attention, meaning and assessment in the context of world political events – in other words, the methods used by actors to influence other actors' perception and assessment of what happens. Pivotally, this usually implies an attempt either to maintain or to problematise the existing political order.

---

7. Even though widely used in other social sciences and well established in social-movement studies in particular (*see*, e.g. Snow 2004), this approach has only recently gained ground in the disciplines of political science and international relations (Watson 2012; Haukkala 2010: 54–6; Aaltola 2008).
8. The subtitle of Goffman's *Frame Analysis* (1986) is 'An essay on the organization of experience'.
9. *See*, e.g. Aaltola 2008: 9–10. It should be noted that the description of framing theory presented here refers only the political applications of the approach. While stemming from Goffman's work, the political applications bear only a slight resemblance to the uses of frame analysis in sociology.

According to Goffman, frames define social situations, providing the principles of organisation that govern events and our subjective involvement in them (Goffman 1986, 10–11). In world politics, a common example is the Cold War frame, which 'highlighted certain foreign events – say, civil wars – as problems, identified their source (communist rebels), offered moral judgments (atheistic aggression) and commended particular solutions (U.S. support for the other side)' (Entman 1993: 52). For framing to succeed in doing all these things, the frame used by the communicator must resonate with a wider background culture – a stock of commonly invoked frames – shared by the communicator and the audience (Entman 1993: 53). In global politics, this poses a special challenge, as a shared cultural background is mostly lacking. Actors may, however, invoke a number of frames that are understandable to all or most global players. In the context of the 'Arab Spring', one specific set of frames consists of the political memories and established interpretations of various previous social movements and revolutions, starting from the French Revolution and including the Iranian revolution and the transitions from communism of 1989. Additionally, there are a number of frames specific to a set of states and other global actors, constituting loose communities such as 'the West', 'North Atlantic democracies', 'the developed states' and so on.

The world opened by each frame is irrefutably real while it is attended to. When the attention moves elsewhere, the reality of the frame relapses. It is therefore particularly interesting to look at framing as a way of capturing attention. It is crucial for different actors – especially major world political players such as the US and the EU – to re-energise the frames they are using in order to recapture attention. In this way, frames function as reminders of the basic tenets of the underlying world order. If key actors fail to re-energise, the frame will eventually break. Creating a dramatic tension is a particularly suitable method for re-energising the frame: 'often what talkers undertake to do is not to provide information to a recipient but to present dramas to an audience' (Goffman 1986: 508). As will be seen in the 'Arab Spring' case, below, the dramatic tension required for the successful management of the flow of events is usually created between progressive and regressive trajectories. The tension between these two extremes provides the overall meaning of the individual occurrences and directs attention to specific features of the events (Aaltola 2008).

Major events are fertile ground for creating such tension. On the other hand, they also present a serious maintenance problem. If events overflow the frame and cannot be properly managed, a break can occur in the applicability of the frame, a break in its governance (Goffman 1986: 347). In the case of the 'Arab Spring', the commonalities and continuities between the European and the MENA region protests represented one such potential break and created pressure on the EU to manage the situation properly.

It should be clear from above that frame analysis as applied here is best characterised as a research orientation combining theoretical and methodological elements, rather than as a clear-cut method in a traditional social scientific manner. Whereas many frame-analytic studies focus on such questions as 'how does the formulation of the issue affect the public's opinions?', implying a conscious choice of frame, the present chapter does not see frames as freely chosen. While deeply rooted in the world-views and power-interests of the actors, frames are not so much selected as semi-automatically adapted. This stance adds to the need for the process of frame analysis to be self-reflective and not automatic. Hence, instead of identifying 'an initial set of frames ... to create a coding scheme' (Chong and Druckman 2007: 107), I will proceed in a more open-ended manner, focusing on an analysis of meanings arising from the identified frames. With the help of the empirical and conceptual literature explicated in the next section, a set of relevant features of the EU as global actor, particularly towards the southern Mediterranean area, will be identified. Using this understanding as a heuristic background, the EU documents are examined and a set of frames identified. The frames are then analysed with a focus on the meaning given to the events and the implications these meanings bear for our understanding of the EU as an actor and, particularly, its location in the world-political-power hierarchy.

Apropos of earlier frame-analytic literature, the present chapter makes some adjustments concerning the conceptual triad of event, occurrence and process. As will be shown in greater detail below, vast political implications – such as whether what happened challenges our established ideas of politics in any significant way – turn on the question of whether something is labelled as an event or as a part of a wider process. My distinction between the two is derived from Hannah Arendt's analyses of 'the social', on the one hand, and of revolutions, on the other. Arendt argued that the French Revolution created an entirely new imaginary and political vocabulary, with twofold consequences. First, the idea that new beginning could be a political phenomenon gained ground. With new beginning is denoted a novel event, which for a moment 'abolishes the sequence of temporality itself' (Arendt 2006: 37, 206).[10] Second, the French Revolution also introduced to politics the idea of irresistible movement. The course of the revolution was seen as uncontrollable and, as a consequence, it was conceptualised through the idea of historical necessity (Arendt 2006: 41–5). In this vein, all subsequent upheavals were interpreted as a continuation of the same movement which began in France (Arendt 2006: 40). While other events have been added to this set (most notably those of 1989), it is still possible to argue that the idea of revolutionary upheavals being part of the same process remains a key aspect of the global 'revolution' frame. As a result, the idea of a properly new beginning has been more or less lost – with the help of modern sciences (social, human and natural) in which processuality[11] plays a key role. As Alexander Barder and David McCourt have rightly argued, in IR theory 'each unique event is downplayed in favor of transhistorical processual occurrences' (Barder and McCourt 2010: 119). As will be emphasised in the present chapter, this is not merely a problem in IR theory; governance institutions also tend to think this way. Secondly, in the same

---

10. The idea of an event as a radical rupture is also present in Alain Badiou's work. In relation to the uprisings of 2011, for instance, he argued that the riots indicated the possibility of a 'new situation in the history of politics', a reopening of history (Badiou 2012: 27, *passim*).

11. The condition of being part of a process and not a discrete event.

vein, a distinction is made between events and occurrences. In this scheme, events that take place – are situated – within the processual imaginary are not, properly speaking, events but 'mere' occurrences. The concept of an event designates a happening on an historic scale, with possible global/universal ramifications and which creates a rupture in the smooth processuality of everyday life. Occurrences, on the other hand, are smaller incidents that set the concrete, short-term course of politics.[12]

The EU, the Mediterranean and earlier uprisings

In the research on the EU's global agency, a 'new agenda' has recently emerged, where the EU's policies are analysed through the concepts of 'normative' and 'ethical' power.[13] Thereby attention has been redirected to the question of how the EU uses its power in global politics instead of asking whether or not the EU can be a unified political actor. The 'ethical power' approach is particularly interested in the ethics of the EU's foreign relations, not as an empirical statement but as a 'new line of critical reflection' focusing on the inter-connections of ethics, interests and power – especially 'soft power' (Aggestam 2008: 2, 8). This chapter contributes to this discussion by examining how the EU constructs its own legitimacy, by framing itself as a normative power and a plausible politico-economic model. The specificities of the Mediterranean area in the EU discourse will also be reflected upon. In the wider context of the book, this discussion also complements the analysis by Kousis of the anti-troika protests in Chapter Seven.

Beginning with the generalities of the EU's foreign policy, we come across a problem particular to transnational actors – the lack of 'thick' cultural background. In building its authority, an actor needs to make sure its framings of reality resonate with each other and, especially, with the available cultural resources that ultimately underpin all political discourse (for example, McNamara 2010: 165, 173). In the European context, the lack of shared language and unitary (invented) tradition poses special challenges for the creation of cultural resonances. One way to solve this problem – as we will shortly see in more detail – is the emphasis put on the effectiveness of EU institutions in managing the problems faced by the Union and the member-states. Some shared cultural resources are also available to the EU. The EU's self-understanding is deeply rooted in European culture (Postel-Vinay 2008: 45). Among such cultural resources can be included such political memories and shared experiences as the legacy of Enlightenment liberalism; the experience of totalitarianism and the subsequent building of democratic governance; memories of 1989; and the conception of Europe as a developed area

---

12. While both events and occurrences can be surprising, only events are surprising *per definitionem*. On these lines, it will be argued below that in the frame that emerged in the EU documents, the 'Arab Spring' was seen as a surprising, yet more or less familiar, occurrence rather than as an event in the sense given to the term here. This framing provided the EU a better basis for presenting itself as a legitimate actor and even as a special authoriser of the events.

13. The concept was first coined by Ian Manners (2002). *See also* Whitman 2011.

(especially in contrast to its southern neighbours).[14] Whereas in the US foreign-policy tradition there is a large stock of semi-religious images, the EU has built on imaginaries of efficient governance, ethical use of power and the spreading of democracy and 'good governance'. The EU presents itself as a good example of the value of practical and peaceful co-operation among different actors and as a proponent of liberal Enlightenment values.

Among more specific cultural resources, a wide array of commonly recognised frames can be invoked in the face of events like the 'Arab Spring'. The inheritance of the French Revolution and, especially, the memory of 1989 and the 'colour revolutions' of the early 2000s have left a definite mark on the European imaginary concerning what a democratic revolution/transition process should look like. From the Western European perspective, it is particularly relevant to note that it is quite easy to read all the revolutions and uprisings that have occurred on European soil as continuations of the process that began with the French Revolution. As a constitutive event of the contemporary EU, 1989 is a case in point. As Milada Anna Vachudová and Tim Snyder have argued, 'the revolutions of 1989 were not bearers of new political ideas. Instead, their shared ideology was one of restored normalcy, of a return to Europe' (Vachudová and Snyder 1996: 1). The revolutions of Central and Eastern Europe were a powerful demonstration of the desirability of the Western European political-economic model. As the European Council declared at the time, the transition 'brings ever closer a Europe which, having overcome the unnatural divisions imposed on it by ideology and confrontation, stands united in its commitment to democracy, pluralism, the rule of Law, full respect for human rights, and the principles of the market economy' (European Council 1990). More recently, this line of thought gained support from the essentially pro-Western 2004 uprisings in Ukraine. Within the EU administration, Ukraine's Orange Revolution was seen as demonstrating its 'European-ness'.[15] There is thus a strong European imaginary concerning popular uprisings, springing from the experiences in and around the present-day EU and supported by the general political structure and nature of the EU and its policies.

Of the latter, it is important to examine the context of Euro-Mediterranean politics as a particular background for the EU's reactions to the 'Arab Spring'. In 1995, the EU launched what is commonly known as the Barcelona Process or Union for the Mediterranean, with the goal of promoting co-operation among and with its Mediterranean neighbours. The stated goals of the Barcelona process included regional stability, economic partnership and socio-cultural partnership (Barcelona Declaration 1995). Both the Barcelona process and the later (2003–4) European Neighbourhood Policy (ENP) were launched with the aspiration of

---

14. In its relations with Third World countries, the European political imaginary is also, no doubt, still under the influence of Orientalism, which has been firmly embedded in European culture from the beginning (Said 2003: 1, 5, 22).
15. This was at least the view of Chris Patten, the former European Commissioner for External Relations, cited in Bulley 2009: 80.

making concrete the idea of the EU as a 'force for good' (for example, Barbé and Johansson-Nogués 2008: 81). In the Barcelona Process particularly, a lot of emphasis was also put on the common cultural heritage and unity of the Mediterranean area. Vasiliki Yiakoumaki has argued that the reappearance of the 'Mediterranean' on the agenda of the EU was, to a large extent, motivated by the Union's 'effort to play a certain role in global economy' and played a central role in the legitimisation of the EU's politics (Yiakoumaki 2011: 46).

Apart from the production of a certain notion of 'cultural unity',[16] the idea of the EU as a force for good in global politics has been played out in the Barcelona Process and, especially, the ENP by a strong emphasis on democracy-promotion. Often seen as the spearhead of the EU's ethical foreign policy, democracy-promotion is one of the key tools with which the Union seeks to augment its influence in its immediate neighbourhood and throughout the world. These policies are based on such keywords as 'partnership' and 'local ownership'. They are supposed to be a reciprocal attempt to build an efficient, transparent and democratic set of political institutions. Officially, the EU's role is to offer funding and technical assistance. Hence, even though directly connected to the project of ethical foreign policy, substantial questions of a normative, political and ideological nature are often disregarded for internal reasons, in order to avoid confrontations between member-states. This has rendered the discussion on democracy-promotion programmatic and technical (Kurki 2011: 351). Nevertheless, many commentators have noted that *in actu*, there are many political presuppositions behind the seemingly technical programmes of assistance. It is worthwhile to explicate these presuppositions briefly, given that they not only provide us with a background on the Euro-Mediterranean relationship but also illuminate the concept of democracy operative in EU discourse. This is particularly relevant in the present context, given that the Arab uprisings were essentially seen as an aspiration for democratic institutions.

This act of depoliticisation in the EU's democracy-promotion and ethical foreign-policy discourse in general can be approached through the concept of the 'anti-politics machine', introduced by James Ferguson in his research on the 'development apparatus'. According to Ferguson, the anti-politics machine depoliticises 'everything it touches ... all the while performing, almost unnoticed, its own pre-eminently political operation' (Ferguson 1990: xv).[17] In other words, it involves presenting political problems as solvable through the application of seemingly technical solutions within a pre-given network of actors. Indeed, critics of the EU's democracy-promotion strategies have pointed out that they are not power-free and that they promote a very specific understanding of what democracy is. They are based on a particular liberal reading of the European experience, coupled with an assumption that this experience can be universalised in a non-question-begging manner (for example, Taylor 2010: 52). Even though they masquerade in the guise

---

16. On this, *see* Yiakoumaki 2011.
17. The concept is thus also related to Barthes' concept of depoliticised speech – *viz.* an attempt to present the political elements of one's discourse as 'natural' (Barthes 1991: 141–3).

of technical and bureaucratic jargon, a form of 'depoliticized speech' (Barthes 1991: 141), there is a clearly noticeable prioritisation of the neo-liberal, 'good governance' understanding of democracy, in which the terms 'good governance' and 'democracy' or 'democratic governance' are used interchangeably (Slocum-Bradley and Bradley 2010: 38; Kurki 2011: 361).[18] Milja Kurki has analysed these policies using the Foucauldian concept of governmentality, concluding that instead of institutional changes, the aim of the EU's democracy-promotion is to 'intervene to effect changes in the views, mindsets and assumptions of target state populations and civil society organisations' (Kurki 2011: 356). Benoit Challand has further argued that the democracy-promotion of Western powers, including the EU, has been exclusively aimed at the 'professional' forms of civil-society activists, thereby creating 'both institutional and discursive isomorphic pressures that contribute to the spreading of a managerial version of civil society that takes the same (Western) organisational and rhetorical forms all over the planet' (Challand 2011: 274). What both these criticisms come down to is a problematic emphasis on the moulding of good neo-liberal citizens, understood as *homines oeconomici* (for example, Challand 2011: 274–5).

Democracy-promotion is only one case among others in which the EU seeks to presents its policies as technical solutions to well defined problems. Arguably, much of its self-image is built on the idea of the institutional structure of the Union being particularly effective and capable of solving problems. Internally, the emphasis on effectiveness of bureaucracy is a method of building the EU's legitimacy vis-à-vis member-states. The EU is needed because it is good at solving problems. Externally, on the other hand, the stress on technicality enables the EU to present itself as an unbiased, 'objective' helper of others, in this sense different from the more 'preaching' United States. It does not openly impose its viewpoints on others but plays the role of pragmatic problem-solver. This is particularly visible in the context of the ENP and the Barcelona Process. These policies have been criticised for being economy-centred, and – the rhetoric of reciprocity notwithstanding – creating a system of EU-led 'hub-and-spokes' arrangements, with the EU more or less presenting its own model of democracy as a good to be exported (Hollis 2012: 81–3; Haukkala 2010: 2). Commentators have also pointed to the latent security aspect of the ENP, particularly in the Mediterranean area, where the EU has expressed worries about the 'unmanaged' flow of people (Barbé and Johansson-Nogués 2008: 86). Indeed, according to Laïdi (2008: 15), the ENP 'constitutes a very classic semi-periphery control policy that aims to set up a virtuous circle encompassing development, democracy and good governance so as not to jeopardise Europe's security and stability'. In this sense, the ENP can very well be said to be the epitome of the intersectionality of ethics, interest and power.

---

18. Starting from criticism of the EU's technical assistance as an instance of the anti-politics machine, we gain a new perspective on the EU's 'normative power'. Instead – or in addition – to being a use of power based on norms, the concept can be seen as an attempt to define what passes as 'normal' in world politics (*see also* Laïdi 2008: 16).

Framing the 'Arab Spring'

From the EU's perspective, the uprisings of 2011 can be characterised as unexpected, sudden and surprising (*see*, for example, Vasconcelos 2012: 7). From a frame-analytic perspective, this kind of event often constitutes what Goffman called 'negative experience', a condition resulting from the inability to non-problematically apply any available frame to the chain of events unfolding before our eyes (Goffman 1986: 378–9). Even though the initial period of bewilderment was rather short, this does tell us something about the magnitude of the uprisings. The frame-analytic question 'what is going on here?' was insistent and created an atmosphere of uncertainty.

This uncertainty was further amplified by the dynamics of diffusion examined elsewhere in the present volume. As opposed to many other protests, the 'contagion effect' in the 'Arab Spring' case was remarkably strong. Not only did the protests spread like a wildfire regionally, they also captured people's imaginations all around the globe (Challand 2011: 271). The Indignados and the Occupy movement were very strongly influenced by the 'Arab Spring' (Vasconcelos 2012: 17). This has been repeatedly confirmed by the demonstrators themselves ('Strike/Riot/Walk Like An Egyptian!'). This posed a special kind of problem for the EU, in that it needed to take special care in managing the meanings arising from the Arab spring in a manner that avoided too strong an association with the protest taking place within its own member states – and, indeed, against the very politics of austerity initiated by EU institutions. There was a strong political motive for interpreting and framing the events in such a manner that would clearly demarcate them from protests within the Union itself. In addition, the status of the EU as major global actor and a regional hegemon created a strongly felt pressure to react convincingly and according to the principles the Union seeks to promote in its foreign policy. In short, it was vital to 'get it right'. It is in such intense moments in world politics that the power-political dynamics of framing are disclosed. In such situations, the pressure to make the right judgments and to have an impact on other actors' judgments and actions is particularly high. In what follows, the EU's communications on the subject will be examined in order to illuminate the ways in which the EU responded to that pressure.

The analysis proceeds as a to-and-fro movement between the data on the one hand and the conceptual tools and background literature on the other. Instead of a document-to-document examination, the communications were examined for commonalities, in order to get a handle on the general features of the EU's response. Based on this analysis, a set of frames was identified. More precisely, this set consists of frames and groups of frames nested within each other. In this nested system, the most important are the hegemonic frame of the liberal world order, shared by the EU and the US, and the frame of the EU as a legitimate and ethical global actor. In a sense, all of the other frames identified can be interpreted as subordinate to these two, as methods devised to uphold them. These two frames constitute the general background frame for EU policies, whereas other frames analysed are specific to the 'Arab Spring' case. Following the conceptualisation presented above, it is argued that the key methods for upholding the idea of 'the-EU-as-a-legitimate-actor-in-a-legitimate-global-order' were the mutually supporting moves of normalisation/depoliticisation and processualisation (that is, anti-eventualisation). The mentioned frames include many familiar features, including the presentation of European values as universal values; temporal blending between current and previous occurrences; the presupposition that European experiences could be transformed into technical expertise; the presentation of the EU itself as a 'success story' and so on.[19]

Most of the frames used emerged early on and had been present in the discourse since the March 2011 Joint Communication 'A Partnership for Democracy and Shared Prosperity with the Southern Mediterranean'.[20] There are few differences between the documents. This, in addition to the actual content of the documents, seems to indicate that the EU's framing of the events emerged almost automatically from the set of previously available frames in the European political imaginary. From a strategic perspective, a key aspect of the EU's reactions to the 'Arab Spring' was an attempt to re-energise the set of frames that present the Union as a legitimate, democratic actor and a plausible economic-political model – a force for good in global politics. The point was to demonstrate that the events re-revealed the legitimacy of the political order and the set of values that the EU represents. In its February 2011 Declaration, the European Council noted that the aspirations of the Tunisian and Egyptian people 'are in accordance with the values the European Union promotes for itself and throughout the world' (European Council 2011a: 14). From this standpoint, an anticipated trajectory that emphasised the hard road ahead but also set forth the rewards at the end of the process was created.

Hence, the need for simultaneous highlighting and containment was addressed by situating the 'Arab Spring' within a specific temporal regime. The outstanding feature of this temporal regime is the emphasis on the protests as part of a continuing process and not as discrete or game-changing 'events', in order to protect the master frame which presents the EU as a legitimate global actor. This implied, above all, the identification of the 'Arab Spring' with previous uprisings in the history of Europe and the EU's neighbourhood. Thereby, as usually happens, the 'negative experience' was quickly replaced by unitary exposition and simplicity. Through an interplay and temporal blending of political memories, cultural and rhetorical conventions and familiar images, a heuristic emerged that seemed to give the Europeans a clear idea of what is going on. This kind of heuristic is partly non-cognitive and escapes exact formulations (Aaltola 2009: 74–5). It is based on hints given by news stories, images and other stimuli, creating connections that are hard

---

19. The relations of these different levels to each other can be thought through via Goffman's argument, according to which 'any strip of activity could be seen as organized into tracks, a main track or story line and ancillary tracks of various kinds' (Goffman 1986: 319). In this chapter, the main track is the interpretation of the 'Arab Spring' as a processual movement into liberal democracy; other frames and methods are ancillary tracks.
20. One notable exception is the concept of 'deep democracy', which is missing from the first communication.

to put in words. For instance, there is a clear visual continuity between journalists' images from the Tahrir Square and those from, for instance, the Ukrainian Orange Revolution – a continuity that goes hand in hand with the stack of other frames that can be invoked in relation to uprisings. When these kinds of connections are made, it suddenly becomes quite clear what is going on. Something similar to a Barthesian myth happens: a blissful clarity emerges, and 'things appear to mean something by themselves' (Barthes 1991: 143). Instead of uncertainty and confusion, we now have clarity based on cognitive and non-cognitive heuristics. What initially was surprising and unknown is now still surprising, yes, but also familiar. Thus, the return to normality did not happen, as Žižek has argued, with the civil war in Libya. It had taken place already with the alignment of Tunisian and Egyptian events to the frame of democratic transitions (*cf.* Žižek 2012: 71).[21] It thereby became advantageous for the EU to actually accentuate the meaning of the events, while simultaneously paying due attention to the management of the meanings given to them.

What was it that was going on in 2011?

In this section I will analyse more closely the EU's framing of events. The section is divided into three parts. The first part discusses the elements of the dramatic tension that can be perceived in the EU's responses. This drama provides the moral background for the interpretation of the events. The second part then analyses the workings of the anti-politics machine in the documents addressing the uprisings. I will point out how the basically liberal understanding of politics, economy and society is depoliticised and presented as a question of effectiveness and technicality. The third part of this section examines the method of temporal blending and normalisation, in which the uprisings become coupled with earlier uprisings and the established framework of the ENP and other such policies. Finally, it is argued that the methods of framing analysed come down to a mutually reinforcing spatio-temporal dynamics of geographical containment and temporal processualisation. All three of the analysed components permitted the element of diffusion to be ignored and the Arab revolts to be treated as wholly unrelated to contemporaneous protests elsewhere. The section closes with reflections on the problems of the processual imaginary in politics.

The drama: Between enthusiasm and alarmism

As was established above, building a dramatic tension is a common method for highlighting an event and re-energising one's own frames. Uncertainty concerning the moral desirability of the outcome helps the actors to involve themselves in otherwise external happenings and creates a sense of urgency in making

---

21. Žižek does note, nevertheless, the connection drawn between the 'Arab Spring' and the Eastern European 'pro-democracy' movements (*cf.* Žižek 2012: 74).

judgments. In the case of the 'Arab Spring', dramatic tension emerged around two opposed trajectories, which drew heavily from the political memories and the stock of frames relating to earlier uprisings.[22] The enthusiastic (or revivalist) interpretation set the events in a continuum with 1989 and other similar events. The uprisings, in this reading, were a strict continuation of democracy-promotion policies and a further step on the road to liberal democracy. They told a familiar story about the spread of practices associated with the EU and the West – freedom, liberty, well managed and efficient governance – and their effects: stability and prosperity. The alarmist imaginary presented the other side of story, to generate tension. Overshadowed by memories of anti-Western revolutions (such as Iran in 1979) and the threat of 'failed states', a negative trajectory was created that sustained the drama and allowed the EU to involve itself in the events. Thus, the EU and its representatives continuously reminded us about the dangers involved. The European Council was following the 'deteriorating situation in Egypt' with 'utmost concern' (European Council 2011a: 14). President Barroso noted that 'we all know the risks in these transition processes very well' (Barroso 2011a: 3, see also ECHR 2011a: 2). The EU pretty much shared Tony Blair's worries about how to ensure the process of change happened with due care, order, and stability.[23] While not explicitly mentioned, an undeniable aspect of the frame is also the fear of losing influence, connected with the general decline of Western power (for example, Gills 2010).

Along the negative trajectory, two issues were particularly 'securitised':[24] migration and energy. While gas and oil supplies were only passingly mentioned, it is clear that considerations relating to energy security were among the strongest strategic interests that the EU had in relation to the transitions (ECHR 2011a: 9). Of the explicitly stated worries, the most persistent was state failure and the likely associated unmanaged flow of refugees. The EU has stated state failure in its neighbourhood as one of the key threats, seeing failed or fragile states as 'ungoverned spaces' where crime and terrorism develop and that function as springboards for unwanted migrants (*see* Hout 2010: 141–5). This is why the EU emphasises the need to build resilient and effective institutions and dreads any political change that is not well managed and stable. In almost all communications addressing the situation, attention was directed to improving the efficient management and control of borders in the region in order to keep irregular migrants out while encouraging the right kind of mobility (Extraordinary European Council 2011: 3–4; ECHR 2011a: 6–7; ECHR 2011b: 11).

---

22. A similar point is made by Vasconcelos (2012: 11).
23. 'Former British Prime Minister Tony Blair discusses the crisis in Egypt and Middle East peace', CNN, 31 January 2011.
24. On the concept of securitisation, *see*, e.g. Wæver *et al.* 1993.

The anti-politics machine: Finding working solutions to well defined problems

The events were seen as an important occasion for the EU to affirm its self-image, to send 'a concrete signal to our neighbours and beyond, that we are 100 per cent committed to supporting democracy and the values upon which the EU was founded' (Ashton, quoted in European Commission 2012). To this end, the EU also sought to highlight its own history of co-operation, pragmatic problem-solving ability and good governance as a 'success story' (ECHR 2011a: 13) and as a model to be followed. Especially the EU's internal unity and the effectiveness of its governance (efficient border-management, for example) were emphasised – for instance: delivering 'the common message and the coherence that will make our actions effective' (ECHR 2011b: 5). Other key words and phrases include 'well managed', 'controlled', 'sustainable stability', 'capacity-building' and so on (ECHR 2011b: 11; Ashton 2011, 2–3; ECHR 2011a, 6–7) The repetition of such words can be interpreted as an effort to highlight the secular, effective and pragmatic nature of the EU. They also neutralise and depoliticise the issues at hand.

A commonly repeated theme in the EU's communications was European experiences in striving for democracy (ECHR 2011b: 21; Ashton 2011: 2; Barroso 2011a: 3). In line with the general ethos of the EU explicated above, it was believed that this experience could easily be transformed into technical expertise. Offering this expertise was seen as a designated task for the EU, not only because of its own values and self-image but because the 'international community' demanded it from the Europeans. The European Bank for Reconstruction and Development was 'responding to calls from the international community – and from the Mediterranean region itself – to apply the 20 years of experience it has built up supporting the process of economic and democratic change in Eastern Europe to a new region undergoing an equally dramatic transformation' (EBRD 2011). The EU was thus able to represent itself as the good-willed technical assistant, while simultaneously promoting an economic-political constellation built on the Western model. Once this model was taken for granted, the EU could assume the role of a judge or supervisor against its southern 'partners'. The problems faced by the Arabs were clearly defined (building a stable democratic system and efficient economy) and the solutions presented themselves quite automatically. These included support for NGOs, political parties, trade unions and suchlike actors (European Commission 2012). Institutionally, it meant the familiar goals: good governance programmes; the rule of law; stronger institutions and effective co-operation between them; and well functioning market economies (ECHR 2011b: 21; ECHR 2011a: 2–9). A particular depoliticised problem/solution pair offered by the EU was economy-related. The joint communication 'Partnership for Democracy and Shared Prosperity', for instance, maintained that the 'unrest in several Southern Mediterranean countries is clearly linked to economic weaknesses'. These economic weaknesses were further identified as problems of purely local quality, with no system or regional level allusions.[25] Hence, the solutions were easily at hand: what was needed were institutional guarantees for a sound business environment and support for small and medium-sized businesses (ECHR 2011a: 7; ECHR 2011b: 7). This shows the strength of the neo-liberal paradigm of governance and economic policy, defined here as a commitment to market-centred economic policy and openness to global capital flows (for example, Reid 2001: 787). Even though questions of wealth-distribution and social justice were mentioned, the focus in terms of solutions was primarily on free-market solutions (*see* Teti 2012: 273). The private sector was seen as the key to better economic performance (for example, Barroso 2011b: 4).

Further, there were worries about democratic aspiration going too far and disturbing economic development. While the protestors contested the desirability of the liberal reading of representative democracy and the 'democracy of experts' of the European institutions (*see*, for example, Chapter One of the present volume), the EU more or less systematically ignored such contestations, focusing on free and fair elections and basic civil rights (European Council 2011a). As Andrea Teti puts it, the framework offered by the EU was 'largely liberal, in the sense that it focuses primarily on a balance between civil society and the state' (Teti 2012: 273). Despite the rhetoric of 'deep democracy' (to be addressed below), calls for more participatory or deliberative democratic practices were not addressed. What was needed was the correct blend of democratic and economic reforms, dispensed in a managed transition to elections-based democracy and encapsulated in the catch-phrase 'money, markets, mobility' (for example, Ashton 2011: 3; Barroso 2011b: 4). In this framing, the EU's role was seen as working together with its neighbours 'to anchor the essential values and principles of human rights, democracy and rule of law, a market economy and inclusive, sustainable development in their political and economic fabric' (ECHR 2011b: 21).

Temporal blending/spatial containment: a politics of processualisation

Fundamentally important vehicles for the normalisation of the Arab protests were their temporal blending with earlier uprisings and their insertion into a continuum with earlier ENP and Union for the Mediterranean (UfM) based policies. This strategy was directly related to the dynamics of diffusion. If sufficiently strong connections can be made to previous events, the pressure of making contemporary connections eases. If the 'Arab Spring' could be aligned to the frame of democratic transitions, too strong an association to the Occupy movement could be avoided. Accordingly, after the initial confusion, the events were rapidly identified as the familiar pro-democracy movements that confirm the superiority of Western models of democracy and economic policies. Similarly to the revolutions of Central and Eastern Europe and to the 2004 uprisings in Ukraine, the Arab revolts were framed

---

25. Teti (2012: 277) interprets the quoted line in the same spirit: 'Here, "unrest" is depoliticised, construed as a result of "economic weakness"'.

as an espousal of the values embodied by the EU institutions, the 'universal values we all share' (ECHR 2011a, 2), such as the rule of law, democracy, good governance and a market economy.

Hence, one of the key aspects of the EU's communications is the framing of the Union as a plausible model to be followed, whose experiences are relevant and valuable for Arabs now striving for the rights and freedoms that Europeans already have. Even though the representatives were very careful to stress that the EU 'does not ask its neighbours to copy our models', these declarations were always accompanied with offers of 'our experience and our assistance' (Barroso 2011b: 3; *see also* Ashton 2011: 2). The EU presented the struggles as a 'quest for the principles and values that it [the EU] cherishes' and offered its 'expertise' in order to help the Arabs to enjoy 'the *same* freedoms that we take as our right' (ECHR 2011a: 2, my emphasis). In the same spirit, the importance of already established policy programmes was repeatedly emphasised while sufficient changes in the content of the programmes was simultaneously signalled. Hence the EU emphasised continuity with its earlier policies, such as the UfM and the ENP (European Council 2011b: 14; ECHR 2011b: 1–2, *passim*; European Commission 2012), while adopting a new rhetoric of 'deep democracy' (ECHR 2011a: 2; Ashton 2011: 2). The latter denotes an understanding of democracy in which 'free and fair elections' are accompanied by 'civil and human rights that many Europeans take for granted' (ECHR 2011b: 2). While 'in the past too many have traded democracy for stability' (Barroso 2011b: 2),[26] the new approach is supposed to give priority to democracy. Apart from the self-evident need to address the radically changed situation in the Mediterranean, the rhetoric of change was also inevitable because a very plausible argument could be made that the EU's policies had played a negative role in the genesis of the 'Arab Spring', by furthering social tensions that erupted into protests (Hollis 2012: 81; Challand 2011: 274). However, as analysts have shown, much of the change can thus be considered 'merely rhetorical'. There was no real change in the EU policies, which remained tied to the same principles as before and expressed a continuation of a Eurocentric approach (Behr 2011; Schumacher 2011: 109–10). Quite simply, the analysis of pre-2011 policy 'does not support the EU's claims to innovation' in the later documents (Teti *et al.* 2013: 64). Hence, the changes are best understood as adjustments within a process. In other words, it is more or less plausible to read the rhetoric of deep democracy as an instant of *plus ça change*, of an outward change keeping the fundamentals constant.

The temporal blending with earlier policies and previous uprisings is part and parcel of an attempt at spatial containment. In the light of the conjunctural analysis and dynamics of diffusion presented by Sotirakopoulos and Rootes in Chapter Eight of this volume, it is rather easy to see why the EU framed the 'Arab Spring' in this particular way. It was, indeed, in the interest of the EU to frame the events so that, first, their origin was identified as the crisis of authoritarian rule and the

---

26. *See also* Behr 2011: 15 on this point.

desire for freedom and not the systemic (legitimacy) crisis of the neo-liberal world economy. Hence, the diffusional dynamics of transmitters (the 'Arab Spring') and adopters (the Indignados, Occupy and so on), for the EU, did not exist, or at least the diffusion did not relate to any shared political issues.[27] To retain its own claims to legitimacy, the EU needed to present Western protesters as a separate strand and to frame the Arab uprisings in a way that makes it difficult to draw connections between them and their Western counterparts. The uprisings needed to be contained within certain spatial limits and the EU needed to decontaminate itself. It was therefore particularly crucial to present the uprisings as something that were – spatially and in the political imagination – distant enough not to have anything to do with the internal politics of the Union.

The method of processualisation, discussed above, becomes particularly visible here. By positing the uprisings within the same process that began in the West with the French Revolution and achieved (partial, for the West) completion with the events of the 1989, the EU created a temporal regime which permitted it to present the events the protests in a light that unquestionably and self-evidently affirmed the supremacy of its own politico-economic model of organisation. As the renowned philosopher Alain Badiou has argued: 'According to [the Western powers], the desire inspiring the riots in the Arab countries is "freedom" in the sense given this term by Westerners ... what is expressed in the riots is what might be called a *desire for the West*. A desire to "enjoy" everything that we ... already "enjoy"' (Badiou 2012: 48). Hence, for example, acknowledging the possibility of the idea of unrest spreading into the heartlands of the West was ruled out from the start. What was happening was an orderly transition to a broad-based government (European Council 2011a) or a part of a much wider transition process, a process that some European neighbours had started during the last decade, while 'others have joined the process only recently' (ECHR 2011b, 21). It is thus a single process, not a series of processes with individual termini, initiated by singular political events.

To a scholar of world politics, this is not entirely surprising. A certain processual temporality of the same kind lurks behind the judgments made of various transitions, particularly those taking place outside the heartlands of the West. As Aaltola puts it in a study of the US hegemony,

> the assumption about the teleological civilizing process leading towards the perfecting of the modern Western international society has acquired a status of a moral judgment: It has become the measuring rod of progress that sets the primitive past apart from the desired future. It prescribes constant transformation and development, and highlights the technological and modernist aspects of Western historical emergence as key features of civilisation (Aaltola 2008: 43).

---

27. For the conceptualisations, *see* the discussion in this volume by Rootes and Sotirakopoulos on Kriesi *et al.* and McAdam and Rucht (Chapter Eight).

A framing via terms such as 'progress', 'plan', 'transition process' and so on further emphasises the notion that each individual occurrence is merely a piece of the puzzle and, as such, incomplete (Aaltola 2008: 61). The processual imaginary reaches even more deeply into the Western imagination. Arendt has analysed the emergence of the modern nation-state and capitalist production as a rise of a processual and circular temporality. Modern sciences (such as economics, history and biology) and the modern political imagination are both held captive by the idea of processes: continuous growth, development, evolution and so forth (*see*, for example, Arendt 1998: 45, 116, 145). Thus, a way of perceiving political time through notions of individually significant events and intervals between such events is ignored, forgotten or suppressed. No radical departures from the overall process are possible.

The framing in which the Arabs are seen as striving for the 'same' freedoms and rights 'we' already have is an act of turning the interpretations of the uprisings towards processuality. At the same time, they are presented in such a manner that the question concerning their relation to the Occupy and Indignados movements does not come up in the first place. While the events were seen as 'historical' and producing 'dramatic changes' (Extraordinary European Council 2011: 1; Ashton 2011: 2), the potential trajectories for the change were presented as more or less given. These revolts were not – even potentially – new beginnings globally, but only locally. In the global context, they are part of the same process that swept over Europe in 1789, 1844, 1989 and so on. The EU may support the unfolding of this process, so that it proceeds with order and stability, but it is safely on the side, as a spectator. These are things that have already happened 'here' and part of an inevitable and necessary process: a 'process of transition that is naturally and inevitably underway';[28] and to which, 'The European Union is determined to lend its full support to the transition processes towards democratic governance, pluralism, improved opportunities for economic prosperity and social inclusion, and strengthened regional stability' (European Council 2011a: 14). As Arendt would have put it, there is 'nothing new under the sun'.

As opposed to this processuality, and following the Kantian and Arendtian thinking previously discussed, a proper revolutionary event can be described as something that disturbs the world political flow of time, abolishes the normal sequence of events and offers the possibility of a novel political imaginary and vocabulary with universal value gaining ground. Such an event, in other words, redefines the terms of political discourse, not only nationally but globally.

Conclusion

In this chapter, I have examined the reactions of the European Union to the events of the 'Arab Spring'. I have argued that the EU's response largely attempted to downplay the commonalities and continuities between the Arab protests and the

---

28. 'Former British Prime Minister Tony Blair discusses the crisis in Egypt and Middle East peace', CNN, 31 January 2011.

European protests. Although not straightforwardly presented as such, this kind of framing can be conceived as political struggle over meanings. As we have seen, conceptions of democratic society are at the core of this struggle. As della Porta and Mattoni argue in the introduction, the 'Arab Spring' testifies in favour of democracy becoming 'the only game in town'. Yet, as della Porta and Mattoni further argue, one of the strongest common traits in the current wave of protests is the elaboration of radical imaginaries and different conceptions of democracy. The EU avoided directly commenting on this trait and did its best, instead, to normalise the uprisings.

From the perspective of the EU, the trajectories of protest events seemed to be to some extent predetermined. While the uprisings may at first have been surprising and even challenging to interpret, they very soon became attached to the idea of a general transitional process, the desire for the Western models of politics and democracy. In the framing of the uprisings as an attempt to achieve the 'same' freedoms and rights 'we' already have, they were deprived of the character of 'event', making them part of a wider process. In this way, the EU also succeeded in isolating the Arab protests from the general, transnational wave of protests taking place at the same time (and covered elsewhere in this volume). Once this interpretation was in place, the problems faced by the Arabs became more or less clearly defined (building a stable democratic system and an efficient market economy). Even more importantly, the outlines of the solutions started emerging. The solutions emphasised by the EU included support for NGOs, parties, trade unions and other such familiar actors. Key phrases such as 'good governance', 'rule of law' and 'efficient economy' were often repeated. The vision of democracy presented by the EU was – claims to the contrary notwithstanding – rather narrow and did not effectually change from earlier democracy-promotion programmes.

From the EU's perspective, the findings of the chapter make problematic its claims to an ethical foreign policy. The strong tendency to align external events to dominant Eurocentric frames interferes with the kind of reciprocity that forms the basis of any kind of ethical action. Similarly, strong, dominant frames tend to limit plurality of debate within and without the polity in question. Any policy proposal, lesson, critique or remedy that transcends the dominant frame easily 'breache[s] the bounds of acceptable discourse' and is unlikely to have any influence (Entman 1993: 55). It seems that, whereas 'movement actors attempt to challenge dominant definitions of political reality by mobilising new interpretations – schemata, frames – of contested social relationships' (Koopmans and Statham 1999: 204), the key global actors, in this case the EU, often tend to do the opposite, even in cases where the protests are not directed against them. The demonstrators themselves, on the other hand, framed the events as radical breaks, not only vis-à-vis the previous regime but also in the sense of producing unforeseen political results. Their action can thus be read as similar to the radical-republican ethos that Arendt identified with revolutionary tradition, involving the creation of public spaces in which everyone has a right to speak and be listened to. Many commentators have indeed pointed out that the subjectivity of the protestors was 'articulated in large parts *against* ... neoliberal programs [of managerial civil society] or *against* the good governance agenda' (Challand 2011: 275). There was, if only momentarily, a possibility of proceeding along 'an unfamiliar non-Western democratic path' (Vasconcelos 2012: 11). There were authentically novel ways in which Arabs framed their revolts and formed a 'leaderless, decentralised, network-like movement' that was 'something new, not only for the Arabs' (Challand 2011: 271; Achcar 2012: 12). These forms of organisation were also a source of great inspiration for the protestors in the West.

References.

Aaltola, M. (2008) *Sowing the Seeds of Sacred: Political religion of contemporary world order and American era*, Leiden: Nijhoff.

— (2009) *Western Spectacle of Governance and the Emergence of Humanitarian World Politics*, New York: Palgrave Macmillan.

Achcar, G. (2012) 'Arab uprisings: geopolitics, strategies, and adjustment. Dina Matar talks to Gilber Achcar', *Middle East Journal of Culture and Communications* 5: 7–14.

Aggestam, L. (2008) 'Introduction: ethical power Europe?' *International Affairs* 84 (1): 1–11.

Amenta, E. and Caren, N. (2004) 'The legislative, organizational, and beneficiary consequences of state-oriented challengers', in D. Snow, S. Soule and H. Kriesi (eds) *The Blackwell Companion to Social Movements*, Malden: Blackwell.

Arendt, H. (1998) *The Human Condition*, Chicago: Chicago University Press.

— (2006 [1962]) *On Revolution*, New York: Penguin.

Ashton, C. (2011) 'Remarks at the senior officials' meeting on Egypt and Tunisia', Brussels, 23 February.

Badiou, A. (2012) *The Rebirth of History: Times of riots and uprisings*, London: Verso.

Barbé, E. and Johansson-Nogués, E. (2008) 'The EU as a modest "force for good": the European Neighbourhood Policy', *International Affairs* 84 (1): 81–96.

Barcelona Declaration Adopted at the Euro-Mediterranean Conference November 27–28, 1995, http://trade.ec.europa.eu/doclib/docs/2005/july/tradoc_124236.pdf (accessed June 2013).

Barder, A. D. and McCourt, D. M. (2010) 'Rethinking international history, theory and the event with Hannah Arendt', *Journal of International Political Theory* 6 (2): 117–41.

Barroso, J. M. Durao (2011a) 'Statement by President Barroso on the situation in North Africa', press point, Brussels, 2 March.

— (2011b) 'Partners in freedom: the EU response to the 'Arab Spring'', speech at the Opera House, Cairo, Egypt, 14 July.

Barthes, R. (1991) *Mythologies*, New York: Noonday Press.

Behr, T. (2011) 'After the revolution: the EU and the Arab transition', Notre Europe Policy Paper 54, available at http://www.notre-europe.eu/uploads/tx_publication/EU_ArabTransition_T.Behr_NE_April2012.pdf (accessed 26 June 2013).

Behr, T. and Aaltola, M. (2011) 'Arab uprising: causes, prospects, and implications', FIIA Briefing Paper 76, available at http://www.fiia.fi/en/publication/174/the_arab_uprising/ (accessed 26 June 2013).

Bosi, L. and Uba, K. (2009) (eds) Special issue on the outcomes of social movements, *Mobilization: An international journal* 14 (4).

Brassett, J. and Clarke, C. (2012) 'Performing the sub-prime crisis: trauma and the financial event', *International Political Sociology* 6 (1): 4–20.

Brassett, J. and Vaughan-Williams, N. (2012) 'Governing traumatic events', *Alternatives: Global, local, political* 37 (3): 183–7.

Bulley, D. (2009) *Ethics as Foreign Policy: Britain, the EU and the other*, London: Routledge.

Challand, B. (2011) 'The counter-power of civil society and the emergence of a new political imaginary in the Arab world', *Constellations* 18 (3): 271–83.

Chong, D. and Druckman, J. N. (2007) 'Framing theory', *Annual Review of Political Science* 10: 103–26.

CNN, 31 January 2011, 'Former British Prime Minister Tony Blair discusses the crisis in Egypt and Middle East peace'.

della Porta, D. and Diani, M. (2006) *Social Movements: An introduction*, Malden: Blackwell.

Dür, A. (2008) 'Interest groups in the European Union: how powerful are they?' *West European Politics* 31 (6): 1212–30.

Earl, J. (2004) 'The cultural consequences of social movements', in D. Snow, S. Soule and H. Kriesi (eds) *The Blackwell Companion to Social Movements*, Malden: Blackwell.

Entman, R. M. (1993) 'Framing: toward clarification of a fractured paradigm', *Journal of Communication* 43 (4): 51–8.

European Bank for Reconstruction and Development (2011) 'EBRD shareholders back expansion to support emerging Arab democracies: Overwhelming approval opens way for start of activities', http://www.ebrd.com/pages/news/press/2011/111005a.shtml..

European Commission (2012) 'The European Endowment for Democracy – Support for the unsupported', press release, Reference: IP/12/1199 Event Date: 12/11/2012.

ECHR (European Commission and High Representative of the EU for Foreign Affairs and Security Policy) (2011a) 'A partnership for democracy and shared prosperity with the Southern Mediterranean', COM(2011) 200 final; 8 March, Brussels.

— (2011b) 'A new response to a changing neighbourhood: a review of European Neighbourhood Policy', COM(2011) 303; 25 May, Brussels.

European Council (1990), 'Presidency conclusions', SN 46/3/90; 28 April, Dublin.

— (2011a) 'Declaration on Egypt and the region', Conclusions, 4 February.

— (2011b) 'Declaration on the Southern Neighbourhood', 23/24 June.

Extraordinary European Council (2011) Declaration, 11 March.

Ferguson, J. (1990) *The Anti-Politics Machine: 'Development', depoliticization, and bureaucratic power in Lesotho*, Cambridge: Cambridge University Press.

Fine, G. A. and Manning, P. (2003) 'Erving Goffman', in G. Ritzer (ed.), *The Blackwell Companion to Major Contemporary Social Theorists*, Malden: Blackwell Publishing, pp. 34–62.

Gills, B. K. (2010) 'Going South: capitalist crisis, systemic crisis, civilisational crisis', *Third World Quarterly* 31 (2): 169–84.

Giugni, M. (1998) 'Was it worth the effort? The outcomes and consequences of social movements', *Annual Review of Sociology* 24: 371–93.

Goffman, E. (1986) *Frame Analysis: An essay on the organization of experience*, Boston, MA: Northeastern University Press.

Haukkala, H. (2010) *The EU-Russia Strategic Partnership: The limits of post-sovereignty in international relations*, London: Routledge.

Hollis, R. (2012) 'No friend of democratization: Europe's role in the genesis of the "Arab Spring"', *International Affairs* 88 (1): 81–94.

Hout, W. (2010) 'Between development and security: the European Union, governance and fragile states', *Third World Quarterly* 31 (1): 141–57.

Imig, D. and Tarrow, S. (2001) *Contentious Europeans: Protest and politics in an integrating Europe*, Lanham, MD: Rowman & Littlefield.

Jahshan, P. (2011) 'The 2011 Arab Uprisings and the persistence of Orientalism', *The Arab World Geographer* 14 (2): 122–27.

Kant, I. (2006) 'The contest of the faculties, part 2, The contest of the Faculty of Philosophy with the Faculty of Law. The question renewed: "Is humankind continually improving?"' in *Toward Perpetual Peace and Other Writings on Politics, Peace, and History*, edited and with an Introduction by P. Kleingeld, New York: Yale University Press.

Kolb, F. (2007) *Protest and Opportunities: The political outcomes of social movements*, Chicago, IL: University of Chicago Press..

Koopmans, R. and Statham, P. (1999) 'Political claims analysis: integrating protest event and political discourse approaches', *Mobilization: An international quarterly* 4 (2): 203–21.

Kumar, K. (1992) 'The 1989 revolutions and the idea of Europe', *Political Studies* XL: 439–61.

Kurki, M. (2011) 'Governmentality and EU democracy promotion: the European Instrument for Democracy and Human Rights and the construction of democratic civil societies', *International Political Sociology* 5 (4): 349–66.

Laïdi, Z. (2008) 'European preferences and their reception', in Z. Laïdi (ed.) *EU Foreign Policy in a Globalized World*, London: Routledge, pp. 1–20.

Lawson, G. (2005) 'Negotiated revolutions: the prospects for radical change in contemporary world politics', *Review of International Studies* 31: 473–93.

Lundborg, T. (2012) *Politics of the Event: Time, movement, becoming*, London: Routledge.

Manners, I. (2002) 'Normative Power Europe: a contradiction in terms?', *Journal of Common Market Studies*, 40 (2): 235–358.

McNamara, K. R. (2010) 'Constructing the authority in the European Union', in D. D. Avant, M. Finnemore, and S. K. Sell (eds) *Who Governs the Globe?* Cambridge: Cambridge University Press, pp. 153–80.

Perthes, V. (2011) 'Europe and 'Arab Spring'', *Survival* 53 (6): 73–84.

Postel-Vinay, K. (2008) 'The historicity of European normative power', in Z. Laïdi (ed.) *EU Foreign Policy in a Globalized World*, London: Routledge, pp. 38–47.

Reid, B. (2001) 'The Philippine democratic uprising and the contradictions of neoliberalism: EDSA II', *Third World Quarterly* 22 (5): 777–93.

Said, E. (2003) *Orientalism*, London: Penguin Books.

Schumacher, T. (2011) 'The EU and the 'Arab Spring': between spectatorship and actorness', *Insight Turkey* 13 (3): 107–19.

Shihade, M., Flesher Fominaya, C. and Cox, L, (2012) 'The season of revolution: the 'Arab Spring' and European Mobilizations', *Interface: A journal for and about social movements*, 4 (1): 1–16.

Slocum-Bradley, N. and Bradley, A. (2010) 'Is the EU's governance "good"? An assessment of EU governance in its partnership with ACP states', *Third World Quarterly* 31 (1): 31–49.

Snow, D. A. (2004) 'Framing processes, ideology, and discursive fields', in D. Snow, S. Soule and H. Kriesi (eds) *The Blackwell Companion to Social Movements*, Malden: Blackwell.

Taylor, I. (2010) 'Governance and relations between the European Union and Africa: the case of NEPAD', *Third World Quarterly* 31 (1): 51–67.

Teti, A. (2012) 'The EU's first response to the "Arab Spring": A critical discourse analysis of the partnership for democracy and shared prosperity', *Mediterranean Politics* 17 (3): 266–84.

Teti, A., Thompson, D. and Noble, C. (2013) 'EU democracy assistance discourse in its new response to changing neighbourhood', *Democracy and Security* 9 (1): 61–79.

Tilly, C. (1998) 'From interactions to outcomes in social movements', in M. Giugni, D. McAdam and C. Tilly (eds) *How Movements Matter*, Minneapolis, MN: University of Minnesota Press.

Vachudová, M. A. and Snyder, T. (1996) 'Are transitions transitory? Two types of political change in Eastern Europe since 1989', *East European Politics and Societies* 11 (1): 1–35.

Vasconcelos, Á. de (2012) *Listening to Unfamiliar Voices – The Arab Democratic Wave*, Paris: European Union Institute for Security Studies.

Watson, S. D. (2012) '"Framing" the Copenhagen School: integrating the literature on threat construction', *Millennium: Journal of international studies* 40 (2): 279–301.

Wæver, O., Buzan, B., Kelstrup, M. and Lemaitre, P. (1993) *Identity, Migration and the New Security Agenda in Europe*, London: Pinter.

Whitman, R. G. (2011) 'Norms, power and Europe: a new agenda for study of the EU and international relations', in R. G. Whitman (ed.) *Normative Power Europe. Empirical and theoretical perspectives*, London: Palgrave MacMillan.

Yiakoumaki, V. (2011) 'On bureaucratic essentialism: constructing the Mediterranean in European Union Institutions', in M. Kousis, T. Selwyn and D. Clark (eds) *Contested Mediterranean Spaces: Essays in Honor of Charles Tilly*, New York: Berghahn Books.

Žižek, S. (2012) *The Year of Dreaming Dangerously*, New York: Verso.

Chapter Six

They Don't Represent Us! The Global Resonance of the Real Democracy Movement from the *Indignados* to Occupy

Jérôme E. Roos and Leonidas Oikonomakis

Introduction: Real democracy now!

The year 2011 was a watershed in modern history. In the wake of the Arab revolutions, a wave of popular protest washed across the globe: from the leafy squares of the Mediterranean to the concrete heart of the global financial empire at Wall Street, and later from the Bosphorus to Brazil, people suddenly started taking to the streets everywhere. By 15 October 2011, millions had mobilised in over 1,000 cities in more than 80 countries to express their indignation at the subversion of democratic processes by corrupt politicians, big banks and powerful corporations. Following three decades of neo-liberal reform, growing inequality and decreasing state responsiveness to popular concerns, the ongoing crisis of global capitalism appears to have thrown liberal democracy into disarray everywhere. A deafening roar now resounds from the squares of the world. After a long slumber, the 99 per cent has risen, with one unifying objective: real democracy now!

From the very start, it was clear that the anti-austerity protesters in Spain and Greece, the Occupiers in the United States and the millions of others who took to the streets around the world in 2011–13 were not the usual suspects of left-wing politics. Refusing to align themselves with any political party or ideology, the movements deliberately avoided making specific demands on the political class. Rather than recognising the authority of those in power, they have largely retained their autonomy and thereby challenged the legitimacy of prevalent power structures at their very core. At the heart of their calls for real democracy, therefore, the movements of 2011–13 not only reveal a profound crisis of representation in democratic capitalist society but also consciously prefigure the creation of a different democratic model, characterised by popular assemblies, horizontal self-organisation and decentralised mutual aid networks (Hardt and Negri 2011; Graeber 2011a). This leaves us with a key question, however: how was it possible for such a radical critique of representation and such an innovative and not very widespread model of direct democracy to spread so rapidly across borders? Or, to paraphrase BBC Newsnight Editor Paul Mason (2012), why was it suddenly kicking off everywhere?

In this chapter, we argue that the transnational struggles for real democracy – which we refer to here as the Real Democracy Movement (RDM) – spread around the globe through a pattern of resonance. In drawing on this concept, we move beyond the traditional literature in social-movement studies, which has, hitherto, identified diffusion as the mechanism by which movements spread from one place to another. As we aim to demonstrate, the concept of diffusion rests upon a number of assumptions that do not appear to hold in the case of the RDM. Building on extensive participatory observation as well as follow-up interviews with key activists in Greece, Spain and the United States, we argue that two conditions must be in place for an autonomous social movement to resonate and spread across borders: first, different countries must share similar structural conditions; and second, they must have pre-existing horizontal movement experience and autonomous activist networks in place to trigger a broader pattern of resonance within their own country. Movements ultimately spread not as a result of the mindless imitation implied by the 'contagion' metaphor but rather because latent potentialities for mobilisation are activated through the inspiration provided by movements elsewhere.

From diffusion to resonance: How do social movements spread?

How do social movements spread across borders? The literature has traditionally approached this question with reference to the concept of diffusion. In the original definition by Katz (1968), diffusion is defined as

> the acceptance of some specific item, over time, by adopting units – individuals, groups, communities – that are linked both to external channels of communication and to each other by means of both a structure of social relations and a system of value, or culture (cited in McAdam and Rucht 1993: 59).

As such, diffusion involves (1) a transmitter; (2) an adopter; (3) an item to be diffused; and (4) a channel through which the item reaches the adopter from the transmitter. The channel of diffusion can be direct, through pre-existing personal contact between transmitter and adopter (relational diffusion); indirect, through the mass media (non-relational diffusion); or some kind of combination or interplay of the two (McAdam and Rucht 1993). Tarrow (2005) notes that, apart from relational and non-relational channels, diffusion can also be mediated through a process of brokerage between two previously unconnected actors, in which a third party assumes the role of broker.

Building on this basic conceptual framework, the academic debate on the transnational diffusion of social movements has centred on two main questions: how movement ideas and practices are transmitted (through relational or non-relational pathways, through a combination of the two, or through a process of brokerage); and how movement ideas and practices are adopted (spontaneously or through conscious leadership) (Andrews and Biggs 2006). Our core argument seeks to move beyond the confines of this debate and problematise the very notion of diffusion as such. We propose that the current conceptualisation – both in its relational, non-relational and mediated varieties, as well as its spontaneous and centrally organised forms – fails to capture the full complexity of how the RDM actually spread so rapidly across borders. The reason for this is that the concept of diffusion ultimately hinges upon the assumption that there is a clear linear relationship between the transmitter and the adopter. Rather, we suggest that there were many cross-directional relationships between multiple transmitters and multiple adopters, and that each national movement studied here at some point fulfilled both of these functions. In other words, each national movement was at once an adopter and a transmitter; both an imitator and an initiator. It follows that the occupations of Tahrir, Sol, Syntagma, Zuccotti, Taksim and elsewhere are better conceptualised as key nodes in a diffuse global network constituted by complex and continuous interaction effects (Castells 2012).

In this sense, the RDM displayed a 'rhizomatic' as opposed to an 'arborescent' nature (Deleuze and Guattari 1980). The different local movements were not branches of a single tree, which would imply a dualistic and hierarchical relationship between the source of the movement and its various national offshoots, between the transmitter of an idea or set of practices and its adopters; rather they assumed the form of a web of intertwined subterranean roots – a decentralised multiplicity that 'ceaselessly established connections between ... organizations of power and circumstances relative to ... social struggles' (1980: 7). The metaphor and concept of the rhizome emphasises the principles of connectivity and heterogeneity, which hold that any one part of the web can be – and in fact must be – connected to any of the others, as well as the principle of 'asignifying rupture', which holds that a rhizome may be broken in any part but still has the power to continue growing in previous or new directions, unlike a hierarchical tree structure, in which the branches necessarily stem from the trunk and die when severed from the main structure. Such a rhizomatic view of the RDM as a horizontal network, as opposed to a family tree, has important implications for the study of its growth and dissemination across borders.

Much more than an imitator movement taking elements of the struggle of some remote vanguard movement elsewhere, something much deeper seems to be at play: a social phenomenon that we describe as the seemingly spontaneous activation of a latent but pre-existing potential for mobilisation through a transnational pattern of 'resonance'. Simply put, a movement may take off in one place not so much because activists attribute similarity and begin to imitate practices but rather because the affective claims and struggles of people elsewhere resonate with their own and provide domestic activists with the inspiration to activate dormant potentialities for mobilisation back home. This concept of resonance first arose in the Invisible Committee's manifesto, *The Coming Insurrection*, which noted that 'revolutionary movements do not spread by contagion, but by resonance. Something that is constituted here resonates with the shock wave emitted by something constituted over there' (Invisible Committee 2008). A budding revolutionary wave 'is not like a plague or forest fire – a linear process which spreads from place to place after an initial spark'. Rather, it 'takes the shape of music, whose focal points, though dispersed in time and space, succeed in imposing the rhythms of their own vibrations, always taking on more density' (Invisible Committee 2008). As Gaston Gordillo (2011) summarises, 'this is not a linear spread, but convoluted, unpredictable dispersion ... involv[ing] rhizomic, non-linear, vibrating patterns of dispersion resembling sound waves'.

In this conceptualisation, then, the emphasis shifts away from the linear model of causation that sees transmitter movement A as responsible for causing the mobilisation of adopter movement B and instead focuses on the endogenous potentiality for mobilisation that was always-already latent in B and that was merely actualised by the resonance of the building wave of mobilisations that previously passed through A. In other words, the concept of resonance explicitly differentiates between the proximate cause of mobilisation – the 'waves' passing through and amplified by movement A – and the deep causes of mobilisation, which always and already lay hidden underneath the social surface in the form of shared structural conditions and pre-existing local movement experience and activist networks. In this vein, Alain Badiou (2012) has referred to the Arab revolutions as a 'resonant event', while the Colectivo Situaciones (2002) – an influential group of militant researchers during Argentina's spontaneous popular uprising of 2001 – has noted that 'there could be resonances between, for instance, Argentinian piqueteros and migrant workers in Western Europe, even if there is no actual exchange of words between them'. John Holloway previously described the phenomenon in an analysis about the inspiration that Mexico's Zapatistas provided to the Global Justice Movement:

> There is no linear progression here. It is not the spread of an organisation that we are speaking of ... Neither is it really a question of the spread of an influence from Chiapas. It is not that the decisions of the EZLN have an influence on struggles in Rome or Buenos Aires. It is rather a question of resonance and inspiration, ... because the themes that the EZLN raise and the orientations they suggest have resonated strongly with the preoccupations and directions of people in the cities (Holloway 2005).

The social-movement literature is already familiar with one form of resonance: frame resonance. In its original formulation by Snow and Benford (1988) as well as Gamson (1992), this concept deals with the question: 'how does a frame resonate with the members of a group it is attempting to mobilize? Does a frame strike shared inner chords or is it at odds with a target audience's values and beliefs?' (Snow and Benford 1988: 198). There is a potentially interesting research agenda here, focusing on how RDM frames like 'They Don't Represent Us!' (of the Spanish Indignados) or 'We Are The 99 Percent!' (of the Occupy movement) resonated among a transversal audience of students, middle-class professionals, indebted home-owners and unemployed workers that would not necessarily have been mobilised by a frame like 'overthrow the bourgeoisie!' or 'workers of the world unite!' In fact, the '99 Percent' frame represents a deliberate choice on the part of Occupy organisers to move beyond the stale rhetoric of the old left and make an active attempt to re-frame contemporary class relations and class struggle under the conditions of late capitalism (Graeber 2013). That said, this chapter does not concern itself with the resonance of frames. Rather it focuses on how the RDM as such – and, in particular, its autonomous and horizontal models of direct democratic self-organisation – spread across borders prior to the conscious development of such movement frames. This forces us to look beyond 'values and beliefs' alone and consider both the structural and local context in which the movements arose.

Methodological approach

We believe that the best way to develop existing concepts is to adopt the methodological framework proposed by its proponents and showing why – even on its own terms – the concept, at least in its current form, fails to describe adequately a substantively important social phenomenon under investigation. In our approach, we therefore follow Tarrow as well as McAdam and Rucht (1993: 62), in shunning a narrow emphasis on case studies and studying our movements in a holistic sense as a 'transnational movement family' rather than as a series of distinct national movements. We believe such a conceptualisation is justified because, despite their local differences and the fact that they are not strictly nationally based, the different national movements in the post-2011 protest cycle do fulfil the remaining criteria proposed by della Porta and Rucht (1995): they share a common world-view and organisational structure and they have often explicitly joined forces for international campaigns, with the Global Day of Action on 15 October 2011 standing out at the clearest example of this common agenda and leaderless organisational structure. As participants in RDM actions in over half a dozen countries, we always considered ourselves to be part of a global movement – a sentiment that was shared by most of our comrades and interviewees.

This chapter is therefore structured thematically while drawing on evidence from multiple local movement sources, in particular Spain and Greece. Our empirical discussion starts with two sections that look at the conditions we hypothesise to be necessary for a movement to resonate across borders, namely that: (a) the different countries share similar structural conditions; and that (b) they have horizontal movement experience and pre-existing autonomous activist networks. It then moves on to a third empirical section that seeks to problematise the assumptions of the diffusion literature by showing that, instead of imitating a single transmitter, each of the national movements actually drew on multiple sources of inspiration and adapted rather than adopted their ideas and practices. In fact, the movements in the different countries inspired one another in a back-and-forth kind of way, with each at some point fulfilling the role of both transmitter and imitator, making these two conceptual categories very difficult if not impossible to disentangle from one another.

Throughout these sections we base ourselves on research data accumulated through extensive fieldwork in Greece and Spain, involving participant observation and in-depth interviews with movement participants; participation in

Occupy actions in six European countries; and direct (albeit remote) engagement with protests in the US and elsewhere through our participation in the Take the Square collective, a transnational platform of RDM activists rooted in the 15-M movement and best known for its co-ordination of the Global Day of Action on 15 October 2011, as well as our work as editors for *ROAR* Magazine, an activist publication that has actively reported and reflected on every major development in the RDM since the Egyptian revolution of 2011.

Shared structural conditions: The crisis of representation

As we noted in the introduction, if there is one thing that the post-2011 movements – at least those outside the Arab world – have in common, it is their emphatic rejection of representative officials and institutions. We argue that this is a reflection of the structural conditions in response to which the RDM emerged: namely the global crisis of representation. The global financial crisis, which was precipitated by the 2008 Wall Street crash whose ripples subsequently spread to Europe in the form of a sovereign-debt crisis and to emerging markets in the form of commodity-price volatility and a growth slump, has exposed a more long-term dynamic in global capitalism. In a word, globalisation has contributed to a situation in which power has become disconnected from politics. As Zygmunt Bauman (2013) puts it, if politics is about the ability to decide what is to be done and power is the ability to actually do it, then the nation state is full of politics but increasingly devoid of power, which has all but evaporated into a supranational realm of global capital flows and global production networks. This, in turn, has exposed a paradox at the heart of democratic capitalist society: elected representatives are still expected to listen to the needs of their own constituencies but the structural constraints imposed by globalisation and financialisation render them increasingly incapable of doing so. In the end, political leaders – whether democratic or authoritarian, left or right – find themselves more and more compelled by market forces to act against the expectations of large segments of the population.

In this respect, we note that the current economic crisis has played an important role in fuelling popular indignation and thereby contributing to the wave of protests of 2011–13. That said, the same cycle of struggles also included very similar protests in countries like Chile, Israel, Mexico, Canada, Turkey and Brazil, all of which were actually perceived to be rapidly growing 'emerging markets'. The fact that both crisis-stricken developed countries and rapidly growing developing countries experienced social unrest seems to indicate that there is more in play than a simple response to austerity measures or economic crisis. What unites these widely varying national contexts is that each of these countries has, over the course of the past decade(s), become increasingly deeply integrated into global capital markets and global networks of production, while following a clear pattern of neo-liberal market reform. These structural changes in the global political economy, combined with the ideological triumph of neo-liberalism, have greatly reduced the responsiveness of state institutions to popular concerns. As John Holloway put it in a recent interview with *ROAR* Magazine:

... one thing that's become clear in the crisis to more and more people is the distance of the state from society, and the degree to which the state is integrated into the movement of money, so that the state even loses the appearance of being pulled in two directions. It becomes more and more clear that the state is bound to do everything possible to satisfy the money markets and in that sense to guarantee the accumulation of capital ... And if that means absolutely refusing to listen to the protests, if it means letting the rioters burn down the cities, then so be it. The most important is really the money markets (cited in Roos 2013).

The global crisis of representation is therefore not just a product of the economic crisis, even if it is closely connected to it. Rather, both are symptoms of a much broader pattern of global capitalist restructuring, including the dual processes of globalisation and financialisation. In this sense, the Occupy movement cannot be reduced to a 'we are here' movement, clamouring for attention amid an economic system that has 'lost its way', as Tarrow (2011) has claimed. Rather, it is a social response to an historical shift in the relationship between capital and the state on the one hand and ordinary citizens and representative institutions on the other. Whether or not a country is seen to be in 'crisis', everywhere people are beginning to feel less and less represented by those who are supposed to be representing their interests in parliament and government. For us, the crisis of representation – and the popular reaction to it in the form of the RDM – is a global and systemic phenomenon that resonates far beyond the borders of individual nation states and therefore cannot simply be reduced to a 'call for attention'.

The movements in Spain and Greece illustrate this well. Although the crises in the two countries took very different forms – the main debtor in Greece was the public sector while in Spain it was the private sector – the social consequences were equally devastating. In both Greece and Spain, popular indignation with politicians runs high: a fact that was neatly confirmed when on 15 May 2011 over 100,000 marched in Madrid and occupied Puerta del Sol; and when, only ten days later, on 25 May 2011 hundreds of thousands more swarmed into and occupied Syntagma Square in Athens. The shared structural conditions between Greece and Spain are fairly straightforward: the two countries share not just the devastating socio-economic fallout of the eurozone debt crisis, with rampant youth unemployment as one of its most visible symptoms, but they also constitute the two most extreme examples of a truly European – indeed global – phenomenon: namely the deepening loss of trust in representative institutions. According to the European Commission, 68 per cent of Europeans do not believe that their voices count in Europe,[1] while a recent Eurobarometer survey found that public confidence in the EU has fallen to historic lows (Traynor 2013). This collapse in public confidence in EU institutions was by far the most pronounced in Spain,

---

1. Speech by vice-president Reding during 'Future of Europe' debate in Lisbon, Portugal on 20 February 2013.

where trust fell from 65 per cent in 2007 to only 20 per cent in 2013, with mistrust soaring from 23 per cent to 72 per cent.

Meanwhile, a study by the Pew Research Global Attitudes Project from May 2013 finds that mistrust is not just limited to EU institutions: 'compounding their doubts about the Brussels-based European Union, Europeans are losing faith in the capacity of their own national leaders to cope with the economy's woes' (Pew Research 2013). Another study by the European Social Survey published in April concludes that rising unemployment, work-related anxiety and a growing sense of social insecurity have gravely undermined public faith in representative politics as such. According to the survey, 'overall levels of political trust and satisfaction with democracy [declined] across much of Europe [and] reached truly alarming proportions in the case of Greece' (Economic and Social Research Council 2013). José Ignacio Torreblanca, who analysed these findings for the European Council of Foreign Relations, remarks that 'both debtor and creditor countries basically feel that they lost control of what they are doing' (Naumann 2013) and concludes that most European citizens 'now think that their national democracy is being subverted by the way the euro crisis is conducted' (Traynor 2013).

This crisis of representation is by no means limited to Europe. The direct backdrop to Adbusters' call to Occupy Wall Street in New York was the fact that the financial crisis of 2008–09 had never truly been resolved, merely moved around: the losses of the big banks had been socialised, while individuals and households remained mired in unaffordable student, mortgage, credit card and medical debts. Moreover, Barack Obama, who had been elected on a progressive platform that promised to take money out of politics, and whose campaign at times took on nearly messianic proportions, gravely disappointed his left-wing and liberal base of young supporters by resolutely swinging to the right immediately upon his inauguration, greatly expanding Bush's bank bailouts as his first major act in office. Even though the Federal government remained committed to a mild form of fiscal stimulus, at the municipal and state levels, authorities were increasingly beginning to pursue harsh austerity measures, feeding into the financial squeeze of individuals and households around the country. Meanwhile, as inequality had sky-rocketed over the past thirty years while social mobility all but stagnated, the political system as such had ceased to function as a representative organ of the sovereign people: even a former IMF chief economist now recognises that Washington has long since been captured by powerful Wall Street interests (Johnson and Kwak 2011). No surprise, then, that OccupyWallSt.org, the unofficial but *de facto* website for Occupy, described the movement to be 'fighting back against the corrosive power of major banks and multinational corporations over the democratic process, and the role of Wall Street in creating an economic collapse that has caused the greatest recession in generations'.

Pre-existing movement experience and activist networks

The second condition we specify as necessary for the widespread resonance of social movements between one place and another is the presence of pre-existing horizontal movement experience and autonomous activist networks. Here, we identify a number of specificities to the Greek, Spanish and US cases that lent themselves to the actualisation of dormant potentialities once an external source of inspiration presented itself to trigger them. In the case of Spain, numerous commentators and activists have, rightly, stressed the precedent of the Egyptian revolution and the occupation of Tahrir Square as a major source of inspiration for the Indignados. When a young Spanish woman was photographed with a sign that said 'Nobody expects the #SpanishRevolution', not only did the hashtag refer to the role of social media in instantaneously disseminating information about the protests, but she was also indirectly alluding to a major source of revolutionary inspiration for the protestors themselves: Tahrir Square.

As one of our friends in Take the Square put it, 'Of course Egypt inspired us! The Egyptians showed us that it was possible to have a revolution without leaders. That it was possible to overthrow a regime through a non-violent occupation of a square. Of course that inspired us.' In this sense, we can extend Badiou's interpretation of the Arab revolutions as a resonant event to the European anti-austerity protests that kicked off in Spain and which resonated to the same frequency of spontaneous and autonomous revolt centred on a main square as the movement's key organisational hub. But while Tahrir clearly played a very important role in inspiring the decision to occupy Puerta del Sol, the idea that the 15-M movement was therefore 'diffused' from Egypt – with the Spaniards simply adopting a set of ideas and practices developed and transmitted by the Egyptians – would be simplistic. After all, the practice of occupying public space is by no means new to Spain. Many of the early participants in #AcampadaSol came directly out of Madrid's lively Okupa movement, including major squats and social centres like La Tabacalera and Patio Maravillas. The latter defines itself as a 'multi-purpose autonomously governed space' and has its own 'HackLab' whose members and material resources were crucial in setting up the movement's basic communications networks, including its websites, live streaming set-ups, Twitter accounts and Facebook pages.

At the same time, these autonomous spaces and social centres were an important source of experience for the practice of *autogestión* – an anarchist and mutualist principle going back to Pierre-Joseph Proudhon that refers to the leaderless self-management of workers or other communities – which is very well established in Madrid and in Spain more generally. Other sources of such horizontal experience include the anarcho-syndicalist union CNT, which rests on the country's anarchist tradition of the 1930s and the strong movement of neighbourhood assemblies that thrived in the 1960s and which was later reinvigorated and reincorporated by the 15-M movement, following the voluntary disbanding of the protest camps and their decentralisation into neighbourhood assemblies. All of this illustrates that the assemblary model of direct democracy did not arrive at Sol out of a vacuum, nor was it directly adopted from abroad. Rather, it was endogenous to local movement experience and institutionalised at a very early stage into the decentralised organisational model of the *Democracia Real YA!* or '*Real Democracy Now!*' (DRY) platform, as well as the many movements and associations that constituted the DRY network. The Juventud Sín Futuro student platform, for instance, grew out of the autonomous student movements against the Bologna process of 2008–9, most of which had been organising through student assemblies for years.

A similar history of movement experience and a roughly comparable panoply of activist networks under-girded the occupation of Syntagma Square on May 25, 2011. Athens is well known in movement circles for having one of Europe's biggest and best-organised anarchist communities. While the hard-core anarchists were initially very reluctant to join the protests at Syntagma for their 'post-political' character, the so-called 'small-a anarchists' (Graeber 2002) were present in the square from the very start and played a key role in setting up the General Assembly, working groups and basic solidarity and mutual-aid networks. Many of these activists frequent or live in Exarchia, an anarchist neighbourhood of Athens that is within walking distance from Syntagma Square and which has been a hub for autonomous movements and activist networks ever since the military junta was overthrown – following the bloody repression of a student uprising that began inside the neighbourhood's Polytechnic campus. As in Madrid, many of the activists in Athens were already familiar with the occupation of public space, from the city's many squats to the struggle over a disused parking lot in Exarchia in 2009, which – after being successfully defended by residents after the municipality announced plans to build a new garage there and ordered police to clear the space – was turned into the well known self-managed Navarinou Park. Also, many Greek protestors were by no means new to confrontation with police, as many had experienced or even participated in the spontaneous urban uprising of 2008, which followed the police killing of 15-year-old Alexandros Grigoropoulos in Exarchia.

Similarly, while the majority of protestors at Syntagma Square were probably novices to political protest, some of the key organisers of the assemblies and other platforms were either disillusioned after years of participation in the stale hierarchies of the traditional leftist parties or had been organising through direct-democratic models in the Global Justice Movement and its various outgrowths, including the No Border Camps and other campaigns to defend the rights of immigrants and refugees. So, while at first sight it may seem self-evident that the Greek movement for direct democracy was simply 'diffused' from Spain, it would be simplistic to ascribe a clear linear or causal relationship between the two. To understand what really animated the occupation of Syntagma, we have to recognise the fact that a wave of protests and strikes had been rocking the country already, ever since the first EU/IMF bailout was announced in early 2010. By May, 2011, a spontaneous outburst of civil disobedience was already underway, with the 'I Don't Pay' movement occupying toll booths and metro stations and allowing drivers and passengers to pass through without paying.

In this sense, the surprise is not that the Greeks eventually occupied Syntagma Square on 25 May 2011, ten days after the Spanish occupied Puerta del Sol, but that they did not do so earlier. If we go back in time, we can therefore immediately see why a pure diffusion-based reading of the Greek protests fails to describe adequately what had already been stirring underneath the surface for months, if not years. On 23 April 2010, Prime Minister Giorgos Papandreou had announced the EU/IMF bailout and, on 5 May 2010, Parliament voted on its first austerity memorandum to meet the conditions for the emergency loan. On that day, Greece witnessed a massive wave of protests that culminated with the tragic arson of the Marfin bank in Stadiou Street in Athens, during which three employees – one of them three-months pregnant – were burnt alive. As one Greek anarchist later told us, the tragedy of the Marfin bank temporarily took the lifeblood out of the resistance, provoking a period of soul-searching and relative absence of anarchists from the movement: 'it really set us back at least a year', he said.

If we dig below the surface, we find a very different story but nonetheless a similar theme in the United States. Like the Spanish and Greek movements before it, Occupy Wall Street did not emerge out of a vacuum. It emerged as part of a growing wave of grassroots struggles and, as such, marked a rapid intensification rather than a radical break with what had come before. On June 9, 2011, a month launching their call to Occupy Wall Street, the Canadian magazine Adbusters had already emailed its followers arguing that 'America now needs its own Tahrir.' Around the same time, a coalition of movements and NGOs called New Yorkers Against Budget Cuts made a call-to-action to set up the so-called Bloombergville protest camp in City Hall Park on 14 June, vowing to 'stay till Bloomberg's budget is defeated'. The protests against Bloomberg's austerity budget were in turn inspired by the Walkerville occupation of Wisconsin workers that had taken place earlier in June, which itself emerged out of the occupation of the Wisconsin State Congress in February, following Governor Walker's move to abolish collective bargaining rights as part of a new austerity budget. Meanwhile, various marches and actions against austerity, like the so-called Bay Of Rage Anti-Cut Marches in the San Francisco Bay Area, were held in numerous other cities across the United States.

Apart from these pre-constituted grassroots anti-austerity movements, Occupy had some deeper roots within the US social fabric. As David Graeber, the anthropologist, anarchist and early organiser in the Occupy movement has recounted, the first meetings of the New York General Assembly in Tompkins Square Park featured 'a smattering of activists who had been connected to the Global Justice Movement' and a large group of young participants 'who had cut their activist teeth on the Bloombergville encampment' earlier that summer (Graeber 2011c). As a result, numerous activists and observers have noted the anarchist roots of the Occupy movement, as well as its relationship to the similarly anarchist-inspired Global Justice Movement (Graeber 2011a; 2011b). Sociologist Dana Williams (2012) has noted that 'the most immediate inspiration for Occupy is anarchism', even going so far as to claim that anarchism constitutes the 'DNA' of the movement, while Michael Kazin, Professor of History at Georgetown

University, has written about Occupy's 'anarchist vision of a future in which autonomous, self-governing communities would link up with one another' (Kazin 2011). This seems to indicate that the RDM's strong emphasis on autonomy from political parties and the state allows not only for its transnational resonance across boundaries; but it also creates possibilities for a form of historical and ideological resonance with the theory and practice of anarchism – a resonance that in turn fed into the widespread participation of anarchists in the RDM.

The movements' multiple sources of inspiration

The fact that Occupy directly drew inspiration from the theory and practice of anarchism is connected to our third main observation: that far from there being an identifiable single 'transmitter' for the ideas and practices of the RDM, what we are really seeing is a multiplicity of inspirational antecedents that simultaneously impinged upon the movement. Still, apart from the endogenous potential for mobilisation that was already there – as a result of the shared structural conditions of the global crisis of representation and the local specificities of pre-existing movement experience and activist networks – struggles elsewhere did play an important role in inspiring Occupy activists to activate those latent potentialities back home. In this respect, the struggles of Tahrir, Syntagma, and Sol clearly resonated across the Atlantic. When it finally launched its call to Occupy Wall Street on 13 July, Adbusters (2011) noted that 'a worldwide shift in revolutionary tactics is underway right now that bodes well for the future'. According to Adbusters, 'the spirit of this fresh tactic, a fusion of Tahrir with the *acampadas* of Spain', was captured in a quote by Pompeu Fabra Professor and 15-M activist Raimundo Viejo:

> The anti-globalisation movement was the first step on the road. Back then our model was to attack the system like a pack of wolves. There was an alpha male, a wolf who led the pack, and those who followed behind. Now the model has evolved. Today we are one big swarm of people (Adbusters 2011).

David Graeber (2011d) has recounted how the European anti-austerity protests were a major source of inspiration for Occupy. In the early days of the movement, on 2 August 2011, Graeber responded to an invitation by a Greek anarchist to join a General Assembly at Bowling Green, where a discussion was to be held on how to respond to Adbusters' call-to-action and how to organise for the occupation of Wall Street on September 17. When he arrived there, Graeber found a number of familiar faces from the Anti-War and Global Justice Movements, as well as a number of Greek and Spanish migrants who had been involved in the RDM elsewhere:

> I quickly spotted at least one Wobbly, a young Korean activist I remembered from some Food Not Bomb event, some college students wearing Zapatista paraphernalia, a Spanish couple who'd been involved with the indignados in

Madrid... I found my Greek friends, an American I knew from street battles in Québec during the Summit of the Americas in 2001, now turned labor organizer in Manhattan, a Japanese activist intellectual I'd known for years ...

In subsequent NYGA meetings in Tompkins Square Park it was decided that

what we really wanted to do was something like had already been accomplished in Athens, Barcelona, or Madrid: occupy a public space to create a New York General Assembly, a body that could act as a model of genuine, direct democracy to counterpose to the corrupt charade presented to us as 'democracy' by the US government (Graeber 2011d).

The Occupy movement thus took its inspiration from multiple sources: from the theory and practice of anarchism to the Zapatistas and the Anti-War and Global Justice Movements, and from the Greek and Spanish anti-austerity family movements and the direct democratic models in the squares of Madrid, Barcelona and Athens, to the Arab uprisings that had just unleashed the global revolutionary wave at the start of the year.

A similar pattern is revealed if we take a more in-depth look at the Spanish and Greek movements. To think that Egypt was the sole source of inspiration for the 15-M movement in Spain, for instance, would be a mistake. Fabio Gándara, the 26-year-old lawyer who set up the digital DRY platform with three friends, has said that he looked to Iceland for inspiration, as did two of the key organisers of Take the Square, one of whom even moved there because of the island's new constitutional guarantees for press freedom and whistle-blower protection. Iceland was a source of inspiration precisely because mass protests in the wake of the country's financial crisis helped to bring down the government and force the state to go after those responsible for the crisis. 'We saw that the public could change things', Gándara told *El País* (Elola 2011). Iceland thus became a major source of inspiration for organisers and participants in the movement. However, such an observation certainly cannot be taken to mean that the movement therefore 'diffused' from Iceland. Rather, just as Egypt's leaderless struggle for democracy resonated with indignant Spaniards, so the Icelandic struggle against the bankers struck a chord with 15-M activists.

The story of the PAH, the Platform of Mortgage Victims, is another example of the multiple sources of inspiration that fed into the 15-M movement. The PAH, which was one of the larger platforms within the DRY network, had already been fighting for the rights of homeowners since 2009, when bank-sanctioned home evictions began to sky-rocket. In late 2010, it started one of its most visible campaigns, Stop Desahucios, which was aimed at stopping or paralysing foreclosures through direct action. The Madrid chapter of the PAH emerged out of the CONADEE – the National Coordination of Ecuadorians in Spain – which had been fighting for the rights of poor Ecuadorian migrants, many of whom were about to be evicted from their homes, since early 2008. We interviewed Aïda Quinatoa, spokeswoman for CONADEE and a key organiser in PAH, who told us that she had fled Ecuador in the early 2000s, in response to that country's devastating debt crisis, only to arrive in Spain in the build-up to yet another debt crisis. This time, however, as the bank was about to evict her from her home, Aïda decided to fight back. She helped set up the Madrid chapter of the PAH on the basis of what she describes as the values of the indigenous peoples of Latin America: a communitarian, leaderless ethos revolving around consensus-based decision-making. Assemblies have formed the organisational backbone of the PAH from the very start and, when the PAH joined DRY two months before 15-M, spokesman Chema Ruiz recounted that, in DRY, 'we found an assembly-like movement without leaders, a heterogeneous group of people, hopeful of changing things' (cited in Elola 2011).

Others have also traced the autonomous roots of the Indignados back to Latin American indigenous movements. The renowned Mexican intellectual Pablo González Casanova (2012), a former rector of UNAM (Universidad Nacional Autónoma de México) has written that 'the movement of the Indignados began in the Lacandon Jungle' of Chiapas, Mexico, where the Zapatista rebellion of 1994 started. As the 90-year-old sociologist poetically put it, 'the Zapatista movement walks through the whole world, not as an echo, but as the voice of the same thoughts and desires'. This observation was confirmed in the more recent wave of protests in Brazil, when the autonomous-anarchist Free-Pass Movement (MPL), whose actions 'sparked' the mass mobilisations, told reporters that they, too, took their inspiration from the autonomous, horizontal and direct-democratic self-management of the Zapatistas. As one MPL organiser put it, 'the Zapatistas have greatly influenced the alter-globalization movement. They are part of a historical process of which we are the fruit' (Farah 2013). It is no surprise, then, that Subcomandante Marcos of the Zapatista Army of National Liberation (EZLN) was one of the first to suggest the idea – in John Holloway's (1996) words – 'for thinking about the unity of struggles as one of frequencies, of being tuned in, of wavelengths, vibrations, echoes'. As Holloway observed, '... dignity resonates. As it vibrates, it sets off vibrations in other dignities, an unstructured, possibly discordant resonance'. It is also no surprise that Greek protestors would hold up a large banner in front of Parliament on 25 May 2011 with the famous Zapatista slogan: '*para todos todo, para nosotros nada*' – 'everything for everyone and nothing for ourselves'. Nearly twenty years since the Chiapas uprising, the Zapatista call for dignity continues to resonate around the world.

Just like their counterparts in Spain and the United States, the Greeks also did not take their ideas or practices from a single transmitter but rather drew inspiration from a multiplicity of movements whose ideas and practices they then translated and reinvented in a way that allowed the protestors to speak of the transnational movement as a 'we' instead of an 'us-and-them'. It would be easy to say that, because the occupation of Syntagma followed the occupation of Sol, the RDM simply diffused from Spain to Greece. But then what about the influence of Egypt and the other Arab countries in revolt? Did they 'pass through' Spain? Or was their role independent? We believe that these struggles cannot (and should not) be disentangled. Instead, they should be conceived of as a wave that passed through all these countries at different points in time and that resonated strongly back and forth; with each individual movement at some point fulfilling both the role of a 'transmitter' of inspiration and of a 'receiver' of inspiration.

Dimitris, who was one of the co-ordinators of the General Assembly at Syntagma, is clear about these multiple sources of inspiration: 'what happened in Egypt, what happened in Spain – it's not irrelevant of what happened here in Greece. Or what's happening now. Or what's going to happen.' He stressed specifically how the struggle of the Egyptians and Spaniards resonated with the revolutionary desires of many Greeks: 'It inspired us. In a way, when you see such radical images, think of the people on the bridge in Egypt, with the police attacking them, and suddenly the people return and chase the police away. You cannot forget these images. They change you.' Asked how these images from Egypt changed him, Dimitris' answer was simple and straightforward: 'They woke us up.'

A similar idea resonated in the Greek response to the rumoured Spanish slogan to be quiet, lest they wake up the Greeks: a large banner was unfurled outside the Spanish Embassy – and later in front of Parliament – reading: '*Estamos despiertos! Que hora es? Ya es hora de que se vayan!*' – 'We are awake! What time is it? Time for them to go!' The reference here was clearly not only to Spain, but also to the famous slogan of protestors in Buenos Aires during Argentina's crisis of 2001–2: '*que se vayan todos!*', 'Away with them all!' A balloon was hoisted carrying an Argentine flag in honour of that country's decision to defy foreign creditors and default on its debt, while banners with helicopters – referring to the helicopter-escape of Argentinian President de la Rua from the Presidential Palace in 2001 – were a common sight on the square. Very often, one could also notice Egyptian, Tunisian or Spanish flags. Meanwhile, in a sign of more historical resonance, the slogan 'Bread, Education, Freedom: the Junta did not end in 1973' was very popular, borrowed as it was from the student occupation of the Polytechnic in 1973, which was violently repressed and marked the beginning of the end of the Dictatorship of the Colonels. Later on, there was also more resonance between Greece and Argentina. When the workers of Vio.Me in Thessaloniki occupied their factory and resumed production under direct-democratic worker self-management in early 2013, Theodoros Karyotis, spokesman of the Vio.Me Solidarity Initiative, told an Argentinian newspaper that they had been inspired by the struggle of Argentina's Recovered Factories Movement: 'the truth is that the workers themselves say there is resonance between what the [Argentinian] FatSinPat workers say and write, and what the Vio.Me workers believe in and struggle against. There is a strong identification' (Chausis 2013).

Conclusion: The struggle comes full circle

The discussion above raises a host of important questions. First of all, if activists in Spain, Greece and the United States all drew on multiple sources of inspiration for their actions, to what extent are we justified to identify one, and not another movement, as the principal 'transmitter' or 'initiator' (McAdam 1995)? Did the movements in Greece diffuse from Egypt or from Spain? Did the direct-democratic models come from Chiapas, Exarchia or from Madrid? And was it really a one-way affair, with the Greeks only taking inspiration from the Spanish, or did the affect between them run both ways? We believe that the relations between the different national movements within the transnational RDM were more complex than the standard theory of diffusion would have us believe and we are therefore inclined to conceive of the RDM's spread in terms of resonance: a situation in which the latent potentialities for mass mobilisation – owing to shared structural conditions between countries and the presence of horizontal movement experience and pre-existing autonomous activist networks within them – are suddenly triggered by the inspiration provided by similar struggles elsewhere.

On 15 October 2011, roughly a month after the occupation of Wall Street, the Occupy movement suddenly burst on to the scene around the world, inspiring protests and occupations in over 1,000 cities in more than 80 countries. At that point, Kalle Lasn and Micah White (2011) of Adbusters wrote that 'the call to Occupy Wall Street resonates around the world'. If Occupy was at once a source of inspiration for struggles around the world, and itself took inspiration from struggles around the world, then to what extent does it still make sense to pose a stark division between the exclusionary categories of the transmitter and the adopter? If Occupy was at once a transmitter of ideas and practices to over 1,000 cities in more than 80 countries and an adopter of ideas and practices from Tahrir, Sol, Syntagma and elsewhere, then how useful can such a sharp dualistic distinction of analytical concepts really be? And, perhaps most importantly, if the distinction between transmitter and adopter becomes blurred, to what extent does it still make sense to conceive of the spreading of social movements as a linear process between the two? To us, it seems to make more sense to conceive of the local movements as nodes in a transnational network than to speak of tree-like branches in different countries. Rather than mindless imitators, perhaps we should speak of a multiplicity of movements collectively experimenting with alternative democratic models and learning new lessons in the process.

As Egypt geared up for a major demonstration on 30 June 2013, with millions of people taking to the streets and heading back to Tahrir Square in the hope of pushing President Morsi and the Muslim Brotherhood from power, we received an open letter from a collective of anti-authoritarian Egyptian revolutionaries called 'Comrades from Cairo' (2013), which claimed that, 'though our networks are still weak, we draw hope and inspiration from recent uprisings, especially across Turkey and Brazil'. Highlighting the transnational dimension of the ongoing revolutionary wave, the authors wrote that 'none of us are fighting in isolation ... it is the same structure of authority and power that we have to fight, dismantle and bring down'. Recurrent activist statements like these, emphasising the importance of (1) shared structural conditions; (2) local movement experience and activist networks; and (3) multiple sources of inspiration, force us to question the linear conception of diffusion in the social-movements literature. After all, if Spain diffused from Egypt; Greece from Spain; and Occupy from Greece (or was it Spain?) – as the linear diffusion theory would have it – then how can we explain the fact that the same call for real democracy now resonates in Brazil, Turkey and then bounces right back to Egypt, which was supposed to have started the line of causation in first place?

In the future, social-movement scholars may want to develop new methodologies for identifying these shared structural conditions, local movement experience and activist networks, and multiple sources of inspiration that characterise the transnational resonance of social movements. While there is no space to develop such a methodology here, it should by now be clear that the linear concept of diffusion is simplistic and fails to capture the full complexity of the process by which movements spread across borders in the twenty-first century. On a recent trip to Chiapas, we saw a quote by Subcomandante Marcos scribbled on to a wall that appeared to capture the essence of the non-linear nature of revolt: 'the struggle is like a circle', it read. 'It can start anywhere, but it never ends'.

References

Adbusters (2011) '#OCCUPYWALLSTREET', *Adbusters*, 13 July.
Andrews, K. T. and Biggs, M. (2006) 'The dynamics of protest diffusion: movement organizations, social networks, and news media in the 1960 sit-ins', *American Sociological Review* 71 (5): 752–77.
Badiou, A. (2012) *The Rebirth of History: Times of riots and uprisings*, London and New York: Verso.
Bauman, Z. (2013) 'Europe is trapped between power and politics', *Social Europe Journal*, 14 May, http://www.social-europe.eu/2013/05/europe-is-trapped-between-power-and-politics (accessed 24 June 2013).
Castells, M. (2012) *Networks of Outrage and Hope: Social movements in the Internet age*, Cambridge: Polity Press.
Chausis, I. (2013) 'La fábrica recuperada griega que se inspiró en la Argentina', *Tiempo*, 6 May [translated by T. van der Putten as: 'The Greek workers who took inspiration from Argentina', *ROAR Magazine*, 9 May].
Colectivo Situaciones (2002 [2011]) *19 & 20: Notes for a new social protagonism*, New York: Minor Compositions.
Comrades from Cairo (2013) 'From Taksim and Rio to Tahrir, the smell of tear gas', *ROAR Magazine*, 29 June.
della Porta, D. and Rucht, D. (1995) 'Left-libertarian movements in context: a comparison of Italy and West Germany, 1965–1990', in J. C. Jenkins and B. Klandermans (eds) *The Politics of Social Protest: Comparative perspectives on states and social movements*, Minneapolis, MN: University of Minnesota Press.
Deleuze, G. and Guattari, F. (1987[1980]) *A Thousand Plateaus*, translation by B. Massumi, Minneapolis, MN: University of Minnesota Press.
Economic and Social Research Council (2013) 'Europe survey shows work and well-being impact of recession', *European Social Survey*, 22 April.
Elola, J. (2011) 'El 15-M sacude el sistema', El País, 22 May [translated by J. Roos as: '15-M movement shakes the system', *ROAR Magazine*, 24 May].
Farah, T. (2013). 'Movimento Passe Livre se inspira em zapatistas do México,' *O Globo*, 23 June 2013 [translated by T. van der Putten as: 'Brazilian movement takes inspiration from the Zapatistas', *ROAR Magazine*, 24 June 2013].
Gamson, W. A. (1992) 'The social psychology of collective action', in A. D. Morris and C. M. Mueller (eds) *Frontiers in Social Movement Theory*, New Haven, CT: Yale University Press, pp. 53–76.
González Casanova, P. (2012). 'The movement of the indignados began in the Lacandon Jungle', *Take the Square*, 20 January 2012 (accessed 1 February 2012).
Gordillo, G. (2011) 'Resonance and the Egyptian Revolution', *Space and Politics*, http://spaceandpolitics.blogspot.nl/2011/02/resonance-and-egyptian-revolution.html (accessed 1 July 2013).

Graeber, D. (2002) 'The new anarchists', *New Left Review* 13: 61–73.
— (2011a) 'Occupy and anarchism's gift of democracy', *Guardian*, 15 November.
— (2011b) *Debt: The first 5,000 years*, New York: Melville House.
— (2011c) 'Occupy Wall Street's anarchist roots', *Al Jazeera*, 30 November.
— (2011d) 'On playing by the rules: the strange success of Occupy Wall Street', *Naked Capitalism*, 19 October.
— (2013) *The Democracy Project: A history, a crisis, a movement*, New York: Random House.
Hardt, M. and Negri, A. (2011) 'The fight for real democracy at the heart of Occupy Wall Street', *Foreign Affairs*, October.
Holloway, J. (1996) 'The concept of power and the Zapatistas', *Common Sense* 19 (June).
— (2005) 'Zapatismo urbano', *Humboldt Journal of Social Relations* 29 (1): 168–178.
— (2010) *Crack Capitalism*, London: Pluto Press.
Invisible Committee (2008) *The Coming Insurrection*, London: MIT Press.
Johnson, S. and Kwak, J. (2011) *13 Bankers: The Wall Street takeover and the next financial meltdown*, New York: Vintage Books.
Katz, E. (1968) 'Diffusion (interpersonal influence)', in D. L. Shills (ed.) *International Encyclopedia of the Social Sciences* (vol. 4), London: Macmillan and Free Press, pp. 78–85.
Kazin, M. (2011) 'Anarchism now: Occupy Wall Street revives an ideology', *New Republic*, 7 November.
Lasn, K. and White, M. (2011) 'The call to occupy Wall Street resonates around the world', *The Guardian*, 19 September.
Mason, P. (2012) *Why It's Kicking Off Everywhere: The new revolutions*, London: Verso Books.
McAdam, D. (1995) '"Initiator" and "spin-off" movements: diffusion processes in protest cycles', in M. Traugott (ed.) *Repertoires and Cycles of Collective Action*, Durham, NC and London: Duke University Press, pp. 217–39.
McAdam, D. and Rucht, D. (1993) 'The cross-national diffusion of movement ideas', *Annals of the American Academy of Political and Social Science* 528 (1), 56–74.
Naumann, N. (2013) 'Trust in European Union hits record low', *Deutsche Welle*, 26 April.
Pew Research (2013) 'The new sick man of Europe: the European Union', *Pew Global Attitudes Project*, 13 May.
Roos, J. (2013) 'Talking about a revolution with John Holloway', *ROAR Magazine*, 17 April 2013.
Snow, D. A. and Benford, R. D. (1988) 'Ideology, frame resonance, and participant mobilization', *International Social Movement Research* 1: 197–217.
Tarrow, S. (2005) *The New Transnational Activism*, New York: Cambridge University Press.

— (2011) 'Why Occupy Wall Street is not the Tea Party of the Left', *Foreign Affairs*, October.
Traynor, I. (2013) 'Crisis for Europe as trust hits record low', *Guardian*, 24 April.
Williams, D. (2012) 'The anarchist DNA of Occupy', *Contexts* 11 (2).

Chapter Seven

The Transnational Dimension of the Greek Protest Campaign Against Troika Memoranda and Austerity Policies, 2010–2012[1]

Maria Kousis

Introduction

The recent spiralling global economic crisis, whose roots can be traced to the US financial crisis of 2008, has had a severe impact on Greece, a high public-debt Southern European country which became the centre of global attention as the first eurozone member-state to threaten the euro by a possible exit. Under unprecedented transnational pressure from global economic and political players, as well as close scrutiny by all major global media, the Greek government, blamed for the country's dire situation, faces historical dilemmas in view of the 'domino effect' and its related adverse implications – not only for the Greek people but for the global economy as a whole – if the country leaves the euro.

The contention in Greece illustrates a shift towards the importance of the financial sector and the impact of the financial crisis on the ever-more-interdependent global economic and political arena of the twenty-first century, involving most economies of the globe. Such consequences are visible in the most recent declining GDP growth figures (Eurostat 2013) and the latest OECD call for structural reforms of the G20 major world economies (OECD 2013).

At the same time, Greek protests highlight the impact of global economic threats and opportunities on national and regional spaces of contention (Kousis and Tilly 2005). Although the immediate causes of the Greek sovereign-debt crisis lie in the *financialisation crisis* of 2007–9, blame has also been attributed to the weak

---

1. The data used in this chapter were, in part, produced from Mediterranean Voices: Oral History and Cultural Practices in Mediterranean Cities (which is a Euromed Heritage II research project (2002–6) on Mediterranean cities, funded by DG EuropeAid), with 80 per cent of funding by the European Commission (DG EuropeAid, contract no. E8/AIDCO/2000/2095–05) and 20 per cent through matched funding by the University of Crete and other sources. The work by Kostas Kanellopoulos (locating media mentions and coding), Marina Papadaki (technical assistance) and Sara Karavasili (data entry) is gratefully acknowledged. Constructive comments by Donatella della Porta, Alice Mattoni and Ari-Elmeri Hyvonen are deeply appreciated.

integration of peripheral countries in the eurozone (Lapavitsas *et al.* 2010). Greece was the starting point of speculator attacks on other eurozone peripheral states, that is, Portugal, Ireland, Cyprus and Spain. Threats to this eurozone periphery led to pressure on Southern European governments from global economic actors to accept bailout packages and implement radical neo-liberal policies involving unprecedented austerity measures.

As seen in global neo-liberal restructuring, economic crises and the growing power of transnational organisations and global economic institutions in Latin America (Almeida 2007), these recent developments in the Southern eurozone offer evidence on how economic change and its impacts are bearers of opportunities or threats for mobilisation (della Porta and Tarrow 2005; Kousis and Tilly 2005; Smith and Wiest 2012). The impact of the recent crisis is even more pervasive given the speed of the recent global economic crisis generated through the neo-liberal and IT- driven mode of capitalism that has been dominant since the 1970s (Hassan 2011). At the same time, however, the development of electronic communications is a new opportunity for social movements of the past decade (McAdam, Tarrow and Tilly 2001; Tilly 2004; Rucht 2005; della Porta and Tarrow 2005; Mattoni 2012).

As witnessed across global regions, neo-liberal restructuring has induced transnational contention. According to della Porta and Tarrow (2005), three features of transnational contention stand out in most studies: 1) *internalisation*, that is, conflicts of external origin playing out on domestic territory; 2) *diffusion*, the adopting or adapting of organisational forms, collective-action frames and targets; and 3) *externalisation*, visible in movement organisations that become active internationally. The Greek case offers new evidence on each of these features. Moving beyond and above the EU as a transnational space of opportunities and threats (Imig and Tarrow 2001), Greece is a clear example not only of resistance mounted against the enveloping impact of the global financial crisis on the national population but also of the intense transnational pressure from the so-called troika – the European Commission (EC), European Central Bank (ECB) and the International Monetary Fund (IMF) – and from other powerful economic forces aiming to preserve the stability of the interdependent global economic and political system.

This chapter offers new, primary data on the Greek campaign against the troika and their austerity measures, which allows the systematic tracing of these three transnational features, from January 2010 to January 2013. Following the related literature review and the presentation of the method, it lays out the analysis in two sections focused on the 32 large protest events (LPEs) that constitute the campaign (Kousis and Diani 2014). The first section illustrates the internalisation and diffusion characteristics of the campaign, with evidence on sequences of actions, troika/government packages, target groups, participating groups, claims and action-forms (including connected actions and direct democracy). The following section of the analysis will offer data and discussion on the externalisation of the campaign, visible in the participation of non-Greek cities.

Transnational economic and political contention

Since the eighties, the impacts of globalisation have been increasingly deep and pervasive in the economic, political, social and cultural spheres, reaffirming the critical importance of structural transformations and dynamics for social-movement development (*see*, for example, Tarrow 2005; Almeida and Johnston 2006; Almeida 2008; Almeida 2010). Neo-liberalism's failure to deliver social protection and collective goods on a variety of fronts, ranging from provision of healthcare to employment, is reflected in the more recent shift of the burden from governments and corporations to individuals, far less capable of bearing them. Globalisation coincides with the intensification of income disparities across countries, while income and wage inequality within countries can in part be attributed to foreign trade and investment (Guillen 2001; Smith and Wiest 2012). The increasing importance of global market forces has also limited the relative importance of state actors (della Porta and Tarrow 2005), which are now confronting constraints on their actions from both domestic and external sources. Thus, global neo-liberalism is steadily heightening pressures to limit government spending for redistribution and welfare, while neither the market nor major economic actors can respond to social demands (Rucht 2003).

The phases of transnational contention: An 'environmental' and relational view

Since the 1980s and before the global economic crisis of 2008, transnational contention can be considered to involve four phases (Bringel and Echart Muñoz 2010). In the first phase, the late 1980s, counter-summits were organised in the EU against the major international financial institutions. Anti-austerity contention under neo-liberal restructuring appears in the global debt crisis of the 1980s, first in Latin America (Strawn 2005; Almeida and Johnston 2006; Almeida 2010; Bellinger and Arce 2011) and Asian regions (Arce and Kim 2011), with the IMF and the World Bank playing a central role in the neo-liberalisation of national economies and its impacts. Anti-austerity protests in the nineties in Latin America, with the above characteristics, have been viewed as 'defensive mobilisations', mobilising broad, cross-class coalitions of working-class groups, unions, public employees, students, peasants, teachers, community-based groups, indigenous and ethnic-based groups, left-wing political parties and anarchist groups, unemployed, informal sector, middle-class groups, church-based groups, environmental groups, women's organisations and armed insurgent groups (Almeida 2007, 2010).

The second phase, of the 1990s, witnessed similar counter-summits organised in South America and North America against NAFTA[2] (Bringel and Echart Muñoz 2010). At this time, neo-liberal restructuring led to European demonstrations against increases in unemployment and neo-liberal globalisation generally. Local

---

2. North American Free Trade Agreement.

and national networks of grassroots activism based on unions, associations and political organisations co-ordinated EU-level mobilisations against European Monetary Union austerity measures, demanding jobs and social inclusion, aiming for another Europe, in another world (Mathers 2007). Anti-privatisation protests in Greece also begin in the 1990s (Kousis 2004), as seen, for example, in the case of nation-wide blockades in 1996–7, by farmers facing increased imports, EU subsidy cuts and increasing debts. The farmers opposed government austerity measures, as the country was taking steps to meet the entry requirements to join the European Monetary Union (Bush and Simi 2001: 106, 121).

The third phase involved the Seattle mobilisations against the World Trade Organization (WTO), G8, the International Monetary Fund (IMF), the World Bank, the EU, the annual Davos World Economic Forum, while the fourth phase includes the transnational activist networks of the World Social Forum[3] (Bringel and Echart Muñoz 2010) and the European Social Forum (della Porta 2009), focused on the global justice against neo-liberal globalisation and neo-liberal restructuring.

A new fifth phase (Kousis 2012; Kousis and Diani 2014) of both transnational and national contention has risen since the 2008 global financial crisis and the spiralling banking sector or sovereign-debt crises across US, European and other regions. It is a period marked by the recent economic struggles encompassing wider populations, such as the Occupy movement, the Arab Spring protests, the Eastern European protests and the Indignados (Kriesi 2011; Goldstone 2011; Smith 2011; Kousis 2012; Beissinger and Sasse 2012; della Porta 2012; Fuster Morell 2012; Shepard 2012). Mobilising both at the national as well as the transnational level, contenders are against financial, economic and political institutions both at home and abroad, and both across and beyond the EU as a space of contention. They are led by broad coalitions calling upon economic and political power-holders to change the *status quo* and offer alternative policies that move towards economic justice and real democracy.

In the fifth phase, the recent global financial crisis has led to a new set of opportunities and threats for the expression of public demands in democratic as well as authoritarian contexts (Smith 2011). Examples include the recent anti-austerity and economic protests in Eastern European (Beissinger and Sasse 2012), Western (Kriesi 2011) and Mediterranean regions (Goldstone 2011).

Features of transnational contention

Della Porta and Tarrow (2005) point out that most studies on transnational contention focus on three main features of movement organisations that become active internationally: internalisation/domestication, diffusion and externalisation. Moving further, they argue that transnational contention involves not only changes in the global environment ('environmental change'), but also 'cognitive

---

3. The WSF was created to draw attention to the misrepresentations of the World Economic Forum: *see* della Porta and Tarrow 2005.

change' towards transnational identities, visible in the spreading of tactics and frames against target transnational organisations such as the IMF. This change is also reflected in domestic or national contexts, where activists are influenced by struggles carried out beyond their borders. Concerning externalisation, activists communicate across national borders and are thus encouraged towards more globalised framing of their claims. 'Relational changes', that is, social-movement–state interactions, are also influenced by the larger international context. Thus, an increasing shift towards a transnational arena of contention also features the rise of transnational organisational networks, synchronised actions and commonly constructed global frames and aims (della Porta and Tarrow 2005: 3–10).

Scholars of the past decade have also pointed out the need for studying how domestic and transnational political opportunities and threats interact and influence social-movement organisation, protest and outcomes (della Porta and Tarrow 2005; della Porta *et al.* 2006; Shekha 2011). Moving beyond the state as a controller of threats as defined by Goldstone and Tilly (2001), neo-liberal economic reforms imposed on governments and national populations by organisations such as the IMF and the WTO often represent political threats to activists who target them for the impacts of their policies (della Porta and Tarrow 2005; Kousis and Tilly 2005; Almeida 2010; 2011).

Common transnational features have surfaced at the Northern-core and the 'new democracies' of Southern-periphery (Kousis and Eder 2001; Kousis *et al.* 2008; Fishman 2011). Northern and Southern European, as well as Eastern European protest agendas converge on central issues such as economic rights, problems created by the crisis in the eurozone, unemployment, migration, violence, democracy and extremist phenomena. However, a new wave of novel and more frequent anti-austerity protests against troika policies and measures implemented by national governments has, since 2010, spread across the eurozone's Southern European/old periphery (including Ireland), more exposed to the global financial crisis of 2008 (Kousis 2012). Protestors are responding to economic and political threats, defined by Almeida as 'collective bads ... taking away existing rights, goods and safety', (2010: 305–6). He distinguishes three types of threat: '1. state repression, 2. erosion in fundamental political rights, and 3. state-attributed economic problems'.

Thus, Southern European anti-austerity protests lead this fifth phase of a new transnational contention rooted at the local and national level. The activists targeted national and transnational financial and political institutions responsible for the drastic social effects of the 2008 financial crisis (Kousis 2012). An eloquent example of organising structures is the case of the Indignados/Αγανακτισμένοι, who participate both as national contender publics and transnational ones (Fuster Morell 2012; Korizi and Vradis 2012).

'Meganetworks' are another important feature of the current economic contention against neo-liberal reforms and austerity policies in Southern European national and, less frequently but steadily increasingly, transnational spaces (Kousis 2012, 2013). These comprise very broad cross-class coalitions that 'facilitate further mobilization by creating and linking prior, tightly-linked within-group networks to each other' (Goldstone 2011). Their importance is even more noteworthy as 'meganetworks' are characterised by both 'contained' as well as 'warring movements' (Tarrow 2011). Contained movements have four basic characteristics. They involve traditional groups (unions, political parties, working classes, unemployed, middle classes, professional associations, church, consumer groups, women, youth/students). They depict an increased politicisation of protest – that is, increasing interactions between movement activists and political parties and elections (Tarrow 2011). They are more widespread and complex, involving an increase in networking (Diani 2011) and an increase in IT-use. These anti-austerity protests also reflect characteristics of 'warring movements', that is, increasing militancy (right, left) and violence (Tarrow 2011).

Systematic studies of the contentious politics of financial crises have just started to appear, for example, on the EU (Kriesi 2011), France (Ancelovici 2011), Eastern European countries (Beissinger and Sasse 2012). Recent work on Southern European crisis-related contention offers fresh evidence but has been focused on a specific set of topics, such as union participation in the Greek protests of 2010 (Psimitis 2011), symbolic memory in Greek and Tunisian protests (Vogiatzoglou and Sergi 2013), the 'M12M,' 'M15M' and 'M15O mobilisations in Spain and Portugal (Baumgarten 2012) and the composition of the 15-M mobilisations in Spain (Fuster Morell 2012). Nevertheless, studies offering systematic data on the transnational dimension of contention are rare or non-existent.

The sections to follow present the applied protest-event analysis approach and a systematic analysis, with new data, of the major features of economic contention of the Greek protest campaign against troika memoranda and austerity policies that took place at the local, national, and transnational levels, for the first three years of the crisis.

Research approach: Large protest events and claims

Aiming to offer a systematic analysis of economic and political contention (Tilly 1978), this chapter will analyse and discuss large protest-events (LPEs) related to the Greek financial crisis by utilising a new methodological approach, which utilizes the Large Protest Event as its unit of analysis. Simultaneously, while protest-events depict one level of contention, the data set of LPEs offer evidence on the development of an anti-austerity campaign at the national level and beyond.

The focus on the national campaign as well as the high frequency of contentious events in Greece[4] occurs in the current 'thickened' period, when 'the pace of challenging events quickens to the point that it becomes practically impossible to comprehend them and they come to constitute an increasingly significant part of their own causal structure' (Beissinger 2002). Therefore, choosing LPEs as the unit of analysis facilitates the systematic tracing of all key events and synchronised actions at the national level, which constitute a national anti-austerity campaign

---

4. *See*, for example, http://www.apergia.gr/ for a day-to-day calendar of protests in Greece.

sparked by neo-liberal adjustment and austerity policies in Southern European countries. Mostly involving demonstration-marches, national strikes and *piazza* protests, with claims against austerity or/and neo-liberal policies, for the first three years of the Greek crisis – January 2010 to December 2012 – the set of LPEs share the following features:

1. Large numbers of participants (minimum 5,000–maximum 500,000);
2. Large number of parallel/synchronised events;
3. Focused on national-level justice claims and resisting structural changes;
4. Broad, cross-class coalitions involving a large number of groups and the general public;
5. Based in Athens' Constitution Square, addressing the Parliament;
6. Accompanied by parallel protests in cities and towns across the country with the same claims.

These LPEs were widely covered by national and transnational media. Thus, as in previous periods of 'thickened history'[5] the best strategy is a 'blanketing strategy' (Beissinger 1998: 290–300), utilising multiple available sources in order to enrich the data set. Initially five major sources were selected: *Eleftherotypia*,[6] leftist *Rizospastis* and *Avgi* as well as alternative e-media sites Indymedia and realdemocracy.gr. They were subsequently supplemented by other Greek national news sources, for example, *To Vima, Ta Nea, Kathimerini, Epohi*, tvxs and Greek blogs such as iskra.gr. Furthermore, for this case of the first (Greek) sovereign-debt crisis in the eurozone, international news sources (the *Guardian*, Reuters, BBC, CNN), provided detailed and steady coverage of the large protest events, in spite of recent general findings on the limited coverage of international newspapers on national protests (Herkenrath and Knoll 2011).

Social media, IT and mobile-phone technology has been used in Greek mobilisations, especially since the catastrophic forest fires of 2007 – mostly mobiles (Karamichas 2007). Such communication tools were especially utilised in the national youth campaign protesting against the fatal shooting of sixteen-year-old Alexis Grigoropoulos by a policeman (Iakovidou, Kanellopoulos and Kotronaki 2010). Facebook and other social media use facilitated organising efforts and contributed to unprecedented levels of protest participation from May to September 2011, especially in relation to the 'movement of the piazzas' (Leontidou 2012).

---

5. The crisis period in Greece witnessed a rapid rise in independent electronic news and media sites, which have been occasionally used in this data set. This may be comparable to the transitional period, witnessing the rapid development of independent newspaper sources (Beissinger 1998).
6. Over a period of more than forty years, *Eleftherotypia*, an independent centre-left, multi-thematic newspaper, with high circulation rates, offered continuous and detailed coverage on contentious issues and social mobilisations (Kousis 1999, 2005); the paper stopped operating from December 2011 to mid-January 2012, due to economic problems.

Based on the analysis of mentions from more than 450 articles, 24 of the 32 LPEs brought together from 25,000 to 500,000 participants. Eight of the 32 were LPEs involving 5,000–24,000 participants, which were either carried out on national commemoration days or on transnational action days, all promoting anti-austerity and anti-liberalism claims. Three of these eight LPEs focused on anti-austerity demands and were carried out on dates commemorating: (1) the refusal of Greece to allow Axis forces to enter Greece and the beginning of the country's participation in World War II on 28 October 1940; (2) the successful University (Πολυτεχνείο[7]) Student uprising against the military dictatorship on 17 November 1973; (3) the unprovoked killing of 16-year-old A. Grigoropoulos by a policeman in the centre of Athens on 6 December 2008.[8] Two of the five related large protest events adopted new, transnational forms of action, while also making claims concerning economic system/crisis-born injustices: one following the Occupy movement on 15 October 2011, the other creating a new solidarity campaign for the Greek people, 'We Are All Greeks,' 'Je suis Grecque,' on 18 February 2012. A 32nd LPE of 10,000 participants on 19 January 2013 had a primary anti-racist focus in addition to an anti-austerity one and was carried out with the participation not only of Greek cities but cities across the globe, following the fatal stabbing of a Pakistani immigrant – even though the LPE was organised well before this occurred.

Researchers examining social claims and actions at a regional, national or cross-national level have adopted Tilly's (1978) protest-event analysis (Rucht and Neidhardt 1998) or related approaches, such as protest-case analysis (Kousis 1999) and political claims analysis (Koopmans and Statham 1999); these have incorporated and expanded the claims' repertoire, not only that of mobilising groups but those of their opponents as well as their supporters (Koopmans and Statham 1999; Kousis 1998, 2005).

Coding

The data set of thirty-two LPEs was created and organised, adapting the rules on protest-event, political claims and protest-case analysis (Rucht and Neidhardt 1998; Fillieule and Jimenéz 2007; Koopmans 2002; Kousis 1998). Thus, in addition to protest characteristics (place, action-forms, participating groups, supporters and challenged groups) the analysis also involved coding related to a) the source/object or (in) activity/ies, of contention; b) the related impacts; and, c) the resolutions proposed by the protesters for the amelioration of problems, including those related to new alternative policies.

The unit of data collection is the mention and the unit of analysis is the LPE and its related claims. Coding of action-forms, actors and claims was done in

---

7. *See*, for example, the November 2010 march with demands about austerity measures and transnational targeted groups: http://www.youtube.com/watch?v=dOqKdSMwAXI.
8. *See* Iakovidou, Kanellopoulos and Kotronaki 2010.

an 'open' manner, that is, using information located in the articles themselves, extended when necessary. The final coding instrument used in this analysis has been through twelve revisions. These different drafts were tested with different samples of protest events and their claims. Overall, at least eight trials of the different versions of the coding instrument were carried out, in February 2012.

The coding instrument designed for crisis- and austerity-related LPE-claims is comprised of parts referring to: the media source; location of the major protest event; claimant-protesters; forms of action; supporting actors; opponent actors and the related economic-crisis claims. In order to retain as much of the information available as possible, all general and specific categories were coded as dichotomous yes/no variables.[9]

Protesting groups

Major coding categories include: challenging actor/s related to Government agencies (such as the various ministries), including non-Greek, such as EU or other international organisations; legislative/parliament; judiciary; executive agencies (police and security); local government authorities; political parties; residential/community citizen groups; employers/economic organisations; church/religious organisations; media and journalists; farmers and agricultural organisations; educational professionals and organisations; students/pupils/parents associations; expert organisations and groups; other professional organisations and groups; unions and employees; economic interest groups; development interest groups; civil society organisations and groups; the general public; and volunteer groups.

Action-forms of protesting-claimant groups

The forms of action related to the political claim and the related coding rules were adjusted to the sphere of crisis politics in Greece. The main categories of action forms and related characteristics refer to direct-democratic action; petitioning; demonstrative protests; confrontational protests; violent protests; number of participants; number of wounded; number of people arrested; properties damaged; as well as amounts of tear gas and chemicals used by the police.

Supporters, opponents and their claims

The instrument allows the coding of EU as well as non-EU member-state groups or networks. It also offers the following general categories for coding challenged groups: Governments (Greek; EU member-state); supranational or intergovernmental bodies; (European Commission; EUROGROUP; ECOFIN; IMF; ECB; troika; G20; G8); Greek/EU legislatures/parliaments; Greek/EU

---

9. If funding is secured, a more developed claims coding scheme is planned, aiming to offer more detailed results.

judiciary; Greek police and security agencies; local government agencies/ authorities; banks; credit-rating agencies; financial/investment agencies; capitalist institutions; church; the rich/οι έχοντεσ/the 1 per cent; political parties or their representatives. Challenged group frames codes relate to bailout packages and policies; eurozone mechanisms; contagion to other economies; impacts of austerity laws-measures; and ways out of the crisis.

Claims of protesting groups

The codes developed on protestors' claims took into consideration Lapavitsas *et al.*'s (2010) account of the eurozone crisis. Given the specific public-sphere policy area, that is, crisis politics, as well as the specific national setting and short time period, four major issue areas surfaced: externally imposed packages; default; external intervention; opposition to unprecedented austerity laws-measures; the impacts of unprecedented austerity laws-measures on Greek society; economy; sovereignty; democracy; and protester resolution-proposals on the debt crisis. In addition to the above, inspired by Gottweis (2007), the codebook includes open- and closed-ended coding categories on ethical/moral and accountability issues.

Transnational features of the greek protest campaign: Internalisation and diffusion

The analysis to follow depicts a protest campaign (Kousis and Diani 2014) unprecedented in size, scale and global media attention (Tzogopoulos 2013), which began in Greece in early 2010, when the troika imposed the first austerity and structural-adjustment measures; it was the IMF's first notable involvement in a eurozone region. Since 2010, the campaign has exhibited not only national but also transnational features in terms of targets, organisational forms and claims and innovative learning practices. Built on previous experiences with mobilisations of the recent past, the campaign has linked to and been influenced by the rhythms of economic and political contention in the Arab, Indignado and Occupy protests. Last but not least, it has also been a campaign promoted by national and transnational networks and alliances through the use of IT technologies.

The section that follows sheds light on internalisation and diffusion processes related to the Greek campaign. The findings illustrate opposition to troika Memoranda, as well as opposition to the Greek government's acceptance of Memoranda imposing harsh austerity policies on the population as conditions of bailout aid packages. Thus the organisation of contentious actions across the country took place before the Greek Parliament voted on Memoranda-related policies. The data in this section reflect on processes related to the adoption or adaptation of organisational forms, collective-action frames and targets, especially in the second phase. The subsequent section focuses on features of externalisation in the Greek campaign.

Timeline of the protests

The waves of large contentious events which mounted in response to a series of structural and financial measures and policies could be envisaged in three different phases, as illustrated in in the data below (*see* Figures 7.1 and 7.2).

The first protest period, February 2010 to February 2011

The first period of anti-austerity protest was triggered by the troika's first Memorandum authorising the first Greek bailout package (110 billion euros, the highest ever given to any country) and associated austerity measures, which gave rise to an escalating wave of strikes and intense protests. This began in February 2010, in response to the first Greek government's stability measures, with a general strike by ΓΣΕΕ[10] and rallies in Athens and other cities. Union Confederations of both private- and public-sector employees (ΓΣΕΕ, ΑΔΕΔΥ) carried out a general strike against the second-largest state financial package in March 2010, two months before the IMF's entry into the eurozone region. At the end of April, credit institution Standard & Poor's downgraded Greece's main debt-rating to junk status (BB+).

On 5 May 2010, there was a third national strike and a wave of demonstrations across the country against the bailout and the related Greek government austerity pledges and measures for their implementation. It is a date marked by the death of three employees in the fire that burned the bank they were working in, while protests occurred in the area. Politicians were harshly criticised in public. Violence was escalating.

On 17 November and 6 December 2010 – on the commemorations of the 1973 University Student uprising against the military junta and of the killing of 16-year-old Alexis Grigoropoulos by a policeman – LPE participants voiced strong claims against the first Memorandum.

On 15 December 2010, a fourth national general strike took place during an LPE that witnessed increasing violence, including a bodily attack on a member of parliament from the right-wing New Democracy party. The general public became a more visible participant in the LPE.

In the February 2011 LPE, with demonstrations and the fifth national strike against the first Memorandum and the third package of economic measures, large amounts of tear gas and related chemicals were used by the police. Participants included tradesmen and self-employed citizens. The country was now deeply in recession.

The second protest period, April 2011 to February 2012

The second anti-austerity period, a time of escalating and intense protests across the country, witnessed more austerity measures under the Multi-Purpose Act and the second Memorandum. These gave rise to a second round of intensification

---

10. Confederations of private sector employees.

148 | Spreading Protest: Social Movements in Times of Crisis

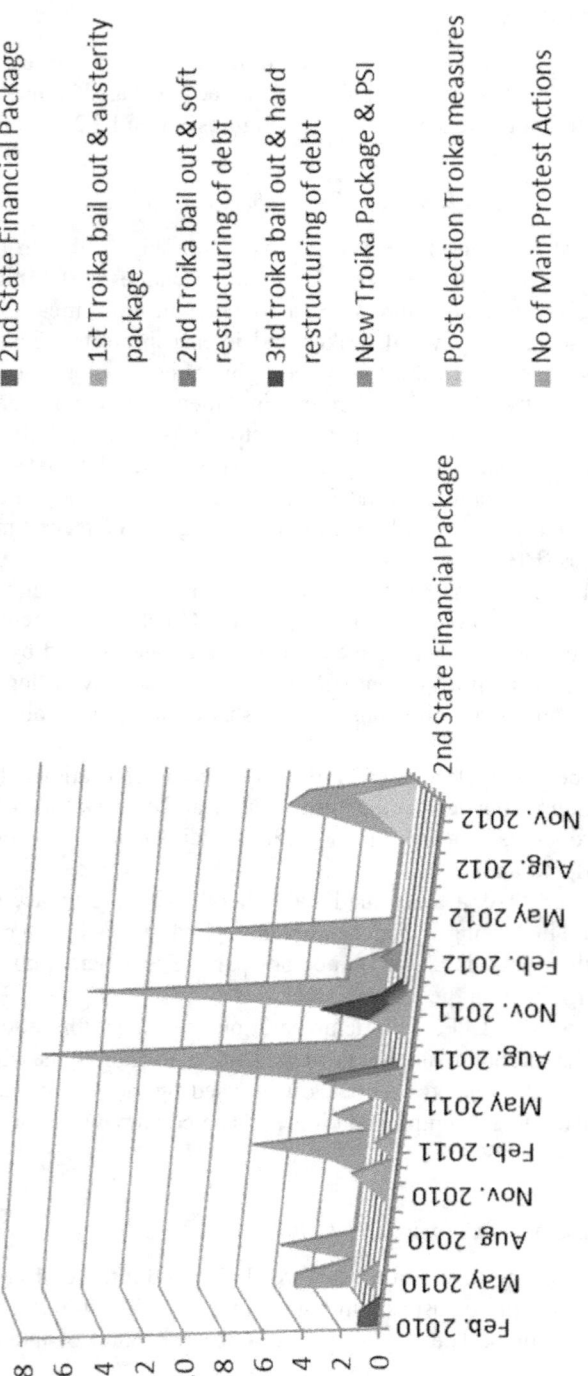

Figure 7.1: Total number of major protest actions and related bailout and austerity packages, Jan. 2010–Dec. 2012

See http://press.ecpr.eu/resources.asp for full colour.

of strikes and protests, with the strong presence of the Greek Aganaktismenoi (Indignados) or, the movement of the piazzas, as well as the beginning of the transnational dimension of the Greek anti-austerity campaign. More austerity measures followed. The number of major actions peaked in May and June 2011, due to novel as well as conventional action-repertoires attracting very broad cross-class coalitions, inspired by and following to a large extent the Spanish Indignados. After this, police repression subsided until early June, violence decreased and political party affiliation and references were dropped.

On 28 and 29 June, the seventh national strike intensified the LPE and activists blockaded Parliament, aiming to stop MPs from passing another set of bailout- and austerity-related legislative measures and voicing their opposition to the measures related to the troika's second bailout package (of 21 June 2011). Protesters encountered high levels of police repression and the use of tear gas and violence erupted at the end of the hitherto peaceful protests. Amnesty International called on the Greek state to restrain police repression.

A similar peak in the number of types of major actions, which include the eighth and ninth national strikes, was reached on 5 and 19–20 October 2011, related to troika's third Greek bailout package of 'hard restructuring' (27 October 2011) and the accompanying measures. In November, Papandreou stepped down as prime minister and was replaced by former ECB vice-president Lucas Papademos.

Fewer major protest events were carried out in the 10–12 February 2012 LPE, which responded to the anti-austerity measures and increased private-sector involvement in all sectors required by the troika's new 130-billion-euro loan-package. Protest events included the tenth national 48-hour strike but, more importantly, protests intensified, while the number of participants were the highest compared to previous levels. This LPE witnessed unprecedented action-intensity and property damage.

There were no LPEs during the first national elections held during the crisis, between March and August 2012. In the national elections of 6 May 2012 and 17 June 2012, widespread economic voting (*see*, for example, Kriesi 2011) was clearly reflected in the dramatic drop in support for the two previous ruling parties of the post-dictatorial period, especially PASOK, which ruled during the period of the crisis, and the rise of SYRIZA (Coalition of the Left) as well as Golden Dawn (the extreme-right party) (Kousis and Kanellopoulos 2014).

The third protest period, September to early January 2013

The third period was one of further austerity through neo-liberal policies and measures, leading to the rejuvenation of economic protest-activity. Six large protest events took place: three national, general strikes (the eleventh, twelfth and thirteenth of the period) by public- and private-sector workers; one workers' rally; two national, general work stoppages (one of which was part of the ETUC European Unions' first strike against austerity) and one march on the commemoration of the University Student uprising against the military junta.

Features of the protests

Reflecting the above timeline of contention, Figure 7.2 illustrates the highest number of participants, with notable peaks in the second phase of the large protests mounted against troika bailout packages and the accompanying austerity measures. The number of participants decreased after the national elections of 2012.

Protesters targeted transnational as well as national power-holders, as seen in Figure 7.3. Mentions of all targeted groups rise sharply during the second period, marked by the 'piazza movement' (Leontidou 2012). The campaign's primary targets were the Greek government, the troika and the European Commission as well as foreign banks. Less frequently mentioned targeted groups include financial institutions and credit agencies, the rich and local-government agencies. Least mentioned were capitalist markets and the G20/G8; in a minority of events, Germany was visible as a target of protest, especially after June 2011.

The great majority of demonstrators' claims were against troika Memoranda and austerity policies, which had lead to overwhelming wage and pension cuts, job cuts, tax increases, new taxes, dramatic unemployment, drastic privatisation of public enterprises, drastic increase of inequality and poverty, aggravated recession, and no growth. While claims on the negative impacts of troika measures on society, sovereignty and democracy increased from period one to period three, accountability claims decreased considerably, followed by a moderate decrease in claims referring to the structural-adjustment measures themselves (Kousis and Diani 2014).

In 27 out of the 32 large protests, people's claims centre on troika policies' impact on democracy, while in 25 of the 32 they point to their impact on Greek sovereignty. Protesters claim, for example, that under these sweeping reforms, the Greek constitution was disregarded, that labour and social welfare laws were annulled and the right to peaceful protest was threatened (People's Assembly of Syntagma Square, 2011). *See*, for example, Figure 7.4.

Figure 7.5 depicts all participating groups involved in the 32 LPEs. They include unions or worker confederations; political parties of the left; anarchist groups; youth groups (students, pupils); justice-oriented groups and networks; Indignados (Αγανακτισμένοι); anti-authoritarian groups; civil-society groups; and professional/educational organisations. Participation in type and numbers escalated and reached its highest peak in the second period, with the new and mounting presence of the Αγανακτισμένοι and the general public.

Thus, there was a steady increase in the number of different types of participating groups and organisations especially in the pre-election period of the second protest phase – as seen in the noticeable peaks of May–June 2011 and February 2012 in Figure 7.5. While the anti-austerity campaign began with conventional/traditional protest groups, such as unions, political parties, teachers and students, a year later new groups, such as Αγανακτισμένοι, or justice-oriented groups (for example, campaigning against paying the new taxes), significantly fortified the broad coalitions of anti-austerity contention.

Figure 7.2: Highest number of participants in main protest actions, Jan. 2010–Dec. 2012

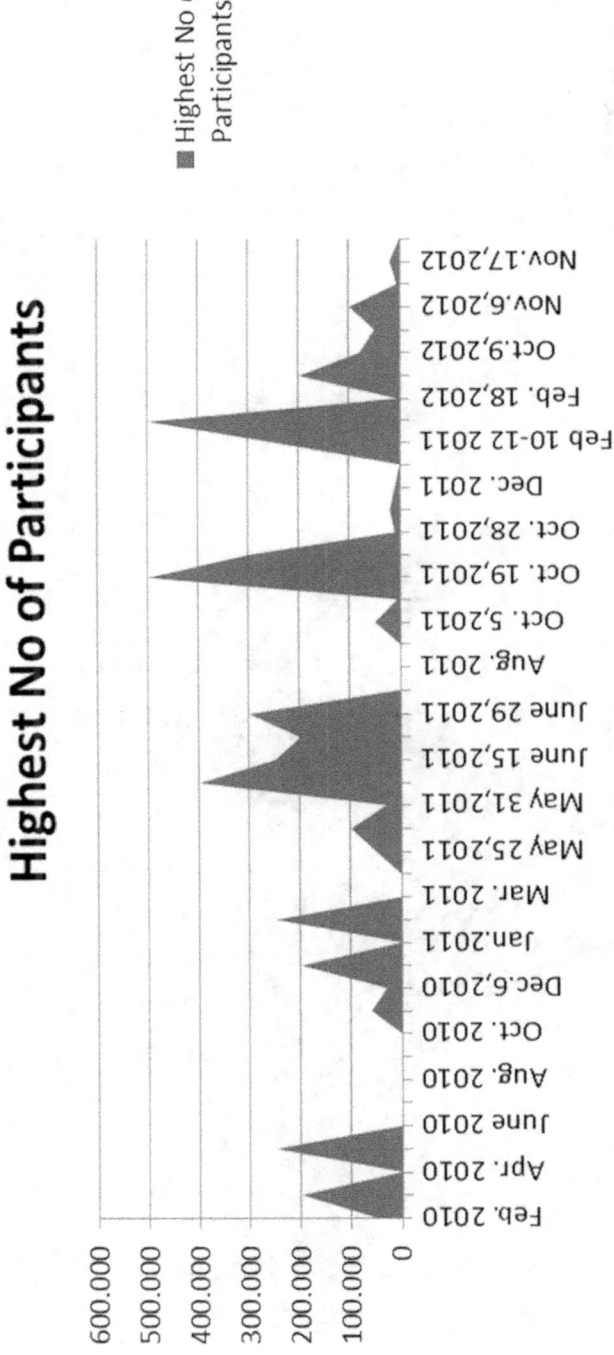

See http://press.ecpr.eu/resources.asp for full colour.

Figure 7.3: Target groups mentioned in LPEs, Jan. 2010– Dec. 2012

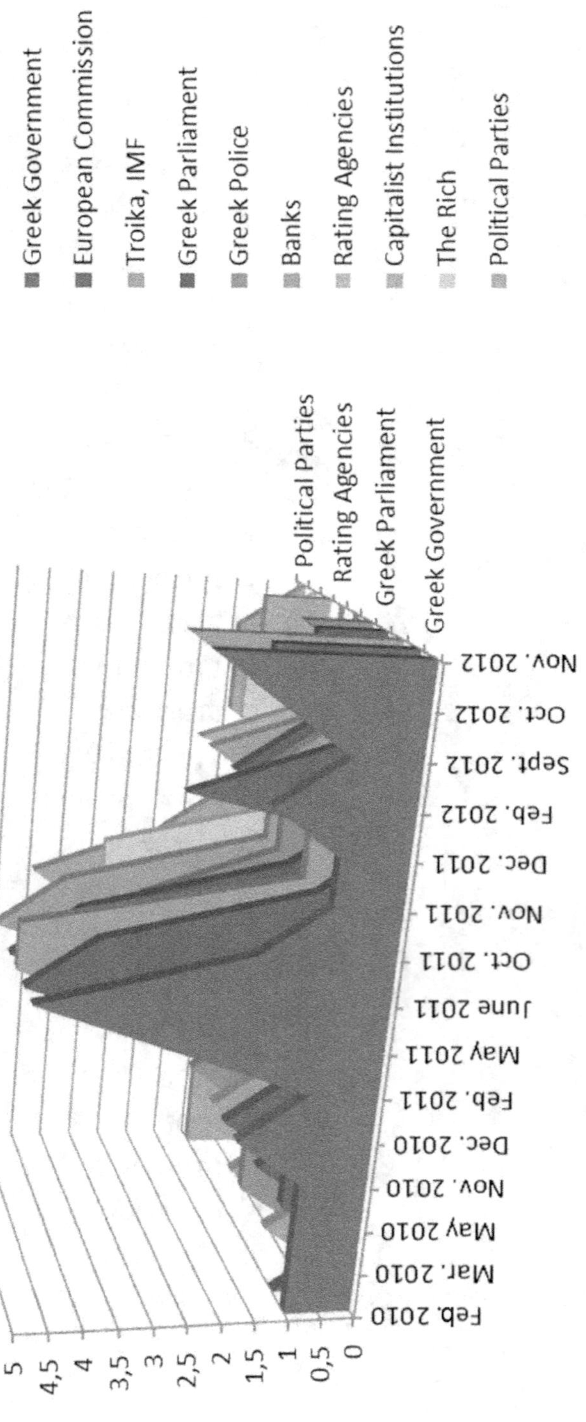

See http://press.ecpr.eu/resources.asp for full colour.

Figure 7.4: Vote of the People's Assembly of Syntagma Square, 27 May

VOTE OF THE PEOPLE'S ASSEMBLY OF SYNTAGMA SQUARE

Athens, May 27 2011

For a long time decisions have been made for us, without consulting us.

We are workers, unemployed, retirees, youth, who have come to Syntagma Square to fight and give a struggle for our lives and our future.

We are here because we know that the solutions to our problems can only be provided by us.

We call all residents of Athens, workers, unemployed and youth, to come to Syntagma Square, and all of society to fill the public squares and to take their lives into their own hands.

In these public squares we will shape our claims and our demands together.

We call on all workers who are going on strike in the coming days to show up and stay at Syntagma Square.

We will not leave the squares until those who compelled us to come here leave the country: the governments, the Troika (EU, ECB and IMF), banks, the IMF Memoranda, and everyone who exploits us.

We send them the message that the debt is not ours.

DIRECT DEMOCRACY NOW!

EQUALITY - JUSTICE - DIGNITY!

The only struggle that is lost is the one that is never fought!

http://commons.wikimedia.org/wiki/File:Vote_of_the_People%27s_Assembly_of_Syntagma_Square.svg

154 | Spreading Protest: Social Movements in Times of Crisis

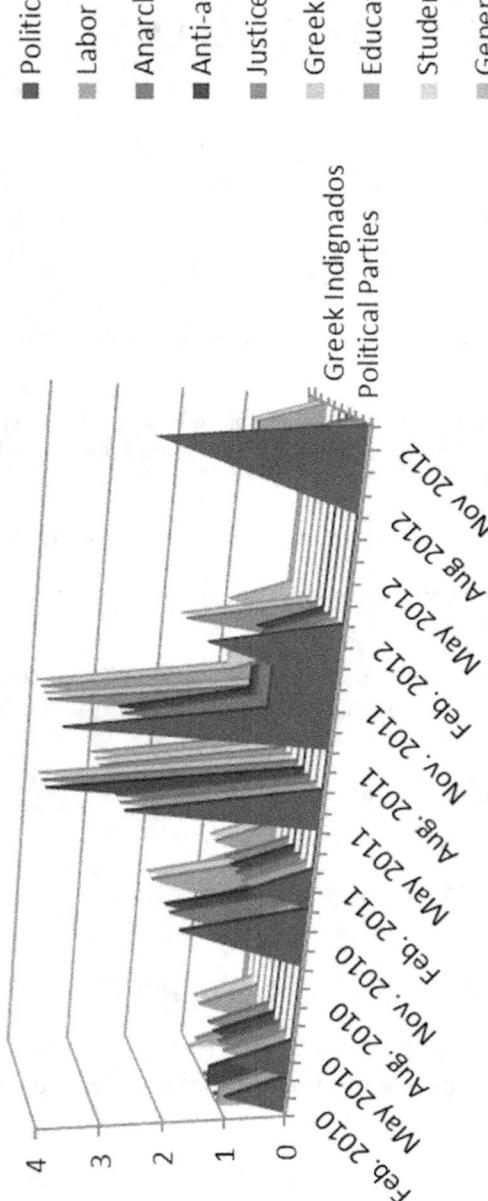

Figure 7.5: Major participating groups in LPEs, Jan. 2010– Dec. 2012

See http://press.ecpr.eu/resources.asp for full colour.

The profile of the initiating groups of the LPEs changes significantly to a more powerful mix from 2010 to 2012. In the starting year, unions and students/youth were the first two initiating groups, while in 2011, these included Αγανακτισμένοι (Indignados), students, Occupy groups, unions, anarchists and the general public (Kousis 2013).

In the past three years, virtual communication and social media played an important role in organising, supporting and spreading anti-austerity resistance in Greece (Tsaliki 2012; Karamichas 2012; Leontidou 2012). This is especially obvious when examining the action forms of the campaign.

Moving beyond conventional protests and influenced significantly from Spanish and Arab protests, major actions are portrayed in Figure 7.7. Following the pattern shown in previous graphs, actions escalated in the second period. From May to June 2011, through calls on Facebook and other social media, a new type of participating group had a strong presence in Σύνταγμα and central piazzas or landmarks of most Greek cities, the Αγανακτισμένοι, inspired by the Spanish Indignados (*see*, for example, Korizi and Vradis 2012; Giovanopoulos and Mitropoulos 2011; Leontidou 2012). Blaming political parties for the country's critical condition, but also showing their disrespect in front of the Parliament (Tzanelli 2011), they rejected political-party affiliations and opted for peaceful events and actions. These led to the participation of thousands of citizens across classes, ages and political beliefs, who joined the two-month-long actions at their Σύνταγμα protest camp in front of the Greek Parliament. Such protest camps were simultaneously set up across most Greek cities, as seen in Figure 7.8, below (Kousis 2013).

For the first time in the post-war period, this 'occupation' of piazzas across the country was marked by a strong presence of citizens against austerity and neo-liberal restructuring (Giovanopoulos 2011). In most of these occupations, co-ordinating groups were formed, meetings were organised on a daily or weekly basis and minutes of meetings were taken (Gazakis and Spathas 2011).[11] Musical and cultural events took place, following the blueprints of 'happenings' and the operating style of Σύνταγμα's 'movement of the squares'. Local issues of grave concern were discussed, such as the selling of ports or gold mines, or the degradation of health services. Σύνταγμα sites real-democracy.gr and amesi-dimokratia.org were linked to the public assemblies of Greek cities and towns via Facebook and blogs. Non-Athenian activists on occasion visited Σύνταγμα (Mpresta 2011: 94–100). Older memories were revived as reflected in the slogan 'Bread, Education, Liberty: The [Military] Junta Did Not End In 1973' (Axelos 2011).

Σύνταγμα Square's more pragmatic but angrier upper piazza and its more progressive and alternative lower piazza were notably different. While the upper

---

11. *See also* http://www.demotix.com/news/714621/tenth-day-greek-protests-athens#media-714579 (accessed 4 March 2014).

156 | Spreading Protest: Social Movements in Times of Crisis

Figure 7.6: Major action forms of the 32 LPEs, Jan. 2010–Jan. 2013

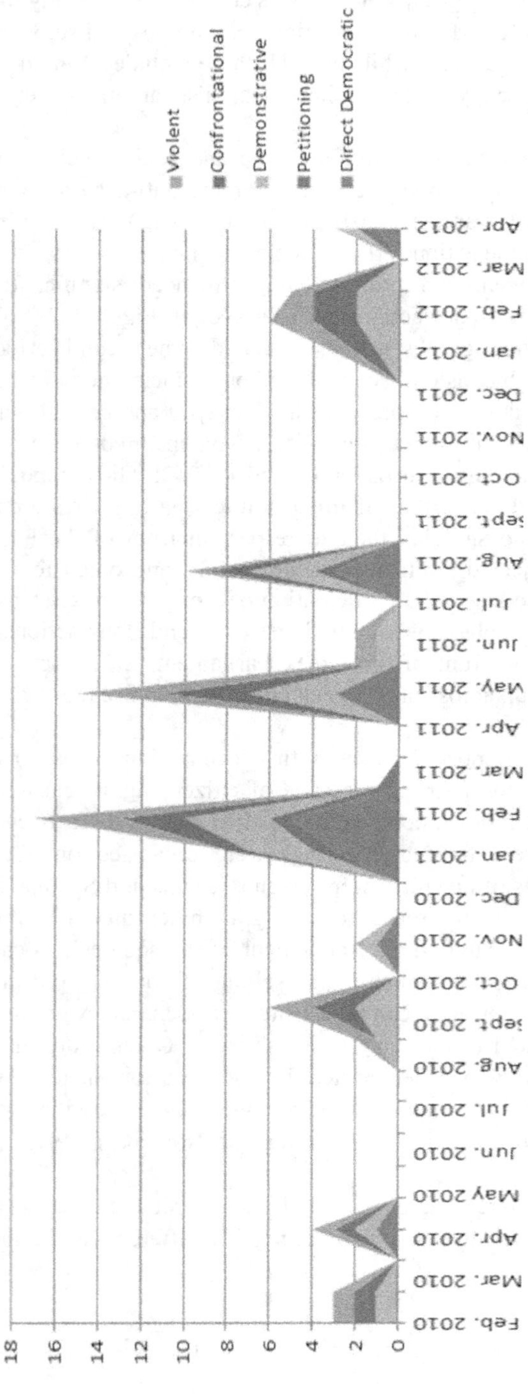

See http://press.ecpr.eu/resources.asp for full colour.

The Transnational Dimension | 157

Figure 7.7: Total number of violent actions, number of injured protesters and number of arrests, Jan. 2010–Dec. 2012

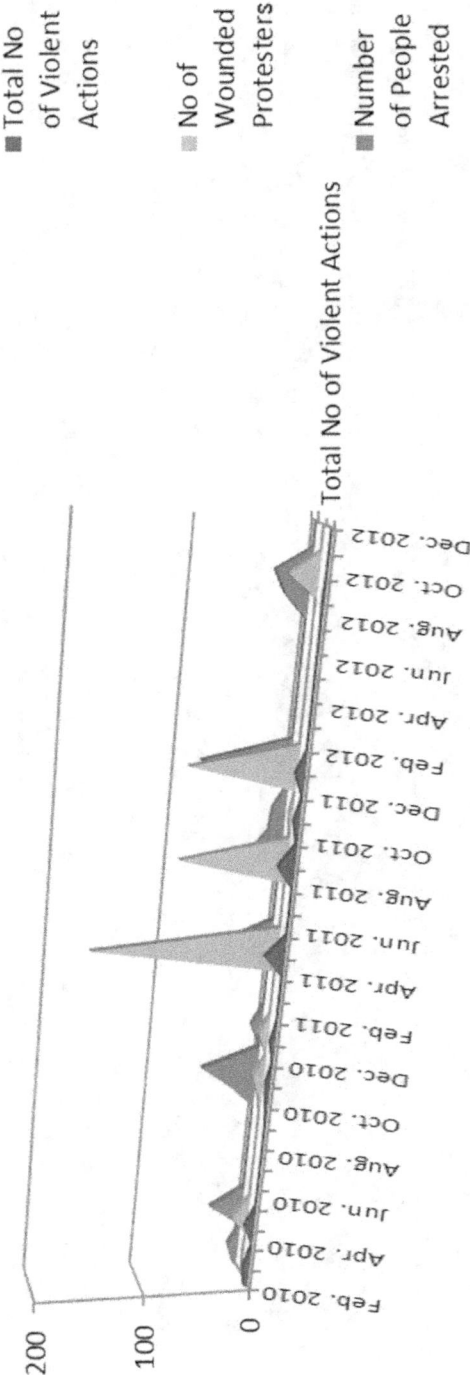

See http://press.ecpr.eu/resources.asp for full colour.

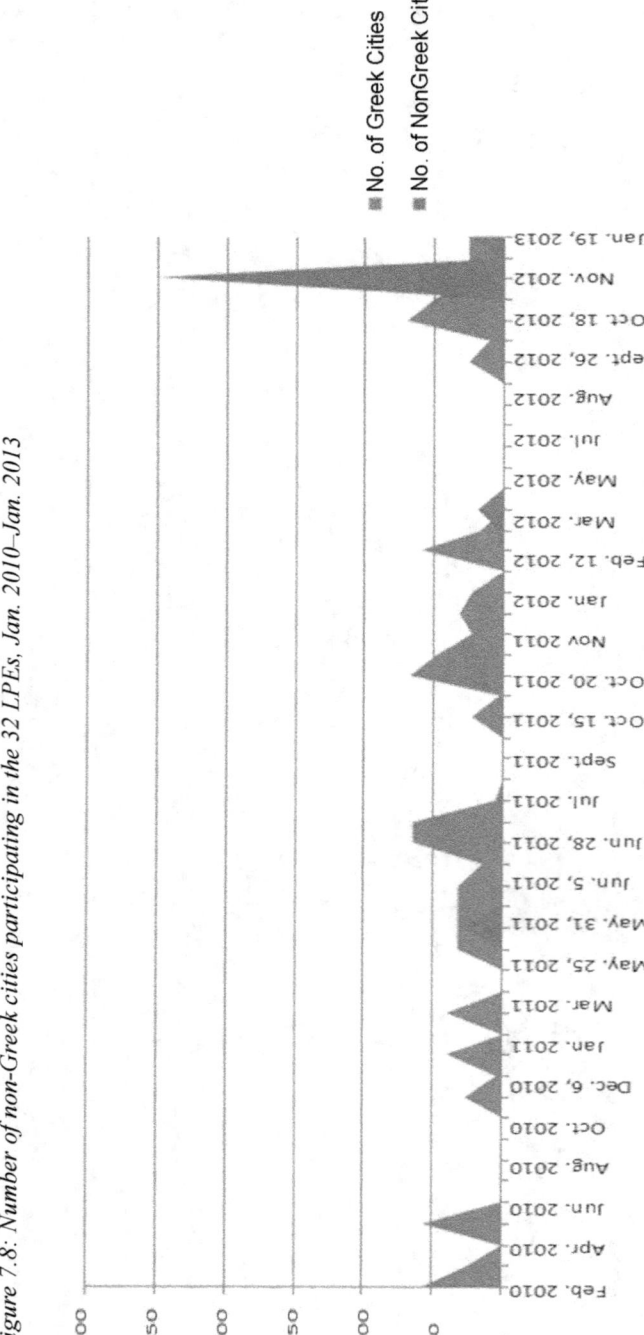

Figure 7.8: Number of non-Greek cities participating in the 32 LPEs, Jan. 2010–Jan. 2013

See http://press.ecpr.eu/resources.asp for full colour.

area attracted demonstrators with more patriotic and populist claims, the lower part hosted the camp and a direct-democratic-oriented 'agora' of highly committed activists, many from radical parties of the left (Sotirakopoulos and Sotiropoulos 2013; Karamichas 2012; Leontidou 2012; Tsaliki 2012; Stavrou 2011).

Although the majority of mobilisations were carried out by the numerous protesters peacefully, violence did occur, usually at the end of the LPEs and on the part of very small groups of activists, as depicted in Figure 7.6. A notable increase is noted for the second period, when the peaceful demonstrations were confronted by violence before and during the voting of significant troika austerity packages in the Parliament, in Syntagma Square.

Most importantly, it is the number of those injured that escalates very greatly during this period. This mounting violence in the summer of 2011 led to a warning by Amnesty International:

> The Greek authorities must prevent the excessive and indiscriminate use of force and other violations by the police in future protests. They must also ensure a thorough, prompt, independent and impartial investigation into all allegations of such abuses (Amnesty International 2011).

Similar, albeit lower, peaks can be noted in the number of arrests. Escalating violence and repression in LPEs involving the troika is line with a tendency to higher levels of violence and repression in cases involving powerful transnational target groups in Greece, for example, in 2003 (Kalonomos 2013).

Transnational features of the campaign: Externalisation

This section focuses on features of externalisation in the Greek campaign against Troika Memoranda and austerity policies, with data on movement-organisation at the international level involving cities across the globe, especially the Global North, during the second phase of the campaign (Kousis 2012; Tsomou 2011). The data shows an expansion in the communication, synchronisation and collaboration tactics used by Greek activists reaching beyond national borders and by activists beyond national borders linking to the Greek protests. Five of the campaign's 32 large protest events were part of huge transnational protest events, in cities in Europe, North America and other regions of the globe. All of these five events occurred during the second, pre-election period.

Figure 7.8 depicts the aforementioned highly concentrated but small number of transnational events, synchronised with Occupy and Indignado or other European action events, across 1,277 transnational urban spaces.

Three of these five LPEs, as shown in Table 7.1, entailed synchronised, parallel actions on global claims, with which the Greek protesters identified, across hundreds of cities, in Europe or across the globe. In 2011, the Greek protesters joined European Revolution of 29 May across European cities demanding 'real democracy now' and on 15 October they participated in the global Occupy Wall

Street event, which was carried out across 951 cities. On November 14, protestors from Syntagma Square in Athens and 25 Greek cities participated in the first European Union Strike Day Against Austerity, which took place across 250 European cities.

Two of the events were organised at the international level but, in contrast to the global anti-austerity claims of the previous three LPEs, they focused their claims on support of and solidarity with the Greek people. Around 18 February 2012 following Parliament's approval of the troika's austerity and structural-adjustment packages and the related highly contentious LPE in the centre of Athens, the transnational solidarity action 'We Are All Greeks' took place in Athens and 19 mostly European and North American cities, from 10–12 February. These solidarity actions targeted Greek embassies and IMF offices.

The thirty-second LPE was carried out on 19 January 2013, two days after the fatal stabbing of a Pakistani immigrant, across 26 cities outside of Greece and 25 within its borders. Participants were against austerity and the subsequent support for fascism that has spread rapidly via support for the ultra-right party Golden Dawn across the country.

As seen in Table 7.2, participating cities in Italy, Spain, France and the United Kingdom were more frequently mentioned in the news sources. They appear mostly in the second but also in the third phase of the anti-austerity campaign. Other than supporting local activists, diaspora communities may have also played

Table 7.1: Transnational events linked to the Greek anti-austerity campaign, Jan. 2010–Jan. 2013

Date of LPE	LPE issue	No. of non-Greek cities involved	No. of Greek cities involved
29 May 2011	European Revolution 29 May All cities of Europe	26	32
15 October 2011	Occupy Wall Street European Indignados Day	951	2
18 February 2012	Transnational solidarity action for Greece: 'We are all Greeks'	19	1
14 November 2012	European Union Strike Day vs. Austerity	250	25
19 January 2013	Anti-fascist and anti-austerity demonstration	26	25

Table 7.2: Names of non-Greek cities mentioned as participating in the transnational events

Country	City mentioned as participant in transnational LPE	Phase 1	Phase 2	Phase 3	Total
Southern EU			11	4	15
Italy	Rome, Bologna, Milano, Genova		4	2	6
Spain	Madrid, Barcelona		4	1	5
Portugal	Lisbon		2	1	3
Cyprus	Nicosia		1		1
Northern EU		1	14	7	22
France	Paris, Bastille, Lyon, La Roche, Marseilles		5	1	6
Germany	Berlin		1	1	2
Belgium	Brussels		2	2	4
Netherlands	Amsterdam		1	1	2
Denmark	Copenhagen		2	2	4
UK	London, Edinburgh	1	3		4
Other			5		5
Thailand	Bangkok		1		1
US	New York, Chicago, Los Angeles		4		4

Note: All but two of the cities in the table participated in the LPE of 8 February 2012, Transnational solidarity action for Greece.

an important role in the organisation of these events.

Conclusion

Transnational contention has moved to a new, fifth phase sparked by the global economic crisis of 2008, following its first four phases initiated in the eighties, according to Bringel and Echart Munoz (2010). The current fifth phase offers a blend of economic and political contention (Kousis and Tilly 2005) across Mediterranean, European and North American arenas. Economic opportunities and threats appear to intensify across the globe, leading at times to both 'contained' and 'warring' movements (Tarrow 2011). The Greek contention is an especially useful case, highlighting the rising interdependence of the twenty-first century's global economy, reflected in the unprecedented global media attention Greece received as a high public-debt, Southern European country whose potential exit from the eurozone would threaten the stability of the zone and, ultimately, of the global economy.

The findings of this chapter reflect the three features of transnational contention: internalisation, diffusion and externalisation (della Porta and Tarrow 2005). All three are visible in the preceding analysis of organisational, relational and claims issues of a Greek campaign involving a high level of contention and a national population engaged in a wider struggle, making collective claims on target authorities as Tilly (2004) and Tarrow (2008) describe. It was a defensive campaign, responding to the economic and political problems produced by the 2008 global financial crisis and to policies imposed on Greece by transnational economic power-holders (such as the EC, ECB, IMF, financial market forces, banks and credit-rating agencies). Thus, although taking place in Greece, this conflict was of external origin.

Organisational features of the campaign include the rise of 'meganetworks' (Goldstone 2011), involving unions, leftist parties, the piazza movement across the entire country and high numbers of the general public in protest against troika policies. The organisational structure of the campaign was deeply rooted at the local and national level and has been enhanced through the use of social media, especially in extending itself to the transnational arena. This is especially visible in the diffusion of the movement of piazzas (Leontidou 2012) from other Mediterranean cities and neighbourhoods to those in Greece, in the second and third year of the campaign, since 2011. However, these processes also reflect common cognitive changes and the rise in transnational identities visible in the similarities in claims-making, synchronised actions and common targets. These also facilitated the diffusion of transnational contention.

Diffusion and externalisation processes have increasingly been gaining ground since 2011, documented in the protesters' adopting or adapting the organisational forms, collective-action strategies and target-awareness of similar struggles across the globe. More specifically, whereas unions and leftist parties were among the major organisers of the LPEs in all three phases, in 2011, the movement of the piazzas, directly and indirectly influenced by the Indignados movement, shows different, autonomous action-organising and identity-building, with alternative visions of how the world needs to be (della Porta and Tarrow 2005; Leontidou 2012; Madden and Vradis 2012). Fortified by the older movement organisers, unions and leftist parties, but also the new, transnationally inspired activists of the piazza movement, the campaign targeted powerful transnational forces of the troika, banks, financial institutions and the Greek state for the dramatic impacts of their policies on the Greek population. Thus the data suggest that activists in national arenas are moved increasingly and steadily by transnational opportunities and threats towards transnational social-movement-organising, identity-building and tactics.

It is in a sense inevitable, therefore, that externalisation processes have been consolidated since 2011, as documented in the growth of organising, networking and claim-making across national borders, offering activists a transnational arena of contention. In the Greek campaign, these transnational actions take two different paths: one of constructing transnational actions and identities; the other building transnational solidarity in support of national campaigns and causes, targeting international and national power-holders.

Following della Porta and Tarrow (2005), evidence from the Greek case shows that the new economic and political context has given rise to new and more violent government tactics when confronting protesters, documented in the number of injuries and arrests. Subsequently, the Greek campaign appears to feature both 'contained movements', involving traditional groups and featuring an increased politicisation of protest, as well as 'warring movements' (increasing militancy on the right and left, and violence) (Tarrow 2011). Based on the above, a shift of targets from national to transnational has been documented in the Greek campaign, followed by a shift of contention from national to transnational arenas.

Finally, the findings from the Greek campaign highlight the EU's increasing interdependence in the global economy, the entry of powerful new economic/financial actors and resulting new contentious economic and political arenas in the first decade of the twenty-first century.

Given the above, it is even more imperative now to study transnational economic and political contention as seen through 'the function of existing legal arrangements, regulatory agencies, network connections, and cultural contexts' (Tilly 2005).

References

Almeida, P. D. (2007) 'Defensive mobilization: popular movements against economic adjustment policies', *Latin American Perspectives* issue 154, 34 (3): 123–39.

— (2008) 'The sequencing of success: organizing templates and neoliberal policy outcomes,' *Mobilization: The international quarterly* 13 (2): 165–87.

— (2010) 'Globalization and collective action', in K. T. Leicht and J. C. Jenkins (eds) *Handbook of Politics: State and society in global perspective*, London: Springer.

Almeida, P. D. and Johnston, H. (eds) (2006) 'Neoliberal globalization and popular movements in Latin America', in H. Johnston and P. D. Almeida (eds) *Latin American Social Movements*, Lanham, MD: Rowman & Littlefield.

Amnesty International (2011) 'Greece urged not to use excessive force during protests', 16 June, http://www.amnesty.org/en/news-and-updates/greece-urged-not-use-excessive-force-during-protests-2011-06-16 (accessed 20 February 2014).

Ancelovici, M. (2011) 'In search of lost radicalism: the hot autumn of 2010 and the transformation of labor contention in France', *French Politics, Culture & Society* 29 (3): 121–40.

Arce, M. and Kim, W. (2011) 'Globalization and extra-parliamentary politics in an era of democracy', *European Political Science Review* 3 (02): 253–78, DOI: http://dx.doi.org/10.1017/S1755773910000408.

Axelos, L. (2011) 'Ψωμί, Παιδεία, Ελευθερία, Η χούντα δεν τελείωσε το '73' ['Bread, education, liberty: the junta did not end in 1973'], in C. Giovanopoulos and D. Mitropoulos (eds) *Democracy Under Construction: From the streets to the squares*, Athens: A/synechia (in Greek).

Baumgarten, B. (2012) '"M12M", "M15M" and "M15O" – Differences and linkages between mobilization in Portugal and Spain', paper presented at the 19th International Conference, Council of European Studies, Boston, 22–4 March.

Beissinger, M. R. (1998) 'Nationalist violence and the state: political authority and contentious repertoires in the former USSR', *Comparative Politics* 30 (4): 401–22.

— (2002) *Nationalist Mobilization and the Collapse of the Soviet State*, Cambridge: Cambridge University Press.

Beissinger, M. and Sasse, G. (2012) *An End to Societal Patience? The economic crisis and political protest in Eastern Europe*, Nuffield's Working Papers Series in Politics.

Bellinger, P. T. Jr. and Arce, M. (2011) 'Protest and democracy in Latin America's market era', *Political Research Quarterly* 64 (3): 688–704.

Bringel, B. and Echart Muñoz, E. (2010) 'Ten years of Seattle, the anti-globalization movement and the transnational collective action', *Ciências Sociais Unisinos* 46 (1): 28–36.

Bush, E. and Simi, P. (2001) 'European farmers and their protests,' in D. Imig and S. Tarrow (eds) *Contentious Europeans: Protest and politics in an emerging polity*, London: Rowman & Littlefield.

della Porta, D. (ed.) (2009) *Another Europe: Conceptions and practices of democracy in the European social forums*, London: Routledge.

— (2012) 'Mobilizing against the crisis, mobilizing for "another democracy": comparing two global waves of protest', *Interface: A journal for and about social movements* 4 (1): 274–7.

della Porta, D. and Tarrow, S. (2005) *Transnational Processes and Social Activism*, Oxford: Rowman & Littlefield.

della Porta, D., Andretta, M., Mosca, L. and Reiter, H. (2006) *Globalization From Below: Transnational activists and protest networks*, London: University of Minnesota Press.

Diani, M. (2011) 'Networks and Internet into perspective', *Swiss Political Science Review* 17 (4): 469–74.http://onlinelibrary.wiley.com/doi/10.1111/j.1662–6370.2011.02040.x/abstract;jsessionid=799B9A95183FA56A9C770CED39B4381E.f03t02-fn1 (accessed 22 April 2014).

Diani, M. and Kousis, M. (2014) 'The duality of claims and events: the Greek campaign against Troika's memoranda and austerity, 2010–2012', under review in *Mobilization.*

Eurostat (2013) 'Euro area GDP down by 0.6% and EU27 down by 0.5%', http://epp.eurostat.ec.europa.eu/cache/ITY_PUBLIC/2–14022013-AP/EN/2–14022013-AP-EN.PDF (accessed 20 February 2014).

Fillieule, O. and M. Jiménéz (2007) 'Appendix A: the methodology of protest event analysis and the media politics of reporting environmental protest events', in C. Rootes (ed.) *Environmental Protest in Western Europe*, Oxford: Oxford University Press.

Fishman, R. M. (2011) 'Democratic practice after the revolution: the case of Portugal and beyond', *Politics & Society* 39 (2): 233–67.

Fuster Morell, M. (2012) 'Composition of 15M Mobilization in Spain: Free Culture Movement a layer of 15M ecosystem movement', 'Occupy' special edition, *Social Movement Studies*.

Gazakis and Spathas (2011) '"The People in the Square are teaching democracy": the indignados movement in the square of the White Tower', in C. Giovanopoulos and D. Mitropoulos (eds) *Democracy Under Construction: From the streets to the squares*, Athens: A/synechia (in Greek), pp.101–10.

Giovanopoulos, C. (2011) 'The squares as a live organism: the resocialization of the Agora', in C. Giovanopoulos and D. Mitropoulos (eds) *Democracy Under Construction: From the streets to the squares*, Athens: A/synechia (in Greek).

Giovanopoulos, C. and Mitropoulos, D. (eds) (2011) *Democracy Under Construction: From the streets to the squares*, Athens: A/synechia (in Greek).

Goldstone, J. A. (2011) 'Cross-class coalitions and the making of the Arab revolts of 2011', *Swiss Political Science Review* 17: 457–62.

Goldstone, J. A. and Tilly, C. (2001) 'Threat (and opportunity): popular action and state response in the dynamics of contentious action', in R. R. Aminzade, J. A. Goldstone, D. McAdam, E. J. Perry, W. H. Sewell, Jr., S. Tarrow and S. Tilly (eds) *Silence and Voice in the Study of Contentious Politics*, Cambridge: Cambridge University Press.

Gottweis, H. (2007) 'Rhetoric in policy analysis', in F. Fischer (ed.) *Handbook of Public Policy Analysis*, London: Taylor & Francis, pp. 237–50.

Guillen, M. F. (2001) 'Is globalization civilizing, destructive or feeble? A critique of five key debates in the social science literature', *Annual Review of Sociology* 27: 235–60, DOI: 10.1146/annurev.soc.27.1.235.

Hassan, R. (2011) 'The speed of collapse: the space-time dimensions of capitalism's first great crisis of the 21st century' *Critical Sociology* 37 (4): 385–402.

Herkenrath, M. and Knoll, A. (2011) 'Protest events in international press coverage: An empirical critique of cross-national conflict databases', *International Journal of Comparative Sociology* 52 (3): 163–80.

Iakovidou, I., Kanellopoulos, K. and Kotronaki, L. (2010) 'The Greek Uprising of December 2008', *Situations: Project of the radical imagination* 3 (2): 145–57.

Imig, D. and Tarrow, S. (2001) 'Studying contention in an emerging polity', in D. Imig and S. Tarrow (eds), *Contentious Europeans: Protest and politics in an emerging polity*, London: Rowman & Littlefield.

Kalonomos, P. (2013) 'Policing protest: approaches, models and interpretive frames. Dimensions of the Greek model of protest policing', MA thesis, department of Sociology, University of Crete (in Greek).

Karamichas, J. (2007) 'The impact of the summer 2007 forest fires in Greece: recent environmental mobilizations, cyber-activism and electoral performance', *South European Society & Politics* 12 (4): 521–33.

— (2012) 'Square politics: key characteristics of the indignant mobilizations in Greece', paper prepared for the 62th PSA Annual International Conference, 3–5 April, Belfast.

Koopmans, R. (2002) 'Codebook for the analysis of political mobilization and communication in European public spheres', Europub.com (HPSE-CT2000-00046), April, http://europub.wz-berlin.de.

Koopmans, R. and Statham, P. (1999) 'Political claims analysis: integrating protest event and political discourse approaches', *Mobilization* 4 (2): 203–21.

Korizi, S. and Vradis, A. (2012) 'From innocence to realisation', *City: Analysis of urban trends, culture, theory, policy, action* 16 (1–2): 237–42, available at: http://dx.doi.org/10.1080/13604813.2012.662364 (accessed 22 April 2014).

Kousis, M. (1998) 'Protest-case analysis: a methodological approach for the study of grassroots environmental mobilizations', the Working Paper Series, No. 570, Center for Research on Social Organization (CRSO), University of Michigan, Ann Arbor, Michigan, May, http://deepblue.lib.umich.edu/bitstream/2027.42/51334/1/570.pdf.

— (1999) 'Sustaining local environmental mobilisations: groups, actions and frames in Southern Europe', *Environmental Politics* 8 (1): 172–98.

— (2004) 'Economic opportunities and threats in contentious environmental politics: a view from the European South', *Theory & Society* 33 (3–4): 393–415.
— (2005) 'State responses as threats and opportunities in Southern European environmental conflicts', in M. Kousis and C. Tilly (eds), *Economic and Political Contention in Comparative Perspective*, Boulder, CO: Paradigm.
— (2012) 'Greek protests against austerity measures: a relational approach' paper presented in Session LOC03: Political Systems Crisis of Legitimacy, 22nd World Congress of the International Political Science Association, 'Reshaping Power, Shifting Boundaries', 8–12 July, Madrid.
— (2013) 'The Greek campaign against Memoranda and austerity policies' *Sociological Review* 1: 33–41 (in Greek).
Kousis, M. and Eder, K. (eds) (2001) *Environmental Politics in Southern Europe: Actors, institutions and discourses in a Europeanizing society*, Dordrecht: Kluwer Academic Publishers.
Kousis, M. and Kanellopoulos, K. (2014) 'The impact of the Greek Crisis on the repertoire of contention, 2010–2012', proceedings of the 1st Midterm International Conference of the Disaster, Conflict and Social Crisis Research Network of the European Sociological Association.
Kousis, M. and Tilly, C. (2005) 'Introduction', in M. Kousis and C. Tilly (eds) *Economic and Political Contention in Comparative Perspective*, Boulder, CO: Paradigm, pp. 1–14.
Kousis, M., della Porta, D. and Jiménez, M. (2008) 'Southern European environmental movements in comparative perspective', *American Behavioral Scientist* special issue: Mediterranean Political Processes in Historical-Comparative Perspective, guest eds C. Tilly, R. Franzosi, and M. Kousis, 51 (11): 1627–47.
Kriesi, H. (2011) 'The political consequences of the financial and economic crisis in Europe: electoral punishment and popular protest', Oxford paper, version 3, November.
Lapavitsas, C., Kaltenbrunner, A., Lindo, D., Michell, J., Painceira, J. P., Pires, E., Powell, J., Stenfors, A. and Teles, N. (2010) 'Eurozone crisis: beggar thyself and thy neighbour', *Journal of Balkan and Near Eastern Studies* 12 (4): 321–72.
Leontidou, L. (2012) 'Athens in the Mediterranean "movement of the piazzas": spontaneity in material and virtual public spaces', *City: Analysis of urban trends, culture, theory, policy, action* 16 (3), 299–312.
McAdam, D., Tarrow, S. and Tilly, C. (2001) *Dynamics of Contention*, Cambridge and New York: Cambridge University Press.
Madden, D. J. and Vradis, A. (2012): 'Introduction to cities in upheaval: from Athens to Occupy and back,' *City: Analysis of urban trends, culture, theory, policy, action* 16 (1–2): 235–6.
Mathers, A. (2007) *Struggling for Another Europe*, Aldershot: Ashgate.
Mattoni, A. (2012) *Media Practices and Protest Politics: How precarious workers mobilise*, Aldershot: Ashgate.

Mpresta, M. (2011) 'The whole of Greece as one square (?)', in C. Giovanopoulos and D. Mitropoulos (eds) *Democracy Under Construction: From the streets to the squares*, Athens: A/synechia (in Greek).

OECD (2013) 'Structural reforms more important than ever for a strong and balanced economic recovery', http://www.oecd.org/newsroom/ ormsmoreimportantthaneverforastrongandbalancedeconomicrecovery.htm (accessed 20 February 2014).

People's Assembly of Syntagma Square (2011) Vote of the People's Assembly of Syntagma Square, 27 May http://commons.wikimedia.org/wiki/File:Vote_of_the_People%27s_Assembly_of_Syntagma_Square.svg (accessed 4 March 2013).

Psimitis, M. (2011) 'The protest cycle of spring 2010 in Greece', *Social Movement Studies: Journal of social, cultural and political protest* 10 (2): 191–7.

Rucht, D. (2003) 'Transnationalization and globalization of social movements', in P. Ibarra (ed.) *Social Movements and Democracy*, London: Palgrave Macmillan.

— (2005) 'The internet as a new opportunity for transnational protest groups', in M. Kousis and C. Tilly (eds) *Economic and Political Contention in Comparative Perspective*, Boulder, CO: Paradigm.

Rucht, D. and F. Neidhardt (1998) *Acts of Dissent: New developments in the study of protest*, Berlin: Edition Sigma.

Shekha, K. R. (2011) 'Determinants of Latin American activism: domestic and transnational political opportunities and threats', *Sociology Compass* 5 (8): 747–62, DOI: 10.1111/j.1751–9020.2011.00396.x.

Shepard, B. H. (2012), 'Labor and Occupy Wall Street: common causes and uneasy alliances', *WorkingUSA: The journal of labor and society* 15: 121–34.

Smith, J. (2011) 'Globalizations forum on Middle East protests: commentary', *Globalizations* 8 (5): 655–9.

Smith, J. and Wiest, D. (2012) *Social Movements in the World-System: The Politics of crisis and transformation*, New York: Russell Sage Foundation.

Sotirakopoulos, N. and Sotiropoulos, G. (2013) ' "Direct democracy now!": the Greek indignados and the present cycle of struggles', *Current Sociology* 61: 443, DOI: 10.1177/0011392113479744..

Stavrou, A. (2011) 'The "Upper Square" or, when the masses speak "Oe, Oe, Oe, get up from the couch"', in C. Giovanopoulos and D. Mitropoulos (eds) *Democracy Under Construction: From the streets to the squares*, Athens: A/synechia (in Greek).

Strawn, K. (2005) 'Political process, economy, and protest in Mexico, 1999–2000: An event centered quantitative analysis of collective action in a structural adjustment society', PhD thesis, Sociology, University of Wisconsin-Madison..

Tarrow, S. (2005) *The New Transnational Activism*, Cambridge: Cambridge University Press.

— (2008) 'Charles Tilly and the practice of contentious politics', *Social Movement Studies: Journal of social, cultural and political protest* 7 (3): 225–246, DOI http://dx.doi.org/10.1080/14742830802485601.

— (2011) 'Global, conventional and warring movements and the suppression of contention: Themes in contentious politics research', *Politica & Sociedade*, 10 (18): 25–49.
Tilly, C. (1978) *From Mobilization to Revolution*, Reading, MA: Addison-Wesley.
— (2004) *Social Movements, 1768–2004*, London: Paradigm.
Tsaliki, L. (2012) 'The Greek "Indignados": the Aganaktismeni as a case study of the "new repertoire of collective action"', talk offered at the 'In/compatible publics: Publics in Crisis-Production, Regulation and Control of Publics' panel, within the Transmediale Media Art.
Tsomou, M. (2011) 'Zoom out: the squares of Greece abroad', in C. Giovanopoulos and D. Mitropoulos (eds) *Democracy Under Construction: From the streets to the squares*, Athens: A/synechia (in Greek).
Tzanelli, Rodanthi, (2011) '"Take Five": understanding Greek manifestations of "disrespect"', published on 17 November 2011 at openDemocracy http://www.opendemocracy.net/rodanthi-tzanelli/%E2%80%98take-five%E2%80%99-understandinggreek-manifestations-of-%E2%80%98disrespect%E2%80%99 (accessed 10 January 2013).
Tzogopoulos, G. (2013) *The Greek Crisis in the Media: Stereotyping in the international press*, Surrey: Ashgate Publishing.
Vogiatzoglou, M. and Sergi, V. (2013) 'Think globally, act locally? Symbolic memory and global repertoires in the Tunisian uprising and the Greek anti-austerity mobilizations', in C. F. Fominaya and L. Cox (eds) *Understanding European Movements: New social movements, global justice struggles, anti-austerity protest*, London: Routledge.

Chapter Eight

Occupy London in International and Local Context

Nikos Sotirakopoulos and Christopher Rootes

Introduction

Occupy London came late to the international wave of contention that in 2011 sprang up in countries as diverse as Egypt, Spain, Greece and the United States. Although this 'International of grievance' might be represented as a transnational reaction to the severe financial crisis that unfolded from 2008, each local instance of protest had characteristics peculiar to it. The difficulty for the scholar of social movements is to understand that wave of contention as a phenomenon with core characteristics and common narratives, without underestimating the special elements of particular cases. In this chapter, we consider Occupy London, which, though it identified itself as the British 'strand' in an international cycle of struggles, bore the burdens and limitations of the social reality and historical specificities that were its local context.

We consider Occupy London as a phenomenon stimulated by three different factors: a 'passing of the baton' from other similar mobilisations around the world (especially Occupy Wall Street); a reaction to the ways in which the crisis has been experienced in Britain; and a link in the long chain of direct-action protests in Britain. We then proceed to observe Occupy London more closely. What kinds of people participated and why? What were the internal characteristics of the protest and how did they influence its outcome? Was it an anti-capitalist protest, as the media portrayed it? Might it be better understood as a social movement, a political mobilisation or as something else? To answer these questions, we will draw upon data derived from direct observation of Occupy London, more than 30 interviews with participants, and survey data, as well as secondary data and literature on the 2011 struggles and Occupy.[1]

---

1. Observations were made at the St Paul's camp on several days over several months, chiefly by Sotirakopoulos but also by Rootes and others. The interviews employed here were conducted by Sotirakopoulos, and the survey data was collected on 9 and 12 November 2011 at St Paul's and Finsbury Square, as part of the international project, 'Caught in the Act of Protest: Contextualising Contestation' (CCC), by a research team from the University of Southampton, led by Clare Saunders. The survey used a questionnaire adapted from the common research instrument of the CCC project by members of the UK partners in the CCC project (led by Saunders at Southampton

The general frame: An international wave of contention

Economic crisis is widely supposed to entail social dislocation and political contention. Just as the economic turmoil associated since 2008 with the global financial crisis has been international, as one would expect in a globalised financial environment, so the contention that has followed the crisis has also been international. Nevertheless, the recent wave of contention can be also understood as a climax in struggles that had been going on for almost a decade, as a symptom not only of the crisis of capitalism but also of the side effects of the cycle of accumulation commonly labelled 'neo-liberalism'.

This contention has taken various forms but the type of discontent on which we focus is grassroots protests of complaint against or direct challenge to the state. These varied significantly in size, orientation and character. The protests of the Arab Spring and Cairo's Tahrir Square, the Indignados movement in Spain, the Outraged of Syntagma Square in Athens and the Occupy movement in its various versions in some cases leant towards violence, even riot, usually, as in Egypt and Greece, as a reaction to state repression. Because of the urgency of the conjunctures they faced (crises of governance, collapsing standards of living and state repression), only rarely did they attempt to articulate a systematic political narrative. In the case of Occupy, unable to formulate a political alternative, the protests had a prefigurative and moralistic character.

From 2011 onwards, the internationalisation and diffusion of protest conformed to the classic model proposed by Kriesi *et al.* (1995: 182): issues shared on a wide international level – in this case the financial crisis and the malfunctioning or lack of democracy – triggering mobilisations that then gained momentum and influenced one another. Such 'eventful protest' (della Porta 2008) produces its own dynamic that not only gives birth to new forms of organisation, narratives and repertoires of action but also challenges and transforms the existing dominant structures. At the risk of exaggerating and oversimplifying, one might say that in 2011 it was not movements that gave rise to protests but, on the contrary, protests sprang up as a reaction to social, economic and political malaise, gained a momentum of their own and gave birth to movements.

Applying McAdam and Rucht's work on diffusion, we might identify the Arab Spring in general and Tahrir Square in particular as the 'transmitter' (1993: 59), the event that inspired the subsequent wave of contention, its repertoire of action, themes, values and cultural symbols (*cf.* Kriesi *et al.* 1995: 182).

The 'trademark' of the recent wave of contention was the physical occupation of space, usually a square. Square occupations spread like a 'meme' (Mason 2012: 150–1). 'Time and again, the impulse to create areas of self-control ... led... to an almost mystical determination by protesters to occupy a symbolic physical

---

and Rootes at the University of Kent). The CCC project was conducted under the auspices of the European Science Foundation as an ECRP collaboration led by the University of Antwerp; UK participation was funded by Economic and Social Research Council (ESRC) grant number RES-062-23-1565.

space and create within it an experimental, shared community' (Mason 2012: 84). A heterogeneous multitude consisting of people from different classes, social backgrounds and political beliefs met in the physical space of a square, having encounters that would be difficult in more traditional forms of organisation and solidarity building, such as the political party or the trade union.

The occupation of the squares fulfilled the criteria that Soule (2007: 302, 303) identified as necessary for successful diffusion of a protest event: it gave advantages to the movement; it was compatible with already existing experiences in the milieu (as were the horizontalist, non-hierarchical, directly democratic elements from the Global Justice Movement); it was simple and came with limited risks (the occupation of a square is easier than taking over a major government building, let alone the state); it did not demand strict commitment (as, for example, does participation in a political party); and it promised to deliver results. This last element is important because a successful outcome in one instance – such as the overthrow of Mubarak – makes diffusion easier (Koopmans 2007: 26).

If Tahrir Square was the 'transmitter', then the most direct 'adopters' were the Spanish Indignados, the Greek Outraged, and Occupy. This was mirrored in the words of the participants of the London Occupy protest, who almost unanimously identified the Arab Spring as the initial inspiration for their action. But if this was diffusion, it was what Tarrow would call non-relational diffusion (2005: 104), diffusion through mostly indirect channels such as the media (and mainly social media), rather than through direct contacts between activists, as was the case in previous cycles of struggle (McAdam and Rucht 1993).

The common themes – a demand for equality and democracy – that can be traced in the recent wave of contention are key to understanding the phenomenon (Tejerina *et al.* 2013). Yet these themes are so vague and devoid of specific content that they risk being an empty form (Rocamadur 2013). There was no specific political platform or programme to unify the heterogeneous masses that filled the squares, beyond some negative consensus in cases like Egypt (against Mubarak) and Greece (against the austerity packages). Equality and democracy were principles to which no one could easily object. Yet it remains unclear what exactly equality meant. In what form, for whom and in what terms: economic, legislative, social? Who would deliver this equality? Likewise, 'democracy' took different forms and meanings, from 'true democracy' in Spain to 'direct democracy' in Athens, with the analogous difference in the scope and radicalism of each concept (Sotirakopoulos and Sotiropoulos 2013: 446). In both cases, however, democracy sounds more like a hopeless gesture or a appeal with an unknown recipient, or one as unwilling to listen as ruling elites in times of crisis have proven to be. Thus it appeared more as a demand for a return to a *status quo ante* than a move towards something new. Similarly, Occupy Wall Street raised demands for reductions in gross social and economic inequality and for democracy but developed no political project (Rowe 2011; Žižek 2012). As Castells (2012; 186) put it, Occupy 'presented more grievances than demands'.

The short winter of Occupy London

Occupy London was a paradoxical protest. It was relatively small and quite moderate in its scope and ambition and, after months of protest, it had clearly failed to live up to the extravagant expectations it had excited. Yet Occupy London attracted an unusual level of media attention and captured the imagination of legions of sympathisers. The fact that it made such an impact and had such resonance with public opinion signals the importance of understanding a phenomenon that has so far remained under-analysed.

Because it was preceded by Occupy Wall Street and the occupations of the squares in Cairo, Madrid and Athens, but also because the London protests of the previous winter had been surprisingly subdued, Occupy London was a protest event that was widely anticipated. Thus, when it kicked off, at least among the radical milieu, it was considered a natural reaction to the crisis. 'I was watching Occupy Wall Street and was thinking how great it was that it was spreading globally and I was desperate for it to come to UK so I could get involved here', said Obi, an activist from St Paul's camp information team (interview 1). In the previous year, student protests and occupations against the increase in university tuition fees, actions by the UK Uncut network against corporations that allegedly failed to pay their fair share of taxes and the massive march organised by the Trades Union Congress (TUC) in London on 26 March 2011, together with the riots of August 2011, had raised expectations of a 'winter of discontent', something anticipated not only by activists but also by the police (Rootes, fieldwork notes). In the event, the winter of 2011–12 brought little more than three months of peaceful and relatively small-scale occupation of two squares and one deserted building in and around the City of London.

It would, however, have been unreasonable to expect a great deal of Occupy London in view of the fact that it was obliged to pick up from the point where other mobilisations had failed. Thus, after the student protests and UK Uncut faced decisive repressive policing in the winter of 2010–11, their activists had little option but to retreat from direct action or come up with new repertoires.[2] The TUC, although it managed to gather a huge crowd on 26 March 2011, failed to keep up the momentum, especially when attention was diverted away from the main event towards violent incidents and small-scale rioting. In addition, the vigorous prosecution of rioters and looters after the turbulent days of August made clear that the government had and was prepared to use all the resources necessary to control the situation, as well as overwhelming public support for the enforcement of law and order. There was a need for something new and different in direct action and the radical milieu in general.

---

2. Interestingly, however, the horizontal organizational structures of the student occupations of 2010–11 and the alter-globalisation movement, and the narrative of UK Uncut's framing of banks and big corporations as enjoying unfair tax and other benefits, were carried over to Occupy London.

Although much inspiration was drawn from the Arab Spring and the Indignados movement, the most direct catalyst for Occupy London was Occupy Wall Street (OWS), which inspired the rapid, global spread of Occupy protests. Clearly, the narratives, forms of action and general outlook of OWS were closer to the direct experience of British activists than were lethal protests for the overthrow of a dictator in Cairo or the violent clashes and Molotov cocktails of the anti-austerity struggles in Athens. On the other hand, Occupy's power rested on the fact that it captured the imagination and spread as a 'meme' and this might explain why such a protest sprang up in London only in October and not earlier, in the immediate aftermath of the Arab Spring or concurrently with the Spanish and Greek Indignados.

OWS had been active for almost a month when a call was circulated via electronic media for a similar gathering outside the London Stock Exchange on Saturday 15 October 2011, the international day of protest called by the Spanish Indignados. However, when protestors attempted to occupy privately-owned Paternoster Square, which faces the London Stock Exchange, the police sealed it off in order to enforce a High Court injunction obtained by the square's owners. A crowd of some 2,000 to 3,000 people then gathered in the neighbouring unfenced paved area, part public and part the property of the Church, in front of and to the west of St Paul's Cathedral. On the pretext of protecting the cathedral, the police briefly 'kettled' (contained) the protestors. However, though police prevented entry to Paternoster Square, after the Canon Chancellor of St Paul's intervened to ask them not to impede peaceful protest, the police announced that they would not act to clear protestors from the area immediately adjacent to the cathedral. Numbers diminished as night fell but some seventy tents were pitched on the flagstones and about 500 protestors remained, with the police overlooking them from the cathedral threshold.

Interviews suggest that few of the protestors who camped outside St Paul's had done so with any intention of staying there for long. 'I was here, like many on 15 October, just to see what's happening and then go home. But police starting kettling us, so I decided, "OK, I'll stay." Next day I got my sleeping bag and I've been staying here ever since.' (Obi, interview 1). Soon there were more than 100 tents and several hundred protestors living on the site, their numbers diminishing at night and peaking at weekends. A media tent and a camp kitchen were quickly set up. A second camp was established 1,500 metres away in Finsbury Square and, in November, activists occupied a nearby empty building, owned by UBS bank, which became known as the 'Bank of Ideas'. Although the 'Bank of Ideas' was evicted in late January, the camp at St Paul's survived until 28 February, and the Finsbury Square camp until June 2012, but the protest was effectively dead long before the last tents were removed from St Paul's.

Everyday life in Occupy London camps was precarious and uncomfortable but the discomforts were often mitigated. Lack of running water and sanitation was an issue, with the solution usually found in the toilets of nearby malls or cafes, but portable chemical toilets were soon installed at the edge of the site. Housekeeping duties were divided according to a rota. Groceries were freely available, thanks to apparently generous donations provided by various individuals, groups and even the Church. A 'Tent City University' was established, where ideas were exchanged, discussions were held and scholars and activists gave lectures. Many workshops took place in the 'Bank of Ideas', which also provided shelter from the London winter (Sotirakopoulos, fieldwork notes).

Occupy London was non-hierarchical, with horizontal (non) structures and precautions to avoid any possible institutionalisation, a tendency a prominent activist referred to as 'institutional panic' (Boni, interview 2). Decisions were taken by a general assembly, by consensus and, in the manner of previous protest camps, open discussion facilitated by hand gestures. There were various thematic working groups that introduced issues for discussion in the general assembly and a tranquillity team to prevent tensions and ensure that the 'safe space' policy was observed.

Soon, besides housekeeping issues, Occupy London had to spend much time managing its legal disputes with the authorities of St Paul's Cathedral and the City of London. In late October, amidst claims, highly publicised in the press, that the Cathedral was losing revenue because visitors were deterred by the proximity of protestors, the Cathedral authorities closed St Paul's on grounds of health and safety. It was widely expected that the police would soon be called to clear the square. As a reaction to such plans and as a gesture of solidarity with the protestors, the Canon Chancellor of St Paul's, Giles Fraser, resigned his post (Butt, Laville and Malik 2011). The backlash against the proposed eviction of the square led to the resignation of the Dean of St Paul's, Graeme Knowles, some days later (Walker 2011). From November onwards, the relationship of Occupy London with the Church was more harmonious, with activists knowing that they could stay at least until New Year's Day.

These controversies with the Church were widely covered by the media and so kept Occupy in the news. Much of Occupy's 'success' in getting attention from the media and the wider public was thus due to the accident that protestors prevented from camping outside the London Stock Exchange ended up outside St Paul's. On the one hand, they were on the doorstep of one of London's main tourist attractions and, on the other, their interaction with the Church gave a whole new dynamic to the protest. 'We are in the middle', Tami said. 'On the left-hand side you have the financial area. On the right side you have the religious side, which is interlinked with the financial powers ... and they shouldn't be. On the board of trustees of St Paul's cathedral you've got Goldman Sachs and HSBC. The fact that we stand between these sides highlights a lot of things' (interview 19). This proximity to St Paul's enhanced religious and spiritual tendencies within the protest camp. Slogans such as 'What Would Jesus Do?' or 'Jesus Would Be With Us' became popular, and a man dressed as Jesus Christ and holding a banner claiming 'I Threw Out The Moneylenders For a Reason' became a media spectacle.

The final blow to Occupy came when the Corporation of the City of London won a High Court order for the eviction of the camp from the public space adjoining the cathedral. The remaining campers refused to leave, and so the eviction was forcible, though with little actual violence (BBC News 2012). The High Court injunction was not, however, the only factor that brought Occupy London to its knees. The rigours of a protest camp during winter, natural fatigue and the exhaustion of initiatives were also factors. After Christmas, fewer and fewer activists were staying at the camps. One activist, Fuzzy, described general assemblies in Finsbury Square in the first months of 2012 that attracted only eight people (interview 3). Homeless people became a larger proportion of the camp's inhabitants. Brendan O'Neill (2012) reported in February that 'Occupy London is now effectively a holding camp for the mentally ill, a space where the psychologically afflicted and deeply troubled can gather to eat, drink and be unmerry.' Fuzzy admits that the camps at some point did indeed look like a 'welfare shelter', although he considered this to be a success of Occupy, as it provided an alternative to inadequate welfare institutions (interview 3).

Even a sympathetic commentator, Laurie Penny (2012), reported in January that

> the protest has become a network of mutual support for the lost and destitute ... Three months of sleeping in tents, washing in the bathrooms of nearby cafes and working around-the-clock to run a kitchen feeding thousands with no running water and little electricity will transform even the most fresh-faced student into a jittering bundle of aching limbs and paranoia.

Penny touches here on one of the factors that doomed Occupy London to remain a small protest – the heavy demands it made on its activists. However, this is only part of the picture. After all, camping in Zuccotti Park in New York was also uncomfortable, yet OWS attracted larger numbers, whilst in other cases in the recent wave of contention, such as in Cairo and Athens, lives were put on the line or police repression was greater. Thus, the relative modesty of the London protest cannot convincingly be explained in terms of the discomforts and rigours of the protest itself, which were in most respects considerably less exacting than those experienced by protestors in other places.

One deeper reason for the small numbers of participants in Occupy London was the relatively mild character of the social and economic crisis that followed the financial crisis in Britain. Although the weakest parts of British society suffered increasing hardships, the social structure remained intact and, for the great majority of people, life had not altered dramatically. Although the rate of unemployment rose from 5 per cent in 2007 to 8 per cent in 2011, this was modest compared with the escalation of unemployment in Greece, for example, where it rose from 8 per cent in 2007 to 18 per cent in 2011 and was accompanied by severe social dislocation. In addition, as we will see shortly, the apolitical or anti-political and sometimes naive narrative of Occupy London probably alienated a critical mass of more conventionally politically interested people who might otherwise have been keener to participate in an anti-austerity movement.

However, Occupy London presents us with another paradox: despite its small size, it survived for several months, longer than its New York exemplar. This was partly because Occupy London managed to stay in the public eye for quite a long time, whether because of its interaction with the Church, the support it attracted from sympathisers, or its disputes with the City of London. This attention fuelled Occupy, insulated it from repressive policing and gave it a *raison d'être* when, politically, it seemed to be at a dead-end. Prominent activist Boni observed that, with protests like Occupy, sometimes it is difficult to call it a day: 'Yes, at some point we became something like a refugee camp, as most of the people with some politics had already gone home. But you could not easily end it. Some people will always stay on' (interview 2).

Occupy London's predicament makes evident the limitations of self-sustained protest camps. Even if a protest overcomes litigation or harassment by the police (which were among the factors that brought OWS to an end), the uncomfortable reality of everyday life in a protest camp will severely narrow its appeal and limit its duration. The idea of an enduring protest camp in the heart of the city, not merely protesting a single issue but calling for a wider change, appeared as a radical innovation in activists' repertoire of action, but its significance was probably overestimated.

Who participated and why

In phenomena like Occupy, which lack a central political line or orientation, the protests are the people who participate in them. Accordingly, information about the social characteristics of the protestors is of particular interest. This section will be mostly based on our fieldwork observations and extracts from interviews, backed up by some quantitative data from the 'Caught in the Act of Protest' survey. From the open-ended interviews, it became clear that the backgrounds of activists are closely related to the bases of their decisions to participate in the protest; therefore 'who participated' and 'why' will be examined together.

It might be assumed that the majority of participants in such a protest would be young people and students. However, in the case of Occupy London, there seemed to be a balance of age groups. Unsurprisingly, most 'full-time' participants, especially in the mornings, were unemployed, freelancers or students. In at least two cases, people gave up jobs or even houses to participate in Occupy; they were, predictably, young and without family commitments.

Occupy protestors were reluctant to define themselves politically. From the open-ended interviews, the majority of activists who answered the question about political affiliation declared some kind of link with the environmental movement, whereas some activists, reluctantly, identified themselves with some sort of socialism, and three declared themselves to be anarchists. Of the 106 activists and sympathisers who responded to the 'Caught in the Act of Protest' survey and declared a present party identification, 47 identified with the Greens, 33 with Labour, 8 with the Liberal Democrats, 4 with the Conservative Party, 4 with the Socialist Workers' Party (SWP) and 1 as a 'Communist'.

In peoples' motivations in taking to the squares, the dominant theme was a sense of injustice and inequality, triggering a feeling of personal responsibility.

The system we live in is fundamentally broken, socially, fiscally and economically. The social contract is broken. We want to show the displeasure of people against the system. (Buenaventura, interview 4).

For Adrian, it was a sense of duty to future generations: 'Something is seriously wrong with our society. I have children and I feel I have a responsibility for their future' (interview 5). The crisis and its consequences operated as a catalyst for some protestors to take action: 'I lost my job and I cannot find another job, and this is why I decided to come here to protest' (John, interview 6). Matthew was quite candid: 'I have a mortgage, VAT has increased and the cost of food has gone up. Had I not been touched by the crisis, I probably wouldn't care for this movement and I would tell them to go get a job' (interview 7). Predictably, others had different motives for participating. 'I was simply interested to join a free and open community' (Nathan, interview 8). A feeling of sharing and of contributing motivated Carmel: 'I cook well, so I came to provide food to people who are here, together with love, smiles and appreciation' (interview 9). Others, such as the wanderer and self-declared 'old hippy', Poet, had more practical concerns: 'I have to stay somewhere overnight. The meditation tent seems just right!' (interview 10).

Most, however, saw participation in Occupy as a gesture of personal protest against what was perceived to be a general injustice. 'I feel strongly against inequality and I'd feel a hypocrite if I hadn't got involved in this' (Spiter, interview 11). The vague calls for equality and democracy that were the general themes of this wave of contention internationally were, in Occupy London, linked with a strong message of emotional dissatisfaction and moral disapproval. The words of a prominent activist at St Paul's (interview 1) – 'we are showing them we are unhappy' – were repeated time and again. This tendency is not new in social movements and contentious politics. What is new is that the expression of this dissatisfaction at St Paul's (and at most protest sites internationally) was not followed by a collective demand for a specific, systematic political programme designed to put an end to the situation against which the protest arose.

Why did the protestors adopt one repertoire of action rather than another? Why did the protest take the particular form of occupying a square? Almost every interviewee mentioned Tahrir Square, the Spanish Indignados or OWS as sources of inspiration. Activists 'renamed' the square outside St Paul's, erecting a sign proclaiming 'Tahrir Square EC4M, City of Westminster' and banners from other countries were used, including one from Syntagma in Athens. At least three long-term participants of Occupy London had previous experience in Spain and Greece. Toby, a Spanish activist, who sold his car so that he could travel to Occupy London, explicitly mentioned his experience in Puerta del Sol (interview 12). Internationalism was one of the values Occupy activists emphasised. Links with other Occupy camps throughout the world were promoted as core elements of the London 'branch', which also adopted the narrative of representing the 99 per cent against the power of the 1 per cent, the common theme of the global Occupy movement (Tejerina *et al.* 2013: 384).

Thus Occupy London adopted (and adapted) some of the forms, codes and repertoires of actions employed elsewhere in the 2011 international wave of contention but it also sprang up as a reaction to a growing feeling of injustice and inequality, accelerated by the conjunctural crisis in Britain. But Occupy London was also a link in the chain of grassroots protests in Britain. A number of tents and banners bore visible signs that they had been used in previous years at the Camps for Climate Action. Not only did the climate camps inspire because they had been innovative, peaceful and inclusive (Saunders and Price 2009; Saunders 2012) but they had also been successful in problematising the burning of coal to generate electricity and the expansion of aviation. However, although the Climate Camps were a space within which more conventional forms of political action were canvassed, their prevailing ethos and strategy was a 'post-political' one that viewed individual responsibility as the primary basis for action (Schlembach *et al.* 2012). It is probably not coincidental that Occupy emerged just as the Camp for Climate Action dissolved in order that activists might engage in the wider society and channel more energy into highlighting the miseries caused by the financial crisis (Camp for Climate Action 2011).

Daniel, an activist with experience from Climate Camps and the Global Justice Movement, said: 'My experience in the Climate Camps made me think I'd be of some help to this movement' (interview 13). On the continuity of direct-action protest in the UK, he commented that

> this form of protest goes back to the anti-roads movement. When you occupy, you reclaim a space for yourself and you prevent others from using it. This concept has grown bigger and bigger ... from squatting rooms to the Climate Camps. Occupy is an incarnation of that concept, but has left behind the idea of preventing other people from using this space.

But what about other, more recent movements?

> The alter-globalisation movement created a space within activism for people doing things in the streets and for its norms and values to become the accepted way of doing protest – consensus in decision-making and occupying a physical space. This is like a second-generation thing. There is some continuation, but without necessarily much connection.

Boni, a key activist in Occupy, accepted the importance of some Climate Camp veterans, but added that 'we have to keep in mind that most people in Occupy London did not have any history in protest. There were people from all walks of life ... even a Conservative Party councillor was there – and of course soon left' (interview 2). According to an activist in his late 40s, and with long experience in direct action,

> the roots of Occupy lay not only in Climate Camps, but go further in the past, to the peace camps, the anti-roads movement, etc. ... Movements come full

circle or reach their limits. But then they re-emerge in different conditions and with different characteristics (interview 14).

Another key activist, Fuzzy, was much younger. His protest history, like that of many others in Occupy, began in the student mobilisations of 2010 and the anti-cuts campaign. Yet he saw himself as part of the rich history of direct-action protest in Britain. To the suggestion that previous direct-action protests with characteristics similar to those of Occupy had disappeared, and asked whether the same would happen with Occupy, he replied that

> it's like waves. When you are wrapped up in a wave, it's impossible to know whether it's high tide or low tide and whether or not this particular wave or this particular tide will be the one that pushes everything over the edge. But what you can always rely on is that there will be a next wave (interview 3).

Thus Occupy London was at the same time a part of a transnational wave of contention, a reaction to the financial crisis as it was experienced in Britain and an event expressing some continuity with previous grassroots mobilisations in Britain.

Squares devoid of politics?

It is now time to examine Occupy's narrative and pose some questions about its character. Was it, as it was portrayed by the media, at least its early stages, an anti-capitalist protest? Should it be understood as a political movement? Or was it perhaps the collective staging of a gesture at the level of consciousness and mainly a prefigurative protest?[3] Deciphering the ideological character of Occupy's narrative is not easy because its activists celebrated diversity and were unwilling to accept a political identity. For this reason, Occupy's 'official' documents serve as a starting point.

According to the 'constitutional' statement on its website, 'Occupy London is part of the global social movement that has brought together concerned citizens from across the world against this injustice and to fight for a sustainable economy that puts people and the environment we live in before corporate profits' (Occupy London 2011a). Thus big corporations are foregrounded as opponents, their pursuit of profit portrayed as responsible for the aforementioned injustice. The reference to a 'sustainable economy' and the 'environment' reveals the Green credentials of Occupy London and hints at economic growth as something problematic. Reference to 'concerned citizens' reveals how much of Occupy's narrative was about the perceived 'apathy of the masses'. The initial statement of Occupy's assembly targets the 'unsustainable system', celebrates diversity and inclusiveness, opposes the cuts, declares solidarity with the oppressed around

---

3. I.e. a protest operating as an example and embodying the participants' values and their vision of a good society.

the world and denounces the environmental degradation caused by the present economic system (Occupy London 2011a). Here, the vague and all-encompassing nature of Occupy becomes evident. It is a narrative that could be incorporated by almost anyone, from political elites to the Green movement.

According to Rochon, the elements that give 'newsworthiness' to a movement are size, novelty and militancy (1990: 108). Occupy London was small and there was nothing militant about it. Even its novelty was limited because a sustained protest camp in the heart of London was not unprecedented; a 'Democracy Village' protest camp occupied Parliament Square for almost three months in May–July 2010 before it was forcibly evicted.[4] It is therefore necessary to search elsewhere for the bases of Occupy's appeal. Gitlin (2012) points out how, in times of crisis, when many members of the public are worried and crave some sort of response, a movement that offers a vague and open-ended narrative can be quite easily accepted by a wide range of people. Another reason for Occupy's noteworthiness is based not in what Occupy was saying but in how the protest was perceived by the media. For O'Neill, Occupy London's all-encompassing message made it possible for other subjects, mainly the media, to project on to it their own worries and agenda. Yet Occupy's promotion by the media was unusual for such a small protest (O'Neill 2011). Prominent Occupy activist Naomi Calvin (2011) was 'extremely pleased by the coverage we've got from the mainstream media. Some of the people in the media team are from UK Uncut and they've been staggered by the amount of attention we've had.'

Interviews did not greatly help to elucidate Occupy's ideological outlook. 'I am a socialist, but we don't want any of these old words' (Chloe, interview 15). 'That's the beauty of this protest, that you don't have a group of people with a certain agenda. We have the Marxists, anti-capitalists, student unions, environmental protesters ... all sorts of people coming together for a common cause' (Charlie, interview 16). Dan seemed unhappy even to address the question: 'It is an inclusive movement, we don't ask people for qualifications or beliefs' (interview 17). For Peter, 'everyone comes here as an individual. There are members of different organisations, such as environmental, feminist, anti-cuts ... but they are coming here as individuals. People don't want organisations and groups to be here' (interview 18). 'Occupy is my ideology; I want no other labels' (Tami, interview 19). 'We are looking forward beyond separatist ideologies. This is the 21st century' (Phil, interview 20). Bill summed up the argument: 'Ideology? Meh ...' (interview 21).

Their diversity of views and unwillingness to accept an ideological orientation was celebrated by Occupy as a virtue, but it attracted criticism. For Frank Furedi (2011), the activists were celebrating their inability to say anything practical and particular at all. Even if Occupy's narrative was, on a rhetorical level, all-

---

4. A peace camp on the pavement at Parliament Square, started by Brian Haw to protest against Britain's participation in the invasion of Iraq, has existed continuously since 2001 but it never involved more than a handful of campers. The 'Democracy Village' numbered about thirty tents.

encompassing and ambitious, the set of demands that was articulated was quite modest and limited to a reform ensuring transparency in transactions in the City of London and the personal liability of high players in the financial sector (Occupy 2011b). As far as the participants interviewed were concerned, two themes emerged as targets for the movement: shifting the public agenda on issues of economic and social inequality and sustaining the protest for as long as possible. Natalia, from the media team, emphasised this agenda-setting element: 'Debate in the media and the rhetoric of politicians was on a *status quo* track, but now this is gradually changing. It's not a massive shift, but it's a shift. In that sense we have achieved something already' (interview 22). For Obi from St. Paul's information team, 'the important thing is that already after some weeks of the protest, people know more about the City of London and how powerful the Mayor has become. We know more about … finally politicians and archbishop talk about equality and justice' (interview 1). On the self-sustaining character of the protest, 'The mere fact that we stand here is a success' (Toby, interview 12) was a motto echoed time and again in Occupy camps. However, although Occupy may have stimulated a debate, it is doubtful whether the terms of the debate about issues of social and economic inequality shifted as a result. Celebrating the mere existence of Occupy risks seeing the campaign as an end in itself.

Was Occupy London anti-capitalist?

A large banner declaring 'Capitalism Is Crisis' was prominently displayed above the tents at St Paul's and, for some time, Occupy was perceived, not least by the media, as an anti-capitalist protest. But the same banner had appeared at the 2009 Climate Camp. Occupy London protestors repeatedly tried to shake off the anti-capitalist label and, before long, a less combative 'Democratise Capitalism' banner took its place.

A key activist, who considered himself anti-capitalist, explained:

> We were afraid of using the anti-capitalist label. We wanted people to come and engage with us, rather than appear as anti-capitalists. We wanted people to come down and meet us, rather than having any pre-given particular political image (interview 2).

Naomi Calvin, one of Occupy's featured activists, in a public debate on 2 November 2011, happily announced that 'the BBC is not anymore calling us anti-capitalist … this is a significant change!' (Calvin, 2011). If, as we have suggested, Occupy London was fuelled mainly by the attention of the mass media and its constant thirst for recognition, the abandonment of the anti-capitalist label may have owed more to the group's public-relations strategy than to any shift in its political analysis. Nevertheless, the muting of anti-capitalist voices seemed to be more consonant with the protest's generally moderate message and aims.

In our interviews with them, activists expressed some anti-capitalist sentiments but they articulated at best a very shallow critique of elements of the prevailing socio-economic system, echoing much of what might be described as romantic anti-capitalism, reminiscent of the reaction by part of the intelligentsia against rapid industrialisation at the dawn of the nineteenth century. Moreover, it was a critique mostly on the moral level, on issues such as bankers' bonuses or the privileged tax regime enjoyed by big corporations, rather than a critique of the capitalist system as such. However, of even greater interest is the fact that a significant number of interviewees did not frame capitalism as a problem at all.

'I am not an anti-capitalist ... capitalism has done great in the past' (Spiter, interview 11). 'Anti-capitalism has been a label, which induces fear in people, and thus it has been adopted by the media to induce this very fear. Through capitalism people get their security and the warmth in their home' (Dan, interview 17). Obi saw himself as 'a capitalist with a small "c"', as he owned a small business. For him, the problem was not capitalism but what he called 'corporatocracy' (interview 1). Dani believed that capitalism could be put to the service of a good cause (interview 23). 'Not all of us are anti-capitalists. Some of us think capitalism is OK, however it shouldn't be about a few businesses swallowing up all the wealth' (Tami interview 19).

Thus it is evident that not only did Occupy fail to engage in a systemic analysis of modern capitalism and how it generated the crisis, or make any attempt to form an alternative plan or vision, but it apparently did not even aspire to do so. There was a limited critique, mainly of aspects of 'neo-liberalism', but neo-liberalism was not seen as a necessary stage for capital's survival nor as the dominant regime of accumulation in this period of crisis; it was instead seen as an elite-driven political project that could be undone without questioning the fundamentals of the capitalist mode of production. Many protestors consciously disavowed the anti-capitalist label, sincerely believing that it was only the derailing of the system from some golden past that had caused the crisis. Occupy might thus be understood as a more or less reformist protest, whose main addressee was the state, in a call for some intervention here and there to restore a (mostly imaginary) lost balance.[5]

A prefigurative rather than political movement

Yet although the reformist element was present in Occupy, it was not the dominant characteristic of the protest. The prevailing ethos of Occupy was not political but moral, emphasising individual rather than social change. Mostly focused on appeals at the level of consciousness, it had a strongly prefigurative character; that

---

5. When asked 'who or what is to blame for the "unsustainable financial system" and lack of social justice?', most of those who responded to the CCC survey mentioned banks/the governments that failed to regulate them: 29 per cent explicitly mentioned banks/bankers/financiers/financial institutions, alone or in combination, but 34 per cent blamed governments/politicians, usually for failing to regulate banks/financial interests effectively. Just 4 per cent explicitly mentioned neo-liberalism/neo-liberal economic policies; and only 17 per cent explicitly blamed capitalism/the capitalist system and, of these, several specified 'flaws in the capitalist system' or government's failure to regulate capitalism.

is, it was keen to serve as a model and as a microcosm for how social relations and interactions ought to operate.

David Graeber, a fierce supporter of the Occupy movement on both sides of the Atlantic, has emphasised the prefigurative ethos of such movements, seeing them as 'theme parks' of direct democracy and egalitarianism and proposing the term 'contaminationism' to signify 'the idea that all people really needed was to be exposed to the experience of direct action and direct democracy, and they would want to start imitating it all by themselves' (Graeber 2007). Graeber saw contaminationism functioning in the Global Justice Movement and he had faith in its potential for Occupy, in which 'the camps were always primarily an advertisement, a defiant experiment in libertarian communism' (Graeber 2012: 427). Boni, a prominent Occupy London activist, emphasised the importance of this:

> People don't only change politics as a result of argument, but also as a result of experience. And Occupy was an experience leading to a transformation, and this is why people will continue being politically engaged. People did not leave the same persons from Occupy (interview 2).

This prefigurative ethos was also evident among other activists interviewed in Occupy London camps. For Carmel, the best thing the movement can achieve is to 'operate as a model and show the world how well a society can work if we all co-operate' (interview 9). George said that he participated full time in Occupy 'to show them that we have created a viable alternative, a system where there is no higher state authority or monetary system and which nevertheless functions perfectly well' (interview 24).

We expected that a protest lacking a political orientation and emphasising the prefigurative element would mainly deliver a message on the level of consciousness and this seems to be validated by our interviews with activists. 'Actually, very little needs to be changed in the system. It's the mindset of the people that's the problem. I see this as a movement of consciousness.' (Adrian interview 5). 'People need to change their minds first. Human greed is the main problem, not capitalism' (Chucky interview 25).

A moralistic ethos prevalent in Occupy went hand in hand with an uneasiness with modern culture, morality and the way of life of the common people. In addition, materialism was considered as one of the main problems of our society. Thus, although Occupy claimed to represent the 99 per cent, for many activists, this 99 per cent was part of the problem. As one Occupier put it,

> We don't need a lot of the comforts that we've become accustomed to ... We don't necessarily need all the technological advancement, as useful as it is, in order to live. The fear of having these things taken away stops us from considering any other options that we have'(Dan interview 18).

As Katie put it, 'The idea of having fun because you have a lot of money needs to change. People need to stop being materialistic' (interview 26).

Bill took this moralism to its logical limit:

> Humankind is the craziest thing in nature and we have moved away from nature and animals, we are going to the supermarket and consuming whatever we want. The system is good in theory, it has worked well for decades until the banks got off track, until they got obsessed with money and other mental disorders (interview 21).

We don't need that much ... *they* make us believe we need all these things. We don't need economic growth. What we need is to spread out what we've got. We don't need to keep making stuff, but spread out what we've got, 'cause we've got enough, we just need to share them. Share, co-operate and not destroy the environment (Chloe, interview 15).

Inca also points to the 'Average Joe's apathy' as one of the main problems:

> There is a spiritual apathy towards fellow men and women. This protest is a plea to people: we are in tents, we are freezing; take courage from what we sacrifice and do something! ... We are trying to inspire a new kind of consciousness that does not need as many material things and does not equate happiness with an enormous amount of material wealth (interview 30).

It seems unlikely that this anti-materialist narrative could ever have wide appeal. Occupy's form and cultural codes, which could not be easily endorsed by most people, are probably the most telling explanation for its small size.

In Occupy, but also generally in the ethos of modern social movements and parts of the Left, more and more, the personal is considered political. This tendency has intensified as the horizon of politics has shrunk and the belief in grand projects of total social transformation and emancipation has waned (Furedi 2005). It flourishes in a consciousness-raising protest such as Occupy. Katie sums it up: 'This is a movement of consciousness. From the relationship you have with people to the furniture you buy ... everything is linked. Bankers and the 1 per cent don't realise that what they do is bad and they think they deserve what they earn.' (interview 26). For Thom, individual choices can strike a blow against the system: 'Get away from multinational companies and get neighbours shopping together, make food co-operatives and put the money together. This will scare them more than any political change' (interview 27). Ginder asserted that

> People have to change their consciousness. We cannot carry on blaming the system for the problems that we take part in. Individuals need to change the way they think and operate within the system. The system only exists because of the mass of people choosing to follow it. If they decide to change the way

they are, for example buy locally, this system will cease to exist because this mass of people will stop feeding it (interview 28).

Predictably, this moralistic attitude coexisted harmoniously with a New-Age tendency to inner exploration and fulfilment; after all, if the personal is political, the self and the body become a subject of immanent importance. This resulted in a shallow spirituality that at times seemed to be an opt-out from the current moment of the social crisis and the political battlefield.

Humanity is detached from itself, no longer self-aware; instead of operating on a level of feeling, we get lost in a mindset of alienating structures, and the more we do that, the more psychopathic in nature we become. It's a mindset (Adrian, interview 5).

Sandy went further:

This is a spiritual movement. We are focusing on the now. Living in the moment is more important than making long-term plans. Forget fear and remember love (interview 29).

Conclusion

Occupy London was a protest phenomenon that can be understood on three levels: as a protest influenced by various protest actions in 2011 in other parts of the world; as a reaction to the financial crisis as it was experienced by elements of British society; and as the latest instance in the long history of grassroots protests in Britain. If Occupy London lacked the political vigour and the challenging character of roughly contemporaneous movements in some other countries, this was, perhaps, because, faced with financial crisis, British society and political culture proved relatively resilient. Despite pay freezes and/or below-inflation pay rises across the public and private sectors, a sharply devalued currency and consequently depressed living standards for the vast majority of Britons, levels of employment in Britain remained surprisingly buoyant. Thus Britain, despite the heroic proportions of its banking and debt crisis and the economic depression it produced, was less severely hit by the financial crisis than some other countries, such as Greece or Spain, where thematically similar movements sprang up. For that reason, it is understandable that the rhetoric, narrative, targets and class resonance of Occupy London should have been more moderate than those of other movements facing a more ominous social predicament. In Britain, dire predictions of mass unemployment and immiseration were not fulfilled and the massive, disruptive protests they were expected to produce did not materialise. Doubtless the moderation of British political culture played a part, but firm policing of demonstrations in 2010–11 and stern judicial sentencing of violent protestors forestalled the escalation of protest when it did occur.

Against this background, Occupy London was mostly a protest at the level of consciousness raising, with an unclear narrative, little in the way of political analysis but plenty of generalisations, moralistic slogans and scapegoating of easy targets (mainly 'greedy bankers' and 'tax cheating' corporations). It claimed to represent the 99 per cent, but it considered the material aspirations of the 99 per cent to be part of the problem. Although its speakers claimed that 'the best way of understanding it is to join in' (Calvin, 2011), the demanding nature of Occupy's form of action made mass participation improbable.

Sympathetic observers praised Occupy's prefigurative character, its organisational horizontality and the strictly egalitarian values it upheld. Yet Occupy London, though it succeeded in building strong ties of identity among a small number of activists, failed to provide a positive vision for the millions who suffered losses as the crisis unfolded. That failure, however, mirrors the ideological and political weakness of the Left in Britain; it would be harsh to condemn Occupy for shortcomings in areas in which political parties, trade unions and even intellectual imagination have also failed.

We are left to reflect on the puzzle of London's place in the transnational diffusion of the 2011 wave of contention. In his account of the 'colour revolutions', Mark Beissinger (2007) suggested that as the wave of mobilisation spread from countries where the structural conditions for political transformation were well laid to those where conditions were less structurally conducive, so the permutations of outcomes of modular action expanded, with a greater likelihood of violent conflict in the latter cases. It might be supposed that, because Occupy London came late in the international sequence and was, in its scale if not its duration, a poor relation to OWS, Britain was less 'structurally conducive' to such mobilisations. Certainly, Occupy London was noticeably less confrontational than its American counterparts.

Platitudes about the moderation of British political culture aside, the explanation is that Britain came not late but early to the wave of contention and that the earliest protests – the student demonstrations of the autumn and winter of 2010–11 – produced a configuration of protest and state response that was profoundly discouraging to large-scale contentious protest. The events of 2010–11 in London demonstrated that, whilst non-violent peaceful protest was tolerated, and generally facilitated, by the police, it was ineffective in changing the austerity policies of the government or the practices of corporations. Confrontational, invasive, disruptive and/or violent protest, however, was not only vigorously repressed by the police and the courts, but, mediated by a predictably hostile press, it also produced a massive public backlash, such that the substance of protest was drowned out by the volume of the condemnation of its forms. By October 2011, no British activist could have harboured any illusions about the will and the capacity of the state to repress disruptive protest.

London activists were inspired and encouraged by, and picked up themes from, protests elsewhere in Europe, North Africa, and the United States; but Occupy London was not simply a product of transnational diffusion. It was, rather, an attempt in the particular conditions of London in late 2011 to fashion an alternative repertoire of action to those that had failed in the very recent past and it was profoundly influenced by the positive legacies, the forms and internal practices of the most recent instances of innovative and successful non-violent protests in Britain – the Camps for Climate Action. Certainly, Occupy London took some of it cues from the transnational wave of protest but its realisation was rooted in the local context and reflected the recent experience of protest in Britain.

The general lesson that might be drawn from this is that the transnational diffusion of protest is an impression fostered by distance. In fact, protest is not so much transnationally modular as it is embedded in local and national contexts and the particular conjunctions of protest action and state response.

References

BBC News (2012) 'St Paul's protest: Occupy London camp evicted', http://www.bbc.co.uk/news/uk-17187180 (accessed 7 September 2013).

Beissinger, M. R. (2007) 'Structure and example in modular political phenomena: the diffusion of Bulldozer/Rose/Orange/Tulip Revolutions', *Perspectives on Politics* 5 (2): 259–76.

Butt, R., Laville, S. and Malik, S. (2011) 'Giles Fraser resignation: I couldn't face Dale Farm on the steps of St Paul's', *Guardian*, 27 October, http://www.guardian.co.uk/uk/2011/oct/27/giles-fraser-resignation-dale-farm (accessed 7 September 2013).

Calvin, N. (2011) 'Contribution to the debate *Occupy: what do they want?*', Frontline Club, London, 2 November, http://www.frontlineclub.com/first_wednesday_15/ (accessed 12 July 2013).

Camp for Climate Action (2011) 'Metamorphosis: a statement for the camp for climate action', http://www.climatecamp.org.uk/2011-statement (accessed 12 July 2013).

Castells, M. (2012) *Networks of Outrage and Hope: Social movements in the internet age*, Cambridge: Polity.

della Porta, D. (2008) 'Eventful protest, global conflicts', *Distinction: Scandinavian journal of social theory*, 9 (2): 27–56.

Furedi, F. (2005) *Politics of Fear*, London: Continuum.

—— (2011) 'Occupy movement: all process and no principle', *Spiked Online*, 15 November, http://www.spiked-online.com/index.php/site/article/11556/ (accessed 13 July 2013).

Gitlin, T. (2012) 'Occupy's predicament: the moment and the prospects for the movement', public lecture, London School of Economics, 18 October, http://www.youtube.com/watch?v=IkJoG2ai9ys (accessed 6 February 2013).

Graeber, D. (2007) 'The shock of victory', http://news.infoshop.org/article.php?story=2007graeber-victory (accessed 14 July 2013).

—— (2012) 'Afterword', in K. Khatib, M. Killjoy and M. McGuire (eds) *We Are Many: Reflections on movement strategy from Occupation to Liberation*, Oakland, CA: AK Press, pp. 425–35.

Koopmans, R. (2007) 'Protest in time and space: the evolution of waves of contention', in D. Snow, S. Soule and H. Kriesi (eds), *The Blackwell Companion to Social Movements*, Oxford: Blackwell, pp. 19–46.

Kriesi, H., Koopmans, R., Duyvendak, J. W. and Giugni, M. C. (1995) *New Social Movements in Western Europe: A comparative analysis*, London: UCL Press.

McAdam, D. and Rucht, D. (1993) 'The cross-national diffusion of movement ideas', *Annals of the American Academy of Political and Social Science* 528, Citizens, Protest, and Democracy: 56–74.

Mason, P. (2012) *Why It's Kicking Off Everywhere: The new global revolutions*, London: Verso.

Occupy London (2011a) 'Initial statement', http://occupylsx.org/?page_id=575 (accessed 12 July 2013).

— (2011b) 'Occupy London calls for an end to tax havens, for lobbying transparency and personal accountability for executives', http://occupylsx.org/?p=1526 (accessed 13 July 2013).
O'Neill, B. (2011) 'How protest became a prisoner of the media', *Spiked Online Magazine*, 29 December, http://www.spiked-online.com/site/article/11932/ (accessed 12 July 2013).
— (2012) 'Occupy London is now basically a holding camp for the mentally ill. It's time to call it a day', *Telegraph*, 23 February, http://blogs.telegraph.co.uk/news/brendanoneill2/100139274/occupy-london-is-now-basically-a-holding-camp-for-the-mentally-ill-its-time-to-call-it-a-day/ (accessed 9 July 2013).
Penny, L. (2012) 'The Occupy Movement: three months on', *New Statesman*, 18 January, http://www.newstatesman.com/blogs/laurie-penny/2012/01/occupy-movement-london (accessed 09 July 2013).
Rocamadur (2013) 'The Outraged movement in Greece (Το κίνημα των Αγανακτισμένων στην Ελλάδα)', *Blaumachen* 6 (Spring): 49–64.
Rochon, T. (1990) 'The West European peace movement and the theory of new social movements', in R. Dalton and M. Kuechler (eds) *Challenging the Political Order: New social and political movements in western democracies*, Cambridge: Polity, pp. 105–21.
Rowe, A. (2011) 'Politics averted: thoughts on the Occupy X movement', http://www.wsm.ie/c/politics-averted-occupy-movement (accessed 28 July 2013).
Saunders, C. (2012) 'Reformism and radicalism in the Climate Camp in Britain: benign coexistence, tensions and prospects for bridging', *Environmental Politics* 21 (5): 829–46.
Saunders, C. and Price, S. (2009) 'One person's eu-topia, another's hell: Climate Camp as a heterotopia', *Environmental Politics* 18 (1): 117–22.
Schlembach, R., Lear, B. and Bowman, A. (2012) 'Science and ethics in the post-political era: strategies within the Camp for Climate Action', *Environmental Politics* 21 (5) 811–28.
Sotirakopoulos, N. and Sotiropoulos, G. (2013) '"Direct Democracy Now": the Greek Indignados and the present cycle of struggles', *Current Sociology* 61 (4): 443–56.
Soule, S. (2007) 'Diffusion processes within and across movements', in Snow, D., Soule, S. and Kriesi, H. (eds), *The Blackwell Companion to Social Movements*, Oxford: Blackwell, pp. 294–310.
Tarrow, S. (2005) *The New Transnational Activism*, Cambridge: Cambridge University Press.
Tejerina, B., Perugorria, I., Benski, T. and Langman, L. (2013) 'From indignation to occupation: a new wave of global mobilization', *Current Sociology* 61 (4): 377–92.
Walker, P. (2011) 'Dean of St Paul's Cathedral resigns over Occupy London protest row', *Guardian*, 31 October, http://www.guardian.co.uk/uk/2011/oct/31/dean-st-pauls-resigns-occupy (accessed 09 July 2013).

Žižek, S. (2012) *The Year of Dreaming Dangerously*, London: Verso.

Interviews

Obi: interview 1, 7 January 2012
Boni: interview 2, 21 October 2012
Fuzzy: interview 3, 8 February 2013
Buenaventura: interview 4, 12 November 2011
Adrian: interview 5, 9 December 2011
John: interview 6, 12 November 2011
Matthew: interview 7, 12 November 2011
Nathan: interview 8, 23 November 2011
Carmel: interview 9, 26 November 2011
Poet: interview 10, 2 January 2012
Spiter, interview 11, 26 November 2011
Toby: interview 12, 2 January 2012
Daniel: interview 13, 26 November 2011
Charles: interview 14, 26 November 2011
Chloe: interview 15, 12 November 2011
Charlie interview 16, 2 January 2012
Dan interview 17, 23 November 2011
Peter interview 18, 12 November 2011
Tami interview 19, 7 January 2012
Phil interview 20, 9 December 2011
Bill interview 21, 23 November 2011
Natalia: interview 22, 19 November 2011
Dani: interview 23, 9 December 2011
George: interview 24, 12 November 2011
Chucky: interview 25, 2 January 2012
Katie: interview 26, 26 November 2011
Thom: interview 27, 9 December 2011
Ginder: interview 28, 26 November 2011
Sandy: interview 29, 19 November 2011
Inca: interview 30, 7 January 2012

Chapter Nine

Breaks and Continuities in and Between Cycles of Protest: Memories and Legacies of the Global Justice Movement in the Context of Anti-Austerity Mobilisations

Lorenzo Zamponi and Priska Daphi

Introduction

Every new movement has to face comparison with its antecedents – both by the media and by scholars of social movements. The comparison with past mobilisations also plays a crucial role in how contemporary activists mobilise and how repertoires, frames and forms of organisation diffuse. This chapter will analyse how activists perceive continuities and discontinuities, in an attempt to deepen our understanding of diffusion across time. We focus in particular on the legacies of the Global Justice Movement for contemporary anti-austerity protests in Italy.

As media scholars have shown, the media tend to represent any episode of social contention as a newer version of something that has already happened in the past, providing the audience with a familiar reference for interpreting something potentially unsettling and threatening, and thus contributing to the cultural construction of a set of canonical narrative conventions (Bird and Dardenne 1988; Cohen, Adoni and Bantz 1990; Edy 2006). At the same time, the media often transmit a narrative of spontaneity and newness, as was mostly the case for the most recent wave of anti-austerity mobilisations.

This is particularly true in the case of the present wave of mobilisation, which involved an articulated set of episodes of collective action, in particular between 2011 and 2012, each one placed in its own political context and cultural setting and characterised by its own set of social roots and goals – the most visible manifestations of which have been the Arab Spring, the European anti-austerity mobilisations and Occupy in the United States.

In particular, several scholars have pointed out continuities between the Global Justice Movement (GJM) of the early 2000s and the European anti-austerity mobilisations. These observations address various aspects of the protest but focus mainly on two nodes: the development of a transnational anti-corporate discourse embedded in the relationship between different social and political actors built on the infrastructures of the GJM (Smith 2012: 374); and the diffusion and evolution of cultures and practices of horizontality, connected with the widespread critique of the traditional mechanisms of representative democracy (della Porta 2012; Maeckelbergh 2012).

Given the geographical, historical, and political context, these continuities are not surprising for anyone, except to those who believe that a global wave of mobilisation may start 'like a fever' (Polletta 2006) and spread automatically via social media. In this vein, David Graeber, one of the most famous Occupiers, wrote in a column in *The Guardian* two weeks after the start of Occupy Wall Street:

> The form of resistance that has emerged looks remarkably similar to the old Global Justice Movement, too: we see the rejection of old-fashioned party politics, the same embrace of radical diversity, the same emphasis on inventing new forms of democracy from below (Graeber 2011).

Do other activists identify similar continuities? This chapter will examine how activists from different movement sectors reconstruct the historical role of the GJM, now that another cycle of protest seems to have started. Do they feel empowered or constrained by the baggage from the past? Addressing these questions provides insight into interesting issues, such as the reciprocal interaction between cycles of protest and the mechanisms of diffusion of repertoires and of contentions through time, as well as the role of collective memory in latent phases and its reconstruction in more contentious ones.

In the last few years, the growing literature on transnational movements has paid considerable attention to processes of diffusion across places. Diffusion across time has taken somewhat of a backseat in this context. Mechanisms of diffusion and the influence of a movement on others, however, have been addressed in the literature on cycles of protest (*see* della Porta and Tarrow 1986; McAdam 1995). This literature usually refers to movements temporally close to each other, connected from the thematic point of view, and oriented towards a common aim (della Porta and Rucht 2002). In addition, the influence of a sometimes remote past of contemporary mobilisation has, to a certain extent, been described by the scholarship on social movements and memory (for a brief literature review, *see* Zamponi 2013).

In this chapter, we are dealing with a case that stands in the middle between these two poles (on the one hand, the reciprocal influence between contiguous movements and, on the other, the role of remote and mediated pasts in present protest): a case of cross-temporal diffusion between mobilisations that scholars do not define, at least for now, as part of a recognisable and united cycle of protest, but that are so close to each other temporally that individual and collective participation in both is not only possible but likely. This case allows us to examine the interaction of memories of the past with interpretations and decisions in present mobilisations: cultural elaboration of symbols and practices referring to the past and actual material links between different mobilisations are active in the same process. In this context, memories can become one of the channels of a broader process of cross-temporal diffusion between movements.

How does this process work? How does memory participate in the cross-temporal diffusion process between different movements? What role do factors such as collective identities, changes in the social and political context and specific mnemonic projects play in this process?

To answer these questions, we exploited the occasion of two events organised by networks of social movement organisations in Italy: 'Genova 2001–Genova 2011: *Loro La Crisi, Noi La Speranza*' ('They Are the Crisis, We Are the Hope'), organised in Genoa in July 2011, on the tenth anniversary of the anti-G8 protests; and 'Firenze 10–10', organised in Florence in November 2012, on the tenth anniversary of the first European Social Forum (ESF). Being both commemorative moments as well as occasions of debate and interaction, these events provided a good opportunity to contextualise the role of the past in contemporary mobilisation. We conducted individual interviews and a focus group, identifying direct dialogue with the activists as the best tool to address the symbolic aspects of collective action and, in particular, the processes of meaning construction (Blee and Taylor 2002).

The following will first provide details on our conceptual model of cross-temporal diffusion and analytical methods. After a short introduction to the GJM and the anti-austerity mobilisations, we will analyse which continuities and discontinuities with the GJM Italian activists identify in 2011 and 2013.

Cycles of protest, legacies and memories

Diffusion, cycles of protests and movements as movements' outcomes

Movements consist of mobilisation cycles, which produce effects on each other. In the last decades, scholarship on cycles of protest and social-movement outcomes has contributed to a critical reconsideration of the myth of social movements' 'immaculate conception' (Taylor 1989): though large protests often surprise observers, they hardly start from scratch. Mostly, they are rooted in previous mobilisations (McAdam 1995). Diagnostic frames, repertoires of action, collective identities, and forms of organisation are readopted and revised – strategically as well as contingently.

Cycles of protest consist of several mobilisations or episodes (McAdam *et al.* 2007). These mobilisations are connected through various processes, including appropriation and diffusion as well as personal continuities. A mobilisation may trigger new mobilisations, so-called 'spin-off' movements, by creating new opportunities and inspirations or factionalisation (Whittier 2004). It may also have 'spillover' effects in which it influences rather than triggers other mobilisations – both contemporary as well as later ones.

In this chapter, we focus on cycles of protest that are particularly close to each other. The literature on cycles of protest has traditionally been centrally concerned with diffusion across time, that is, diffusion that happens between two different but temporally associated mobilisations. In fact, even if both the Global Justice Movement and the contemporary wave of mobilisation have challenged scholars into analysing more and more cases and mechanisms of cross-spatial (in particular, transnational) diffusion, cross-temporal diffusion is not less important in understanding the development of mobilisation cycles.

Seminal definitions of diffusion reveal that diffusion takes place not only across space but also across time: 'Diffusion ... [is] defined as the acceptance of some specific item, over time, by adopting units – individual, groups, communities – that are linked both to external channels of communication and to each other by means of both a structure of social relations and a system of values, or culture' (Katz 1968). In this vein, McAdam and Rucht emphasise: 'protest makers do not have to reinvent the wheel at each place and in each conflict. ... they often find inspiration elsewhere, in the ideas and tactics espoused and practiced by other activists' (1993: 58). Diffusion should not be analysed as a linear process of transmission; instead, one needs to take into account the relevance of the processes of reception and re-contextualisation of mobilisation frames (Roggeband 2010). The development of a cycle of protest is usually considered the standard setting of cross-temporal diffusion, both in national contexts (della Porta and Tarrow 1986; McAdam 1995) and in cases of transnational diffusion (McAdam and Rucht 1993). McAdam (1995) describes the diffusion process inside a cycle of protest, arguing that 'initiator movements have a culturally catalytic effect on later struggles' and 'latecomers ... [are] creative adapters and interpreters of the cultural "lessons" of the early risers' (McAdam 1995: 229). In particular, he refers to the civil rights movement as the initiator of a long cycle of protest in the United States, with the 'identification of latecomers with the movement that triggered the cycle' – that is, with the Afro-American civil rights movement – expressed through slogans like 'Women Are the Niggers of the World' (McAdam 1995: 233).

But what happens when a process of cross-temporal diffusion takes place between mobilisations that are not currently recognised as part of the same cycle of protest, as in our case? In our hypothesis, we see the coexistence of direct continuities between the different cycles and of a different channel of diffusion, that is, memory. The following sub-section will present this approach, with an emphasis on processes of interpretation with respect to activists' memories.

The past in the present: Diffusion and collective memories

Various mechanisms and dynamics intervene in latent phases and, in general, in the relationship between different cycles of protest. The past goes on having an influence on collective action through different mechanisms, which are situated at different levels and which need to be analysed through conceptual lenses drawing from different scholarship traditions. In this paper, we examine processes of cross-temporal diffusion with a focus on activist memories. Memories constitute a particular channel of diffusion and they do so centrally through linking past and present events. In this way, memories identify legacies of the past – identifying both what is similar now (continuities) as well as what is different (discontinuities).

We have already referred, in our previous work (Zamponi 2013; Daphi 2013), to the role of collective memory in social-movement studies, using, in particular, the sociology of memory based on the seminal work of Maurice Halbwachs (1992). The success of this line of work in the scholarship on contentious politics is primarily connected with the widespread interest in the processes of construction of collective identities and in the symbolic dimension of collective action (Polletta and Jasper 2001; della Porta and Diani 2006; Daphi 2011). Accordingly, the contribution of the literature on memories to our understanding of processes of diffusion is the emphasis on activists' interpretation of reality: memory-approaches highlight that what happened in the past is not an objective fact but a social construction – which selects, highlights and omits events. And, as Halbwachs (1992) emphasises, this past is constructed in a certain present set of social relations. The act of remembering is a narrative act situated in the present, while the object of remembering is in the past. In this vein, memories are not a mere mirror of past events but reveal insights into present sets of interpreting reality.

The present approach to collective memory, rooted in the Durkheimian sociological tradition, tends to focus on 'public discourses about the past as wholes' and on 'narratives and images of the past that speak in the name of collectivities' (Olick 1999: 345). In this context, memory is usually defined as the set of symbols and practices referring to the past, which are shared by a community of people. Analysing memories, hence, allows us access not only to individual interpretations of the past but also to collective ones. In this paper, we are particularly interested in activists' perceptions of continuities and discontinuities with the GJM, together constituting the legacy of the GJM. When we refer to legacies, we refer to something that comes from the past but is situated in the present.

Of course, various collectives' memories play an important role in connecting phases of visibility and intense activity – including public memory. However, in this chapter we focus on memory produced and transmitted by social actors participating in the cycle of protest. We do not investigate public memory and its role in shaping the symbolic environment of mobilisation. We focus more on movement culture than on the public sphere. Notwithstanding this analytical focus, we acknowledge that movements live in a symbolically constructed world and that the borders between what happens inside and outside the movement are never neat and regular. Movement cultures tend to develop in a dialogic and dialectic relationship with the rest of their symbolic environments:

> Rather than looking for distinct frames or ideologies that challengers pit against dominant frames, or assuming that resistant cultural practices are harboured in a detached subversive subculture, dialogic analysis argues that much contention occurs within a discursive field heavily structured by the dominant genres (Steinberg 2002: 213).

In this vein, it is important to note that memory, in this work, plays different roles. It is a *source* of our research, both in its individual (even if socially mediated and constructed) aspects (that is, activists' individual accounts of their movement experience) and in its collective and public aspects (the public commemoration of past protest events). It is an *object* of our research, given that we analyse the organisation of the two anniversaries as specific cases of mnemonic work. It is the *context* of our research, given that we chose to set our interviews in the context of public commemorations, aiming at exploiting the climate of collective reflexivity on the past that this kind of event tends to enhance and, in this way, to collect individual accounts that have a deep connection with the collective movement culture. And finally, memory is a *channel* of diffusion identifying past experiences that are important in mobilisations today, or not. A sense of victory and defeat, for example, associated in the public discourse with a past protest event, can enhance or constrain the use of certain repertoires of protest or organisational forms in contemporary mobilisation.

Methods

In order to analyse the conceptualisations of the past and the processes of meaning-construction referring to the relationship between the GJM and the current wave of mobilisation in Italian activists, we interviewed former activists of the GJM at two points in time: on the one hand, previous to the anniversary of the counter-summit in Genoa (2001) in July 2011 and, on the other hand, shortly after the commemoration event of the first European Social Forum in Florence (2002) in November 2012.

Anniversaries – Context and comparison

The context of these two anniversaries was selected for analysis because commemorative events trigger intensive consideration and discussion of the past. These events provide the space for reflecting on the relevance and meaning of past mobilisations (see details on the events, below). The anniversaries of Genoa and Florence, in particular, provided the chance to evaluate continuities and discontinuities. They also provided the opportunity for establishing relationships and building communication among activists and collective actors that have been active during different cycles of protest.

Hence, interviews conducted closely before or after these events allow extensive insight into perspectives on the role of the past in present mobilisations. Furthermore, we compare two different anniversaries in order to identify changes over time. While only a year separates the two events of commemoration in 2011 and 2012, the context of mobilisations has changed considerably in this time – changes that can be expected to affect activists' memories of the GJM. First, the explosion of the crisis in Italy – which provoked a change in government and the passing of harsh austerity measures dictated by the European Commission – took place between the first and the second set of interviews. Second, the surge of the anti-austerity mobilisations took place in 2011, including the Indignados in Spain, Occupy Wall Street and mobilisations in Italy, for example around the Global Day of Action on 15 October 2011.

Activist interviews and focus group

In order to assess activists' memories, we conducted individual interviews and a focus group. Direct dialogue with activists is a highly useful tool for addressing the symbolic aspects of collective action and, in particular, the processes of meaning-construction (Blee and Taylor 2002). As individual remembering is embedded in a collective's meaning-making, individual interviews provide a way of tapping into collective discourse. While individually retold, memories reflect collective patterns of interpretation – a result of interaction as well as an influence on it. Hence, individual interviews represent a fruitful way of assessing collective memories. Therefore, we treat interviews like 'memory texts' able to 'voice a collective imagination' (Kuhn 2000: 191). Individual stories are linked to a broader (and, of course, intrinsically plural and contentious) collective narrative, taking into account that 'the psychical and the social, if formally distinct, are in practice always intertwined' (Kuhn 2000: 192).

In the context of the tenth anniversary of the counter-summit in Genoa in July 2001, four interviews were conducted a few weeks previous to the events and one focus group was conducted during the anniversary itself. In the context of the tenth anniversary of the European Social Forum in Florence in 2002, Firenze 10+10, we interviewed five activists in the two weeks after the event had taken place.

All interviewees and focus-group participants were active in the main phase of the GJM and took part in the respective commemorative events. These activists were and (partially) still are organised in different groups and movement sectors, even if their itinerary of militancy has been evolving during the decade that separates the events from each other.

In the first group (Genoa anniversary), two of the interviewees belonged to groups of the anti-neoliberal sector – a critical union and an NGO – and are still active in them. The third interviewee was and still is active in a large eco-pacifist organisation, which played a central role in the GJM mobilisations in Italy and remains strongly involved in World Social Forums today. The fourth interviewee is part of the anti-capitalist sector – she was mostly active in a social centre[1] in southern Italy and today remains active in issues of education. Similarly, the participants of the focus group come from different sectors: two of the participants were active in the anti-capitalist sector, one from a social centre in Southern Italy, the other active in the Disobbedienti, a post-autonomous network of social-centre activists, with the youth organisation of Rifondazione Comunista. The first is still active in a Southern social centre, while the other is now active in a small union. The third focus group participant was involved in Rete Lilliput – a network of Catholic and peace groups belonging to the eco-pacifist sector that remains active in the area of fair trade. The fourth was active in the steelworkers' union FIOM (anti-neoliberal sector).

In the second group of interviewees (Florence anniversary), four belonged to the anti-neoliberal sector of the movement in 2002, though with different focuses:

---

1. The expression 'social centre' in Italy refers to squatted, post-autonomous spaces.

one was an activist in the collective of his own school, one was a member of ATTAC Italy, one was an activist of a student union, and the fourth was a spokesperson of a local social forum. The fifth interviewee belonged to the anti-capitalist sector – he was participating in the Disobbedienti network as a member of the youth of Rifondazione Comunista. As with the first group of interviewees, all activists went on participating in politics after 2002. But their itineraries of activism differ: two of them got primarily engaged in the movement to reclaim public water, culminating in the referendum of 2011; one went on as a student union activist; and two participated in party politics with Rifondazione Comunista, although both of them left party politics after the split of Rifondazione in 2008.

Interviewees differ not only with respect to movement sector. They also vary in terms of age, geographical origin and intensity of engagement: In the first group, four activists were in their 20s back in 2001, two in their 30s, and one each in their 40s, 50s and 60s. Two interviewees of the second group were in their late teens in 2002, one was in their 20s, one in their 30s and one in their 40s. These activists had different roles within the GJM mobilisations: some were centrally involved in the organisation of the counter-summits in Genoa and /or the ESF in Florence (less than half), while most participated as attendees, even if in a couple of cases they belonged to organisations involved in the process, either in 2001/2002 or 2011/2012. Furthermore, activists came from different cities and regions in Italy – three in the North, five in the centre, and four in the South.

Method of analysis

In order to identify the definitions and significance of past GJM mobilisations for today, we distinguished between two forms of legacies in the interviews and focus groups. First, we examined what activists consider to be continuities between the GJM and present mobilisations. Second, we looked at the discontinuities activists identify between the GJM and present mobilisations. Then, we compared continuities and discontinuities across time and movement sectors, trying to identify some meaningful variation that could have been produced by what happened between the first and second set of interviews. Furthermore, we tried to link differences in perception and expression of continuities and discontinuities to the different collective identities that activists propose for contemporary mobilisations; and also to connect them to the organisation of the two commemorative events as attempts at mnemonic work.

Introduction of cases

The GJM in Italy

While various labels for the Global Justice Movement circulate (for example, 'alter-globalisation movement', 'no-global movement'), those who study these activists generally agree that the movement comprises a network of groups engaged in collective action of various kinds, based on the shared goal of advancing economic, social, political and environmental justice in opposition to neo-liberal globalisation (della Porta 2007). Along with national neo-liberal policies and transnational corporations, the GJM opposes international institutions such as the World Bank (WB), the International Monetary Fund (IMF) and the World Trade Organization (WTO). A wide range of groups and activists constitute the GJM: its social configurations, sets of mobilising structures (ranging from trade unions to grassroots groups) and geographic locations are heterogeneous (Andretta et al. 2003).

Mobilisations against neo-liberal globalisation started to develop in Italy against the background of the break-up of old alliances between institutional politics, third-sector organisations and social movements. The collapse of the traditional party system in the early 1990s, as well as the turn of the successor of the communist party (PCI) towards more moderate (and neo-liberal) policies, facilitated new alliances and contributed to the development of grassroots trade unions (cf. Reiter et al. 2007). In this context, alliances began to build between third-sector associations – in particular voluntary associations of the Catholic and communist subculture – social-movement organisations of the 1970s and 1980s, radical grassroots groups (centrally, the social centres) and unions (Reiter et al. 2007). Accordingly, unions (both grassroots and institutional) have been centrally involved from the start, while access to institutional politics was low due to marginal alliances with parties.

Networks between these various groups were consolidated and expanded in a series of campaigns and counter-summits in the late 1990s – such as the G7 counter-summit in Naples in 1997. The (successful) protests against the WTO meeting in Seattle in November 1999 crucially furthered this co-operation around the issue of global justice. Launched at the first World Social Forum in Porto Alegre in early 2001, a large coalition bringing together around 800 different groups began to prepare the protests against the G8 summit in Genoa in July 2001 (cf. Reiter et al. 2007). These meetings and protest events not only constituted a crucial organisational infrastructure of the movement (Haug 2013; Rucht and Roth 2008), they were also highly influential with respect to transforming cultural and social meaning, creating and sustaining networks, as well as facilitating mutual learning feelings of belonging (cf. Sewell and McAdam 2001; della Porta 2008)

Among these transformative GJM events, the counter-summit in Genoa in 2001 and the European Social Forum in Florence in 2002 have been particularly influential in Italy. The Genoa counter-summit[2] had strong repercussions for politics in Italy and elsewhere, due to its size (around 300,000 people participated in the march on 21 July), the high level of media attention and the ensuing violence.

---

2. The main protest events took place between 19 and 21 July. The counter-summit started off with a large demonstration, between 10,000 and 20,000 participants, on 19 July. On 20 July, various (direct) actions were organised: activists met in different squares (so-called 'thematic squares') and in different marches. On the last day, 21 July, the largest march, with around 300,000 participants, concluded the official programme of the counter-summit.

While some groups (especially the more radical groups) became less involved after Genoa (centrally, due to disagreements about forms of protest), the coalition grew stronger as a result of the broad denunciation of police violence. The large participation at the first European Social Forum in Florence in 2002 clearly revealed this growth: one million people took part. In terms of participation, the movement peaked with the mobilisations against the war in Iraq on 15 February, with three million participants (though several more radical groups that were still involved in Florence did not participate). After this event the movement – for various reasons that will be discussed below – lost much of its momentum.

Following Andretta *et al* (2003) and della Porta *et al* (2006), three sectors of the GJM can be distinguished: an anti-neoliberal sector, an eco-pacifist sector, and an anti-capitalist sector. The anti-neoliberal sector is composed of groups that aim to control the market through politics; it includes trade unions, political parties, Attac, and other NGOs. The eco-pacifist sector encompasses environmentalist groups and organisations as well as secular and religious peace and solidarity groups. The anti-capitalist sector is composed of more radical groups, ranging from squatters to anarchist and Trotskyist groups that oppose capitalist structures and often refuse negotiations with institutional politics.

The anti-austerity mobilisations in Italy

The first explicitly anti-austerity mobilisation in Italy was the student protest of 2008 (Caruso *et al.* 2010), which included the financial crisis in its discourse, in particular through the slogan '*Noi La Crisi Non La Paghiamo*' ('We Won't Pay For The Crisis'). The protest was the beginning of an intense wave of mobilisation, culminating in the fall of 2010 with a gradual broadening of the claims and of the social composition of the movement. From a students' and researchers' protest against the university reform proposed to the government, mobilisations turned into a complex and broad movement, including the steelworkers' union FIOM, social centres and the committees to reclaim public water. These were kept together by a shared anti-austerity and anti-neoliberal discourse.

In this way, the Italian student movement anticipated some of the characteristics of the anti-austerity movements of 2011, playing a unifying role that cut across political identities and was recognised by a wide spectrum of social and political actors. In this process, the movement went over the thematic borders of education, building a powerful narrative on the social condition of the Italian youth as a 'precarious generation' hit by crisis and austerity and, therefore, sympathetic to a strong demand for radical social and political change (Zamponi 2011).

Despite the policy defeat of the student mobilisation (on 23 December 2010 the parliament approved the Gelmini Law), its addressing of issues of precarity and austerity can be traced in various political events during the spring of 2011, including the national demonstration of women (13 February), the day of action of precarious workers (9 April), the general strike (6 May), the election in Milan and Naples of radical mayors (29 May) and the unexpected victories of the referendums for public water and against the nuclear energy programme (13 June 2011).

For reasons that we have investigated elsewhere, no movement in Italy managed to achieve the level of mass participation, symbolic strength and transversal recognition necessary to develop a general anti-austerity movement. Among these reasons are: the peculiar situation of the national government (which, differently from Spain and Greece, did not include progressive forces, but only Silvio Berlusconi's populist right and Mario Monti's technocratic cabinet); the internal divisions in the movement after the violent outcome of the demonstration of 15 October 2011; and the failed diffusion of the Indignados identity (Zamponi 2012). Nevertheless, 2011, the year of the Arab Spring, of Spanish 15-M and Occupy Wall Street, was a contentious year in Italy as well, with claims and recurrent topics that resonated with those of the global wave of mobilisation (della Porta *et al.* 2012; della Porta and Andretta 2012). The huge number of participants in the Roman demonstration in occasion of the Global Day of Action on 15 October 2011 and the significant participation of students and precarious workers in the European workers' strike of 14 November 2012 show that anti-austerity mobilisations are possible without a united and visible anti-austerity movement. Rather, this mobilisation is characterised by the activism of different social actors, each one significantly contentious in its one field of action. Only in particular situations did these actors manage to participate in a joint protest event, basing their claims on a previously developed shared anti-austerity discourse. The main protagonists of these mobilisations were the student movement, some trade unions (in particular the steelworkers' union FIOM), the committees to reclaim public water and the social centres (della Porta *et al.* 2012). These mobilisations have some continuities and differences with the GJM coalition that will be discussed in the following part of the paper.

Introducing the anniversaries

In commemoration of the July 2001 Genoa counter-summit, an anniversary was organised in 2011 with exhibitions, panel discussions and a large demonstration. Called '*Loro La Crisi, Noi La Speranza*' ('They Are the Crisis, We Are the Hope'), the event was launched in September 2010 with a public document signed by national and Genoan activists. From this document an ambitious agenda emerged for the event, around four main points: 1) the statement that 'We Were Right': the movement denounced, ten years ago, the risks of neo-liberal globalisation, and now the crisis shows that it was a correct forecast; 2) a commemorative element, the will to remember what happened ten years ago (the police violence and so on); 3) the will to bring back to interconnected activism the people who were in Genoa ten years ago; and 4) the existence of wider support, now, thanks to the crisis, for the anti-neoliberal globalisation struggle and the need to organise it. The event, hence, built on the commemoration of the counter-summit of years ago, basing its legitimacy on the fact that the proposers of the initiative were active in that context. Nevertheless, it aimed to play a significant political role in contemporary mobilisation: in fact, as a document circulated by the Italian delegation in the International Council of the World Social Forum in May 2011 states, the event in Genoa was planned as a 'forum in due occasion of the 10th anniversary of the G8 of 2011 and an international assembly for the re-connection of the local and national struggles with the global agenda'. Furthermore, it was a commemorative event with a specific frame on the events of ten years ago, that is, based on the statement 'We Were Right' – so much so that the 'multimedia exhibition on the last 10 years of history' organised in Genoa was titled 'Progetto Cassandra', from the character in Greek mythology who foresaw calamities such as the destruction of Troy but was cursed never to be believed. This is the specific mnemonic project of Genoa 2011.

The event on the occasion of the tenth anniversary of the first European Social Forum, organised in Florence in November 2002, was first planned by former activists of the local Florence Social Forum, which called for a national meeting in February 2012 to launch the event entitled 'Firenze 10+10: Joining Forces For Another Europe'. The international appeal was circulated at the beginning of June, with some common traits to the Genoan document – in particular the 'Cassandra' element, the will to bring back to action activists and networks, the commemoration-based legitimacy of the organisers, and the emphasis on the need for a new transnational interconnection of struggles. Nevertheless, the tone is much more diplomatic: on the one hand because it recognises the existence of struggles and mobilisations around the world that originated outside the WSF setting; on the other hand, it aims to give the event a role of instrumental contributor to a broader process, stating that the process of building a European alternative public space 'is, by all means, building itself', regardless of the organisation of the event. The mnemonic project is very similar to the other, because it links a political goal (the rebuilding of transnational networks of resistance to neo-liberalism) to the legitimacy of the anniversary. Nevertheless, hints can be detected in the launching documents of the two events at how what has happened in the meanwhile (the crisis in Italy and the peak of the anti-austerity mobilisation) is influencing this process of memory construction.

Analysing activist memories

Remembering Genoa and Florence and the GJM more generally

Both events – the counter-summit in Genoa in 2001 as well as the European Social Forum (ESF) in Florence a year later – constitute crucial culmination points of the GJM in Italy and beyond (for example, on repercussions in Germany, see Daphi 2013). Accordingly, both events are identified by activists as crucial moments, revealing the movement's size and strength.

Activists identify the counter-summit in Genoa 2001 as the point of departure of the movement (unlike activists in other countries; *see* Daphi 2013): though in terms of participants it was not the largest,[3] it is identified as a turning point in terms of coalition-building (different groups join forces – many of them previously in conflict), new (horizontal) forms of organisation, repertoires and relations with institutional politics. Emblematic of the centrality of this event is that activists mostly determine which (other) groups form part of the movement with respect to the members of the Genoa Social Forum, the committee that prepared the counter-summit in Genoa in 2001. In particular, activists stress Genoa's role in learning to work together:

> Everybody was feeling free to be part of that, no matter where he/she came from, in terms of personal history, politics, service, political participation and so on. Therefore the movement, no matter how diversified and all the people were coming from different areas, like the Catholics and the unionists, the positive thing was that you did not ... have the pieces fighting one against the other, the challenge for hegemony within this framework and the competition because everyone was sure to have better ideas than the others, this is something which would have killed that ... (2011, focus group, participant 2).

Similarly, the European Social Forum in Florence is presented as an important manifestation of the movement's breadth and strength. Particularly for the youngest activists, the European Social Forum was the *début* of protest politics, the moment in which they first realised the size and the relevance of the movement and felt a sense of belonging to something so big and important.

> More than everything it was the dimension of the community in complex, there were many people that were there for the event itself and not to represent someone, and that was something that in many assemblies later has not happened. ... I had probably a more ingenuous attitude, it was the first time that I saw something so big, the first big national demonstration, in general the first international event in which I participated, but the feeling I had was that, yes, there was the aspect of organisations which constituted an element of supporting structure, but it favoured a much larger participation (2012, interview 9).

In both 2011 and 2012, however, the role of Genoa and Florence in the movement's further development is interpreted differently across movement sectors. Genoa is seen both as a peak, after which the movement started to decline, and as a first event in a longer series of peak events: activists from the anti-capitalist sector consider the movement's decline to have started already with Genoa in 2001, since the reaction to police repression caused splits within the coalition. The strong repression by the state, especially during the counter-summit in Genoa, defeated the movements' efforts and led to internal conflicts about repertoires.

---

3. Demonstrations during the European Social Forum had more participants, as did the demonstrations against the war in Iraq on 15 February 2004.

Activists from eco-pacifist groups and anti-neoliberal groups identify Genoa more as a beginning than an end, defining a later point of decline.

In this vein, Florence is interpreted more positively by the activists from the anti-neoliberal sector than by those having an anti-capitalist background. In the accounts of those coming from the anti-neoliberal sector, Florence is interpreted as something the movement needed in order to overcome the problem of the violence-repression spiral after Genoa:

> The risk was that after Genoa there was an effect similar to the one of 15 October of last year, that was an effect of disintegration, and that fear prevailed. The repressive strategy partly worked: many people I know had a trauma, from that moment on they have never demonstrated any more. Therefore, first of all, it had the function of relaunching and giving continuity to the movement ... To overcome Genoa it meant to overcome the trauma for many people that were in Genoa, it meant also to overcome a completely mistaken image that the media had spread, that was the image of a violent movement, in a nihilistic sense, the image of the black bloc (2012, interview 6).

In contrast, (the) anti-capitalist activist(s) remembers how his sector distanced itself from the ESF and presents it as a strategic choice that is now considered a mistake:

> We, as *Disobbedienti*, made a quite poor choice, that was to have an experience close to the *Fortezza da basso*, but not inside, in order to point out a difference. Everything had to have a high level of contentiousness. We did not understand the fact that we could build the weapons of critique, in the social forum, without needing to have a demonstration every time. We did not get this element, and it was massive, because that demonstration against the war in Florence was huge, even in days in which the debate in the press was particularly strong (2012, interview 8).

The GJM's end

The sectors' different ways of contextualising the events are crucially linked to the question of when and how the GJM's main phase ended. While activists generally agree in considering the main phase of the Global Justice Movement to be over, they disagree about when and how this happened – both across time and across movement sectors. This issue will be picked up in the following sections. Here, however, we want to provide a general overview of the explanations activists provide for the end of the cycle of protest characterised by Genoa and Florence.

All activists mention the failure[4] of the anti-war demonstrations from 2003

---

4. Most activists consider these protests to be failures since they did not stop the war, despite the very high number of participants.

to 2005 as a crucial factor in weakening the movement. Institutional politics' lack of reaction to anti-war claims discouraged activism. In particular, many see the mobilisations against the war in Iraq as demonstrations of the movement's ineffectiveness, along with the divisions within the movement linked to the question of supporting the Prodi government around 2006 (*see* Daphi 2013). In this context, activists mention in particular the choice of Rifondazione Comunista, a party that had played a significant role in the movement, to form a centre-left coalition. This process started in the second half of 2004 and ended with the narrow victory by the centre-left coalition over Silvio Berlusconi's Right in 2006.[5] Two painful years of the Prodi II cabinet followed – a process activists describe as something able to break collective and personal relationships, changing the role of Rifondazione inside the movement and bringing back the old debate on the relationship between movements and parties. The elections provided new opportunities: for the actors supporting the centre-left coalition, the chance to negotiate and obtain some results on the GJM issues; for the ones opposing it, the chance to inherit the whole strength of the movement in opposition to the new government. For both sides, the movement became more a field for the struggle for hegemony of different actors than a common enterprise.

> I would put the breakdown of that experience in the experience of Bertinotti, because that was when we started to fight brutally with each other, impacting on the movement. ... We fought brutally on what the cooperation between party and movement, in the sense of autonomous actors in the movement, meant (2012, interview 5).

Together with the perceived failure of the anti-war mobilisations and the division over the centre-left government, another lethal factor for the movements was, in the activists' perspective, the gradual retreat of some relevant SMOs from their investment in the movement.

> The movement phase ended and the organisations pass to the collection phase. The movement phase could perhaps go on, but at a certain point it was decided that it was over, because a new cycle was opening, a new political phase, with the centre-left coalition. One part said 'let's bring something home from this government', another said 'there are no friendly governments' and saying this it also said to the other part of the movement that there was an incompatibility between them (2012, interview 9).

---

5. In 2005, the decision was passed through the national convention of the party and the regional elections (in which Nichi Vendola, a member of Rifondazione Comunista, became president of Apulia, supported by a broad centre-left coalition). In the same year, it was confirmed at the national centre-left primaries, in which the secretary of Rifondazione, Fausto Bertinotti, was defeated by former Christian-Democrat Romano Prodi. In 2006, the centre-left coalition won the elections, Prodi became Prime Minister and Bertinotti Speaker of the House.

These observations suggest that activists largely consider the GJM's main phase to be over, transiting to a new phase of mobilisation. Exactly how new this phase is considered to be, the following sections will unearth.

Legacies: Continuities between the GJM and anti-austerity mobilisations

Activists in both contexts identify several aspects of the GJM that are continuing. In contrast to what we expected, the identified continuities of the GJM are surprisingly stable over time. Activists in both 2011 and 2012 point, in particular, to continuities in horizontal forms of organisation, in addressing issues of democracy and with respect to co-operation of certain networks of activists.

Horizontal forms of organisation

Activists highlight continuities in forms of horizontal organisations. In this vein, an activist from a social centre stresses the legacy of communication and organisation – in particular, forms of horizontal networking – during the focus group conducted in Genoa in 2011.

> Well, I think that there was a cycle, which consumed itself between 1998 and 2003 in the West. Of course I also think that any movement leaves some things behind. Surely we learned a lot of things about how communication and organization within social movements work ... Forms are repeating themselves, organizational forms, practices, languages and using a lot the social networks and so on, linkages among groups rather than organizations (2011, focus group, participant 1).

Activists interviewed in the context of the Florence anniversary also stress continuities with respect to horizontal organisation in most recent mobilisations. This form of organisation derives from a political culture built on the reciprocal interpenetration of different political and organisational cultures and the ability to keep together collective actors and individuals.

> In my opinion there are many things in common. ... In the explosion of altermondialist movements there were two components that were already co-habitating: a more organised component, formed by organisations that chose a spokesperson and that participated to the process in their own way, but you also had already then a huge quantity of people who followed an *indignados* model, that is 'nobody represents me, I represent myself, I participate to the social forum as an individual' (2012, interview 6).

Democracy

Linked to the emphasis on horizontality, activists also see continuity in addressing the issue of democratic rule, including a critique of representative democracy. In the interviews conducted in the context of the Genoa anniversaries, anti-austerity mobilisations (mainly abroad) are seen as a continuation of the GJM as they (also) address the issue of who gets to decide what and how. In this vein, an activist from a social centre explains during the focus group that democracy is a central aspect of the GJM and links it to present anti-austerity struggles in Greece:

> In my opinion [a] shared goal is democracy inside and outside the movement. I mean not only regarding this leadership thing – and this is a problem which is felt by everybody – the point is how we decide things inside the movement. This is something ineluctable in the sense that this has always existed. The issue of democracy, of course also towards the outside dimension. The G8 were, they were also deciding the Greek events, the political economies and so on. Who decides this, how and against who (2011, focus group, participant 2).

Similarly, activists interviewed in 2012 emphasise that the GJM's addressing of issues of democracy is very similar in such recent mobilisations such Occupy Wall Street.

> Now Occupy Wall Street says 'We are the 99 per cent, you are the 1 per cent.' In Genoa we said: 'we are 6 billions, you are 8 assholes', the logic is exactly the same. I see an element of continuity between the two points. ... The cycle that was opened by the experience of the mass irruption of 2001, Seattle, then Genoa, and so on, I don't think it is over and another has opened. I think that there has been the dissemination of a critical culture. ... There is no rupture, there is a dissemination, that now, in Italy, has to deal with the economic crisis, in a totally different condition than 2001 (2012, interview 8).

Continuing networks of co-operation

Activists also point to continuities with respect to activist networks (in particular, those connected to the anti-neoliberal sector). Certain activist groups continue the co-operation built in the context of the GJM in present mobilisations, especially in the campaign against the privatisation of water.

In the context of the Genoa anniversary, for example, an activist from the anti-neoliberal sector emphasises that in Genoa, different groups learned to work together, adding that such a coalition was achieved again in the recent campaign against the privatisation of water:

> Everybody learned before, in 2001 that, if he ... likes to work very well about his specific thing, the specific aim to win, to go ahead, was possible only [by] staying with other, because it was impossible to change the situation only in

its specific local situation, specific situation, everything was international and because the globalization changed completely the world, ... so we decided we need to stay together if we everybody want to obtain some result in his specific sphere, this was the must ... We, [which] means all the different groups together were able to ... to take one million four hundred thousand signatures to defend public water. ... the people were the same people that were in Genoa and after in Florence. And it was an occasion where all these people came out another time together and on the local dimension (2011, interview 2).

In the context of the Florence anniversary, as well, activists argue that the water movement developed directly from a sector of the GJM, recycling its organisational infrastructures (while following an evolution towards a pragmatic and locally rooted single-issue struggle, *see* below):

Furthermore, from there some projects were born, that indisputably went on in the following years. The project on common goods, on water as a symbol of common goods, was born in Florence, and it developed starting from there. ... Most part of the group against the privatisations of the [Florence] social forum, it was called 'WTO group', became in fact the embryo that built the first water forum, that then drafted the first regional bill against the privatisation of water, then, with a document signed together with others, it formed in Tuscany the Italian Forum of Movements for Water, then the national bill and the referendum. There has been a transformation, the social forum model became something else. At the end of the day the model of the Italian Forum of the Movements for Water is fundamentally a development of that one (2012, interview 6).

Legacies: Discontinuities in 2011 and 2012

While the quotations above show that activists emphasise several continuities, all point to a caesura: the movement as it was in 2001 and 2002 with the counter-summit in Genoa (and the events leading up to it) and the European Social Forum in Florence is now over. While activists have different views on why this is the case – also across time – most activists agree on a main difference from present mobilisations: mobilisations today are more local and concrete as activists returned to their groups, issues and places. However, there are significant differences with respect to how this change is evaluated.

Similarities 2011/2012: Mobilisations now more local and concrete

According to the activists, the processes of localisation and of focusing on concrete issues rather than broad themes has a structural reason: the economic crisis focuses the public debate on materialist topics and calls for urgent mobilisation. On the other hand, GJM activists' political reorientation is also seen to play a large role in this development: starting from the decline of the GJM in Italy, they say, activists leaving the movement brought back home the baggage of knowledge and experience produced in the mobilisation and invested in local, concrete and pragmatic struggles, most notably the movement against the privatisation of water. This reorientation is crucially linked to activists' critical reflections on the inefficacy of the strategy of the GJM, which, while able to break the unanimous support for neo-liberalism in public opinion, failed when engaged in a specific struggle with a specific goal (stopping the war in Iraq). As a consequence, activists left the search for huge demonstrations and media attention on global topics, focusing more on locally rooted issues and pragmatic struggles.

In this vein, all of the activists interviewed in the context of the Genoa anniversary see the main difference today in localisation: mobilisations today are more locally rooted and divided as activists returned to their groups and places:

> Now the strongest, and the most interesting and the most participated [in] campaign, mobilisation, fight, you can find it at the local level and mainly promoted by local coalitions, you know, local movements or specific movements which were born to deal with that question. And they are spread all over Italy and most of them are really concentrated on their issue and they have not a national perspective. ... Which is very important because all the local struggles are the ones, who are able, for example, to reach the citizen (2011, interview 3).

> Therefore between 2007 and 2010 this conflict became much more rooted, also in its transnational form. For I think that some things repeat themselves, for example in Greece, or with respect to the environmental issues, but the forms of linkages that the no global phase had, and the forms of comprehensibility which allowed the big localized fights to take place simply did not repeat themselves (2011, focus group, participant 1).

Similarly, activists interviewed in 2012 underline the territorial rootedness of present mobilisations, in particular, the water movement:

> All those activists, when the movement as a national movement entered in a crisis, went back in their territories, but bringing with them the consciousness and the acquisitions of that experience. ... Those are the years in which this country sees loads of territorial struggles, many of which linked to environmental issues. .... And of all these movements, I think that the only one which has managed to build, on the base of a specific issue, a strong territorial rootedness and also a big national struggle, it was the water movement, that then it arrived to the referendum. ... The second phase was ... a retreat but also a concrete territorial construction of alternatives on specific issues, I'm referring also to the No Tav movement, to the struggles related to energy, etc. (2012, interview 7).

Differences 2011/2012: Distinguishing opinion vs material, global vs European and pessimism

While activists interviewed in 2011 and 2012 agree that processes of localisation constitute a major difference between GJM mobilisations and those today, they frame and evaluate this change differently.

Opinion vs material

First, activists interviewed in 2012 distance themselves more clearly from GJM's immaterial 'opinion' approach (a term which can only be found among anti-capitalist activists in 2011). The GJM opinion movement is represented by the activists as something in radical opposition to the current social and political phase, from different points of view. The activists argue that the crisis has pushed social movements towards a more down-to-earth attitude, showing the practical effects of neo-liberal globalisation and calling for urgent and radical action. The GJM, conversely, is considered an opinion movement, that is, a wave of mobilisation linked more with ethical values of justice than with the everyday problems of protestors. In this vein, the GJM is attributed a discursive nature composed of three different factors: ethical values as motivation to action; opinion-sharing as level of commitment; and proposal of alternatives in the public discourse as goal. Accordingly, the main goal of the GJM, which the activists consider achieved, was the break-up of the unanimous consent around neo-liberal globalisation that characterised the 1990s:

> In those years, the so-called *pensée unique* was even stronger than now. The idea not only of conquering a part of public opinion, but even to have the chance to say that there were alternative thoughts, recipes and concepts in respect to the ones imposed by the dominant dogma, it was already considered a success.

In particular, some activists tend to represent their past activity in the GJM as something romantically far from their concrete daily life and more connected to big global topics:

> The school collective had a platform that was frankly exaggerated for a students' representative: it went from stopping the war in Afghanistan to everything could come to someone's mind. ... Then I was interested above all in Middle East, peace ... I followed in particular topic related to Turkey, the Kurdish question, the Ocalan case (2012, interview 5).

In the same vein, some of the interviewees characterise the period of the GJM as a time in which the harsh reality of the crisis had yet to present itself and activists were more prone to intellectual speculation and delusional suggestions. They represent the development of mobilisation between the two cycles of protest as a moment of awakening, a passage from a phase characterised by ideological analysis and theorisation – sometimes, according to them, even out of touch with reality – to a period in which the materiality of the crisis has forced everyone to be more concrete and in which social elements are more important than ideological ones. The following quotation is one of the most brutal examples of this kind of self-criticism:

> Watching it today, unfortunately, the protest against globalisation had more an ethical characterisation than a real fulfilment in the youth question, and so also the topic of precarity was born inside that movement, but it didn't have an element of subjectification. ... [It was] more ethical-political than [based on] a social rootedness. ... The most critical point it was the lack of the tendency to choose pragmatic goals and pursue them. ... Today, instead, there are assemblies in the factories, in the schools, and so one, there is a totally different situation. ... A part of the movement, in its analysis of work, then, made the apology of autonomous work and flexibility. I had read 'The End of Work' by Jeremy Rifkin and that influenced my point of view. Workers didn't exist anymore in our head, not only blue-collars, but actually the young steelworker. Precarity was still considered partly an opportunity. ... In that phase there were also some analyses, post-70s, in particular on labour topics, that didn't take into account reality. Now everyone has to take reality into account. This is the difference (2012, interview 8).

In contrast to the GJM, the activists interviewed in 2012 represent the current events as a more serious, extreme and almost tragic phase, in which there is no more space and time for ethical considerations and opinion-building. Instead, there is an urgent need for action and solutions. The activists tend to use words like 'drastic', 'extreme', 'radical', 'urgency', 'rupture'. This 'urgency' is interpreted as one of the main factors determining a shift from the 'altruistic' approach of the GJM to a more materialistic point of view.

> In 2001 in Genoa there was a strong youth component, even an angry one, the anxiety for the future did not arrive overnight. ... But you had also a strong dimension ... of Western guilt, for the fact that my well-being was linked to the exploitation of other people like me in the rest of the world, therefore there was a much more 'altruistic' dimension. This thing from 2008 on disappears (2012, interview 9).

> The difference now is that the crisis of the model has become extreme, and therefore there is no more room for mediation. ... The mobilisation will need to be much more radical, not in terms of forms, but surely in the urgency of change. Today there is no more room for a governance of the present phase that tries to keep together stuff. Either there is a rupture, [I'd say] of the revolutionary kind, if the word wasn't so used up... (2012, interview 7).

Global vs European

Second, activists interviewed in 2012 emphasise that contemporary mobilisations left behind the GJM's emphasis on global analyses of problems. In the interviews conducted in the context of the Genoa anniversary in 2011, several activists across all sectors still identify global thinking as a central legacy of the movement. In this vein, an activist from a social centre argues that, while a new phase of mobilisation began, the global thinking coined in the GJM continues in the context of the European MayDay, migrant struggles and student movements:

> And so, this does not mean that the political experience died, completely died in Italy but maybe starts a new phase, a new era, and a new experience was born. What still remained from Genoa was the need to think about in transnational context, to think about politics in international context. And for example the experience of the mayday ... there was this [initiative] sometime to build up the European process. And, also about the migrant struggle there was a transnational build-up, collective and a network of experiences that makes some really interesting action, also. Also about students there is student struggle there is the idea, the need that you have to be, you have to think about in a European, at least European context (2011, interview 4).

> So I would say that the movement certainly left a legacy behind it, for example regarding the more transnational character of these protests, rather than international. Because there is more of a global relation, between global and local, and less a dimension of international organization (2011, focus group, participant 1).

In 2012, in contrast, activists largely consider transnational analysis and organising to be over. The focus on more concrete, material issues results in less attention to international solidarity and a lack of a global point of view in contemporary movements. Activists do not deny the existence of a transnational wave of mobilisation but they tend to criticise the lack of an organisational culture of transnational protest in the anti-austerity mobilisation, pointing out how, in comparison with the GJM, communication has now been substituted for organisation. This is not meant in the sense of communication being a useful tool for organisation (*cf.* Mattoni 2012). Instead, communication is understood to hide a lack of organisation, especially at the transnational level. According to some activists, contemporary movements are very good at representing their struggle as united, while they do not achieve enough in terms of concrete co-ordination. The transnational nature of the current wave, according to activists, has shifted from the level of real co-ordination to one of representation: activists feel more engaged in constructing *ex post* the narrative of a united transnational mobilisation than in building an actually shared agenda.

There were movement infrastructures which allowed protest, ... the social forums were tools thanks to which relationships were established, sometimes among activists, mostly among organisations, small, medium and big ones, which allowed then to communicate one common mobilisation. At the student level we had the definitional of international days of action, like the 17 November of 2004 and 2005. ... Now the international dimension of the struggles is very disintegrated, without legitimate places that belong to everyone ... the construction of international mobilisations is not a participated construction at the international level. There is the lack of a supra-national level. ... People try *a posteriori* to construct a unity of sense, because there are struggles around the world, and the fact that we communicate more quickly and better allows to see everything as connected. ... The international dimension doesn't exist in actual terms, there is potentially and it is narrated. ... (2012, interview 9).

In fact, activists interviewed in 2012 also regard the present mobilisations' focus on European issues critically as a step backwards from the global conscience of the GJM and consider it a case of Eurocentrism:

I think that the economic discourse now is totally Eurocentric, while at the time of the social forum it was really a global discourse. Now when we talk about crisis, we do it above all from the point of view of Europe (2012, interview 6).

Then we opposed the conditionality mechanisms of the IMF, now we oppose the conditionality mechanisms of the troika to access loan packages, it is exactly the same mechanism. ... The truth is that since then we have always tried to put the rights of the people of the Global South in relationship with ours, always saying that they're two sides of the same coin, that either you manage to put into place a mechanism of global justice or there won't be justice for anyone.

Pessimism

Third, activists interviewed in 2012 are more pessimistic about mobilisation potentials than are activists interviewed in 2011, as some of the quotes above indicate. Present capacities to build a broad and powerful movement are considered very low in 2012, while in 2011 some activists still utter hopeful expectations in this regard. This change is most clearly illustrated with respect to activists' view of the anniversaries of Genoa and Florence: while in 2011 about half consider the anniversary of Genoa to be a chance to rebuild a broad movement, in 2012 none of the activists interviewed express such expectations.

Activists evaluate the anniversary in Genoa in 2011 differently. Activists from more moderate groups of the anti-neoliberal and eco-pacifist sectors see the event predominantly as an opportunity to get together again and renew some of the energy of working together that was present during the time of the counter-summit in Genoa in 2001. In this way, the anniversary is presented as a possible new cycle of mobilisation after a phase of less joint activity. The ten years' distance from past events (and clashes between groups) is seen as a help in pacifying conflicts within the movement and bringing the different groups together again. In addition, the time (of financial crisis) is seen to have proven the GJM right.

> So, in July in Genoa we'll organise the 10th anniversary of Genoa 2001. And we try to put all together ... this passage Genoa July is very important, because if we organise something strong, we can go together and so on next year. I don't know if we succeed, we can succeed to organise a forum in July without any battle against the, inside us. If we succeed it's possible that we propose Italy as the next venue for the [social forum] (2011, interview 1).

> Ok... I tell you an important thing. We are organizing the meeting ten years after .... 10 years ago in Genoa, we said exactly what will ... be happening in the future. ... they didn't believe us and now the situation is terrible. ... We said ... ok... We were right ten years ago ... [it] is absolutely necessary to link another time between us because we must stop this terrible run to the disaster of the world and of Italy. ... It's not so easy, because Genoa left a lot of scars, ... [but] I think that we will be able to put together now, after ten years (2011, interview 2).

Activists from the anti-capitalist sector, instead, have a more sceptical stance towards the anniversary event in 2011. They underline the reductionist pitfalls of commemoration and emphasise the need for critical reflection and concrete campaigning.

> There is [the] idea to commemorate. ... a lot of stuff changed and I don't know ... actors changed so it would be interesting if on this commemoration we can talk about common points and differences. But, if we are just talking about how it was nice, how it was ten years ago, when we were younger, I mean, I think that is not very useful for anybody. Not for us, neither for younger people that will not have a chance to understand well what is going on now (2011, interview 4).

> I think there is a sort of obscuring risk in the ... anniversaries, especially those with round numbers like 10 years, 20 years, and I think these are mechanisms which are not very connected to reality ... I mean, I was fearing a commemorative and reductionist dynamic and I have to say that until now my impression is ... 50/50. ... I think it is very strange that we did not refer yet to other present situations like the Val di Susa issue and ... the other thing is that the final judgment for many of the protesters of 2001 is now pending ... I still have not hear any single word about it (2011, focus group, participant 1).

Activists interviewed in 2012, instead, mostly consider the anniversary of Florence a failure. Only the oldest activists, also being the most involved in the organisation of Firenze 10+10, see the anniversary event also as a positive experience, mostly in building and strengthening networks across Europe and useful to address the lack of international co-ordination and the Eurocentrism we described before.

All the activists, however, share the impression that the anniversary events – both with reference to the anniversary in Genoa and the one in Florence – failed. This failure is largely attributed, on the one hand, to the lack of links between activists of different cycles of mobilisations within Italy. In particular, activists refer to the lack of participation of people 'who are active now' – mainly with respect to the Italian anti-austerity mobilisations – in the anniversaries. From the point of view of some activists, there is a significant difference between the people and groups who coined the GJM and those of the current wave of protest – and the anniversaries, while situated in the latter phase, were mainly promoted by the former actors:

> I found disappointing Genoa last year, because it was almost fundamentally based on memory and nostalgia, partly comprehensible, because the emotions, both positive and negative, felt in Genoa, are incomparable. But to me it seemed really only watching backward, and stop. ... Both Genoa and Florence have been promoted by networks that certainly belonged to the movement of Genoa and Florence but that today are not part of the main struggles, and, vice versa, some movements did not participate, or did marginally, to those events, for example, the No Tav movement, the territorial struggles, etc., they were in Florence but not in Genoa. Those events have been built mostly by who were there then, while for me they should have been built by those who are active now, because they are the only ones that can say how much of today's experiences comes from then (2012, interview 9).

> The same structures which participated to that experience are not protagonists of these phase, or some are, but some aren't. Today there is more an element of subjectification, for example, of students, if I had to look at what's happening now [the anniversary events in Florence and Genoa made] no sense. None. They were less or more the same structures of the previous time, when they have a massive rootedness in society, now they don't have it any more. It made no sense to do it. It could make more sense to have a convergence point among those who are active in Italy (2012, interview 8).

Bringing together mostly groups active in the past, the anniversaries are described as something artificial – a description that is also linked to the protests on 15 October 2011. In fact, some activists tend to refer to the Italian demonstration linked to the 'United For Global Change' mobilisation launched by the Spanish 15-M movement in connection with the initiatives for the anniversaries of Genoa and Florence, seeing in these events a similarity in the attempt to impose an artificial framework of mobilisation to the movement. Such comparison is based on the fact that, in both occasions, they see attempts to artificially produce specific elements of mobilisation: in the former case, they see the attempt to forcefully recreate in the Italian context a framework coming from elsewhere in space (importing into Italy the model of the Spanish 15-M or Occupy Wall Street), while in the latter they see the same mechanism happening in time (importing, to 2011, the model of 2001). Some activists are particularly concerned with the spontaneity of movements and with the necessity to avoid forcing on them external models. Furthermore, 15 October partially reinforced this fear: as we have briefly discussed elsewhere (della Porta and Zamponi 2013), how, in the controversial political debate that led to the 15 October demonstration in Rome, there were tensions between, on the one hand, the actors who had been in the first row in the GJM and returned with the anniversary and, on the other hand, the protagonists of the anti-austerity protests of 2008–10.

> I consider Genoa one of the milestones of my political history, but I don't think that we should spend years remaking Genoa, let's build something else. ... I hope that 15 October made a clean sweep, I don't say this because I liked that day, I found it obviously devastating, but I hope that everyone understood that that day was exactly the result of constructing artificial mobilisations, in which deeply different interests and dynamics pretend to build a common space to let everyone have its own, and the result was the total explosion. ... 15 October was the result of an artificial attempt to reconstruct a dynamic that wasn't into place. And I hope that everyone understood that these things shouldn't be done any more (2012, interview 7).

On the other hand, the failure is attributed to the inability to connect, not only with activists from different generations of activism but also with those from a different mobilisation experience abroad – in particular, Occupy and Indignados activists. Some interviewees, especially, stress the incommensurability between the activists belonging to the GJM and those engaged in the Occupy/Indignados struggle, based on a fundamental difference in terms of movement culture and structure of participation. In fact, the Occupy activists are considered by some of the interviewees as the carriers of a culture of total refusal of organised forms, with whom it is impossible to communicate for someone who grew up inside the organisational structures of the GJM:

> In my opinion Firenze 10+10 was quite a failure. ... I've seen exactly this incapacity to meet, between those who came from yesterday, that are those who have been bringing forth their projects for a long time, and those who arrive now, with Occupy. I had a guest in my house, a Dutch guy who got politicised through Occupy, etc. and we are unable to communicate, we have no political meeting point of any kind, he refers to a network of assemblies, etc. of Occupy, which I blatantly ignore, while I refer to experience that I've

known for 10 years which he blatantly ignores. In my opinion this was visible, in the sense that …there was little communication between these two separate worlds … (2012, interview 5).

Conclusion

In this contribution we aimed to illuminate the recent explosion of anti-austerity mobilisations with a focus on temporal diffusion between cycles of protests. In particular, we analysed activists' collective memories in order to explore such diffusion. Activists' memories, we argued, constitute a crucial channel through which diffusion takes place between cycles of contention – especially across time. In memories, continuities and discontinuities of present and past mobilisations are constructed – so-called movement legacies – which crucially connect different phases of mobilisation.

Our analysis of interviews with activists of the GJM did not only show that commemorative events are an important opportunity for activists' reflection on the past. Crucially, it revealed the relative permanence of collective memories: despite the different political and social contexts in which interviews were conducted (before the anti-austerity protests in 2011 and afterwards in 2012), memories of the GJM and its perceived legacies change only in a limited way. Activists evaluate the legacies of the GJM in present mobilisations similarly, with respect to both continuities and discontinuities: they identify continuities mainly with respect to organisational structures – in particular, horizontal forms of organisation – as well as critical culture – in particular regarding issues of representation – as well as continuing activist networks. Discontinuities are predominantly identified with respect to the more local and concrete nature of present mobilisation, as opposed to the more global framing of the GJM mobilisations.

While similarities are predominant, the comparison also revealed significant changes in activists' interpretations of the GJM's legacies, which differ with the evolution of a cycle of protest across time. In particular, the emphasis on the GJM being an opinion movement is much less pronounced in the earlier interviews, while the difference between anti-austerity struggles and more global campaigning comes to the foreground between 2011 and 2012. Activists interviewed in the context of the anniversary of the counter-summit in Genoa in 2011 consider building broad coalitions and thinking globally as crucial continuities of the GJM. In contrast, those interviewed a year later in the context of the anniversary of the European Social Forum in 2012 – and a year that had seen several anti-austerity mobilisations – emphasise differences in this regard: present mobilisations are much more concrete and local today. Accordingly, the chances (and desirability) of rebuilding a broad coalition as in the days of Genoa and Florence are seen much more pessimistically than in 2011.

This difference seems to have much to do with the changed social and political context. In fact, in July 2011 the acute phase of the Italian fiscal crisis was still in its initial phase (the turning point is usually set on 11 July, when the spread between the interest rates of German and Italian bonds arrived at 300), Silvio Berlusconi's cabinet was still in power and the mobilisations of 15 October had not yet taken place. The set of events linked to the explosion of the financial crisis seems to have made activists become, sensibly, more pessimistic. The implementation of austerity measures dictated by the European Central Bank (ECB) and the difficult development of anti-austerity protests are central reasons for this more negative view. The development of this pessimistic perspective had the paradoxical effect that the anniversaries, which, in 2011 were welcomed with mixed views but with a general favour, even by the most radical activists, in 2012 are strongly criticised even by their own organisers. Analogously, the acute phase of the crisis enhances the divergence between a global and altruistic GJM and a nation-centred and concrete anti-austerity movement. In this vein, activists' accounts are contradictory in describing the continuity between GJM and anti-austerity protest in terms of organisational culture. At the same time, activists criticise the anniversaries as unable to attract contemporary activists due to different organisational cultures. This has most probably to do with the fact that Italy did not see the presence of a unified anti-austerity movement in a similar form to the Spanish 15-M. Accordingly, when people mention 'Indignados' or 'Occupy', they do not refer to the protagonists of Italian anti-austerity mobilisations but to activists coming from abroad or to members of the small and isolated attempt to build an Italian version of the Spanish movement, characterised by very specific elements in terms of organisational culture.

In addition to some differences in memories across time, the analysis also revealed different memories of the GJM across movement sectors. In this respect, perspectives on continuities and discontinuities of the GJM perceptibly differed between the more moderate and radical groups. With respect to the anniversary, for example, more moderate activists from the anti-neoliberal and eco-pacifist sector interviewed in 2011 see in the anniversary a chance to join cross-sectorally. This is linked to the fact that these activists see the reason for the movement's decline primarily in the lack of co-operation between groups from different movement sectors. Anti-capitalist activists interviewed in 2011 are more sceptical about the anniversary, as they attribute the decline to fundamental conflicts about repertoires and forms of organisation. In this vein, we also showed that activists from the anti-capitalist sector stress the necessity for concrete action and campaigns in anniversaries and contemporary mobilisation much more than activists from other sectors do, implying that not enough attention has been paid to them in the past.

Based on these findings, this contribution more generally showed that current mobilisations are connected to and draw on the past in several ways. More specifically, it revealed that memories provide activists with crucial interpretative frameworks for understanding mobilisations and demarcating them from others. The relative permanence of activists' memories in particular points to the fact that memories are not only socially constructed; they also provide relatively stable interpretative schemes that affect social interaction.

In this way, memories have been shown to channel diffusion: memory is a crucial element in diffusing forms of organisation and issues addressed across waves of mobilisations. This is because memories crucially shape how elements of diffusion are interpreted: were the forms of organisation, frames, and repertoires that were employed successes worth continuing or aberrations better not to pursue? Hence, the contribution also showed that movements produce effects on later cycles of mobilisation, outcomes, so to say, through memory.

In fact, such interpretations – as this analysis unearthed – are group-specific, both to the movement at large (across time) as well as to specific sectors within the movement. Memories, at least in our case, are influenced by social and political change, given the visible relationship between the acceleration in crisis, austerity and protest that took place between the two groups of interviews and the growing stress on the discursive nature of the GJM and on the sense of urgency of the contemporary situation in activists' accounts. However, at the same time, there is a persistent narrative of the GJM, probably linked to the centrality of the story of Genoa in the discourse of the Italian social-movement landscape in the last decade.

Accordingly, this contribution reveals more generally the role of the social appropriation of the past (Harris 2006) in social-movement dynamics. In this vein, further research on memory as a symbolic resource and outcome as well as on the symbolic relationship between different cycles of protest is required. In addition, we hope to have shown that analysing movement memories is a fruitful way in which to explore processes of diffusion. Further research is needed on the interaction of memory work and diffusion. Furthermore, this contribution calls for an approach to memory that systematically considers the conditions that constrain and enable its construction. This seems particularly accurate in cases of short-term memory like the present case, in which the persistence of mnemonic representations is evaluated over a period of one year.

References

Andretta, M., della Porta, D., Mosca, L. and Reiter, H. (2003) *No Global – New Global: Identität und Strategien der Antiglobalisierungsbewegung*, Frankfurt and New York: Campus Verlag.

Bird, S. E. and Dardenne, R. W. (1988) 'Myth, chronicle, and story: exploring the narrative qualities of news', in J. W. Carey (ed.) *Media, Myths and Narratives: Television and the press*, London: Sage, pp. 67–88.

Blee, K. M. and Taylor, V. (2002) 'Semi-structured interviewing in social movement research', in B. Klandermans and S. Staggenborg (eds) *Methods of Social Movement Research*, Minneapolis, MN: University of Minnesota Press.

Caruso, L., Giorgi, A., Mattoni, A. and Piazza, G. (2010) *Alla ricerca dell'Onda. I nuovi conflitti nell'istruzione superior*, Milano: Franco Angeli.

Cohen, A. A., Adoni, H. and Bantz, C. R. (1990) *Social Conflict and Television News*, Newbury Park: Sage.

Daphi, P. (2011). 'Soziale Bewegungen und Kollektive Identität. Forschungsstand und Forschungslücken', *Forschungsjournal Soziale Bewegungen*, 24 (4).

— (2013) 'Collective identity across borders: bridging local and transnational memories in the Italian and German Global Justice Movements', in L. Cox and C. Flesher Fominaya (eds), *Understanding European Movements: New social movements, global justice struggles, anti-austerity protest*, London and New York: Routledge.

della Porta, D. (2007) 'The Global Justice Movement in context', in D. della Porta (ed.) *The Global Justice Movement: Cross-national and transnational perspectives*, Boulder, CO and London: Paradigm.

— (2008) 'Eventful protest, global conflicts', *Distinktion: Scandinavian journal of social theory* 9 (2): 27–56.

— (2012) 'Mobilizing against the crisis, mobilizing for "another democracy": comparing two global waves of protest', *Interface: A journal for and about social movements* 4 (1): 274–77.

della Porta, D. and Andretta, M. (2012) *Il conflitto dei lavoratori nell'ultimo anno del governo Berlusconi*, paper presented at the SISP conference in Rome, 13–15 September.

della Porta, D. and Diani, M. (2006) *Social Movements: An Introduction*, Blackwell Publishing.

della Porta, D. and Rucht, D. (2002) 'The dynamics of environmental campaigns', *Mobilization* 7 (1).

della Porta, D. and Tarrow, S. (1986) 'Unwanted children: Political violence and the cycle of protest in Italy. 1966–1973', *European Journal of Political Research* 14 (6): 607–32.

della Porta, D. and Zamponi, L. (2013) 'Protest and policing on October 15th, global day of action: the Italian case', *Policing and Society* 23 (1): 65–80.

della Porta, D., Andretta, M., Mosca, L. and Reiter, H. (2006) *Globalization from Below: Transnational activists and protest networks*, Minneapolis, MN: University of Minnesota Press..

della Porta, D., Mosca, L. and Parks, L. (2012) 'Same old stories? Trade unions and protest in Italy in 2011', *OpenDemocracy* [online], 11 October.
Edy, J. A. (2006) *Troubled Pasts: News and the collective memory of social unrest*, Philadelphia: Temple University Press.
Graeber, D. (2011) 'Occupy Wall Street rediscovers the radical imagination', *Guardian* 25 September, http://www.guardian.co.uk/commentisfree/cifamerica/2011/sep/25/occupy-wall-street-protest (accessed 23 February 2012).
Halbwachs, M. (1992) *On Collective Memory*, Chicago, IL: University of Chicago Press.
Harris, F. C. (2006) 'It takes a tragedy to arouse them: collective memory and collective action during the civil rights movement', *Social Movement Studies* 5 (1): 19–43.
Haug, C. (2013) 'Organizing spaces: meeting arenas as a social movement infrastructure between organization, network, and institution', *Organization Studies* 43.
Katz, E. (1968) 'Diffusion (interpersonal influence)', in D. L. Shils (ed.) *International Encyclopedia of the Social Sciences*, London: Macmillan and Free Press, 4, pp. 78–85.
Kuhn, A. (2000) 'A journey through memory', in S. Radstone (ed.) *Memory and Methodology*, Oxford: Berg, pp. 179–98.
McAdam, D. (1995) '"Initiator" and "spin-off" movements: diffusion processes in protest cycles', in M. Traugott (ed.) *Repertoires and Cycles of Collective Action*, Durham, NC: Duke University Press.
McAdam, D. and Rucht, D. (1993) 'The cross-national diffusion of movement ideas', *Annals of the American Academy of Political and Social Science*, 528 (1): 56–74.
McAdam, D., Tarrow, S. and Tilly, C. (2001) *Dynamics of Contention*. Cambridge Studies in Contentious Politics, Cambridge and New York: Cambridge University Press.
— (2007) 'Comparative perspectives on contentious politics', in M. Lichbach and A. Zuckerman (eds) *Ideas, Interests and Institutions: Advancing theory in comparative politics*, Cambridge: Cambridge University Press 2007.
Maeckelbergh, M. (2012) 'Horizontal democracy now: from alterglobalization to occupation', *Interface: A journal for and about social movements* 4 (1): 207–34.
Mattoni, A. (2012) *Media Practices and Protest Politics: How precarious workers mobilise*, Farnham, Ashgate.
Olick, J. K. (1999) 'Collective memory: the two cultures', *Sociological Theory* 17 (3), 333–48.
Polletta, F. (2006) *It Was Like a Fever: Storytelling in protest and politics*, Chicago, IL: University of Chicago Press.
Polletta, F. and Jasper, J. M. (2001) 'Collective identity and social movements', *Annual Review of Sociology* 27: 283–305.

Reiter, H., Andretta, M., della Porta, D. and Mosca, L. (2007) 'The Global Justice Movement in Italy', in D. della Porta (ed.), *The Global Justice Movement: Cross-National and transnational perspectives*, Boulder, CO and London: Paradigm, pp. 52–78.

Roggeband, C. (2010) 'Transnational networks and institutions: how diffusion shaped the politicization of sexual harassment in Europe', in R. K. Givan, K. M. Roberts, and S. A. Soule (eds) *The Diffusion of Social Movements: Actors, mechanisms, and political effects*, Cambridge: Cambridge University Press.

Rucht, D. and Roth, R. (2008). 'Globalisierungskritische Netzwerke, Kampagnen und Bewegungen', in R. Roth and D. Rucht (eds), *Die sozialen Bewegungen in Deutschland seit 1945. Ein Handbuch*, Frankfurt/Main: Campus-Verl.

Sewell, W. H. Jr. and McAdam, D. (2001). 'It's about time: temporality in the study of social movements and revolutions', in R. Aminzade (ed.) *Silence and Voice In the Study Of Contentious Politics*, Cambridge Studies in Contentious Politics, Cambridge and New York: Cambridge University Press, pp. 89–125.

Smith, J. (2012) 'Connecting social movements and political moments: bringing movement building tools from global justice to Occupy Wall Street activism', *Interface: A journal for and about social movements* 4 (2): 369–82.

Steinberg, M. W. 2002. 'Toward a more dialogic analysis of social movement culture', in D. S. Meyer, N. Whittier, and B. Robnett (eds) *Social Movements: Identity, culture, and the state*, Oxford: Oxford University Press, pp. 208–25.

Taylor, V. A. (1989) 'Social movement continuity: the women's movement in abeyance', *American Sociological Review* 54: 761–75.

Whittier, N. (2004) 'The consequences of social movements for each other', in D. A. Snow, S. A. Soule, and H. Kriesi (eds) *The Blackwell Companion to Social Movements*, Oxford: Blackwell.

Zamponi, L. (2011) 'La rivolta della conoscenza: il movimento studentesco', in B. Maida (ed.) *Senti che bel rumore. Un anno di lotta per l'università pubblica*, Torino: Accademia Press.

— (2012) '"Why don't Italians occupy?" Hypotheses on a failed mobilisation', *Social Movement Studies* 11 (3–4): 416–26.

— (2013) 'Collective memory and social movements', in D. A. Snow, D. della Porta, B. Klandermans, and D. McAdam (eds) *The Wiley-Blackwell Encyclopedia of Social and Political Movements*, Wiley-Blackwell.

Interviews

1. Interview with activist, Rome, 12 May 2011 (conducted in English)
2. Interview with activist, Florence, 18 May 2011 (conducted in English)
3. Interview with activist, Rome, 11 May 2011 (conducted in English)
4. Interview with activist, Bologna, 14 April 2011 (conducted in English)
5. Interview with activist, Florence, 13 November 2012 (conducted in Italian)
6. Interview with activist, Florence, 20 November 2012 (conducted in Italian)
7. Interview with activist, Rome, 23 November 2012 (conducted in Italian)
8. Interview with activist, Rome, 30 November 2012 (conducted in Italian)
9. Interview with activist, Roma, 2 December 2012 (conducted in Italian)

Focus group conducted with four activists, Genoa, 22 July 2011(conducted in Italian).

Chapter Ten

Towards a 'Non-Global Justice Movement'? Two Paths to Re-Scaling the Left Contention in the Czech Republic[1]

Jiří Navrátil and Ondřej Císař

Introduction

A new wave of political protest targeting economic and social justice issues has arisen recently, as a response to the consequences of the global financial and economic crisis, the way these consequences were dealt with and the way these decisions were legitimised. It is hard to resist the temptation to treat this phenomenon as some kind of a resurrection of the Global Justice Movement (GJM), which was at its height at the beginning of the new millennium and has declined since then. However, a closer look reveals important differences. The cases of the Occupy Wall Street movement in the United States or Indignados in Spain suggest that a strong national or even local dimension of protest has been present; consequently, the claims-making of these movements has focused on national and local rather than transnational and global publics and authorities. This may come as a surprise, for one of the interpretations of the crisis on the part of the media, politicians, academia and activists has attributed the blame to deregulated financial markets, relaxed political control over the activities of the banking sector and, more generally, to the global prevalence of neo-liberal policies in many spheres of social life. Therefore, one might ask whether and why the claims of contemporary leftist social movements targeting the austerity policies used in responding to the crisis in many countries lack the transnational dimension of the GJM or, at least, the original internationalism of the 'old' left; and ask why they remain mostly on the local and national levels.

This paper focuses on this problem through a case study of leftist protest politics in the Czech Republic. As suggested above, however, it explores processes that might also have taken place in other democratic countries. Our main goals are to describe and understand the various paths by which the trajectory of claims-

---

1. This work was supported by the project 'Employment of Newly Graduated Doctors of Science for Scientific Excellence' (CZ.1.07/2.3.00/30.0009) co-financed from European Social Fund and the state budget of the Czech Republic, and is a part of the research project Collective Action and Protest in East-Central Europe (code GAP404/11/0462), funded by the Czech Science Foundation.

making of Czech left activism changed and remained 'nationalised' or 'localised', even during times of global financial and economic crisis, and to discuss the possible determinants of these processes. Our analytical focus is on the period after 2000, for two reasons. First, by then the economic and political transition from the socialist regime was basically over, leading to the establishment of a consolidated democracy (Hasselmann 2006; Klingemann *et al.* 2006). Second, the first massive transnational mobilisation took place in Prague, leading to the temporary fulfilment of the transnationalisation process of the Czech left movements. We deal with this exceptional moment of heightened transnational mobilisation to illustrate the theoretical framework and to contextualise our analysis of the period after it.

On a more general level, we deal with the interrelated mechanisms of diffusion and scale-shift.[2] As Sidney Tarrow (2005: 124–36) points out, contention often diffuses together with shifts in scale: while Islamism, for example, diffused upward from its originally local roots to the global level, social forums have diffused downwards from the originally global to the continental, national and local scales. Moreover, Tarrow stresses that unlike diffusion of innovations, contention diffuses and shifts in scale in relation to institutions, which provide opportunities for contention and its transmission to different levels. According to Tarrow (2010: 205), 'diffusion is seldom self-generating out of the claims and inventions of activists; it results from their interaction with, and often mirrors, the institutions they attack and their practices'. In the Czech case, we differentiate between two time periods. In a nutshell, we argue that during the first period, international financial institutions created opportunities for both diffusion of alter-globalisation claims and frames to the Czech context and for the transnationalisation of the domestic left. Subsequently, due to the lack of international institutional opportunities in the second period, the Czech left has not connected internationally in its resistance to the consequences of economic crisis; it shifted its agenda and framing downward in response to the state's national austerity policies.

Furthermore, in our analysis of shifts in the agenda and framing of leftist social movements in reaction to austerity measures and economic crisis, we differentiate between two modes of left activism – the moderate (social-democratic, trade-unionist) one, and the radical (anarchist, Trotskyite, communist) one. They consist of both organisations that were carried over from the socialist regime (trade unions, communist parties) and those newly established (Trotskyites, anarchists) or re-established (social-democrats) after its fall. Despite these similarities, the two modes represent entirely different ways of organising, goals, strategies and means of contentious interaction with elites or other actors.

The structure of the paper is as follows. After presenting the data and methods used, the paper aims at a theoretical framing of the problem. It introduces major approaches conceptualising the rise of transnational collective action, but also its localisation, and the key social and political processes and conditions that contributed to the rise of transnational/local non-state actors and contentious

---

2. 'Scale-shift' refers here to 'the coordination of collective action at a different level than where it began' (Tarrow 2005: 32).

politics. We conclude by summarising the various responses of collective actors in terms of the scale of issues they deal with and the scale of their framing.

This theoretical framework is applied to the case of Czech radical and moderate left actors, in order to analytically describe their transformation between the Prague International Monetary Fund/World Bank (IMF/WB) summit in September 2000 and the later imposition of austerity measures and coming of economic crisis to the Czech Republic. Here, we draw on data on protest issues, social embeddedness and, particularly, on the scale of frames and issues of the Czech radical left and labour in order to show different trajectories of these two modes of left contention.

Finally, we discuss two important downward shifts that took place in the case of the radical left. The first started after the withdrawal of global justice activists from massive engagement in protests against the wars in Afghanistan and Iraq (2005) and continued during their subsequent involvement in domestic anti-war activism (2006), when the rebirth of a revived symbolic conception of 'national democracy' effectively weakened the previous global framing. The second shift downwards accompanied the start of the economic crisis (2009), when the radical left transformed into a counter-movement acting primarily against local events organised by the domestic radical right; and thus further shifted the scale of contention to the local level. On the other hand, Czech labour unions and employees followed an upwards shift during their general process of internalisation, when they raised their concerns from the local to national level as a consequence of the escalating politicisation of economic debates related to national austerity reforms and the global financial/economic crisis.

Data and methods

Our inquiry is based on a protest-event analysis. The protest event is defined here as either an actual gathering of at least three people convened in a public space in order to make claims that bear on the interests of an institution/collective actor or a petition addressed to an institution/collective actor (see also Tilly 1995). Only real episodes of collective action are included; threats of resorting to collective action, such as strike alerts, were excluded.

We used the electronic archive of the Czech News Agency (CNA) and searched the news between January 1989 and December 2010 for selected keywords. There is a potential bias in the source we used for analysis. First, use of data from a nationwide press agency may cause local events (namely, those organised by the radical left) to be under-represented. Second, events with controversial and violent content may be over-represented (which may also apply to the ratio of events where the radical left was targeting the radical right). Generally, one can conclude that the CNA represents 'what is considered as noteworthy by the media and therefore reaches a broad audience ... one should keep in mind that for many analytic purposes, it is not so much the actual level of protest but its composition and trends over time that are of interest' (Koopmans and Rucht 2002: 247). Even if there might be a bias in CNA data, it is systematic and does not invalidate the results of our analysis, particularly in terms of long-term trends and their changes. The CNA consistently reports what it regards as relevant from the point of view of the media at a particular point in time; thus it pre-selects data according to its general relevance (for a broad audience).

The following variables were coded for each event: date; place; duration; collective participants and organisers; number of individual participants; main issues and framing and their scale; target of the claim; repertoire; reaction of elites; and police activity. All news items covering any protest event were selected and coded. The whole dataset, consisting of 6,235 protest events, was used to sample out events that have taken place since 2000 and in which one of the organisers was a left-wing actor (labour unions, social-democratic and communist parties, radical-left SMOs) or employees, which resulted in a dataset with 668 events (the PEA Left database). For most of the analyses we split the dataset according to its organisers into events organised by the moderate left (N=394 – trade unions, social-democratic parties and their youth organisations) and radical left (N=274 – anarchists, Trotskyites, Marxist and communist groups, communist parties and their youth organisations). There were only ten events that were jointly co-organised by the moderate and radical left SMOs (two in 2000, one in 2003, two in 2007, two in 2008, two in 2009 and one in 2010), which further supports the analytical distinction in this paper between the two modes of activism (see Introduction). These joint events were coded as organised by the moderate or radical left according to the prevailing type of organisers of the event. We consider the year 2009 to be the start of the contention related to the global financial/economic crisis, as the first claims explicitly related to the crisis appeared in January 2009.

Four key variables were used in the present analysis. First, the framing scale was coded as local, national or transnational according to the prevailing interpretation of the event on the part of its participants (the diagnostic framing was coded; that is, who was held responsible by the activists for the issue or problem). Second, the issue scale of the event was coded as local, national or transnational depending on the scope and origin of the main issues the protesters were raising. Third, two main protest issues[3] of each event were coded and the first of them was used for analysis. Fourth, event attendance was recorded. In cases when the exact number was not available (several dozen, several hundred and so on), its lower boundary was coded (20,200 and so on). Petitions were excluded from the analysis of event attendance.

Shifting the scale of contention: a theoretical framework

The international dimension of collective mobilisations against capitalism and unfavourable economic developments on a large scale was probably first introduced by the nineteenth-century communist, socialist and anarchist organisational networks, which succeeded in framing their struggle as international and therefore

---

3. The items were: the performance of state institutions and the quality of democracy; historical justice/recognition; the EU; economic issues; industry; urban-planning; social policies; cultural and sport policies; agriculture; consumer issues, domestic security, foreign policies and war; environment; women rights; LGBT rights; minority rights; other human rights; and religion.

built joint co-ordinating and mobilising platforms (the International[s]). While the supranational dimension of these mobilisations lay in their framing and their level of co-ordination, their issues remained mostly on the national and even local levels. Despite the left's internationalist rhetoric, the state remained its primary target.

This changed in 1968 at the latest and, more recently, during the first wave of mass mobilisations against international economic institutions and their policies in the second half of the twentieth century. Targets of protests in the field of economic distribution started to be framed supra-nationally in both recently industrialised and developed countries during the 1970s and 1980s; yet co-ordination of challengers remained predominantly on the national and local scales (Walton and Ragin 1990: 876–7; Gerhards and Rucht 1992; Routledge 1996; Rothman and Oliver 2002).

However, truly transnational collective action arose when both issues of protest were framed as transnational, and inter-organisational co-ordination crossed the boundaries of national states (Ayres 2004). This kind of collective action therefore consisted of co-ordination among international campaigns against both national and supra-national actors; and it can be observed starting around the end of the twentieth century (della Porta and Tarrow 2005: 7). Waves of protest against economic developments that began to cross national boundaries reached Western countries mostly during the 1990s; and it flourished there, partly because of growing transnational communication, organisational and institutional ties and the opportunities provided by some international institutions (*cf.* Keck and Sikkink 1998; Smith 2008: 94–5).

These developments in collective action became possible because of changes in the broader social and political environment after the Seattle anti-WTO mobilisation in November 1999; the ensuing movement was labelled 'anti-neoliberal', 'anti-global' or 'global justice' (GJM). Collective actors considered as separate or even in competition until then (unions, ecologists and so on) joined together and organised a series of successful events challenging a symbol of economic globalisation, the WTO. The combination of success (closure of the WTO meeting) and extensive media and public attention made Seattle 1999 a founding myth and the 'coming out' of the GJM, at least in the West (Smith 2002; Munck 2007: 57; Juris 2008: 33). The Seattle event demonstrated that the movement is a diverse network of organisations, groups and activists, characterised by innovative strategies and repertoire. These were based on the GJM's rejection of existing models of interest-representation and a preference for grassroots politics.

This preference has complicated the picture of GJM as an example of a fully transnational actor or even as a real global movement (Graeber 2002; McDonald 2006; Wissenburg 2004) and some students of social movements have pointed out that there are differences between the way the movement is imagined and its real activities 'on the ground'. Therefore, many activists may still understand the world more in national or even local terms (Williams 2008). Consequently, scholars also suggest that the opposite scale-shift – the localisation of contention – may have taken place (Hamel *et al.* 2001; Köhler and Wissen 2003; Starr and Adams 2003; Chesters and Welsh 2006). As Wood (2005) and Auyero (2003) have shown, the scale of contentious responses to the impacts and symbols of the globalised economy and its neo-liberal proponents has varied significantly, ranging from transnational to national on down to local activities and symbols. The building of transnational coalitions and cross-border solidarities and identities has therefore not been an automatic outcome nor the only 'dream' goal of GJM actors; and localised contention has not automatically or exclusively given way to international and transnational contentious action. Quite the contrary, challenging the local impacts of the globalised economy and mobilising communities made some actors shift their focus downwards, towards the grassroots (Maiba 2005; Routledge *et al.* 2006). As Tilly and Wood suggest, there are numerous possible trajectories for social movements with regard to their scale – starting from the local and going up through the regional, national, international and global dimensions (Tilly and Wood 2009).

In other words, it seems that both the upward and downward scale-shifts by the left social movements became possible after the formation of GJM. Expectedly, the new scale-shift upward has become the favoured object of inquiry. As was pointed out, transnational activism generally and global justice activism in particular were enabled by a combination of factors both external and internal to the movement(s). Three categories of changes seem to have been particularly important (della Porta and Tarrow 2005: 7–10). The first, an external factor, was the change in the international political environment after the fall of the socialist regimes in Central and Eastern Europe, which opened the space for diverse cross-border non-state collective actors, both in civil society and the economy, and which was further accelerated by the declining cost of international communication and transportation. The second, an internal factor, consisted of the social movements' reflexivity and their ability to recognise the importance of supra-national actors, events and processes and to develop responsive framing. The third factor, also internal, was SMO coalition-making activities that interacted with the process of new identity-formation on the supranational level.

According to Tarrow (2005), there are three sets of political processes that led to the constitution of transnational activism. The first of them takes place on domestic turf and consists of the mobilisation of international or global symbols to frame domestic conflicts in response to the supranational and foreign pressure caused by actions taken in domestic politics (global framing and internalisation). The second set of processes focuses on the connection between domestic and international contention: the first is the transfer of claims from one site to another; the second is the co-ordination of contention at a different level from where it was launched (diffusion and scale-shift). The final set of processes is situated entirely on the international level and consists of the projection of domestic claims on to international institutions and actors (externalisation) and coalition-making among actors from different countries (Tarrow 2005: 32–3; for the case of the Czech Republic, *see* Císař and Vráblíková 2013). As a result, Tarrow differentiates between different types of transnationalisation taking place between the international/global and national levels.

In this paper we draw on Tarrow's insights, employ the notions of localised or 'global' contention and focus on the scale of two key aspects of domestic contention – issues and their framing – understanding them as two dimensions for analysis of the dynamics of Czech left social movements. There are three basic directions of shift in the scale of social movements' issues and frames (*see* Figure 10.1). First, the diagonal captures the shift from local contention towards fully transnational activism (and *vice versa*). Second, while the issues that social movements deal with may remain local or national, they may frame them in more universal or global terms as their transformed imagery becomes deployed (*see* the vertical shift in Figure 10.1). Third, social movements may raise global or transnational issues but frame them on the level of the community or nation-state, in order to make them comprehensible or politically relevant at the grassroots level (*see* the horizontal shift in Figure 10.1).

The upper-left position in the diagram (Figure 10.1) captures purely local contention, defined by local framing and the local scale of an event's issue; the lower-right position defines the exact opposite, that is, events politicising supra-national issues and also drawing on global and international symbols, such as globalisation, regulation of global economic relations or the international trade regime. The upper-right position contains events that use local/domestic symbols

Figure 10.1: Dynamics of issue and frame scales

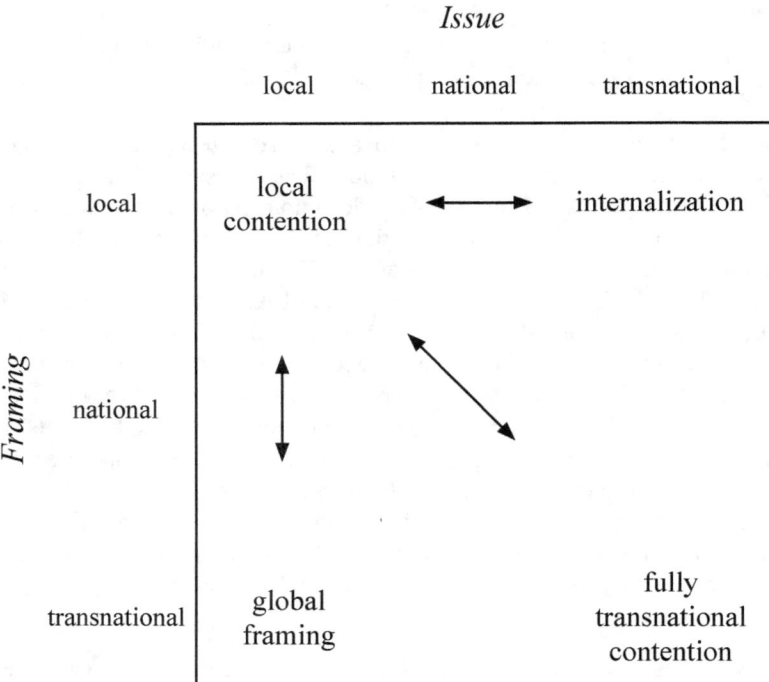

to frame international issues and the problems they entail. One example might be a protectionist framing of a protest against the closure of a firm due to the global economic crisis. The lower-left position in the diagram contains protest events that use an international framing, for example, universal human rights or global justice, for domestic/local political issues.

Processes of scale-shift by Czech left social movements before 2000

The above-discussed theoretical framework can now be applied to the period before the momentous Prague events of 2000 (the IMF/WB counter-summit and its preparation) in order to identify the core conditions related to collective actors themselves that enabled the emergence/activation of the transnational dimension of social movements. Several milestones in this process may be identified:

November 1989	Fall of the socialist regime
1990	Social Democratic Party regains full membership in Socialist International
December 1992	Break-up of Czechoslovakia
1993–5	Trade unions enter European Trade Union Confederation
1995	Social Democratic Party becomes observer in Party of European Socialists
May 1998	'Global Street Party' (Prague)
July 1998	Social Democrats form the first left-wing Czech government after 1989
August 1998	'Local Street Party' (Prague)
1999	Launch of co-ordination activities for anti-IMF/WB protests
September 2000	Anti-IMF/WB protests in Prague

Some of the first signs of the transnationalisation of Czech left after 1989 can be identified on the moderate left: the trade unions. The largest Czech labour platform, the Czech-Moravian Confederation of Trade Unions (CMCTU), was a long-term member of the International Confederation of Free Trade Unions (ICFTU) and the International Trade Union Confederation (ITUC); it became an observer at the European Trade Union Confederation (ETUC) in 1993 and a full member in 1995. However, despite its formal ties to and formal membership of these international networks, the transnational dimension of Czech trade unions remained rather weak and insignificant.[4] The main scope of their activities remained on the domestic (national or local) level with corresponding framing scale: specifically, CMCTU did not raise transnational issues; did not set issues into their broader framework; and did not mobilise foreign partners into their activities.

The genuine process of transnationalisation on the Czech left might be traced to protest events organised in the late 1990s by the anarchist and radical environmentalist scene that gradually took on and internalised the global frames

---

4. Generally the responses of these trade unionist networks to economic globalisation were perceived as inadequate and criticised as such (Waterman 2008).

of reference of foreign/transnational GJM actors (Císař and Koubek 2012). One illustration of the contention inspired by foreign events may be found in an early (late 1990s) protest form of the Czech radical left – street parties.[5] These represented local resistance against broader cultural and social patterns that were seen as detrimental to local and national values: consumerist culture, cultural globalisation, corporate ownership of public spaces and cars as the dominant mode of transportation and urbanism. Here, the process of internalisation intertwined with another process – the diffusion of the various forms of protest – as these (sub-)culturally oriented events explicitly imitated the repertoire of People's Global Action (PGA) and Reclaim the Streets (Císař and Slačálek 2007: 2) and were co-ordinated with similar events in other countries in their timing.

Almost simultaneously with the processes of internalisation, the process of the global framing of collective action appeared. New frames of protest particularly focused on resistance towards the icons and proponents of economic globalisation. This resistance was initially limited to protests against the local (cultural and environmental) consequences of global processes. More specifically, general political-economic issues (international division of labour, social impacts of transnational neo-liberal policies, capitalism) were less emphasised at the beginning and their importance grew only just prior to the end of the millennium (Kolářová 2008: 4; Růžička 2007: 37).

The combination of these processes in turn led to a development of new (although instant) identities fostering transnational coalition-formation and -activation. This stage of Czech GJM represents its peak, particularly the Prague protests in 2000. The preparations for the event started in 1999 and gradually led to the creation of an unprecedentedly wide coalition of domestic and foreign SMOs in a close co-ordination with PGA, Indymedia and other networks (Welsh 2004). The event clearly revealed the ability of various domestic and foreign SMOs and platforms to broker both domestic and transnational coalitions (Welsh 2004). Some evidence of externalisation processes was seen during the event, when local environmental and political claims were shifted upwards; as a result, they drew close attention from abroad. This open critique of the international economic system and the successful mobilisation of a large number of people was enabled by the strong transnational dimension of the event, making this event something very different from other domestic protests by the Czech GJM (*cf.* Císař 2008: 148; Kolářová 2009: 50–5).

The event was also noticed by key representatives of the moderate left. Czech trade unions actively took part to an unprecedented extent, framing their own claims and the claims of their international networks on a global scale, thus forming a genuine transnational coalition. They organised an extra summit of domestic members at which an extraordinarily critical memorandum commenting

---

5. Gatherings or marches organised on the streets or squares, which combined non-violent political protest and cultural performance (music, theatre) and entailed a more or less explicit aim of liberating the public space from state authorities, commerce or overloaded traffic.

on IMF/WB policies was drafted. The document sought to depict the consequences and dangers of IMF/WB policies regarding the rise of poverty and inequality in the former Third World and to introduce the programme of international labour organisations on how to humanise economic globalisation. During the summit, clear examples of the process of externalisation can be identified, for example, when the process of the transformation of the Czech economy in the early 1990s was framed as part of the IMF policies of privatisation and deregulation in developing countries.

An important lesson can be learned from the story of the transnationalisation of the Czech left movements (*see* Figure 10.2). It seems that while there were some earlier signs of transnational strategies and interactions by Czech moderate left, the process itself started later and was a complicated combination of interactions among various processes and sub-processes leading to transnational collective action. Two of these processes were particularly important and served as a precondition for the other ones: (1) developing a cognitive sensitivity towards global processes and events that enabled actors to understand and interpret conflicts they were involved in as a part of broader social and political reality; and (2) the ability to use this sensitivity to challenge foreign and supra-national political actors, institutions and processes, at least on the local/domestic level. Therefore, the main question to be answered is how these key domestic processes of transnational collective action (internalisation and global framing) evolved after 2000 and whether these processes might be identified until and after the coming of the global financial/economic crisis.

Evolution of left-wing activism and its context (2000–2010)

Radical and moderate left followed different protest cycles after 2000. The Czech radical left went through three different key periods/campaigns after 2000. The first was the anti-war campaign, which started with the protests against the NATO summit in Prague in November 2002 and followed with protests against the wars in Iraq and Afghanistan. The second period started in August 2006, with the official request of the US administration to build a National Missile Defense base in the Czech Republic. The third period started in January 2009, with the occurrence of the first protests explicitly related to the financial/economic crisis. In all these campaigns, radical-left groups dominated both in terms of organising and of participation. Trade-union activism (and protest by employees) followed a slightly different trajectory after 2000. Basically, these reflected the government's economic and social policies and economic cycles on the domestic level. Even though there were left-wing or centre-left cabinets between 1998 and 2006, some significant conflicts broke out: in 2003 the social-democratic government proposed cuts in the welfare system and a plan to cut the wages of state employees was introduced in 2004. After a right-wing government came to office, between 2007 and 2008 it launched several large-scale policy reforms, which aimed to cut welfare expenditure and reform the tax system.

Figure 10.2: Dynamics of issue and frame scales of Czech left movements (1990–2000)

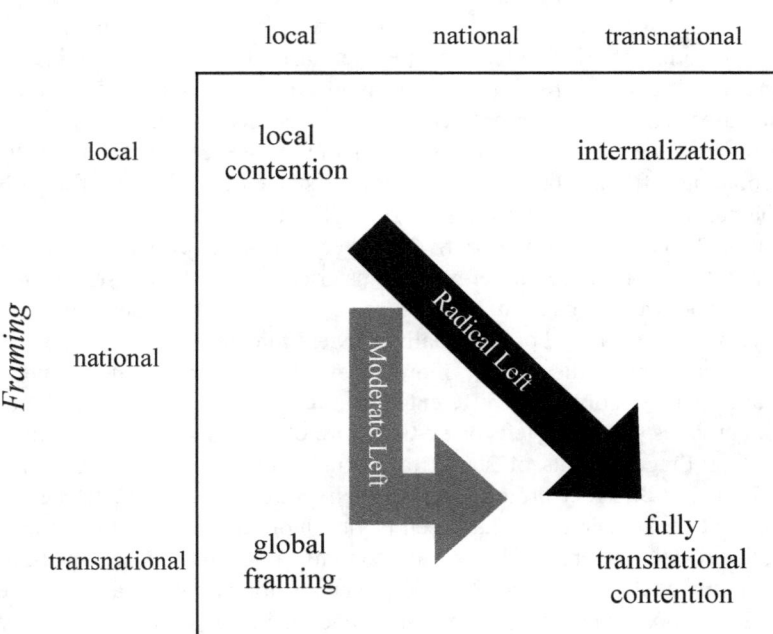

The impact of the global economic crisis on the Czech economy and society consists of several components and is hardly separable from domestic policies. While the measurable economic effect of the crisis on the national economy before 2009 was far from dramatic, the right-wing Czech government was employing the discourse of crisis as early as late 2008 – quite paradoxically – to push through further liberalisation and fiscal restrictions in economic, healthcare and social policies that would otherwise have been adopted only with significant political costs and difficulties. The first austerity measures were proposed in 2007 and became effective in 2008. Their imposition was framed as 'stabilising the budget' and they were not explicitly related to the emerging financial and economic crisis in the US and Western Europe. The measures consisted of lowering business and capital taxes and social benefits, establishing a pseudo-flat-rate income tax, raising consumption taxes and introducing brand-new 'regulatory fees' in the healthcare system. The reform provoked intensive public debate, deepened socio-economic cleavages and was even subjected to review by part of the constitutional court. Eventually, it remained in place in the original form in which was proposed by the government.

By the end of 2008, the first signs of economic recession following the global financial crisis were apparent and, at the beginning of 2009, a recession was confirmed, with a decline in GDP and investments and an increase in unemployment. The strategy of the government was double-edged: on the one hand, since 2007 the government had repeatedly denied that the Czech economy could be threatened by the coming financial/economic crisis in any way; on the other hand, after 2009 it used the notion of crisis to legitimise earlier austerity measures and threatened citizens with 'the Greek road' if there were no further economic restrictions and tax increases. The right-wing political parties succeeded in framing the financial and economic crisis as the 'last chance' to avoid the scenario of 'spendthrift and debt-booming left-wing policies'; and they persuaded the public sufficiently to win the parliamentary elections in mid-2010. The election result was interpreted as a national consensus for a restrictive fiscal economic policy, which encouraged the government to proceed further with its austerity agenda. Anti-austerity protests in this period were organised both by radical left SMOs, labour unions and employees; and new broad protest coalitions were founded.

The fluctuations in the number of protest events organised by the left between 2000 and 2010 confirm two different dynamics (*see* Figure 10.3). While the protest activities of radical left (or ex-GJM) are clearly in steep decline after the momentous Prague events of 2000, trade unions and employees seem to have been following different protest cycles. Their protest peaks in 2003 and 2008 suggest that the moderate left has been paying more attention to the policies of the national government (welfare and economic reforms imposed by Špidla's social-democratic cabinet in 2003 and Topolánek's liberal-conservative cabinet in 2008). The imposition of austerity measures and the impact of the economic crisis clearly have had a differentiated impact on protest mobilisation of the left: while the moderate left seems to have reduced their protest activities after mass protests against the pre-crisis reforms, there is nonetheless some upward movement in 2010, indicating a change in the trend. On the other hand, the radical left seems to be continuing in its downward trajectory.

Another key indicator of the evolution of a social movement is its mobilising capacity (*see* Figure 10.4). This is one of the key characteristics that differentiates the radical from the moderate left (not only) in the Czech Republic: the radical left's mobilising capacities (and social embeddedness) remain constantly low. One of its major mobilisation successes (the 2000 Prague summit) was enabled by its capacity to form vertical transnational ties and to attract participants from abroad. Its mobilisation capacity is based on relatively small sub-cultural communities that are usually unwilling to co-operate (Císař and Koubek 2012). The only exception is the communist part of the movement, which relies on a relatively high party membership.[6] On the other hand, labour unions and employees rely on stable and broad mass support and an organisational infrastructure that is largely inherited from the socialist past. Therefore, the mobilising capacity of trade unions and employees remains much higher, despite considerable fluctuation and even though the mass strikes of the early years of the decade (particularly 2003) were

---

6. The current estimate is 50,000 members.

Figure 10.3: Frequency of protest events by Czech radical and moderate left actors (2000–2010, N=668)

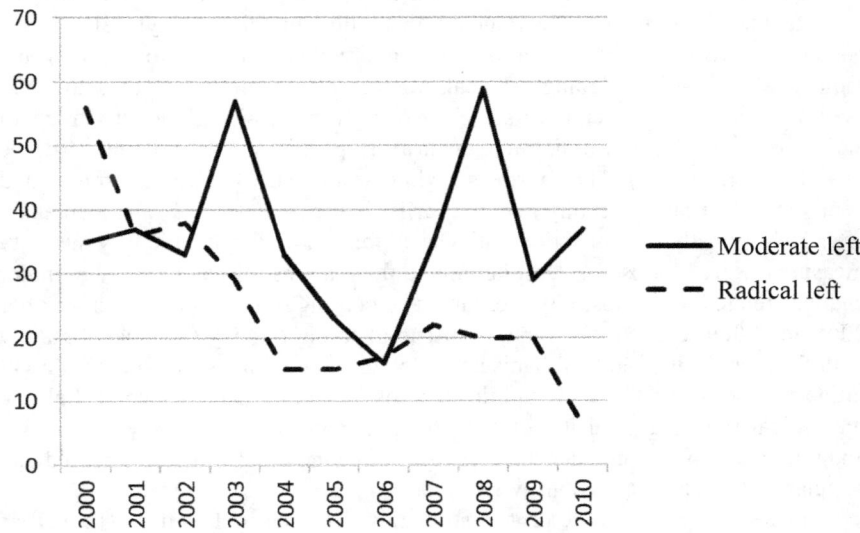

Source: PEA Left

Figure 10.4: Average protest event participation (2000–2010, N=668)

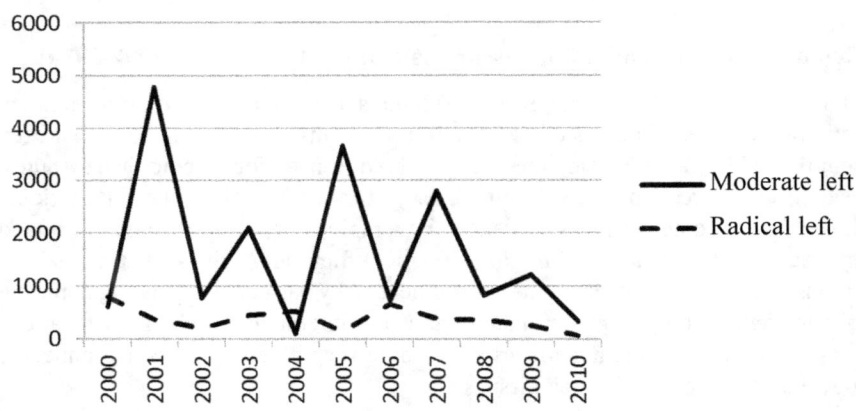

Source: PEA Left

not repeated during the era of neo-liberal policies (2008). Apparently, neither the political nor the economic impact of the financial crisis played any role in changing the existing quantitative patterns of protest participation.

Regarding the issues raised by radical left SMOs, three of them were most important (*see* Figure 10.5): the radical right (following this issue typically means becoming involved in confrontations with nationalist or racist movements); the radical left (pursuing ideological goals of the left – celebration of May Day, events promoting the agenda of social justice, events praising equality, freedom and so on); and foreign policy and security (typically, anti-war issues, critique of US foreign policy). The fourth most important issue – state institutions and democracy – became partially relevant earlier in the period (2001) and then again after 2008 (mostly in connection with Czech foreign policy and the way austerity measures were imposed). Despite many fluctuations, there were two major changes related to the austerity measures and coming of the economic crisis after 2008 and 2009 respectively. First, the issue of foreign policy (associated mainly with the wars in Iraq and Afghanistan and with the possible deployment of a US military base in the Czech Republic) has lost its importance.[7] Second, fighting the radical right regained its relative strength, with the rise of new nationalist and populist movements after the first signs of economic downturn appeared and popular discontent began to grow.

For the last ten years the protest strategies of Czech trade unions (as well as employees) have constantly focused on the issues of the economy and social policy. However, there seems to be some joint mechanism connecting the employment of these two issues, as their relative importance seems to be negatively correlated (*see* Figure 10.6). While the 'usual' trade union protest activities tended to focus on maintaining the *status quo* in social welfare and social entitlements, the more radical and far-reaching austerity measures that followed the crisis (after the economic reforms of 2003) made the unions switch their protest agenda: the economic system itself – and not only its partial outputs in the form of particular welfare policies – became the subject of debate and contention.

Evolution of framing and the issue scale of the Czech left (2000–2010)

Immediately after the Prague events of 2000, some change in both transnational activities and the capacities of Czech left movements could be observed. The key coalition of SMOs organising the event suffered from serious ideological disputes, leading to its breakup a few months later. A further decline of the transnational dimension of contention was evidenced by a rapid decrease in the number of and attendance at street parties with global (justice) framing. At the same time, labour unions returned to their role of the government's key partner in regulating domestic labour conflict; they remained members of the international labour associations but their focus also retreated to particular domestic problems and issues connected to welfare and economic/social issues.

---

7. The anti-war campaign was definitely halted after Obama officially announced the suspension of the project in September 2009.

Figure 10.5: Evolution of key protest issues of the radical left (2000–2010, N=274)

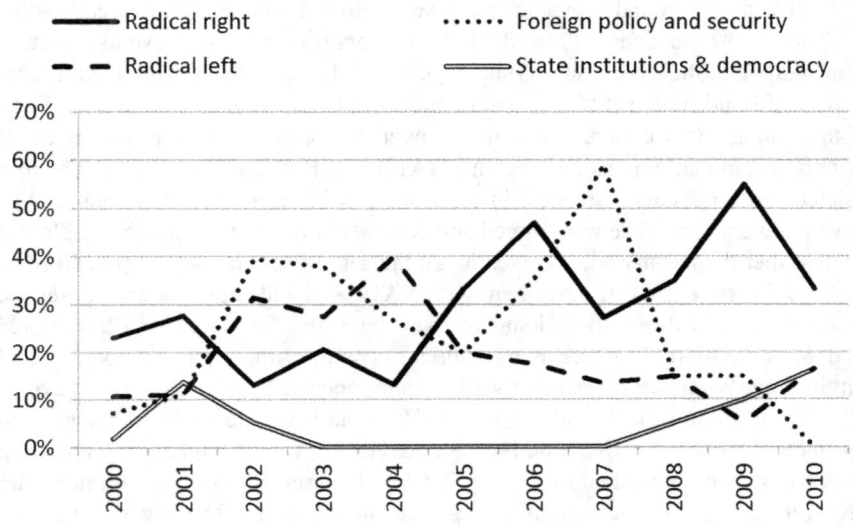

Source: PEA Left

Figure 10.6: Evolution of key protest issues of the moderate left (2000–2010, N=394)

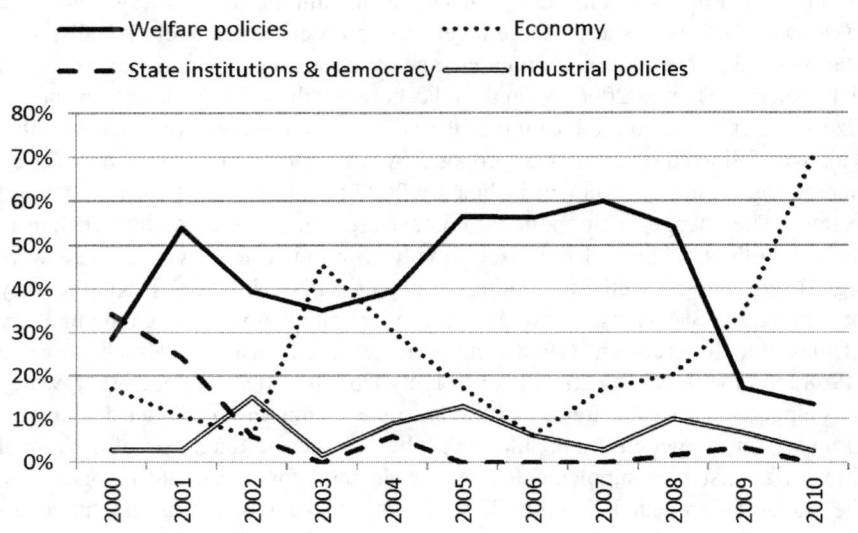

Source: PEA Left

The radical left

The data on the evolution of scale of issues and framing of the radical branch of the Czech left social movements reveal a rather dramatic picture (*see* Figures 10.7 and 10.8). Between 2000 and 2004, the proportion of protest events targeting transnational policies or issues is substantially higher than those targeting national and local issues (even if their absolute numbers have declined after 2002). Even if the Prague 2000 counter-summit was over, the preparations for another event with transnational dimension – against NATO – started in the same year. The first related protest events were held in September 2002. Protest claims consisted of several layers. The issue was framed and perceived on the international (or global) scale rather than as national or even local: the summit in Prague was perceived as an occasion to register disagreement with NATO's global character and strategies, rather than as a threat to national or local interests. The issue was interpreted and perceived largely in terms of political economy; threats to democracy and environment were seen as relatively minor components. The series of protest events against the summit itself and against NATO as an institution may be understood as an overture to the anti-war activism related to the wars in Afghanistan and Iraq; the protests were launched in January 2003 and continued until the summer 2006 (Navrátil 2012). The campaigns against wars in Iraq and Afghanistan brought no significant change related to the framing or issues of protest. The frameworks of the international political economy, corporate power, imperialism and exploitation were further amplified and the process of global framing was further supported by the dissemination of some key foreign slogans into the Czech environment ('No Blood For Oil' or 'Not In My Name').

The profound change in this trajectory took place in 2005 (when the first wave of anti-war protests against US policies and institutions faded away). Between 2006 and 2008, issues at all three levels are represented relatively equally. This was a consequence of an important change in the scale of the anti-war campaign that took place in mid-2006, when the talks between the US administration and the Czech government on the location of the US anti-missile base were made public. This was followed by an official proposal by the United States to the new Czech liberal–right-wing government in January 2007 to join the US National Defense system. The change in the political context brought a corresponding change in the symbolic strategies of the actors involved in anti-war activism. There were significant changes both in framing strategies and their scale. From the very beginning, the SMOs organising the 'anti-radar' campaign employed the imagery of the Munich agreement (1938), the Warsaw Pact invasion of Czechoslovakia (1968) and the threat to national sovereignty from the Russian Federation, which all helped construct the frames of threat to the nation and to Czech democracy. Drawing on the general unpopularity of the project, the diagnosis of a national threat was instantly supplemented by the demand for a national plebiscite on the issue. This created a symbolic mix that can be labelled as the 'national-democratic' framing, which effectively displaced the previous transnational or global dimension in agenda-setting and framing. The anti-radar campaign gradually vanished during late 2008 and early 2009 in the (correct) expectation that the new Obama administration would change US military strategy. However, the arrival of the economic crisis seems to correlate very closely with a significant increase in the share of events raising local issues at the expense of issues on the other two levels.

The evolution of radical left protest framing reveals two interesting features (*see* Figure 10.8). First, during the first half of the period under study, the single most important framing level was the transnational one. The decline of framing on this level between the Prague summit and the rise of protests against the US-led wars in Iraq and Afghanistan in 2002 was followed by another decline in 2005; the rise of a different anti-war issue – a national one – in 2006 prevented its recovery to the preceding level. What is more important, however, is that even the coming of the economic crisis did not change the trend of retreat from the transnational imagination of the radical left. Next, there is an interesting dynamic between the employment of national and local symbolism: trends in the number of events framed on these two levels have been closely intertwined since 2003; only in 2005 and 2009 did locally framed events became more frequent. The coming of the crisis was marked by an immediate rise in locally framed events.

The moderate left

Until 2002, trade unions declared themselves 'apolitical' but they maintained intimate and peaceful relations with the cabinet. When the country started its recovery from the economic hardships of the late 1990s, the leader of CMCTU publicly announced that the government was not to be blamed for the deeds of its (right-wing) predecessor. The tripartite[8] mechanism was reinforced and deepened, and some trade-union experts were even employed at high levels in some of the ministries. Surprisingly, the first large-scale conflict with the government broke out after former Minister of Social Affairs Špidla, a social democrat, won the parliamentary elections in 2002 and formed a coalition with Christian democrats and liberals. During 2003 the Ministry of Finance articulated a plan for 'healing the budget' that anticipated radical cuts in the welfare system. Trade unions responded with massive strikes that lasted for several months. The response was repeated – albeit on a reduced scale – in 2004, after the announcement of cuts to the wages of state employees. The rest of the term of this central-left government was calm.

The second period started after the parliamentary elections in 2006, when Topolánek´s liberal-conservative government was established. Right after its installation, the government announced a plan to launch ambitious budgetary reforms in the areas of taxes, healthcare, education, social services and pensions. The reform laws were passed in August 2007. Between mid-2007 and mid-2008 a series of protest events were launched against the reforms, combining mass

---

8. A body composed of representatives of the government, trade unions and business, who meet to discuss and review the key steps in economic and social policies in the country.

Figure 10.7: Evolution of the issue scale of protest events organised by the radical left (2000–2010, N=274)

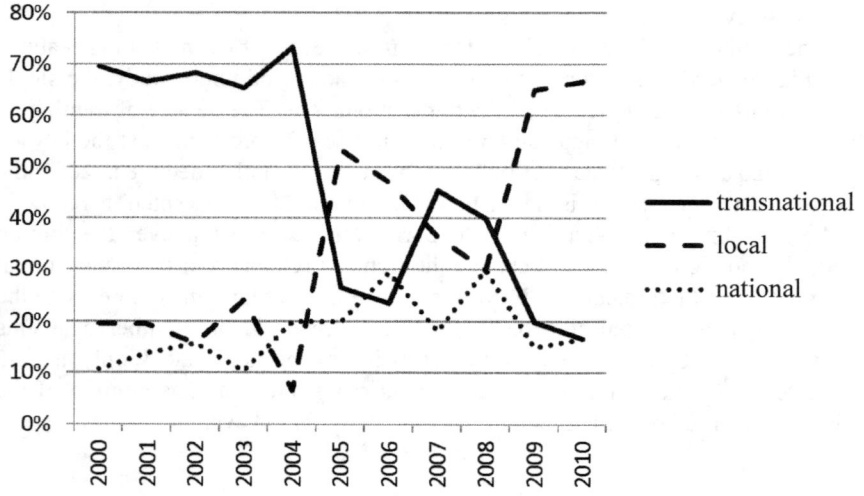

Source: PEA Left

Figure 10.8: Evolution of framing scale of protest events organised by the radical left (2000–2010, N=274)

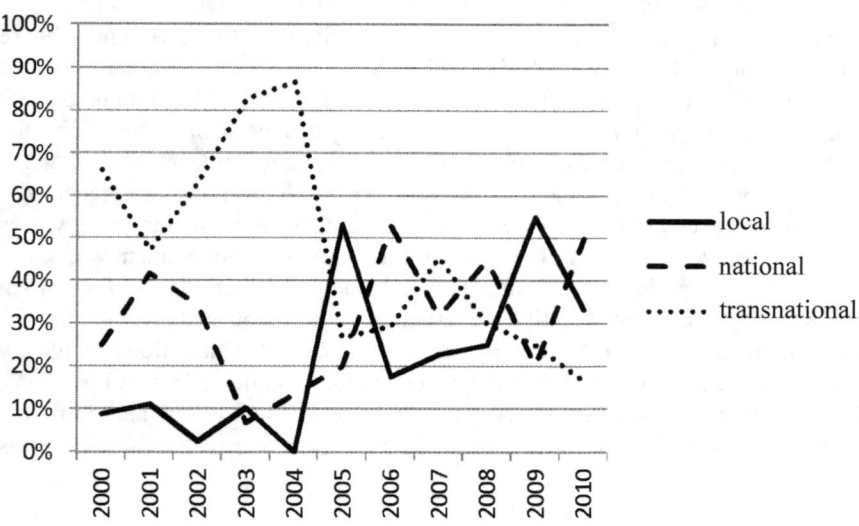

Source: PEA Left

demonstrations and 'happenings'. Most of the claims targeted the reforms as being too restrictive and 'simple-minded' and 'worsening the situation of 80 per cent of employees'. However, unions also targeted the worsening of the dialogue with the government itself. During their campaign, which united all the major Czech trade-union networks, the unions also received symbolic backing from abroad, when the General-Secretary of the ETUC and some trade unionist leaders from neighbouring countries came out in support of the demonstrations. However, the framing of the most of the events up until 2008 remained at the national level and no significant public attempts to introduce more universal concepts or foreign examples of the failure of strict fiscal reforms in other countries appeared.

The evolution of the scale of protest issues at the events organised by the moderate left is different from that of radical activism (*see* Figure 10.9). There are basically three important shifts. The first two are nearly identical: in 2005 and 2007 there was a steep increase in focus on local issues at the expense of other scales. The third important shift followed the introduction of domestic austerity measures, when, for the first time since 2000, national issues became more important than local or transnational ones. Generally, supranational protest targets are lacking or their frequency is insignificant – both in absolute and relative terms. The only moment of an upward scale-shift in issues may be identified with the coming of the crisis in 2009 but the change is quite small and only temporary. Side by side with this small short-term increase in transnational issues in 2009, there has already been a momentary decline in nationally-oriented protests and an increase in local ones; but events raising national issues clearly prevailed at the end of the period.

The second key indicator of the shift towards (or away from) transnational collective action is the scale of framing used in protest events, or the extent to which the local, national and supra-national symbols are used to identify a problem.

The analysis of framing strategies used by moderate-left actors shows that its predominant scale is the national one, and that the use of transnational framing has been rare throughout the period under study, which is not particularly surprising (*see* Figure 10.10). Still, two factors are remarkable here. First, the Prague events in 2000 did not stimulate the highest peak of transnational framing, either in relative or absolute terms; this symbolic level was relatively strongest in 2002 (mostly in connection with the necessary regulation of some industries to fulfil EU accession criteria but also with rising awareness of EU labour regulations) and in 2009 (particularly in connection with the EU and the global financial/economic crisis and with foreign/international owners of companies). From the country's accession to the EU in 2004 until the coming of the crisis in 2009, transnational framing became insignificant. Second, between 2002 and 2005, local framing (blaming particular companies or regional institutions) was equally as important as the national context. An important shift occurred in 2006, with the politicisation of social dialogue in the nationwide discourse due to parliamentary elections and a heated electoral campaign, which amplified socio-economic cleavages. The national level of framing has become predominant since then: symbolic activities aimed at local institutions, processes and actors (companies, local authorities)

Figure 10.9: Evolution of the issue scale of protest events organised by the moderate left (2000–2010, N=394)

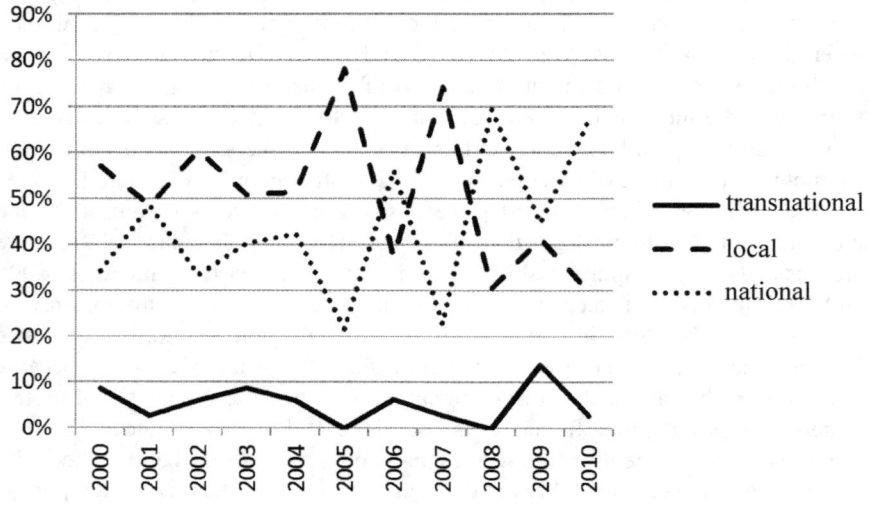

Source: PEA Left

Figure 10.10: Evolution of the framing of protest events organised by the moderate left (2000–2010, N=394)

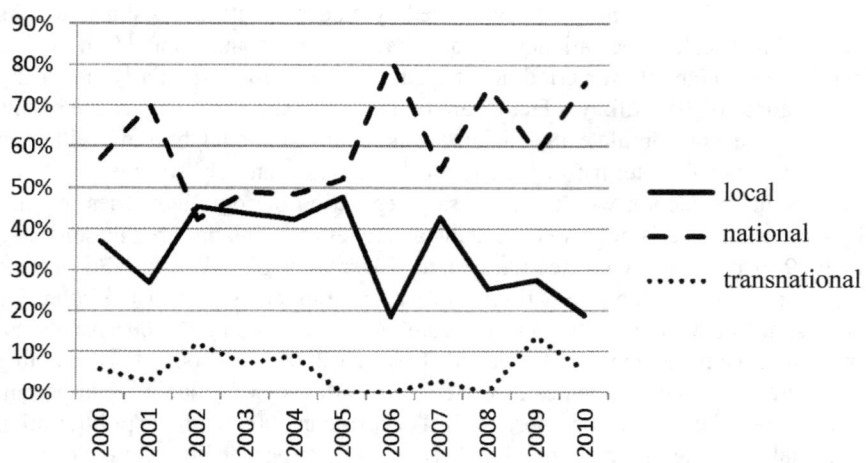

Source: PEA Left

increased the year after the elections and have declined since then. To conclude, it seems that the election of the right-wing government in 2006 and the imposition of austerity measures in 2008 led to a dramatic decrease in events with local framing and contributed to contention on the national level. Even if the first year of economic crisis led to the most remarkable increase in transnationally framed events, protests framed at the national level clearly remained the most important.

To sum up, while Czech trade unions and employees dealt most often with national issues, it was only after 2008 that they started to frame them on the national, and not on the local scale. Next, while local, national and transnational issues were very evenly represented in the protest activities of the radical left after its engagement in domestic anti-war activism after 2005, it was the local framing of its activities that became by far the most dominant after the onset of the economic crisis in 2009. The only sign of transnationalisation might be identified in the framing-scale of the moderate left. However, what seemed to be a shift by trade unions towards more transnationally framed events turned out to be just a temporal swing at the expense of national framing.

Discussion and conclusion

Our exploratory analysis has suggested that the two main branches of Czech left-wing movements have reflected transnational influences in different ways. While the Trotskyite, anarchist and communist groups have generally shifted downwards from transnational to local issues, trade unions behaved differently. Here the scale-shift took the exact opposite direction: both the issue and the scale of framing shifted upwards from the local to the national level. While radical-left actors participating in the successful transnational collective protests of 2000 scaled down from the transnational to the national and from the national to the local level, locally embedded trade unions scaled up to the nationwide arena (*see* Figure 10.11). Generally, even after the onset of the global financial and economic crisis, no conclusive evidence was identified in our data of any processes of internalisation or global framing. No evidence of the processes of transnational contention nor of the 'glocalization'[9] of contention after 2008/2009 can be found in the data. This is an interesting conclusion, as macro-opportunities defined for the rise of transnational contention remained present after 2000 and both of the processes of transnational contention on the domestic level were present in the Czech case at the end of the 1990s. Therefore one could have expected them to be more easily re-launched in the case of an imminent threat of transnational significance.

Instead, the radical left's strategies at the time of the crisis seem to have targeted another movement's reactions to the economic crisis and the related social uncertainty and friction: the radical right. While this issue has always been strongly present in the Czech radical left's programme, it has become even

---

9. The term refers here to efforts to bridge the gap between the local and transnational scale of movement´s activities.

more pronounced than other issues during the last few years. This narrowing of the issue scope is closely connected to the decline in the scale of framing: as radical-right parades and protests usually take place in particular locations and cities, resistance to them is usually framed as a local issue: protecting 'our city and our neighbourhood' from fascism and racism. The relatively shallow social embeddedness of the radical left in Czech society (with the only exception being the Communist Party) enabled this shift from the previous transnational to the local level. In 2000, the non-existence of a broad popular base for the movement on the national level (that would expect and reward particular gains and practical policies) made the employment of a radical universalist framing of global issues relatively easy. Likewise, the same shallow embeddedness made it possible for radical-left actors to shift easily from global/glocal to local issues.

After 2008, trade unionists faced a similar situation to the one they experienced in the economic reforms of 2003: the expectation of a rapid worsening of social conditions among their massive social base (including non-members that support trade-unionist activities), which was either initiated on the national level (2003 and 2008) or transmitted from the transnational arena through the national level (2009), forcing the movement to re-scale its strategies and symbols. One of the reactions was the issue shift. The economy itself, its content, adjustment and meaning became the problem which enabled (or forced) the movement to rescale its framing from local advocacy and contesting against particular employers to a broader realm. Despite the fact that the Czech labour movement is rather self-contained, hierarchical and highly structured, it has also changed its orientation towards co-operation with other non-state actors, even some foreign ones. The shift of issues and frameworks of trade-unionist protest on to the national level was a response to the strategies of the government. The government made two important steps in this regard: first, it claimed that the domestic economy would not be harmed by the financial/economic crisis and, later on, declared itself to be the responsible actor in preventing the economic downturn and imposing a solution (in the form of austerity measures). In other words, it became a visible target tied to the crisis's negative economic impact. This made the movement shift upwards to the nationwide arena but, at the same time, prevented it from linking the problem to the structures and processes of global capitalism.

To conclude, our analysis focused on the dynamics of diffusion and scale-shift mechanisms behind the mobilisation of Czech left movements. It has showed that, while the opportunities provided by international financial institutions contributed to the transnationalisation of domestic contention in 2000, the subsequent time period witnessed the left active on the local and national levels. Consequently, transnational diffusion occurred in the first period and hardly played any role in the second one, in which the left remained within the scope of domestic political institutions, their actors and strategies. Although the financial crisis and subsequent economic downturn represented a chance for the left to point out the supranational roots of national and local hardships, it has not been utilised (not only) in the Czech Republic. There is a strong path-dependency in Czech social movements that influences the readiness and swiftness of their response to new challenges.

With the partial exception of the radical left at the beginning of the period under study here (which was largely driven from abroad), in terms of issues and framing, the Czech left has been self-centred and nation-state-dependent and has tended towards local contention, even in the present era of intensified internationalisation and globalisation. Even if the particular trajectories of the two left components – the moderate and radical left – were very different, both of them focused more on the imminent consequences of global economic friction than on its more universal origins.

Figure 10.11: Dynamics of issue and frame scales of Czech left movements during financial crisis

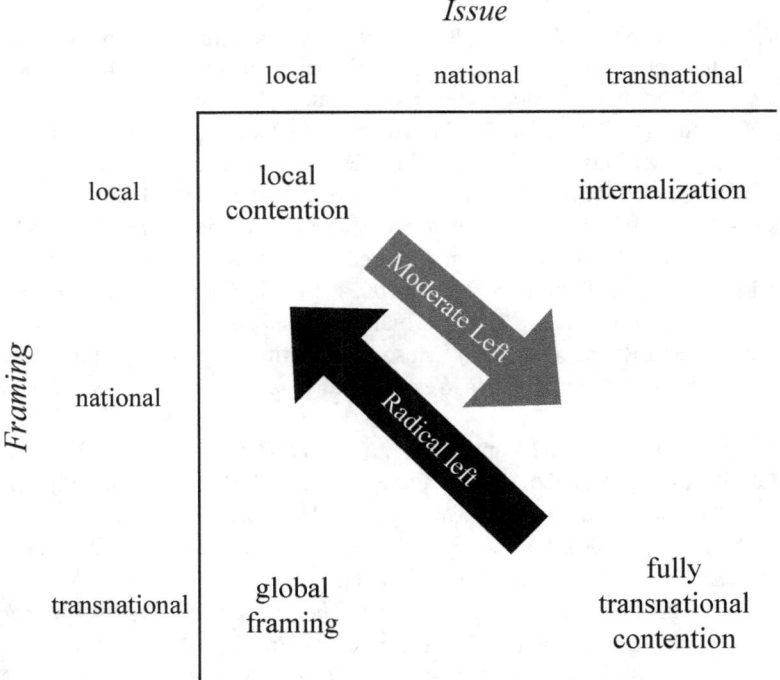

References

Auyero, J. (2003) 'Relational riot: austerity and corruption protest in the neoliberal era', *Social Movement Studies* 2: 117–46.
Ayres, J. M. (2004) 'Framing collective action against neoliberalism: the case of the "anti-globalization" movement', *Journal of World-Systems Research* 10: 11–34.
Císař, O. (2008) *Politický aktivismus v České republice. Sociální hnutí a občanská společnost v období transformace a evropeizace* [*Political activism in the Czech Republic. Social movements and civil society in the period of transformation and Europeanisation*], Brno: CDK.
Císař, O. and Koubek, M. (2012) 'Include 'em all? Culture, politics and a local hardcore/punk scene in the Czech Republic', *Poetics: Journal of empirical research on culture, the media and the arts* 40: 1–21.
Císař, O. and Slačálek, O. (2007)'The alter-globalization movement and democracy in the Czech Republic', paper presented at the ECPR Joint Session of Workshops, Helsinki, Finland, 7–12 May.
Císař, O. and Vráblíková, K. (2013) 'Transnational activism of social movement organizations: the effect of European Union funding on local groups in the Czech Republic', *European Union Politics* 14: 140–60.
Chesters, G. and Welsh, I. (2006) *Complexity and Social Movements: Multitude at the edge of chaos*, London: Routledge.
della Porta, D. and Tarrow, S. (eds) (2005) *Transnational Protest and Global Activism*, Lanham, MD: Rowman & Littlefield.
Gerhards, J. and Rucht, D. (1992) 'Mesomobilization: organizing and framing in two protest campaigns in West Germany', *American Journal of Sociology* 98: 555–96.
Graeber, D. (2002) 'The new anarchists', *New Left Review*, 13: 61–73.
Hamel, P., Lustiger-Thaler, H., Pieterse, J. N. and Roseneil, S. (eds) (2001) *Globalization and Social Movements*, Houndmills: Palgrave.
Hasselmann, C. (2006) *Policy Reform and the Development of Democracy in Eastern Europe*, Aldershot: Ashgate.
Juris, J. S. (2008) *Networking Futures: The movements against corporate globalization*, London: Duke University Press.
Keck, M. E. and Sikkink, K. (1998) *Activists Beyond Borders: Advocacy networks in international politics*, London: Cornell University Press.
Klingemann, H.-D., Fuchs, D. and Zielonka, J. (eds) (2006) *Democracy and Political Culture in Eastern Europe*, Abingdon: Routledge.
Köhler, B. and Wissen, M. (2003) 'Glocalizing protest: urban conflicts and the global social movements', *International Journal of Urban and Regional Research* 27: 942–51.
Kolářová, M. (2008) 'Antiglobalismus [Antiglobalism]', *Socioweb* 4: 3–5.
— (2009) *Protest proti globalizaci. Gender a feministická kritika* [*Protest against globalization. Gender and feminist critique*], Praha: SLON.

Koopmans, R. and Rucht, D. (2002) 'Protest event analysis', in B. Klandermans and S. Staggenborg (eds) *Methods of Social Movement Research*, Minneapolis, MN and London: University of Minnesota Press, pp. 231–59.

Maiba, H. (2005) 'Grassroots transnational social movement activism: the case of Peoples' Global Action', *Sociological Focus* 38: 41–63.

McDonald, K. (2006) *Global Movements: Action and culture*, Oxford: Blackwell.

Munck, R. (2007) *Globalization and Contestation*, Abingdon: Routledge.

Navrátil, J. (2012) '*Vývoj českého hnutí za globální spravedlnost v kontextu protiválečného aktivismu v letech 2002–2009. Analýza procesů transformace kolektivních aktérů*' ['Evolution of Czech Global Justice Movement in the context of antiwar activism between 2002–2009. Process tracing of collective actors' transformation'], PhD thesis, available at: http://is.muni.cz/th/52823/fss_d/ (accessed 28 April 2014).

Rothman, F. D. and Oliver, P. E. (2002) 'From local to global: the anti-dam movement in Southern Brazil, 1979–1992', in J. Smith and H. Johnston, *Globalization & Resistance: Transnational dimensions of social movements*', Lanham, MD: Rowman & Littlefield, pp. 115–32.

Routledge, P. (1996) 'Resisting and reshaping the modern: social movements and the development process', in R. J. Johnston, P. J. Tailor, and M. J. Watts (eds) *Geographies of Global Change: Remapping the world in the late twentieth century*, Oxford: Blackwell, pp. 263–79.

Routledge, P., Nativel, C. and Cumbers, A. (2006) 'Entangled logics and grassroots imaginaries of global justice networks', *Environmental Politics* 15: 839–59.

Růžička, V. (2007) *Squaty a jejich revoluční tendence* [*Squats and their revolutionary tendencies*], Praha: Triton.

Smith, J. (2002) 'Globalizing resistance: the battle of Seattle and the future of social movements', in J. Smith and H. Johnston (eds) *Globalization and Resistance: Transnational dimensions of social movements*, Boulder, CO: Rowman & Littlefield, pp. 207–27.

— (2008) *Social Movements for Global Democracy*, Baltimore: Johns Hopkins University Press.

Starr, A. and Adams, J. (2003) 'Anti-globalization: the global fight for local autonomy', *New Political Science* 25: 19–42.

Tarrow, S. (2005) *The New Transnational Activism*, New York: Cambridge University Press.

— (2010) 'Dynamics of diffusion, mechanisms, institutions, and scale shift', in R. K. Givan, K. M. Roberts and S. Soule (eds) *The Diffusion of Social Movements: Actors, mechanisms and political effects*, Cambridge: Cambridge University Press, pp. 204–19.

Tilly, C. (1995) *Popular Contention in Great Britain 1758–1834*, Cambridge, MA and London: Harvard University Press.

Tilly, C. and Wood, L. (2009) *Social Movements, 1768–2008* (2nd edn), Boulder, CO: Paradigm.

Walton, J. and Ragin, C. (1990) 'Global and national sources of political protest: third world responses to the debt crisis', *American Sociological Review* 55: 876–90.

Waterman, P. (2008) 'A trade union internationalism for the 21st century: meeting the challenge from above, below and beyond', in A. Bieler, I. Lindberg, and D. Pillay (eds) *Labour and the Challenges of Globalization*, London: Pluto Press, pp. 248–63.

Welsh, I. (2004) 'Network movement in the Czech Republic: perturbating Prague', *Journal of Contemporary European Studies* 12: 321–37.

Williams, G. (2008) *Struggles for an Alternative Globalization: An ethnography of counterpower in Southern France*, Aldershot: Ashgate.

Wissenburg, M. (2004) 'Globotopia: the alternatively global movement and utopianism', *Organization & Environment* 17: 493–508.

Wood, L. (2005) 'Taking to the streets against neo-liberalism: global days of action and other strategies', in B. Podobnik and T. Reifer (eds) *Transforming Globalization: Challenges and opportunities in the post 9/11 era*, Leiden: Brill, pp. 69–81.

Chapter Eleven

Flap of the Butterfly: Turkey's June Uprisings

Kivanc Atak

Introduction

'Predictability: Does the flap of a butterfly's wings in Brazil set off a tornado in Texas?' was the title of the presentation by Edward N. Lorenz, one of the pioneers of chaos theory, at the 139th meeting of the American Association for the Advancement of Sciences. The underlying idea was that a minor meteorological event in one place may cause major meteorological consequences in another, distant place on the planet. The mathematical sophistication behind this theoretical model does not seem to be fully applicable to the understanding of social phenomena. Yet certain phenomena that are hardly predictable in nature, such as mass uprisings and revolutions, perhaps do rely on a similar logic, as indicated by this example from a totally different field of science.

This chapter discusses mass uprisings in Turkey in June 2013. In fact, several countries and regions in the world have been shaken by mass upheavals since 2011, from the Arab Spring to the Occupy Wall Street (OWS) protests and further to crisis and anti-austerity mobilisations in Europe. The eruption of the Gezi protests in Turkey came as yet another episode within the global wave of mass protests; but due to substantial differences in Turkey's socio-economic and political conditions, hardly anyone predicted a large-scale mobilisation in this country. Indeed, it is daunting to try to provide a convincing answer as to why protests erupted at this particular moment. Instead of focusing on this question, I examine the Gezi protests from the 'diffusion' perspective, one which can also offer some insights into the 'why now?' question. The chapter is based on my ongoing research. I have been collecting empirical material from interviews, participant observation, a public survey by the private enterprise KONDA[1] and from secondary sources, such as magazines dedicated to Gezi and news media. In this respect, I make

---

1. KONDA is a private research enterprise that carries out public opinion surveys and provides consultancy services in Turkey. This enterprise conducted a survey on 6 and 7 June 2013 inside the Gezi Park with 4,411 individuals. Findings are definitely illustrative yet the survey is limited, in spatial and temporal terms, considering the number of neighbourhoods and towns in involved in protests as well as potential late-comers who joined the protests after the first week. For further information, *see* www.konda.com.tr.

the following propositions: in terms of their contentious origins and structural conditions, uprisings in Turkey differ from the Arab Spring, OWS and crisis-oriented mobilisations in Europe. By the same token, they resonate more with the revolts in Brazil and some countries in the Balkans,[2] which also developed mostly around existing urban struggles. However, explicit parallels in terms of action-repertoires, particularly in the case of public forums, between Gezi and the preceding protests indicate that *emulation*, if not so much *similarity attribution*, might work also across the borders of contextually different countries. I claim that the incremental use of the Internet and social media drastically shapes what 'critical communities' in one place take as an *example* or success story, which plays a profound role in the *adoption* of ideas and practices. The chapter empirically discusses and differentiates between *intra-national* and *transnational* diffusion as regards the ideas and practices related to the uprisings.

I start with a brief review of the main assumptions in the diffusion approach and its link to social-movement studies. I continue with short remarks on the role of the Internet and social media in contemporary forms of diffusion. Then, I locate the Gezi protests within the broader frame of the global uprisings. In the last section, I elaborate on the practices and frames that diffused in the course of the Gezi events and also highlight why we should pay increasing attention to social media, which enabled rapid diffusion, not only in the intra-national but also in the trans-national sphere.

Diffusion and social movements

The diffusion of innovative ideas, policies and practices has been subject to scholarly investigation for several decades. From biology and medicine to technology, mass consumption and public policy, diffusion has a powerful analytical purchase in understanding the spread of miscellaneous phenomena. In the field of social movements, the concept of diffusion has a relatively more recent history – however, one that has already proven highly relevant for analysis. Indeed, the fact that certain repertoires of contention, frames and strategies of protest and mobilisation travel across borders is a major reason why diffusion is a central notion for the study of contentious politics as well.

Under what conditions do ideas and practices diffuse? It goes without saying that this is the compelling question for any researcher who wants to examine the diffusion of a certain phenomenon. As regards social movements, mass upheavals,

---

2. Even though this volume does not discuss the uprisings in Brazil and the Balkans specifically, I refer to them here due to their relevance for the uprisings in Turkey. Indeed, recent protests in Brazil are similarly rooted in urban struggles that date back to the mid-2000s. These involve issues ranging from public transport to forced evictions from and discrimination against the inhabitants of *favelas*. Most recently, large construction projects for the World Cup and Olympics cross-cut increases in bus fares, which altogether cemented public resentment towards budgetary allocation and use of resources. In the Balkans, the sources of public dissent vary considerably; among other issues, resentment with urban policies and corruption scandals related to them has been one of the underlying motives behind the street mobilisations across the region.

and revolutions, it further makes sense to paraphrase this question as follows: why do we observe the spread of a rebellious mobilisation from country A to country B (and C further to D) but not to country E?[3] Since non-phenomena are no less interesting than phenomena themselves, one may also wonder: why do we *not* observe diffusion – for instance in the case of a revolution – at all? Such inquiries emanate from the plausible assumption that social movements and mass protests do not always occur in a splendid isolation from the rest of their environment. Rather, they are somehow related to preceding or contemporaneous episodes in socially and politically comparable, if not identical, circumstances. In other words, 'protest makers do not have to reinvent the wheel at each place and in each conflict' (McAdam and Rucht 1993: 58). That is why an adequate interpretation of the revolution in Egypt requires looking beyond the borders of Egypt in its proximity to the uprisings in Tunisia, just as one cannot properly understand the ongoing civil war in Syria or protests in Yemen without reference to what is and was happening in Egypt or Libya. To recall a more historical example, successful and unsuccessful attempts in the East European revolutions in 1989 need to be analysed in conjunction with each other, perhaps most notably with the Solidarity Movement in Poland. The same holds true for the resonance between Occupy Wall Street (OWS), the Indignados and anti-austerity protests in Europe, as well as between upheavals in Brazil and Turkey, and also across the recent mass protests in the Balkans.

Usually, diffusion starts with an *innovative* action, idea or practice. Traditionally, innovation used to designate the modernity of the centre and the acknowledgement that it will spread to the periphery. As Chabot and Duyvendak (2002) critically assess, nevertheless, the direction of diffusion from centre to periphery implies a superior and a linear relation between them – an implication which should be challenged on both an intellectual and an empirical level. Indeed, the mere fact that the self-immolation of Muhammad Bouazizi in Tunisia triggered an unprecedented chain reaction that not only transcended borders in the Middle East and North Africa (MENA) region but also inspired mass protests across different continents is self-explanatory in this respect. Setting this debate aside, innovation travels in the hands of a set of *adopters* who implement an idea or practice in their own context. The nature of these adopters varies according to the speed and timing of the successful or failed transfer of the diffusing item.[4] In a similar vein, some scholars in the social-movement literature coined the terms 'initiator' and 'spin-off' movements (McAdam 1995). While movements in the first group 'signal or otherwise set in motion an identifiable protest cycle', the latter 'draw their impetus and inspiration from the original initiator movement' (McAdam 1995: 219).

The next step would be to investigate the mechanisms through which the relationship between innovators (or initiators) and adopters is established.

---

3. Needless to say, one can ask the same question on a sub-national, regional, or local level.
4. Indeed, they can be early-adopters or late-adopters as well as non-adopters.

Previous research underscores two main avenues for diffusion to take place: *direct* (or relational) and *indirect* (non-relational) network ties. Whereas direct ties 'facilitate diffusion via point-to-point contact between people via communication' (Soule 2013: 350), indirect ties usually entail mediated contact through a variety of channels such as mass media, or through cognitive attributions or certain institutional terrains (Strang and Meyer 1993). In general, it is argued, successful cases of diffusion involve both direct and indirect network ties at the same time.

The intellectual or behavioural engagement of certain key actors in movement experiences in places other than their own local or domestic environment fosters the transfer of knowledge, ideas, frames and tactics between different social settings. Sean Chabot (2000), for instance, elaborates on the pioneering role by intellectuals, emissaries from India and Afro-American leaders who purposefully visited India, in the dissemination of the Gandhian repertoire into the civil-rights movement in the United States. Along similar lines, McAdam and Rucht (1993) shed light on the ways in which the New Left of the 1960s in Germany embraced some notions from the discourses of the American New Left around the same period, thanks to the experiences of certain figures from the socialist student organisation (SDS) in Germany. More recently, Gemma Edwards (2014) underlines the personal network ties of two suffragettes in the British Suffrage Movement in the early twentieth century, to explain why the tactic of militancy is adopted in one case but not in the other. It is also noteworthy that in situations of direct personal contact, 'weak ties' are considered more influential than strong ties (Granovetter 1978), because exchange of new ideas and information is less likely among people who are already well connected than among those who are proprietors of different experiences and knowledge.

The remaining question is: when is a successful diffusion more likely? The literature I covered juxtaposes at least two interrelated conditions under which diffusion may succeed. First, when the adopters share a position of what is called *structural equivalence*. The term originates from Burt's (1987) proposition that actors who are not directly tied to each other but related through a third party tend to carry out innovative practices, due to their similar structural positions and competition (Strang and Soule 1998: 274). To invoke East European revolutions once again, dissident populations that were perhaps not related to each other with effective direct or indirect ties were, however, connected through a third party, the Soviet regime, which was the 'common enemy', so to speak, and this definitely invigorated the regional diffusion of the breakdown of regimes (Bunce and Wolchik 2006). In the same direction, Soule's (1997) work on the student divestment movement in the United States emphasises the structural commonality rather than geographical proximity between university campuses whereby the shantytown protest tactic could diffuse. The second condition that frequently appears in previous studies is *similarity attribution* and *emulation*. In one sense, these pertain to cultural/cognitive processes whereby potential adopters attribute their subjective interpretations and perceptions to the diffusing item. In other words, 'adopters are not passive recipients, but actively choose to adopt a particular innovation or not' (Koopmans 2006). This idea significantly borrows from the 'framing' school in social movements and several scholars discussed the 'dislocation' and 'relocation' of frames from one context to another, to follow Chabot and Duyvendak (2002), ranging from the spread of decolonisation to the diffusion of the Japan-based Buddhist movement (Snow 1993; Strang 1990). Even though structural equivalence and similarity attribution might be at stake, however, this does not guarantee a successful diffusion. As Seifert (2013) has recently shown in the case of open-field destructions as a high-cost protest method against GMOs in France, Germany, and Spain, domestic factors such as the legal framework and level of state repression may hamper the successful adoption of a contentious strategy.

Bearing this conceptual background in mind, one may still wonder to what extent diffusion is possible when it is hard to attribute social and political similarity across borders or when structural equivalence is hardly visible if not entirely absent. I contend that an adequate response lies in the growing salience and transformative power of the Internet in the realm of social relations.

Internet revolution and revolution via Internet: Diffusion reconsidered

It is noteworthy that the bulk of the literature on diffusion as well as on its various applications to contentious politics dates from before what can be termed the Internet revolution. Obviously, the worldwide spread of Internet and social media more recently, is phenomenal and subject to a burgeoning field of research. Thus, it is interesting to wonder whether online forms of communication and information exchange have been altering mechanisms of diffusion, to the extent that there is a serious intellectual task of revising our theoretical knowledge and concepts in this field ahead.

In terms of diffusion mechanisms, the Internet in general and social media in particular *facilitate* diffusion through indirect ties; but their functioning also cements direct ties between potential initiators and adopters. Indeed, online portals, news agencies, blogs, forums, and so forth transform unrelated individuals into mass audiences for each other and into directly linked networks of people. Therefore, the pivotal role of face-to-face personal contacts in the diffusion of social movements and patterns of mobilisation might be outweighed by the rising tide of the Internet and social media. Fifteen years ago, Ayres (1999) contended that it is 'certainly not clear, first of all, that the Internet can replace the importance of cultural and interpersonal linkages for the sustained diffusion of protest across geographic boundaries' (Ayres 1999: 141). Today, I believe, this statement needs revision. Given that individual use of the Internet has skyrocketed in the last ten years in many countries,[5] together with the emergence of Facebook and Twitter,

---

5. A few examples from countries that have joined the global wave of protests since 2011 illustrate why I emphasise this point. The percentage of individual Internet usage between 2000 and 2012 increased from 0.64 to 44.07 (Egypt), from 2.87 to 49.85 (Brazil), from 1.08 to 65.96 (Bosnia and Herzegovina), from 9.14 to 56 (Greece), from 5.37 to 55.15 (Bulgaria), from 13.62 to 72 (Spain), from 2.75 to 41.44 (Tunisia) and from 3.76 to 45.13 (Turkey), to count but a few. *See* International Telecommunication Union 2013.

let alone other forms of social media, no one can deny the expansion of horizontal, or what Oikonomakis and Roos in Chapter Six of this volume refer to as the 'rhizomatic' nature of diffusion.

In this respect, what do recent findings on the use of online tools tell us about diffusion practices? Are we entering a new age in which diffusion becomes a cause more than an effect for *offline* contentious mobilisation around the world? For the time being, it seems too early to reach this conclusion. Jennifer Earl (2010) suggests that Internet surely has an amplifier effect for information diffusion, yet it did not entirely change the main mechanisms for social-movement activity.

> As such, I argue that the implications of the online diffusion of information fit squarely into a larger body of work that together suggests that the introduction of the Internet and /or rising levels of Internet use will not require a major reformulation of well-honed social movement hypotheses. ... Rather, Internet usage is thought to accelerate existing and well-known theoretical processes. ... information would diffuse faster and potentially farther allowing even tighter framing consistency and even wider coverage for those frames. I refer to this view on the consequences of Internet usage as 'super size' model of Internet activism ... (Earl 2010: 213).

Earl claims that the Internet has wider theoretical implications for *online* rather than offline forms of protest, but this is a separate issue. Recent empirical analyses, on the other hand, lend support for the accelerated nature of information diffusion on the Internet that also reflects on protest participation. In the case of the Egyptian uprising in 2011, Starbird and Palen (2012) demonstrate that the low-risk activism provided by tweeting information from the ground connected individuals in front of their screens with those on the streets and nourished social solidarity with the revolutionary cause. Again on Egypt, another recent research piece suggests that 'those who used blogs and Twitter for both general information and for communicating about the protests were more likely to attend on the *first* (italics mine) day, as were those who used the telephone, E-mail, and Facebook to communicate about the protests' (Tufekci and Wilson 2012: 375). An underlying assumption in these findings is that the uprisings might not be orchestrated online in the initial stages but that individual participation would probably not have grown so rapidly and exponentially in the absence of online channels. For instance, on the spread of OWS protests in the United States:

> A related, equally important finding is that the effect of online activism on offline protests increases over time. We argue that this is because early protests are likely to be organized in communities with activists who know each other through direct personal ties and, therefore, are less dependent on social media usage. As protests spread to communities with fewer experienced activists, protests require more planning and online social networking increases in importance (Vasi and Suh 2013: 36–7).

To say that there is a significant positive association between the penetration of social media into public life and the rise of social movements and mass upheaval would be, for the time being, a strong statement (Rane and Salem 2012). I would argue that the core assumptions and concepts in the diffusion theory have lost their analytical validity on the verge of the Internet revolution. But there is also no doubt that scholars will be more and more occupied with horizontal, non-linear and rapid (transnational) diffusion of information, ideas, and frames, as well as practices in social-movement activity, thanks to the unmistakable growth of the use of the Internet and social media in contemporary societies.

Already in the Arab Spring, social media proved to have an engineering role in the spread of the protests across the region. As I will show below, this effect became amplified to the greatest extent in the course of the Gezi uprisings. Yet our task should not only be to highlight the scope of information exchange but also to investigate why and how the Internet and social media facilitate the diffusion of certain frames and practices but not others.

A global diffusion of uprisings

In light of this debate, how can we understand the Gezi mobilisations in Turkey? For the time being, I position myself between two lines of thought. The first is that there has been a global wave of rebellion since 2011, spreading, roughly speaking, from the eruption of the Arab Spring to OWS, the anti-austerity protests and the Indignados movement, further to the uprisings in the Balkans and to mass mobilisations in countries such as Brazil and Turkey. This assumption would suggest that public contention in these different contexts is a manifestation of a shared phenomenon and that one needs to consider Gezi within the transnational diffusion of protest on a global scale. Alternatively, one can deny a logical sequencing in these different waves of mobilisation and focus on the (mostly) regionally concentrated nature of those episodes, which might be coherent and diffusive in a narrow scope but unrelated from a global perspective. I position myself closer to the first way of thinking yet I also acknowledge that the second assumption is not entirely implausible.

Concerning the social and political origins of the uprisings, the differences between the revolutionary situations in the MENA region and Occupy protests are hardly negligible. Indeed, in one case it was the long-standing, corrupted autocratic regimes that were at the centre of public resentment, whereas in the other it was financial capitalism and its institutions that cemented the grievances of the '99 per cent'. By the same token, it is counter-intuitive to suggest that the uprisings across the globe have nothing in common but a temporal coincidence. Obviously, OWS was primarily inspired by the Arab Spring in terms of the frames and repertoires of action.[6] In a similar vein, the resonance between Zuccotti Park, Plaza del Sol and Syntagma cannot be ignored.

---

6. 'The #occupy movement, originally initiated by a call from *Adbusters* to 'Occupy Wall Street,' was inspired by several international protests, most notably, the Arab Spring protests' (Occupy n.d.).

The necessity to highlight the distinctive character of the uprisings also applies to the Gezi Park protests. Given that the protests were rooted in pre-existing urban struggles rather than financial crisis or autocratic rule, it is plausible to differentiate Gezi from the Arab Spring and the OWS in terms of the sources of dissent. In this respect, the June 2013 demonstrations in Turkey converge more manifestly with the recent rebellions in Brazil and in some of the countries in the Balkans that also originated to varying degrees from existing urban contention. Yet, the growing salience of the Internet and social media is likely to challenge the assumption that *emulation* of protest behaviour is merely contingent on the prerequisite of *similarity attribution* and *structural equivalence*. In other words, the rapid diffusion of ideas and practices that was hard to imagine, if not improbable, two or three decades ago is becoming less and less unrealistic simply because of the expansive flow of information, emergent networks and ties through online platforms. In this fashion, initiation of certain practices in one place reaches more easily to a multiplicity of what Rochon named 'critical communities' (quoted in Chabot and Duyvendak 2002); that is, 'networks of excluded citizens who identify new social problems, formulate new modes of thinking and feeling, and develop new political and cultural solutions' (Chabot and Duyvendak 2002: 706).

In a nutshell, the recent uprisings across the globe indicate that, for certain forms and frames of mass protest to diffuse, it is not compelling to assume similarity between the sources of dissent, nor is it necessary to have a third party that connects unrelated collective actors to each other. In this sense, to reiterate, the increasing impact of the Internet and social media is a major factor which may transform unlikely scenarios of diffusion into imminent narratives. In his analysis of post-communist revolutions between 2000 and 2006, Beissinger (2007) argued that 'prior cases of revolutionary success have encouraged a widespread transnational borrowing of revolutionary modes of confrontation, inciting action where it otherwise would have been unlikely' and that 'in the context of modular change the rising weight of example can in fact turn what might otherwise seem like an impossible structural situation (a high threshold in Kuran's model, *see* Kuran 1989) into a seemingly propitious one (a significantly lowered threshold)' (Beissinger 2007: 273). Depending on how 'success' and 'example' are perceived and recognised by critical communities across a wide geographical scope, therefore, I think that mass upheavals, tactics and frames of protest might still travel due to the expanding online networks, even across societal settings that do not fully resonate with each other.

In what follows, I discuss the Gezi protests in Turkey in light of the conceptual framework drawn so far. First, I offer a short narrative of the uprisings to underline how things started and evolved. I then move on with an empirical investigation of diffusion by particularly looking at frames and actions in circulation. In this respect, I distinguish intra-national and trans-national diffusion, yet I do not treat them as mutually exclusive but as cross-cutting processes.

Gezi: From out of nowhere?

The June 2013 uprisings in Turkey came, unsurprisingly, as a 'surprise'. In comparison to Arab Spring countries, Turkey was not subject to a long-standing autocracy whose rule was further discredited by a combination of issues, among which impoverishment was in the first place.[7] As opposed to the countries in Southern Europe, in a similar vein, Turkey was not suffering deeply from the financial crisis or the consequent austerity measures that, together with high levels of unemployment, imposed devastating effects on societies in the southern Eurozone. Prior to the Gezi upheaval, the Justice and Development Party (AKP) was enjoying growing support – on the margins of 50 per cent of the electorate – and the domestic economy had been portrayed as a 'success story' by mainstream intellectual circles – even though critics were pointing to a variety of problems such as the chronic current-account deficit, which is one of the highest in the world (World Bank 2014). On another front, ongoing negotiations with the imprisoned (Kurdish Separatist) PKK leader and the temporary ceasefire by PKK's military leadership in Northern Iraq were considered as a promising step toward the resolution of the historically rooted Kurdish question. To be brief, the political trajectory in Turkey did not seem to resonate much with the context of the uprisings in the Arab Spring or with political settings juddered by financial turbulence and its societal repercussions. In other words, the Gezi protests are yet another example of why structural predictability of mass upheavals, or the lack thereof, is not a theoretical safe haven for scholars of social movements.

In fact, contrary to the conventional wisdom, the protests that centred on the demolition of the Gezi Park next to Taksim Square have a longer story. Chambers of architects and urban planners as well as several trade unions were already involved in a struggle against the municipal plan for urban transformation in Taksim and the Beyoglu district that dates back to 2009. Notably, the umbrella network called Taksim Solidarity, which became globally known in the course of the Gezi events, is actually 'a platform by more than 80 organisational components that came together one and a half years ago against the project of pedestrianisation in and the reconstruction of *Topcu Barracks* next to the Taksim Square' (Firat 2013: 36). In the meantime, various attempts at collective action were carried out at the initiative of architects and urban planners, together with some shopkeepers in the neighbourhood, particularly after the construction site in Taksim Square was first erected (Atalay 2013: 30). Above all, similar attempts at collective action addressing urban policies existed prior to the project in Taksim: popular struggles in the Sulukule district of Istanbul or in Dikmen in Ankara in the preceding years also revolved around exclusionary urban transformation and rent-seeking activities. Hence, the contentious mobilisation in Taksim is nested within a longer tradition of struggles related to large-scale urban policies in several towns in Turkey.

---

7. This by no means suggests that these structural conditions determined the uprisings in the Middle East; it is noteworthy that until very recently, autocratic stability in the region, despite deep-rooted socio-economic problems in these societies, was a resilient puzzle for political scientists.

By the end of May 2013, early attempts to block the working of bulldozers in Gezi Park were set in motion by a handful of activists who were already involved in protests and knew each other in this contentious struggle. At that time, there was neither much public attention to the resistance, nor extraordinary social-media activity to counteract printed and televised news.

> Over the night of May 27th, around 10 p.m., an e-mail was circulated by *IMECE Societal Urban Movement* with the message: 'they are cutting the trees'. 10–15 people went to the park immediately; from 7 a.m. the next morning, calls for support were announced; those who came were the ones already involved in the network; we were around 30 people in the next morning. At the beginning, we did not know what would happen, but we were thinking that we had to stay and sit down here (Firat 2013: 36).

Although the next day, 28 May, more people started to come to Gezi for solidarity, it was precisely when, before sunrise on both 30 and 31 May, police and municipal security forces (*zabita*) cracked down on a few dozen young dissenters who decided to put up tents inside Gezi Park, that things took a different turn.

> We did not expect the police operation at 5 o'clock in the morning and the fierce attack by security forces on an issue which seemed to have strong public credibility. Among us there were people, who do not have any trust in the state; but we did not expect this, we were not ready for it. ... At the end of that evening, 1000–1500 people stayed overnight. We realized that compared to previous night more riot police arrived. There were more than 10 police buses, and two–three TOMAs.[8] ... This time we were more crowded. It was likely that people could fall down from the ramp around the Divan Hotel, the evacuation ladder was too narrow and at the end it collapsed. ... They fired too many gas bombs (Özgür 2013: 32–3).

While the mainstream media provided fairly limited coverage of what was going on in Taksim, visual material documenting police violence entered social media platforms, together with newly opened Facebook and Twitter accounts disseminating up-to-date information. In fact, many people who did not know about or who had nothing to do with the ongoing struggle learned about and decided to participate in the protests thanks to these online channels.

---

8. Multifunctional water tanks at the disposal of the Turkish police. They are extensively used during public demonstrations in Turkey.

My husband had to be in Iznik[9] on Friday, 31st of May, for business reasons. We decided to spend the weekend there and I joined him as well. During the day on Friday, since we did not use the Internet, we found out about the reach of the events only at night, and we decided to return the next morning. It was my husband who said 'we should go there' when we saw the extent of the situation. I have never participated in a protest, politics has never been my field of interest, and I am one of those who are raised with 'oh my dear, stay away from this' type of warnings. Even though the first day I was thinking that 'we also should do something now', actually I went there not to let my husband alone while being very much concerned about what could happen to us.[10]

At the end of the week and over the weekend, therefore, hundreds of thousands of people took to the streets with the ultimate aim to reach Taksim. The police kept firing gas bombs and pressurised water on the growing crowd; unusually, however, heavy coercion did not succeed in deterring the masses of people who proved to be determined not to disperse. On Saturday afternoon, then, riot police withdrew from Taksim. The square and Gezi Park was thus liberated from state coercion and turned into a 'commune', if you will, surrounded by barricades.

Protests continued over the next few weeks and months, albeit to a lesser extent and gradually on a more minor scale. Gathering on Taksim Square and in the Gezi Park became a daily routine frequented by thousands – until the Park and the Square were closed to any attempt at gathering – while clashes with police from behind the barricades, particularly in the nearby Besiktas district, continued into the late hours of the night. Meanwhile, a number of spokespersons from Taksim Solidarity met with Prime Minister Erdogan; however, the meeting proved inconclusive in terms of the list of demands addressed to the government regarding the municipal project, police coercion and freedom of assembly in the first place.

It is beyond the purpose and limits of this chapter to provide a detailed narrative of the Gezi protests. Suffice it to say that a minor protest against a municipal project turned into a mass upheaval. How was this possible? Who took to the streets? In order to conceive the rapid diffusion of Gezi Park protests domestically, one may plausibly start with this question. In fact, participation in Gezi can be analysed along two axes: individuals and organisations. To continue from the last quote above, it is hard to deny that Gezi brought together a variety of people who did not have an activist profile and some of whom were taking part in a demonstration for the first time. For instance, the survey by KONDA reveals that almost 45 per cent of the interviewees inside the Gezi Park on 6 and 7 June confirmed that this was their first protest-event activity. This is reminiscent of the high number of 'first-comers' in OWS protests as well. Besides that, approximately 80 per cent of the interviewees claimed no affiliation with an organisation such as a political party

---

9. A small town in the Marmara region, a couple of hours distant from Istanbul.
10. Written interview IST1, date of response 12 December 2013.

or association. What is equally striking is that, despite notable differences in their political orientations, people attached themselves to the idea of 'resistance' and this seems to be the benchmark of the widely used template, *Gezi spirit*, affirmed by many protestors.[11]

> I do not know why and how it came to happen, but from the first day onward, we were heading over the roads leading to Gezi with friends who have very different life styles and political stances. This also continued in the later days. The atmosphere was really striking. There was a peaceful, sharing and solidarity-oriented spirit. And it was certainly not discriminatory. I think that just like '68 generation, Gezi spirit will be debated and remembered for years.[12]

In fact, organisational variety in the uprisings confirms this observation as well. On the one hand, one could see activist groups who usually appear together in big demonstrations as in May Day: political parties (for example, SDP and ESP),[13] labour unions (for example, DISK and KESK[14]), associations (for example, Halkevleri[15]), student initiatives (such as Ogrenci Kollektifi, Genç-Der[16]), leftist factions (such as Kaldirac, BDSP[17]) and so forth. On the other hand, there were also networks of groups which, also active in street protests, vary considerably in ideology and political orientations: Kemalists (such as, Turkish Youth Union or TGB), LGBTT groups, anti-capitalist Muslims (such as the Association for Struggling against Capitalism) and, to a more modest extent, pro-Kurdish activists (for example, the Peace and Democracy Party or BDP). This also reflected in the slogans, which ranged from 'Stand Together Against Fascism!' to 'We Are Soldiers of Mustafa Kemal!'

It is reasonable to suggest that the shared resentment against Erdogan, even more than his government and the AKP, made it possible for people with similar and dissimilar political orientations to 'co-resist'. One could easily infer the level

---

11. At the time this chapter was drafted, we knew less about the protest participants in smaller towns and more provincial places, since public and intellectual attention focused overwhelmingly on the largest urban centres such as Istanbul and Ankara, which also shelter significant variety at the neighbourhood level. Thus, I refrain from making a strong claim due to the yet limited nature of the empirical material.
12. Written interview IST2; date of response 23 November 2013.
13. The Socialist Democracy Party and the Socialist Party of the Oppressed.
14. Confederation of Progressive Trade Unions of Turkey and Confederation of Public Employees Unions.
15. People's Houses: they were established in the 1930s by the single-party regime to promote the modernist nation-building project; after the transition to the multi-party regime, however, they were outlawed by the Democrat Party government in 1951. Since the 1960s, People's Houses have been active in associational life as a civil society organisation, except for a seven-year break from 1980 until 1987 following the military coup on 12 September 1980.
16. Student Collectives and Youth to the Squares Association.
17. *Kaldirac*, literally meaning 'lever', is a leftist magazine which frequently mobilises on the street. The abbreviation BDSP stands for Independent Revolutionary Class Platform.

of anger with Erdogan from the sudden mushrooming of miscellaneous graffiti everywhere. It is absolutely true that this shared resentment, or 'common enemy', to echo the widely used expression, had different political roots and meanings for those on the streets. Yet, the generally peaceful environment helped people concentrate on the idea of resistance as a common denominator, rather than on the contradictions embedded in those different political orientations.

Diffusion in cross-cutting spheres

This shared position enabled a mass base to develop for Gezi Park mobilisations throughout Turkey. But we still need to answer the questions of what exactly has diffused in the course of the uprisings and in what ways the diffusion was facilitated, other than by the common resentment of various groups. Here, it might be useful to introduce intra-national and transnational diffusion as distinct but closely related processes. Indeed, the Gezi protests confirmed that ideas and practices do not travel in the hands of passive recipients who simply replicate those ideas and practices. Rather, the diffusing items are transformed, reshaped, and tailored in the process of adoption. Therefore, intra-national and trans-national diffusion need not be mutually exclusive. In the following, I structure my discussion by looking separately at diffusing frames and actions. I stress what seems to be a case of intra-national versus transnational diffusion, without claiming that they are disengaged from each other.

Diffusing frame: Diren! (Resist!)

The overarching frame across Gezi mobilisations was *Diren!* (*Resist!*). Even though websites and social-media accounts proliferated under the label of 'Occupy', this did not become an equally powerful frame for the vast majority of Gezi sympathisers. Indeed, *Diren!* captured aptly the sense of resisting outrageous levels of state coercion as well as the authoritarian tendencies of the incumbent political leadership. It also helped in bridging the different collective and individual positions described above. There is no doubt that one of the most popular slogans of the protests was 'Everywhere Taksim, Everywhere Resistance!' The adoption of *Diren!* thus shows that the parallels between action-forms, namely OWS and 'occupying' Taksim Square and Gezi Park, did not automatically translate into identical frames. The relative weakness of the Occupy frame, in other words, seems to be due to the stronger 'cultural legitimacy' of *Diren!* in the intra-national sphere.

Interestingly, *Diren!* as a sort of master frame travelled not only across platforms that are somewhat related to Gezi but also across social circles which were quite sceptical about or hostile to the Gezi phenomenon itself. As regards the first dimension, the frame was adopted by several local actors who supported Gezi with protests and uprisings outside Istanbul. As I also discuss below, protests erupted in many other cities and neighbourhoods, in big urban centres most remarkably. In Ankara, for instance, clashes with police reached intense levels, specifically in Dikmen, and '*Diren Ankara!*' (*Resist Ankara!*) immediately became the resonant voice from the capital. Needless to say, this was replicated in numerous towns and districts throughout the country. The gendarmerie's attack on peasants who were protesting against the construction of a highly protected military station in a sub-province of Diyarbakir, Lice, to give another example, had a similar effect. A mass protest was organised in several cities to display solidarity with the peasants, using the frame '*Diren Lice!*' (*Resist Lice!*) (*Radikal* 2014). Even after the Gezi protests began to decline, many other episodes of contentious action resorted to the same frame, as we have seen in the Middle East Technical University (METU), the Armutlu neighborhood in Istanbul, Tuzlucayir in Ankara and so forth.

That said, discursive manifestations of *Diren!* also appeared in the language of social actors who denounced Gezi protesters for being 'provocative', 'violent' and 'threatening' for the democratic order. For instance, the Association for Free Opinion and Educational Rights (*Ozgur-Der*) has been pejorative about Gezi from the onset, and the central branch of the association publicly condemned the protests 'as an attempt to revive the Kemalist despotism' (Haksoz Haber 2013). Following the military takeover in Egypt in July 2013, however, Ozgur-Der launched a public campaign to support Mohammed Morsi and the Muslim Brotherhood against the Egyptian armed forces, using the frame '*Diren Mursi, Diren Misir!*' (*Resist Morsi, Resist Egypt!*). The pro-AKP government newspaper, *Yeni Safak*, which also harshly criticised Gezi as an international plot against the government, lent its intellectual support to the Muslim Brotherhood by using the frame of *Diren!*. Overall, this shows that a powerful frame can not only be adopted by the sympathisers of the original cause but also by its opponents for their own cause.

After all, the adoption of *Diren!* offers hints to the coalescence of intra-national and transnational diffusion. A transnationally embedded form of protest paved the way to a master frame that appealed to different publics in Turkey more than 'Occupy'. This seems to be largely due to the stronger fit of a 'resistance' frame to the uprisings as the common denominator of public dissent.

Transnational diffusion of action: Public forums

The Gezi protests are generally associated with Taksim, the central square in Istanbul where Gezi Park is located. However, mass protests spilled over to eighty out of eighty-one administrative provinces in the country. In cities such as Ankara, the physical encounters between the police and protestors were no less tense than in Istanbul; barricades were placed in several major urban centres. Most woefully, Ali Ismail Korkmaz (Eskisehir), Ethem Sarisuluk (Ankara), Ahmet Atakan (Hatay), Adbullah Cömert (Hatay) and Mehmet Sari (policeman, Adana) died in the course of the protests in different cities, and Mehmet Ayvalitas was crushed to death by a car driving through the midst of the crowd in Istanbul. Official records announced by the news media reported that from the end of May until the first days of September 2013, nearly 6,000 protests took place across the whole of Turkey, involving more than three million people (Sardan 2013).

The spatial diffusion of Gezi mobilisations entered a new phase with the public forums. In fact, forums clearly constitute a case of *transnational* diffusion.

General assemblies were held throughout the OWS and 15-M movement in Spain. Prior to these recent examples, moreover, popular assemblies characterised earlier struggles such as the Piqueteros in Argentina (Wolff 2007). Thus, protesters in Turkey did not have to invent forums from scratch; rather, they capitalised on accumulated experiences in previous mobilisations.

As I mentioned above, Taksim and Gezi Park developed a 'commune' spirit after the riot police withdrew from the square. Shortly following the meeting between Solidarity's spokespersons and the Prime Minister on 15 June, however, the police returned to Taksim and brutally evicted people until the Square and the Park were entirely emptied. Just before the police intervention, Taksim Solidarity proposed the idea of organising forums inside the Gezi Park but the forceful eviction ruled out all attempts to gather there. In order to prevent the 'Gezi spirit' from dying out abruptly, components of Taksim Solidarity thus decided to set up public forums in different locations. Initially, forums were centred in Besiktas (Abbasaga Park) and Kadikoy (Yogurtcu Park) districts; but in a couple of days, forums spread to hundreds of public parks in dozens of cities. The idea was to meet regularly, possibly on a daily basis, and promote discussion and deliberation on a variety of issues in a participatory framework.

> We have a lot of questions ahead such as; how local forums can contact each other and bring together common demands, what the working principles of the forums should be, what kind of solidarity practices can emerge out of the forums, to what extent social media can be used to coordinate forums at the provincial and country level, what kind of roles working groups and workshops can play for the functioning of the forums as a body of more effective discussion and decision making (Mustereklerimiz 2013).

In other words, discussions oscillated between technical, organisational, and infrastructural matters, on the one side, and political demands and proposals on the other. The practice of 'open stage' was set in motion, whereby individual participants could briefly address the crowd. Particularly at relatively large gatherings in Besiktas and Kadikoy, communication was carried out via hand signals that were reminiscent of the OWS and 'with origins as various as Quakerism, ancient Athens, the *indignados* of Spain (some of whom were present) and the spokescouncils of the 1999 anti-globalization movement' (Schneider 2011).

It goes without saying that the first days of the forums witnessed vivid and enthusiastic crowds. Due to the lack of substantial experience, nonetheless, it was not an easy task to run the forums, and 'even (relatively) simple technical matters as to whether forums will be cancelled on certain dates and whether a decision is taken in that direction tend to create confusion' (Tugal 2013). Still, meetings in the forums contributed to a new form of public awareness, if to a limited extent. Meanwhile, the infrastructure of the forums, namely announcements and minutes, had also been transmitted to online platforms, some of which are still active several months after their inception.[18] At any rate, the parallels of this exercise with previous experiences recently are hard to ignore:

> I believe they would never have taken off had it not been for the various global precedents, such as the Occupy movement. Our local park forums adopt the methods of global justice movements such as Occupy. The hand gestures to enable communication among crowds without creating noise have been emulated at some of the forums with larger participation. The open stage where individuals queue for and take turns to express their thoughts, ideas and vision freely, is another element of this movement's repertoire that is becoming more and more common (Inceoglu 2013).

However, the promising participatory climate of the forums eventually led to problems in decision-making. The endless debates and proposals from the open stage proved to be counter-productive in the absence of effective mechanisms to work on the proposals.

> When people drift apart from action and start discussing, conflicts become more visible. For example, nationalists impose their nationalism. Or those from the Kurdish national movement feel obliged to underline the word 'Kurdistan' and this creates tensions ... Second, a lot of proposals are placed on the open stage but there was no pool to aggregate those proposals. I think that people had the following feeling: 'My word does not have any value. I make a proposal, but days pass and it is not taken seriously.' Every day, numerous proposals were written down, but they solely remained in the minutes. Thus, the proposals could not be implemented (Dogan 2013).

In *Yogurtcu Park*, for example, those who stayed in the park after the forum meetings finished organised 'co-ordination groups' to discuss further and deal with the proposals. 'But the Coordination could not handle the amount of work', says Deniz Polat (2013), perhaps due to the lack of appropriate methods. In addition, established groups and organisations began to compete with each other in order to put their own stamp in the decisions. Yet this seems to have alienated many people. To tackle such issues, working groups and neighbourhood committees were established to address specific issues such as legal questions. However, these efforts did not eliminate tensions between different groups and activists had to face declining popular interest in the forum-related activities.

Obviously, these concerns are not peculiar to the uprisings in Turkey. Difficulties in making collective decisions and establishing effective organisational structures

---

18. In fact, the forum exercise deserves a deep ethnographic perspective for a thorough analysis. In this chapter, I only refer to it very briefly in order to highlight the diffusion of a particular practice in the course of the mobilisations. Obviously, the ways in which people organise these forums and discuss questions, the range and content of issues debated and to what extent these vary across different forums can certainly become a separate research agenda.

were also formidable in the case of the OWS and Indignados, not to mention others (for a comparison with Spain, *see* Maeckelbergh 2012). This tells us that transnational diffusion is not confined to the actions and practices; rather, it also spreads to problems and dilemmas that are enshrined in those actions and practices.

Intra-national diffusion of action: 'Iftars' on the street

The uprisings in Turkey also witnessed the diffusion of a locally embedded action in the intra-national sphere: *iftars* on the street. In the Muslim tradition, *iftar* refers to the daily break in fasting during the month of Ramadan. It follows the sunset, and Muslims have their meal as soon as the evening call for prayer (ezan) is recited from the mosques. When street protests started to decline after the first couple of weeks of Gezi, the beginning of Ramadan in the early days of July yielded a political opportunity to popularise what is called '*iftars* on the street' as a peculiar form collective action.

In fact, there were several reasons to suspect that mass protests could not be sustained for very long, particularly due to the increasing levels of repression and control by security forces. Indeed, protests ebbed gradually, if not entirely, toward the end of June. Ramadan, which started at the beginning of July in 2013, also played a role in the erosion of street mobilisations: fasting during the day and the general hike in religious consciousness among pious citizens undermined incentives to maintain rebellious protest, at least to a certain extent. However, the onset of Ramadan rejuvenated a subtle and certainly less confrontational action-form, which markedly incorporated the spirit of Gezi into an originally Muslim practice. To the best of my knowledge, the idea of street *iftars* was first introduced in 2011 by the Labour and Justice Platform, an activist initiative that challenges the alienation of socialist and Islamist perspectives from each other and promotes their collaboration. The Platform started to organise *iftars* on the street in front of luxurious hotels, to criticise consumer culture and the commercialisation of Ramadan. Members of the platform performed this practice in several places including Gezi Park, together with socially excluded and working-class people specifically (Emek ve Adalet Platformu 2013).

In July 2013, however, this exercise became popularised in the context of Gezi, thanks to public calls by figures such as Ihsan Eliacik, a leftist-Muslim author and activist, who also provides intellectual encouragement to the Association for Struggling against Capitalism (previously known as the Anti-Capitalist Muslims). As in the case of public forums, *iftars* on the street rapidly diffused in the entire country as a distinctively protest-related action-form, while mass protests were in decline. Arguably, what made this practice adopted widely is its transformation of a custom embedded in Muslim culture into a political challenge, which is socially inclusive and does not discriminate against people based on their beliefs. The logistics of this practice rested both on individual contributions of food and drink and on the organisation by neighbourhood committees closely linked to the public forums. Needless to say, social media played a pivotal role in the dissemination of information about the times and places of the *iftars* as well as logistical issues.

In a nutshell, street *iftars* are emblematic of intra-national diffusion of action. Even though this exercise was invented long before the eruption of the Gezi Park uprisings, it became popular and diffused rapidly in the context of Gezi. This shows us that in order for a practice to diffuse, it might not be sufficient that the practice has cultural legitimacy in society. The rebellious environment created by Gezi worked as a facilitator, or political opportunity, for an already existing form of action to be suddenly embraced by a much larger audience.

Tweeting resistance: Social media within and across borders

I started following the initial protest in Gezi Park via the Internet, before it turned into a mass upheaval. At that time, I was trying to finish the final draft of my dissertation in Florence but strongly distracted by what was going on in Istanbul. Besides the fact that I do research on social movements, it was also difficult not to show a political interest in the happenings. In practice, this meant long hours spent in front of the screen. On 31 May, for the first time in my life, I started following Twitter while at the same time watching Taksim on alternative media portals that provided live broadcasts of the incidents. After an exhausting night, on the morning of 1 June, I read in Facebook and Twitter that masses of people were pouring into Taksim Square, without noticing that some of the pictures posted were actually fake. At any rate, I decided to book a flight to Istanbul that very day and rushed to the airport in Bologna.

Many people, whether or not they have an activist record, followed a similar path in their decision to participate in the protests. The mysterious quiescence of the mainstream media concerning the police violence on the peaceful protest in Taksim was attacked in the Internet and social media, to draw more attention to the protests. The KONDA survey reveals that around 70 per cent of the informants in the Gezi Park learned about the incidents in Taksim through social media. Indeed, it is hard to believe that things could have developed in the same way two or three decades ago. In this respect, the Internet in general and social media in particular strongly facilitated the diffusion of information in the *intra-national* sphere, whereby people became not only passive recipients of circulated news but also active reporters from the ground.

'What is unique about this particular case', states the report by SMaPP (Social Media and Political Participation Lab at New York University), is that unlike some other recent mass revolts, 'around 90 per cent of all geolocated tweets are coming from within Turkey, and 50 per cent from within Istanbul' (SMaPP 2013, 2). This provides a striking contrast to the Egyptian revolution, where only 30 per cent of the tweeting activity came from within the country (Starbird and Palen 2012). In addition, the hashtag *#direngeziparkı* has been used in more than 1.8 million tweets as of 3 June, while 'the hashtag *#jan25* was used in less than one million tweets during the entire Egyptian revolution' (SMaPP 2013: 3).

To nobody's surprise, the number of hashtags and Facebook pages that include the word *diren* (*resist*) has increased exponentially since the end of May 2013. Despite the strong implications of this intense social-media activity for horizontal

Figure 11.1: Temporal distribution of web searches from Turkey, using Google Trends

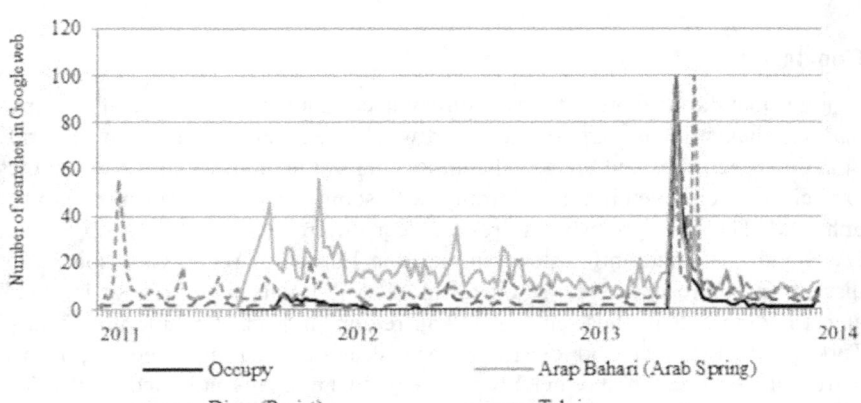

ties and communication, certain actors such as public figures were probably more influential than others, warning us about hierarchical relations that might be disguised by the multitude of Twitter and Facebook users (SMaPP 2013: 5). At any rate, further social-media- and network-analysis can systematically inform us about the ways in which the diffusion of information and frames worked in the case of the Gezi protests. Such systematic analyses can also highlight the *transnational* linkages between Gezi and other uprisings elsewhere in the world.

In terms of public attention, a quick and simple analysis of certain items that appeared in a Google search from Turkey, for instance, could be a useful start. In this sense, Figure 11.1 shows that the searches for 'Occupy', 'Arab Spring' (in Turkish) and 'Tahrir' peaked around the same period when the overarching frame of the Gezi protests, *Diren!*, skyrocketed in online platforms as well. This can be interpreted as a crude indicator of public attention that constructs cognitive linkages between Gezi and other uprisings such as OWS or the Arab Spring.

After all, the Internet and social media did not only facilitate the intra-national diffusion of rebellious protest and the frame of *diren* in particular. They also enabled the *transnational* diffusion of practices, above all, the public forums. Notwithstanding horizontal networks encouraged by online activism, it is hard to overlook that some actors are more influential than others in conveying knowledge and strategies. In other words, those who are more active users of the Internet and social media, and who also have been more closely following or politically/intellectually engaged in previous experiences of mobilisation such as OWS or *Indignados*, must have contributed to the adoption of ideas and practices that travel across borders. Even if the recipients do not adopt them automatically, as in the case of the relative strength of *diren* over the 'occupy' frame, it would be much more difficult to experience the rapid diffusion of a practice such as public forum in the absence of the Internet and social media. Hence, further research can single out the ways in which certain influential actors made use of online channels to promote trans-nationally embedded frames and action repertoires.

Conclusion

To argue that the Gezi protests have nothing in common with the wave of uprisings that has shaken many parts of the world would be an underestimation. In terms of action repertoires and the social composition of the mobilisations, Gezi shows explicit parallels, even if not uniformity, with some other recent episodes of mass upheaval. The Gezi protests also reveal clear differences from the Arab Spring, OWS and crisis and anti-austerity protests in Europe as regards the sources of dissent. In this respect, Gezi resonates more visibly with the uprisings in Brazil and, to some extent, those in the Balkan region. Indeed, the June uprisings in Turkey developed around existing urban struggles that involved established activist networks and unpredictably evolved into a mass revolt joined by a variety of social and political actors. Therefore, Gezi neither posed a popular challenge to a longstanding autocratic regime, unlike the Arab Spring, nor to the supremacy of financial institutions protected by governments at the expense of austerity measures imposed on populations across a wide geographical scope.

In the theoretical framework of diffusion, it is hard to claim that the mechanism of *similarity attribution* or the position of *structural equivalence* was at stake in the course of Gezi, with regard to the Arab Spring, OWS and anti-austerity mobilisations in Europe. This is largely due to the aforementioned reasons. In Brazil and some countries in the Balkans, however, the eruption of Gezi seems to have fostered *emulation* by activist circles which had already been on the streets for a while, if on a less massive scale. Explicit references in slogans that embody attributes to Turkey are self-explanatory in this respect.[19] That said, the exercise of *public forums*, most notably, implies that Gezi resonated with a larger context of global uprisings.

A systematic analysis of how transnational diffusion of ideas and practices worked precisely in the case of Gezi will lay bare a more comprehensive picture. For the time being, it is plausible to assert that the role of direct personal ties in the traditional sense of the word, and of indirect ties enabled by conventional mass media, are outweighed by the increasing penetration of the Internet and social media into individual and public cognition and practices. This phenomenon remarkably facilitates and accelerates diffusion processes, not only between

---

19. 'The Turkish resistance movement exerted a vivid influence on uprisings in Brazil. First, because, like Brazil, Turkey is a country where one rarely sees violent street demonstrations, despite the abject living conditions of much of the population. Chants like "It's over love, so here will turn Turkey" echoed in Pôrto Alegre, Rio de Janeiro, São Paulo, and other cities. Demonstrators adopted tactics of urban confrontation from the Turkish resistance: barricades of burning garbage, gallons of water in which to submerge tear gas canisters.' Anonymous reflections by 'grupelho' (faction) actively involved in the Brazilian uprisings (CrimethInc 2013).

similar contexts of contentious politics but also between societal settings that do not resonate strongly.

At this I point, I think it is useful to recall Beissinger's observation on revolutions: a success story or an *example* has the capacity to trigger revolutionary sentiments under political settings which, in fact, do not really favour or render a revolutionary situation a probable scenario. If we decide not to focus on revolutions *per se*, but look at mass uprisings in general, we could also argue the following: a success story or an example does not have to be a revolution, overthrow of governments, replacement of political leaders or a wholesale policy transformation, to name but a few. The mass uprising itself, together with the constellation of narratives, written and visual material attached to it, could become an example or a success story on its own. Most certainly, the Internet and social media play a profound role in the circulation of these materials to an audience whose magnitude was hardly imaginable a few decades ago. It goes without saying that *emulation* that is invoked on the basis of an example is more likely when social and political similarities can be attributed, or when *existing* collective struggles engage with an example, if not an identical one.

Obviously, there was already accumulated knowledge of the frames and action repertoires that spatially diffused on an intra-national as well as transnational scale throughout the Gezi mobilisations. There is also no room for doubt that social media played a profound role in accelerating the diffusion over a wide geographical reach. Still, more sophisticated analysis is needed to identify patterns of diffusion more precisely – particularly with respect to networks and influential actors. This would, indeed, unveil to what extent diffusion took place in a horizontal fashion and whether there were subtle hierarchies in the transfer of information and ideas.

Gezi has also shown that in order for a contentious exercise to diffuse more successfully, it is important that the exercise have *cultural legitimacy* in the eyes of the adopters. The widespread adoption of *Diren!* as a master frame, in the first place, by a politically diverse group of protest participants was due to the broadly embraced legitimacy of 'resistance' in the face of coercive policing that, ironically, contributed to the solidarity among different actors. The same holds true for the '*iftar* on the street'. Even though this innovative practice was introduced beforehand, it became popularised, on the one hand, thanks to the overlap of Gezi uprisings with the beginning of Ramadan in July 2013 and, on the other, due to the high legitimacy of this culturally embedded practice in an overwhelmingly Muslim society.

After all, the question as to why uprisings in Turkey erupted in that particular point in time is daunting. A deeper examination of diffusion processes may offer us more hints which could help with addressing this question more adequately.

References

Atalay, C. (2013), interview with, 'Hukuksuzluga Karsi Yurttas Hareketi' ('Citizen Mobilization against Lawlessness'), *Express* 136 (June-July): 30.

Ayres, J. M. (1999) 'From the streets to the internet: the cyber-diffusion of contention', *Annals of the American Academy of Political and Social Science* 566 (1): 132–43.

Beissinger, M. R. (2007) 'Structure and example in modular political phenomena: the diffusion of Bulldozer/Rose/Orange/Tulip Revolutions', *Perspectives on Politics* 5 (2): 259–76.

Bunce, V. J. and Wolchik, S. L. (2006) 'International diffusion and postcommunist electoral revolutions', *Communist and Post-Communist Studies* 39 (3): 283–304.

Burt, R. S. (1987) 'Social contagion and innovation: cohesion versus structural equivalence', *American Journal of Sociology* 92 (6): 1287–1335.

Chabot, S. (2000) 'Transnational diffusion and the African American reinvention of Gandhian repertoire', *Mobilization: An international quarterly* 5 (2): 201–16.

Chabot, S. and Duyvendak, J. W. (2002) 'Globalization and transnational diffusion between social movements: reconceptualizing the dissemination of the Gandhian repertoire and the "coming out" routine', *Theory and Society* 31 (6): 697–740.

CrimethInc (2013) 'The June 2013 uprisings in Brazil. Part 1: New alliances, age-old struggles', http://www.crimethinc.com/texts/recentfeatures/brazilpt1.php (accessed 6 January 2014).

Dogan, T. (2013), interview with, 'Yogurtcu Forumu: Bir Bilanco Denemesi' ('Yogurtcu Forum: a trial for an account'), in *Park Gazetesi*, http://parkgazetesi.com/2013/12/08/yogurtcu-forum-sureci-ve-mahalleleri-degerlendirirsek/ (accessed 3 February 2014).

Earl, J. (2010) 'The dynamics of protest-related diffusion on the web', *Information, Communication & Society* 13 (2): 209–25.

Edwards, G. (2014) 'Infectious innovations? The diffusion of tactical innovation in social movement networks, the case of suffragette militancy', *Social Movement Studies* (forthcoming): 1–22.

Emek ve Adalet Platformu (Labour and Justice Platform) (2013) 'Biz kimiz' ('Who we are'), http://www.emekveadalet.org/biz-kimiz (accessed 5 January 2014).

Firat, Z. (2013), interview with, 'Sonuc Ne Olursa Olsun Biz Kazandik' ('Whatever the result will be, we won'), in *Express* 136 (June-July): 36–8.

Granovetter, M. (1978) 'Threshold models of collective behavior', *American Journal of Sociology*: 83 (6): 1420–43.

Inceoglu, I. (2013) 'The Gezi spirit and the forums', *Open Democracy*, 17 July, http://www.opendemocracy.net/%C4%B0rem-%C4%B0nceo%C4%9Flu/gezi-spirit-and-forums (accessed 21 December 2013).

International Telecommunication Union (2013) 'ICT Facts and Figures 2013', http://www.itu.int/en/ITU-D/Statistics/Pages/stat/default.aspx (accessed 7 January 2014).
Koopmans, R. (2006) 'Protest in time and space: the evolution of waves of contention', *The Blackwell Companion to Social Movements*, Malden, MA: Blackwell Publishing, pp. 19–46.
Kuran, T. (1989) 'Sparks and prairie fires: a theory of anticipated political revolution', *Public Choice* 61 (1): 41–74.
McAdam, D. (1995) '"Initiator" and "spin-off" movements: diffusion processes in protest cycles', *Repertoires and Cycles of Collective Action*, Durham: Duke University Press, pp. 217–39.
McAdam, D. and Rucht, D. (1993) 'The cross-national diffusion of movement ideas', *Annals of the American Academy of Political and Social Science* 528 (1): 56–74.
Maeckelbergh, M. (2012) 'Horizontal democracy now: from alterglobalization to occupation', *Interface: A journal for and about social movements* 4 (1): 207–34.
Mustereklerimiz (2013) *Hemzemin Forum Postasi* issue 1, 20 June 2013, http://hemzeminposta.org/2013/06/20/sayi-1-20-haziran-2013/ (accessed 3 December 2013).
Occupy (n.d.) 'Learn about Occupy', http://www.occupytogether.org/aboutoccupy/ (accessed 5 January 2014).
Ozgur, D. (2013), interview with, 'Gercek Katarsis' ('Real catharsis'), in *Express* 136 (June-July): 31–4.
Ozgur-Der (2013) 'Ozgur-Der'den Taksim Aciklamasi' ('Statement about Taksim by Ozgur-Der'), *Haksoz Haber*, http://www.haksozhaber.net/ozgur-derden-taksim-aciklamasi-37977h.htm (accessed 4 March 2014).
Polat, D. (2013), interview with, 'Yogurtcu Forumu ve Demokratik Isleyis' ('Yogurtcu forum and democratic functioning') http://parkgazetesi.com/2013/11/22/yogurtcu-parki-forum-ve-demokratik-isleyis/ (accessed 3 February 2014).
Radikal (2013) 'Tum yurtta "diren Lice" yuruyusleri' ('"Resist Lice" marches in the whole country'), 30 June, http://www.radikal.com.tr/politika/taksimde_diren_lice_yuruyusleri-1139720 (accessed 23 November 2013).
Rane, H. and Salem, S. (2012) 'Social media, social movements and the diffusion of ideas in the Arab uprisings', *Journal of International Communication* 18 (1): 97–111.
Sardan, T. (2013) 'Gezi'den kalanlar ve farkli bir analiz' ('Residues of Gezi and a different analysis'), *Milliyet*, 25 November, http://gundem.milliyet.com.tr/gezi-den-kalanlar-ve-farkli-bir/gundem/ydetay/1797280/default.htm (accessed 6 December 2013).
SMaPP (2013) 'A breakout role for twitter? The role of social media in the Turkish protests', SMaPP data report, Social Media and Participation Lab, New York University, http://smapp.nyu.edu/reports/turkey_data_report.pdf (accessed 11 January 2014).

Schneider, N. (2011) 'From Occupy Wall Street to Occupy Everywhere', *Nation* (October), http://www.thenation.com/article/163924/occupy-wall-street-occupy-everywhere# (accessed 23 February 2014).

Seifert, F. (2013) 'Transnational diffusion of a high-cost protest method: open field destructions in France, Germany and Spain', *Interface: A journal for and about social movements* 5 (2): 213–39.

Snow, D. A. (1993) *Shakubaku: A study of the Nichiren Shoshu Buddhist movement in America, 1960–1975*, New York: Garland.

Soule, S. A. (1997) 'The student divestment movement in the United States and tactical diffusion: the shantytown protest', *Social Forces* 75 (3): 855–82.

— (2013) 'Diffusion and scale shift', *The Wiley-Blackwell Encyclopedia of Social and Political Movements*, Chichester, West Sussex and Malden, MA: Wiley-Blackwell, pp. 349–53.

Starbird, K. and Palen, L. (2012) '(How) will the revolution be retweeted?: Information diffusion and the 2011 Egyptian uprising', *Proceedings of the ACM 2012 Conference on Computer Supported Cooperative Work*, Seattle, pp. 7–16, http://dl.acm.org/citation.cfm?id=2145212 (accessed 15 January 2014).

Strang, D. (1990) 'From dependency to sovereignty: an event history analysis of decolonization', *American Sociological Review* 55: 846–60.

Strang, D. and Meyer, J. W. (1993) 'Institutional conditions for diffusion', *Theory and Society* 22 (4): 487–511.

Strang, D. and Soule, S. A. (1998) 'Diffusion in organizations and social movements: from hybrid corn to poison pills', *Annual Review of Sociology* 24 (1): 265–90.

Tufekci, Z. and Wilson, C. (2012) 'Social media and the decision to participate in political protest: observations from Tahrir Square', *Journal of Communication* 62 (2): 363–79.

Tugal, C. (2013) 'Gezi hareketinin ortak paydalari ve yeni orgutluluk bicimleri' ('Common denominators of Gezi movement and new forms of organization'), *T24* news portal, 3 July, http://t24.com.tr/haber/gezi-hareketinin-ortak-paydalari-ve-yeni-orgutluluk-bicimleri/233416 (accessed 4 December 2013).

Vasi, I. B. and Suh, C. S. (2013) 'Protest in the internet age: public attention, social media, and the spread of "Occupy" protests in the United States', paper presented at the Politics and Protest Workshop at the Graduate Center, CUNY, http://politicsandprotest.ws.gc.cuny.edu/files/2012/07/PPW-2-Vasi.pdf (accessed 15 January 2014).

Wolff, J. (2007) '(De-)mobilising the marginalised: a comparison of the Argentine Piqueteros and Ecuador's indigenous movement', *Journal of Latin American Studies* 39 (1): 1–29.

World Bank (2014) 'Current account balance', http://data.worldbank.org/indicator/BN.CAB.XOKA.CD (accessed 5 January 2014).

Chapter Twelve

Adapting Theories on Diffusion and Transnational Contention Through Social Movements of the Crisis: Some Concluding Remarks[1]

Alice Mattoni and Donatella della Porta

Chapters in this volume addressed diffusion in contemporary mobilisations from different conceptual frameworks and employing a diverse range of methods. Indeed, the attributes of social movements that are diffused, the territorial levels and the historical moments in which they mobilise, and the way in which they spread across space and time might vary considerably. As a result, diffusion processes and their underlying mechanisms are inherently multi-dimensional – requiring scholars to employ an heterogeneity of theoretical perspectives and research methodologies. Unlike other collective volumes on diffusion in social movements (for example, Givan, Roberts and Soule 2010), however, this volume has addressed the topic as it applied to one specific wave of contention. Despite variations on the what, how and why questions about the spread of such mobilisations, focusing on the same time-frame and, to some extent, the same types of mobilisations across different countries offers us the opportunity to compare diffusion mechanisms as they occurred (or not) within a quite homogeneous set of case studies, albeit considered from different perspectives.

In this chapter we go a step further in addressing diffusion processes. Also building on the findings presented in the previous contributions in this volume, we address two questions that are relevant, at both the theoretical and the empirical levels, to understanding current social-movement protests and their future evolution. We first consider how the diffusion processes and mechanisms that characterised anti-austerity and pro-democracy protests put into question more traditional models of diffusion; and we suggest potential new ways to rework such models. We then consider the very notion of transnational social movements: in particular, we discuss to what extent current protests, and the diffusion processes that characterised them, might bring to light some transformations relevant with regard to the transnational aspects of present and future mobilisations.

---

1. The two authors discussed and wrote the present chapter collaboratively and equally. However, Alice Mattoni is the principal author of 'Adapting theories of diffusion' and Donatella della Porta is the principal author of the sections 'Introduction' and 'From thick transnational movements to thin transnational mobilisations?'

Adapting theories of diffusion

Chapters presented in this volume pointed at some relevant aspects with regard to diffusion processes, underlining the need to broaden our understanding of what happens when practices and ideas travel from one context to another. Overall, they suggest the need to expand and redefine traditional conceptual frameworks about diffusion in three main directions.

Exploring uncharted territories of diffusion

Literature on diffusion in social movements traditionally focuses on positive cases, considering countries in which protest actions and frames spread, often successfully. In this way, social-movement scholars have been able to assess under what conditions and through which mechanisms diffusion processes happened in past and present cycles of contention. We know much less, however, about what happens when ideas and actions are not able to travel from one country to another, despite the presence of a pervasive wave of mobilisation and apparently favourable structural and contextual conditions. Anti-austerity and pro-democracy protests are a good case study in this regard: while the frames of the 2011 protests moved successfully from Tunisia to Egypt and thence to Spain, Greece, and the United States, they did not travel well to countries which, like Germany or France or the United Kingdom (Sotirakopolous and Rootes, in Chapter Eight of this volume), seemed less badly hit by recession; to those such as Italy, where protests happened but took different forms (della Porta and Andretta 2013; della Porta, Mosca, and Parks forthcoming 2014); or to the Czech Republic, where protests were intense but localised (Jiří Navrátil and Ondřej Císař in Chapter Ten of this volume).

In fact, some of the chapters in this volume indicate the need to pursue empirical research on countries in which diffusion processes failed to happen, either completely or partially, beginning to explore uncharted territories in the field of diffusion. Mobilisation did not spread in those countries where the economic crisis had less dramatic effects. While some *acampadas* were organised in Brussels, London, Amsterdam and Berlin, their capacity to mobilise remained very limited. As Mark Beissinger (2002) had observed in his analysis of the breakdown of the Soviet Union, and Valerie Bunce and Sharon Wolchik (2011) in their research on the Orange revolutions, while ideas might also spread where conditions are less propitious, their capacity to produce successful mobilisation is limited. Assessment of similarities, which is a relevant conducive condition for cross-national diffusion, is jeopardised by structural differences. Finally, the financial crisis had different characteristics in different countries: public debt was, for example, very high in Greece and Italy but very low in Spain; while Greece carried high levels of debt with foreign banks, this was not the case in Iceland and other countries.

A first explanation for selective diffusion could be found in a distinction between movement of opportunities versus movement of crisis. Research on the labour movement had already indicated that waves of strikes are more likely in situations of full employment, when the working class is structurally stronger. In new social-movement theories, material well-being has been considered as a precondition for the emergence of collective action on 'post-materialistic' issues. This does not mean that there are no protests in moments of crisis, when threats to protestors' very survival are more serious: movements of the unemployed have emerged during peaks of economic recession and peasants have rebelled in times of famine. These movements were, however, characterised by few (material and symbolic) resources; they were more reactive than proactive in their claims and remained rather local, spontaneous and volatile. While the Global Justice Movement denounced a crisis-to-be, the movements against austerity measures reacted against fully developed crises, but with few hopes and resources. Further research on the so-called negative cases of diffusion might contribute to developing further knowledge on the mechanisms and processes by which protest spread in some countries but not in others. Some of the chapters in this volume began to pave the way for such an endeavour.

For instance, Jiří Navrátil and Ondřej Císař focus on a case study, the Czech Republic, in which protests occurring in 2011 did not resonate with the anti-austerity and pro-democracy mobilisations that were crossing many countries around the world. In short, the chapter presents an intriguing case of lack of diffusion – of both practices and ideas – in which the transnational dimension of protest was absent, especially in comparison to mobilisations linked to the Global Justice Movement that occurred in the Czech Republic about a decade ago. Along the same lines, although from a different perspective, Nikos Sotirakopoulos and Christopher Rootes suggest that transnational diffusion also failed in the case of Occupy London: compared to their North American counterparts, the protest camp and related actions were not only much less confrontational but also unable to resonate broadly within British society. The time dimension, the authors suggest, partially explains such a failure. Occupy London came into existence late in the wave of Occupy protests across the world, as the levels of protests elsewhere were declining. Even more importantly, perhaps, Occupy London was organised after a wave of student protests and university occupations in 2010–11, against the raising of tuition fees in higher education, that achieved much higher participation. Finally, Daphi and Zamponi's chapter sheds light on another case of incomplete diffusion, Italy. Recent research shows that protests against austerity measures did happen in this country, evoking some of the collective-action frames developed in Spain, Greece, and the United States (della Porta and Andretta 2013). However, one of the most characteristic features of the 'movements of the crisis' did not spread significantly within Italy, where the *acampadas*, or protest camps, were not successful (della Porta and Andretta 2013.). In Chapter Nine, Daphi and Zamponi consider the important legacy of the Global Justice Movement in Italy, and activists' memories of some past protest events linked to it, as one of the obstacles to the diffusion of protest. Taken together, these chapters show that negative cases – that is, countries in which contentious actions did not spread during a wave of global mobilisations – might also be relevant in explaining why diffusion processes develop in other countries.

Another important aspect of diffusion processes is the role of supranational actors positioned outside the social-movement milieu. In this respect, Ari-Elmeri Hyvoen suggests a promising line of research for understanding the international level of anti-austerity and pro-democracy protests: the diffusion of protest frames outside the social-movement milieu and their instrumental re-appropriation by supranational institutions such as the European Union. While most of this volume focuses on how diffusion processes took place within social-movement networks, and amongst individual activists, Ari-Elmeri Hyvoen moves his gaze a step beyond, focusing on how practices and, in this particular case, ideas might also spread within other sectors of society. At the more theoretical level, this chapter also illustrates how the study of diffusion might be further expanded by including literature on social-movement outcomes: in analysing the way in which the European Union reframed the Tunisian and Egyptian uprisings, it explores an important yet neglected aspect of protest outcomes when it comes to the global level of contention: the impact of social movements at the level of the global 'polity'.

The cross-time dimension of protest

Diffusion happens in space but also in time. Although this second path is still a silence in the literature, some of the chapters presented in this volume address diffusion not only across countries but also between different moments in time. In Chapter Two, Flesher Fominaya and Montanes discuss the spread of the *escrache* across time and space. They highlight the challenges that diffusion processes imply when they travelled from one protest context – post-dictatorial mobilisations in Argentina against crime perpetrators during the dictatorship – to another: protests against house evictions in Spain after the economic crisis that erupted in 2008. Diachronic diffusion is also at the centre of Donatella della Porta's Chapter Three, which focuses on cross-time diffusion of both the ideas and the practices of participatory-deliberative models of democracy across two waves of protest: the Global Justice Movement that emerged late in the 1990s and the anti-austerity protests and pro-democracy protests that developed in many regions of the world in 2011. The emphasis here is on the mechanisms of adaptation, as a relevant aspect of learning processes that occur when ideas and practices travel across time, from one protest wave to another, suggesting that organisational changes in social movements are also a by-product of diffusion processes and the adaptation mechanisms they bring with them.

This chapter shows that for diffusion to happen across time as well as across space, translation mechanisms must first occur, allowing a specific protest tactic to be dislocated from its original context into another; experimentation mechanisms then enable the same protest tactic to be relocated within the new social, cultural and political context (Chabot 2010: 106). Translation and experimentation, indeed, are entrenched within the learning processes that activists develop when engaging with ideas and practices rooted in social-movement experiences that took place in different historical moments and/or countries. As Donatella della

Porta also suggests in her chapter, today translation and experimentation are however embedded in a different media ecology from the one that surrounded, and sustained, the diffusion of other protest tactics in the past – such as the diffusion of Gandhian non-violent tactics in the United States in the 1930s (Chabot 2010). We can also add, as Lesley Wood (2012) observed with regard to the Global Justice Movement in North America, that translation and experimentation require a third step for diffusion to happen: processes of deliberation that become all the more important when considering social-movement organisations that are non-hierarchical, which engage in protest actions that might be risky and whose goals are broad and fuzzy (Wood 2012: 10). From this perspective, the learning processes highlighted by Donatella della Porta acquire an even more important role in the spread of practices and ideas from one social movement to the next. Learning from each other's experiences, but also reinterpreting them, passes through practices of remembering and comparing present and past protest contexts on the side of activists. Again, the Global Justice Movement is put into relation with present anti-austerity and pro-democracy protests in the chapter written by Daphi and Zamponi, who tackle another relevant element when it comes to diffusion across time: memory, which seems to be relevant in explaining how the memories of past protest events might act as lenses able to shape the reception, and therefore the diffusion, of mobilisations occurring in other countries.

These chapters bring about more reflection on a double process of diffusion of practices and ideas, which steer the developments of movements' forms and frames. Together with a process of diffusion that proceeds cross-nationally, there is one which moves cross-temporally. While national differences had, of course, been noted in research on the Global Justice Movements as well (*see*, for example, della Porta 2007; della Porta *et al.* 2006), the new waves of protest made it even more clear that ideas do clearly travel – but not everywhere and at any time. While, besides the degree of severity of the crisis, the opening or closing of political opportunities can contribute much to explain these differences, the specific movements' cultures and traditions also played a role (*see* Table 12.1). While activists travelling between countries brought emerging ideas, the activists reactivated from previous waves of protest brought their specific visions and experiences. While new technologies mediated (facilitated and constrained) the cross-country spread of information, memory acted as a filter in the reception of the new mobilisations occurring in other countries.

Table 12.1: Transnational channels of diffusion

	Across time	Across borders
Relational diffusion	Reactivated activists	Travelling activists
Non-relational diffusion	Memory	New technologies

In short, these chapters illustrate how taking into consideration the cross-time dimension in diffusion processes adds yet another layer of complexity to, and increases the explanatory power of, traditional theories of diffusion. Of course, some methodological challenges are posed by studying the past in the present: combining archival data on previous protests with in-depth interviews with current activists seems to be a reasonable strategy for grasping diffusion processes with regard to their temporal dimension. However, the combination of other methods of data-collection and -analysis might pave the way to an even more in-depth reconstruction of the diachronic perspective in diffusion theories within the field of social-movement studies.

Social-media platforms in diffusion processes

That media connect is a well known truth. The extent to which different media selectively facilitate diffusion, however, has not been a major topic of investigation. Many of the chapters in this volume implicitly or explicitly suggest that social-media platforms also had an important role in diffusing imageries, symbols, frames and ideas, from one country to another but also within the same country.

In his discussion (Chapter Four) of the creation of injustice-symbols in the global public sphere, for instance, Thomas Olesen claims that new media technologies contribute to the quick dissemination of visual memes across borders, as in the case of Neda Agha-Soltan – who was killed in Iran during the 2009 protests against the government after the contested presidential elections – as well as the Egyptian blogger Khaled Said, killed by police in Alexandria on 6 June 2010 (Olesen 2013) and the self-immolation of Mohamed Bouazizi, who set himself on fire and died shortly after this extreme act, quickly becoming a symbol able to capture the injustices that triggered the Tunisian uprising (Lim 2013).

Social media also intertwine with diffusion processes with regard to protest frames and actions. In his chapter about the Gezi protests in Turkey, Kivanc Atak underlines the transformative role of social-media platforms with regard to the mechanisms of diffusion between previous anti-austerity and pro-democracy protests across the world and the Gezi protests. Conditions usually considered necessary to diffusion were lacking in this case: 'structural equivalence' and 'attribution of similarity' did not seem to apply with regard to the Gezi protests and the preceding mobilisations in the MENA region, Southern Europe and North America. But social-media platforms, the author claims, might also function as relevant actors in diffusion processes, hence necessitating for a reconsideration of the mechanisms and conditions that support the spread of protest ideas and practices from one context to another. As Tarrow suggested elsewhere, indeed, 'the outcomes of diffusion vary according to the mechanisms that drive it' (Tarrow 2010: 211). Roos and Oikonomakis in Chapter Six of this volume also suggest that the complex flows of communication and information that enclosed and permeated anti-austerity and pro-democracy mobilisations put into question the usual distinction between the transmitter and the adopter in the traditional model of diffusion. Indeed, the channels through which communication and information circulated changed considerably with respect to past mobilisation, with social-media platforms and smart phones quickly multiplying the dissemination of protest materials, including accounts of actions and frames of protest. Such changes, hence, call into question the linearity of diffusion; the more circular – and rhizomatic – patterns of diffusion in contemporary protests may suggest the need for further reflections on the role of information and communication technologies, and in particular of social-media platforms, with regard to diffusion processes.

In other words, these chapters signal a need to reconsider diffusion processes going beyond the mass media as brokers of diffusion (Tarrow 2005), focusing also on new forms of mediated communication like those enabled by social-media platforms. The massive use of social-media platforms and smart phones, often combined, also blurs the usual difference between relational and non-relational diffusion that characterises the spread of protest actions and ideas from one movement to another. The personal contacts and exchanges that characterised relational diffusion more and more frequently occur through computer-mediated communication: mailing-list servers and Google Groups were employed to organise actions at the local, regional and transnational levels in recent protests (Karpf 2014; Mattoni 2013).

At the same time, mass media are no longer the only source of inspiration when it comes to the diffusion of protest tactics and ideas at the intra-national and transnational level: the creation of the world-wide web back in the 1990s made it easier for activists to spread their protest actions and ideas through alternative information websites such as Indymedia; today, social-media platforms might function as broadcasting media that allow content to travel quickly across individual users and collective groups. Of course, activists who travel from country to country still continue to function as relevant actors in relational diffusion. At the same time, images and videos of protests move rapidly from one country to another due to mass media, from global satellite television networks to the local printing press, hence fostering non-relational diffusion of both protest tactics and ideas. However, the presence of social-media platforms seems to become pervasive when it comes to diffusion processes, and their underlying mechanisms, at the local, national, and transnational levels.

While in the traditional model of diffusion the presence of media was to some extent relegated to non-relational diffusion, in which mass media had a central role, today's media technologies and channels seems relevant for the whole spectrum of diffusion mechanisms; this seems to call for a reconsideration of the way in which diffusion processes work at large. In short, there is the need to reconsider to what extent well established mechanisms of diffusion are transformed, possibly augmented, through social-media platforms. However, social-movement scholars also need to engage in further research to understand if new mechanisms of diffusion are also emerging and with what consequences for social movements and their transnational dimension. Literature shows that although language differences are usually seen as barriers to diffusion (Tarrow 2013), even before the rise of social-media platforms, information and communication technologies might actually have been helping to overcome such obstacles: the interplay of computer-mediated communication and face-to-face transnational meetings during European protests against precarity,[2] for instance, functioned well in the diffusion – and translation – of political concepts elaborated in one country and then actively transferred to another national context (Doerr and Mattoni forthcoming 2014). This, of course, occurred even more frequently within current pro-democracy and anti-austerity movements, especially with regard to the diffusion of a common language (Tarrow 2013). Indeed, some insights on this are already on their way through scholarly work rooted in media and Internet studies.

A recent empirical study on Twitter during Occupy Wall Street (Bennett, Segerberg and Walker 2014), for instance, investigates the mechanisms that sustained the coherent organisation of the crowd-enabled network behind the Occupy Wall Street protests. In doing this, the authors highlighted the role of three different Twitter-enabled mechanisms, nested one into the other: first, the production of Twitter content, such as simple texts but also links embedded in the 140-character tweets; second, the curation of Twitter contents that other users had already produced, through the practice of re-tweeting messages created by others, so that the short lifespan of such tweets was, to some extent, increased; third, the dynamic integration of Twitter content into previously separated networks of Twitter users, usually through the use of #hashtags within tweets that hence had the potential of connecting social-movement organisations and also, increasingly, individual users, otherwise disconnected. These methods, in turn, facilitated the passage of information across different social-movement actors at least vaguely interested in Occupy Wall Street. This last mechanism, in particular, seems to work at the level of the mediated mechanism of diffusion, according to which a broker acts as a connective agent so that protest tactics and ideas might pass from one (social-movement) actor to another. Although Bennett, Segerberg and Walker (2014) only focus on one specific social-media platform used during one specific mobilisation, their work already shows that media and Internet studies might be fruitfully combined with the knowledge produced in social-movement studies to expand and deepen the understanding of recent and future transformations in political participation and mobilisation.

From thick transnational movements to thin transnational mobilisations?

In the previous section, we outlined three main directions that seem worth considering in the adaptation of already existing theories of diffusion: some uncharted territories of diffusion, including cases in which diffusion processes failed to happen, and the diffusion of social-movement actions and frames within supranational institutional actors; the cross-time dimension in the spread of protest practices and ideas across different cycles of protest; and the role of social-media

---

2. 'Precarity', existence in conditions of uncertainty, insecurity and vulnerability, especially in relation to employment conditions, is an issue that has been included on the agenda by global justice activists since the early years of this century.

platforms in the rapid diffusion of information and hence, again, of contentious performances and collective action-frames, across different protest contexts. In this section we go a step further, to discuss another relevant subject in social-movement studies – transnational contention – starting from the current wave of protest and the diffusion processes that characterised it. To understand diffusion processes and mechanisms within the current mobilisations is also a relevant step towards an understanding of the transnational dimension in current social movements.

In fact, several chapters presented in this volume also implicitly or explicitly address the following question: what do we mean when we speak about transnational social movements today? As we pointed out in the Introduction, theories and models of transnational contention and social movements have flourished in the last decades, in part due to the rise of the Global Justice Movement, whose transnational stance was quite self-evident in two of its most common and recurrent manifestations: the counter-summits and the social forums. It was somewhat natural, then, to speak about the transnational dimension of social movements, the creation of international networks of activists who travelled from country to country to plan common days of struggle. This was clear, and evident, especially to scholars who did ethnographic work on these movements (for example, Juris 2008). Although reflections around the transnational dimension of social movements should not be dismissed as such, the present movements of crisis demand that scholars revise some of their analytical tools, as well as posing different research questions about the meaning and consequences of the transformation of the transnational dimension in current protests. In other words, the concepts related to the transnational dimension of protests that scholars have elaborated so far in social-movement literature should not be dismissed; we can reflect on these concepts, revisiting them to see how they can be useful for understanding current movements.

According to della Porta and Tarrow (2005), diffusion has been one pivotal process on which the transnationalisation of the Global Justice Movement developed in the past decades, allowing the transfer of several social-movement features – including, of course, forms of organisation and forms of contention – from one context to another. As the chapters in this volume show, diffusion processes occurred in the movements of the crisis too. During his inaugural lecture at the Centre on Social Movement Studies at the European University Institute on 30 April 2012, Sidney Tarrow observed that thin processes of diffusion were at work in the Occupy Wall Street protests across the United States. Following this insight, we also differentiate between *thick* and *thin* processes of diffusion, with the latter being more common today than in the past, partly due to the spread of information and communication technologies.

In particular, when looking at differences in forms of transnationalisation, the Global Justice Movement was an example of thick diffusion, based on a global organisational network in which social-movement organisations as well as grassroots activist groups had a relevant role in supporting (and spreading) transnational mobilisations such as counter-summits. Partially supported through information and communication technologies managed within the social-movement milieu and, in particular, by activist mailing lists and alternative informational websites, this global organisational network was also thickened due to transnational, but also national, gatherings like the social forum, whose practices rested on a collective conception of politics based on activist groups and organisations. In contrast, the recent wave of protests has been an example of thin diffusion: information travelled quickly from individual to individual through social networking sites, frequently in combination with portable mobile devices such as smart phones. The ability of individuals to communicate the content of protests was therefore important to spreading imageries in the global wave of protest. More important than social-movement organisations and social-movement groups were activists who designed and provided web platforms able to function as content aggregators, to navigate the impressive amount of information produced in the framework of protests. The diffusion of information on the protest was therefore characterised by a weak organisational process of transnationalisation. Occasions for face-to-face communication might have improved in time at the individual level – activists travelling cheaply and often – but collective arenas for transnational encounters, such as the social forum, were less central. Indeed, the protest camps like the Spanish *acampadas* quickly achieved world visibility but were mainly national, if not local, in the range of people involved.

Table 12.2: Paths of diffusion in the two waves of global protests

	Global Justice Movement	Anti-austerity and pro-democracy protests
Diffusion processes	Thick	Thin
How spread: infrastructure of diffusion (people)	Social-movement networks and coalitions	Individual activists and protest participants
How spread: infrastructure of diffusion (technologies)	Activists mailing lists and alternative informational websites	Commercial social media platforms and global satellite television networks
What spread	Social forums	Protest camps
Where spread	Worldwide diffusion	Selective diffusion

The understanding of the transnational dimension in social movements does not only pass through the analysis of diffusion processes. In fact, according to Tarrow (2005), two other processes characterised transnational contention in the past decades: domestication/internalisation; and externalisation. In addition, a third relevant process of transnationalisation was peculiar to the Global Justice Movement: transnational collective action (della Porta and Tarrow 2005). Further empirical research is, hence, needed with regard to other processes of transnationalisation that were at work in the Global Justice Movement and, most probably, were also present, although transformed, within the anti-austerity and pro-democracy protests that happened in the past few years. In the absence of solid empirical investigations on the subject matter, in what follows we simply speculate that processes of internalisation/domestication, externalisation and transnational collective action also differed from those that characterised the Global Justice Movement as well as the social movements that preceded it.

First, internalisation/domestication processes might be seen at work when international pressures are transferred at the level of domestic politics; this shift may create discontent, and frequently massive protests, against the national governments implementing the policies demanded by supranational institutions (Tarrow 2005: 80). This happened to a great extent in the case of Southern European countries, in which the so-called Indignados protests quickly developed against domestic political elites, blamed for swiftly implementing the austerity measures handed down by the European Union, the European Central Bank and the International Monetary Fund. While internalisation processes were less central within the Global Justice Movement, anti-austerity protests in countries like Spain and Greece consolidated around a strong opposition to supranational institutions and national governments. Focusing again on Europe, the renovated trend in internalisation seems more in line with protests against the European Union, and the domestic implementation of its directives and policies, that occurred from 1993 to 1997 (Imig and Tarrow 2001), before the Global Justice Movement emerged and spread across the globe.

Second, externalisation processes occur when contention at the domestic level is brought within international arenas, so that social-movement actors can overcome their lack of opportunities to be heard by their national governments and institutions (Tarrow 2005: 32). In Europe, recent anti-austerity protests aimed at targeting an intricate combination of governmental domestic responses to international economic and political pressures. The example of Greece, in this respect, is particularly apt. Indeed, Maria Kousis, in Chapter Seven, suggests that externalisation has been at work and consolidated from 2011 onwards. However, when looking at the type of transnational protest events listed by the author, and their targets, it seems clear that externalisation occurred in a spurious way, probably also due to the presence of both domestic and supranational institutions blamed for anti-austerity measures. The day of transnational solidarity actions organised in about nineteen non-Greek cities on 18 February 2012, for instance, targeted both local branches of the International Monetary Fund and Greek embassies across Europe. Therefore, representatives of domestic governmental bodies were still at the centre of protest actions, although at the international level and with the aim of gaining visibility and solidarity beyond the Greek borders. About one year later, another day of transnational solidarity was organised to oppose not just anti-austerity measures but, especially, the growing violent activities of the extreme right-wing Golden Dawn formation. On 19 January 2013, solidarity rallies and actions in front of Greek consulates and embassies were organised in 26 cities across the world, while demonstrations also occurred in 25 cities within Greece. Again, in this case, the externalisation process was partial, since the international arena had a relevant role in terms of visibility as well as in raising the global awareness of fascist violence in Greece. But protestors did not target supranational governmental bodies, focusing instead on the institutional representation of Greece abroad.

Finally, transnational collective action has been considered the unprecedented process, with regard to processes of transnationalisation, that characterised the Global Justice Movement (della Porta and Tarrow 2005). While domestication/internalisation, externalisation and diffusion were also at work in past cycles of contention across the globe, transnational collective action was a peculiar and specific trait of the mobilisations against corporate globalisation. The same cannot be said with regard to anti-austerity and pro-democracy protests, in which transnational collective action had only a marginal role. With regard to the European context, for instance, it is true that supranational governmental bodies such as the European Central Bank and the International Monetary Fund, together with economic actors such as credit-rating agencies, had a clear role in anti-austerity protests, as processes of domestication also show. It is also true that international claims referring to other countries were present in domestic demonstrations, as in Portugal, for instance, where:

> a special focus is set on social movements from other countries facing austerity measures and heavily indebted. The protests in Greece have been used as a thread, claiming 'We consider ourselves Greek.' The slogan 'Spain! Greece! Ireland! Portugal! Our struggle is international!' was prominently proclaimed during the 2011 demonstrations. It was meant to show the international dimension of the protest and similarities in the political and economic framework (Baumgarten 2013).

Activists linked to the 15-M mobilisation in Spain, moreover, co-ordinated a Global Action Day against capitalism and austerity: on 15 October 2011, about 951 cities in 82 countries participated in such protest action, organising a variety of demonstrations and other protest events across the globe, under the slogan 'United For Global Change' (Perugorría and Tejerina 2013). Protesters involved in Occupy Wall Street also joined the protests, with 15 October becoming the very first day of public protests, culminating with the establishment of the protest camp for many local activist groups and networks adhering to Occupy Wall Street. Finally, on 14 November 2012, traditional trade unions organised a European strike against austerity that involved the major unions in Portugal, Spain, Greece, Italy, Cyprus and Malta. Both the Global Action Day, which was repeated in 2012, and the European strike, however, occurred through demonstrations and other protest events organised at the national level although within a transnational framework. While these mobilisations certainly had a transnational flavour, they did not imply the gathering of activists coming from various European countries within the same protest site, as regularly happened in the case of the Global Justice Movement.

Only in 2012, from 16 to 19 May, did something similar to the transnational demonstrations that characterised the Global Justice Movement happen in the framework of the anti-austerity protests in Europe. The four Blockupy days of protests, organised by a transnational network of activists already participating in their respective national movements, had the aim of disrupting the activities of the European Central Bank in Frankfurt in order to denounce the financial policies and austerity measures implemented in many European countries. The experience was repeated at the end of May 2013. Activists travelled from various European countries to reach Germany and engage in several protest actions, including an attempt to peacefully blockade the European Central Bank. It remains to be seen to which extent upward scale-shift might happen as challenges are perceived as more and more supranational. Transnational events such as the European elections could have this triggering effect.

References

Baumgarten, B. (2013) 'Geração à Rasca and beyond: mobilizations in Portugal after 12 March 2011', *Current Sociology* 61 (4): 457–73.

Beissinger, M. (2002) *Nationalist Mobilizations and the Breakdown of the Soviet Union*, Cambridge: Cambridge University Press.

Bennett, W. L., Segerberg, A. and Walker, S. (2014) 'Organization in the crowd: peer production in large-scale networked protests', *Information, Communication and Society* 17 (2): 232–60.

Bunce, V. and Wolchik, S. (2011) *Defeating Authoritarian Leaders*, Cambridge: Cambridge University Press.

Chabot, S. (2010) 'Dialogue matters: beyond the transmission model of transnational diffusion between social movements', in R. K. Givan, K. M. Roberts, and S. A. Soule (eds) *The Diffusion of Social Movements: Actors, mechanisms, and political effects*, Cambridge and Malden, MA: Cambridge University Press, pp. 99–124.

della Porta D. (2007) *The Global Justice Movement in Cross-National and Transnational Perspective*, New York: Rowman & Littlefield.

della Porta D. and Andretta, M. (2013) 'Protesting for justice and democracy: Italian Indignados?', *Contemporary Italian Politics* 5 (1): 23–37.

della Porta D., Andretta, M., Mosca, L. and Reiter, H. (2006) *Globalization from Below*, Minneapolis, MN: University of Minnesota Press.

della Porta D., Mosca, L. and Parks, L. (2014 forthcoming) '2011: a year of protest on social justice in Italy', in M. Kaldor (ed.), *Subterranean Politics in Europe*, Basingstoke: Palgrave Macmillan.

della Porta D. and Tarrow, S. (2005) 'Transnational protest and global activism: An introduction', in D. della Porta and S. Tarrow (eds) *Transnational Protest and Global Activism: People, passions, and power*, Lanham, MD: Rowman and Littlefield, pp. 1–20.

Doerr, N. and Mattoni, A. (2014) 'Public spaces and alternative media networks in Europe: The case of the Euro Mayday Parade against precarity', in R. Werenskjold, K. Fahlenbrach, and E. Sivertsen (eds) *The Revolution Will Not Be Televised? Media and protest movements*, New York: Berghahn Books.

Givan, R. K., Roberts, K. M. and Soule, S. A. (eds) (2010) *The Diffusion of Social Movements: Actors, mechanisms, and political effects*, Cambridge and Malden, MA: Cambridge University Press.

Imig, D. R. and Tarrow, S. (2001) *Contentious Europeans: Protest and politics in an emerging polity*, Lanham, MD: Rowman & Littlefield.

Juris, J. S. (2008) *Networking Futures: The movements against corporate globalization*, Durham, NC: Duke University Press.

Karpf, D. (2014) 'Comment on "Organization in the crowd: peer production in large-scale networked protests"', *Information, Communication and Society* 17 (2): 261–3.

Lim, M. (2013) 'Framing Bouazizi: "White lies", hybrid network, and collective/connective action in the 2010–11 Tunisian uprising', *Journalism* 14 (7): 921–941.

Mattoni, A. (2013) 'Beyond celebration: toward a more nuanced assessment of Facebook's role in Occupy Wall Street', *Fieldsights – Hot spots, cultural anthropology online*, http://www.culanth.org/fieldsights/84-beyond-celebration-toward-a-more-nuanced-assessment-of-facebook-s-role-in-occupy-wall-street (accessed 10 February 2014).

Olesen, T. (2013) '"We are all Khaled Said": visual injustice symbols in the Egyptian Revolution, 2010–2011', in N. Doerr, A. Mattoni and S. Teune (eds) *Advances in the Visual Analysis of Social Movements,* vol. 35 Research in Social Movements, Conflicts and Change, Bingley, UK: Emerald Group Publishing Limited, pp. 3–25.

Perugorría, I. and Tejerina, B. (2013) 'Politics of the encounter: cognition, emotions, and networks in the Spanish 15M', *Current Sociology* 61 (4): 424–42.

Tarrow, S. (2005) *The New Transnational Activism*, New York: Cambridge University Press.

— (2010) 'Dynamics of diffusion: Mechanisms, institutions, and scale shift', in R. K. Givan, K. M. Roberts and S. A. Soule (eds) *The Diffusion of Social Movements: Actors, mechanisms, and political effects*, Cambridge: Cambridge University Press, pp. 204–20.

— (2013) *The Language of Contention: Revolutions in words, 1688–2012*, Cambridge University Press.

Wood, L. J. (2012) *Direct Action, Deliberation, and Diffusion: Collective action after the WTO protests in Seattle*, Cambridge: Cambridge University Press.

Index

Page numbers in italics refer to Tables and Figures

acampadas 10, 12, 43, 48, 51–4, 63, 286
  assemblies, role in 51, 52–4
    consensus in 53–4, 57, 63
  as cross-time evolution 44, 57
  as democratic experiment 48, 56–7, 61–2, 63
  as new action form 57
  organisational formats 61–2, 63
  dimensions of democracy in *49, 50–1,* 61
  inclusivity/equality and 51, 61, 63
  public sphere reconstruction 50–1
  emotions, role in 54–5
  new technologies, role in 62
  'politics of becoming' in 57
  Puerta del Sol model 52
  social forums differences 48–9, 50–1, 58
    organisational models and 60
  as 'square movements' 44, 63
  see also protest camps
Adbusters 124, 127, 128, 132, 259 n.6
Agha Soltan, N., death of
  background to 77–8, 83
  Iranian de-symbolisation of 82–3, 84–5
  media presentation 78
    sacrificial theme 80–1
  social media, use of 78, 282
  as symbol of injustice 71, 72, 76, 81, 282
    character traits, role in 83–4, 85
    globalisation of 84–5
    Iranian interpretive package 77, 78–9, 80, 82, 83, 84
    political-cultural formation of 79–80, 82
    resonance infusion in 77, 82, 85
    visual dimension of 85, 282
    women's rights, role in 83, 84, 85
  US reaction to 80
Amnesty International 149, 159
anarchism 125, 126, 127–8
Apartheid (South Africa) struggle 86
Arab Spring 2, 3, 13, 72, 73, 91, 102–12, 117, 140, 172, 175, 193, 203
  diffusion dynamics of 102, 107–8, 129, 130, 146, 173, 253, 254, 261, 272
  social media, use of 259, *271*
  international significance of 91–2
  framing of 92, 96, 102
  see also European Union, protest events analysis
  as resonant event (Badiou) 125
Arendt, H. 94, 97, 110, 111
Argentina 11–12, 19, 22–3, 25
  Dirty War (1976–83)19, 20, 21, 22–3, 34
  escrache technique in 11–12, 19, 22–3, 33, 280
  see also under Spain
  financial policy (2001) 23
  piqueteros 33, 120, 267
  2001–2 crisis protests 131
austerity, protests against 2, 3–4, 5, 122, 138ff., 171, 220, 228, 229, 238, 247–8, 277ff.
  transnational diffusion of 3, 16, 48, 60, 125, 128, 129, 138–42, 175, 193–4, 255, 259, 272, 277ff.
  see also under individual countries; names of movements
autogestión 125

Balkans, protest in 254, 255, 260, 272
Barthes, R. 94, 101, 104

Biko, S. 86
Bouazizi, M. 71, 73, 74
Bosnia 3
Brazil 1, 3, 117, 122
   Free-Pass Movement (MPL) 130
   inequality in 2
   protest in 2, 132, 254, 255, 259, 260, 272
Bulgaria 3

campaign, protest 6, 7, 34, 121, 126, 129, 201
   see also European Social Forum; Global Jusice Movement; Indignados/ 15 M; World Social forums
Canada 122
Chile 23, 122
Colau, A. 28, 29, 31, 33, 34
Colectivo Situaciones 120
collective action 3, 14, 45, 196, 201
   material well-being and 279
   meaning construction in 199
   symbolic dimensions of 195, 197, 199, 221
   transnational 228–9, 231, 286, 287–8
      externalisation of 287
      localisation of 228, 231
   see also transnational contention
collective identity, construction of 197
   collective memory, role in 194–5, 196–7, 199
consensus democracy 11
crisis, economic/financial see financial global crisis (2008-)
Cuba, revolution in 45
Czech Republic 15, 227–49, 278, 279
   Afghan/Iraq war protests, effect on 229, 242
      radical left framing of 242, 243
   Czech News Agency (CNA) 229–30
   data/methods used in 229–31
      issue/framing scales 229, 230, 232–4, *237*, 243–6, *249*

   media use 15, 229–30
   protest-event analysis 229
   financial crisis in 15, 228, 229, 236, 237–8, 247
      anti-austerity protest 228, 229, 238, 247–8
      austerity measures 229, 237, 240, 247
      foreign policy changes and 240
      nationalism/populism emergence 240
      right-wing frames use in 238
   moderate left activism in 228, 229, 230, 236, 238, *239*, 240, *241*, 243, 245–7
      EU accession (2004) effect on 245
      issue framing in 245–6, 247, *249*
      social welfare reform protest 243, 245, 248
      2000–2010 protest 236, 238, *239, 241*, 243, 245, *246*
      union upwards shift in 245, 247, 248
   moderate/radical differences 228, 229, 230, 236, 238, *239*, 240, *241*, 242, 245, 248–9
   post crisis domestic economic focus 240
   Prague IMF/WB (2000) 229, 234, 235–6, 238, 240, 242, 243, 245
      economic globalisation issue 236
   protest event analysis 15, 227–49, 278, 279
   radical left activism 228, 229, 230, 236, 238, *239*, 240, *241*, 242–3, *244*
      anti-war activism 242–3, 247
      framing scale evolution *244*, 249
      national-democratic framing evolution 242, 247, 248
      2000–2010 protest participation 236, 238, *239, 241*, 243, *244*
      transnational scaling down of 243, 247–8
   socialism, transition from 228, 234
   transnational activism (2000–09) 15, 227–8, 234–6, 247–9, 279

Index | 295

decline of 240–1, 243, 247–8
global/new frames, processes of 234–5
Prague GJM (2000) effect on 235–6, 245
process milestones 234
trade unions and 234, 235, 240, 243, 247
see also left activism
Cyprus, protest in 138, *161*, 288

deliberation 10, 281
through consensus 53
deliberative democracy 5, 10, 12, 47
protest groups and 57
participatory-deliberative model 47, 280
democracy
crisis of representation 117, 122, 123–4
'real democracy', call for 117
new visions/models of 10–11
in protest movements 12, 48, 56–7, 63–4
participatory 5, 10, 11, 12, 48, 57
representative 10, 11, 12, 64
see also deliberative democracy; Real Democracy Movement (RDM)
democratisation, waves of 45
diffusion processes 2, 8, 11, 13–14, 16, 19, 20, 33, 35–6, 44, 162, 172, 194–6, 228, 254–5, 277–8
channels/pathways of 118, 198
brokerage, process of 118
memory as 198, 220–1, 281
relational/non-relational 33, 118, 173, 256, *281*, 283
concept/definition of 2, 118–19, 196
cross-border diffusion perspective 72 n.2
conditions of success 256–7
emulation/similarity attribution in 254, 256, 260, 272, 273, 282
innovators/adopters 254, 255–6
structural equivalence and 256–7, 260, 272, 282
cross-temporal perspective 194, 195–7, 280, 281–2, 284
adoption/adaptation 44–7, 61–4, 196, 280
collective identities and 195, 197, 232
collective memory, role in 194–5, 196–7, 219, 220–1, 281
see also case study under Italy
cycles/waves of contention 2, 4, 11, 172, 194, 195–6, 259, 284
framing/counter-framing and 35, 281, 282
cultural construction of 35, 197, 281
dislocation/relocation of 257
re-contextualisation and 196
initiator/spin-off movements 255
Internet/social media, role in 254, 257–9, 260, 270–2, 273, 282, 283–4, 284–5
amplifier effect of 258
'critical communities' in 254, 260
direct/indirect ties of 257–8, 272
language translation in 283–4
intra-national 254, 260, 269
as different from transnational 254, 260
spin-off/spillover movements 195
thin/thick processes of 16, 285–6
in waves of global protests *286*
transnational 5–6, 15, 19, 20, 33–4, 35, 37, 46, 91, 117–18, 188, 189, 194, 196, 227–8, 232, 269, 278, 281, 286
activist networks 118, 120, 121, 125, 132, 283, 286
cultural translation and 20–1, 34, 35, 37, 280
horizontal movement and 118, 119, 121, 125–6, 132, 194
internalisation/externalisation in 286–7
resonance pattern of 118, 119–20, 255

structural conditions and 118, 121, 188, 256–7
transmitter/adopter model 132, 172, 173, 282
see also Real Democracy Movement (RDM); transnational contention
direct democracy 52, 64, 117, 184
DRY (Democracia Real YA!) network 126, 129, 130
  digital platform of 129
  see also PAH

Eastern European, protests 13 n.2, 45, 99, 104 n.21, 107, 140ff., 255, 256
  see also Czech Republic protest analysis
economic crisis *see* financial global crisis (2008-)
Egypt 1
  Comrades from Cairo collective 132
  Khaled Said, death of 73, 84, 282
  protests/revolution in 7, 8, 10, 43, 63, 122, 125, 131, 132, 255
    Internet usage, effect on 258, 270
    Tunisian diffusion 8, 278
  Tahrir Square camps 44, 50, 54, 55, 103, 119, 125, 132, 172
    diffusion of 44, 119, 125, 131, 173, 179
    emotions in 55
    slogans used in 54
    social media use in *271*
    social relations in 56
Eliacik, I. 269
Eurobarometer surveys 123
  EU public confidence 123–4
European Central Bank 220, 287, 288
  2012 protests 288–9
European Commission 91, 123, 137 n.1, 138, 150, 198
European Court of Justice 24
European Neighbourhood Policy (ENP) 94 n.5, 99–100, 101
European Revolution (29th May 2011)
159, *160*
European Social Forum (ESF) 7, 50, 58–9, 140, 195
  democracy, conceptions of in 58
  autonomous spaces and 58
  European Preparatory Assembly 58, 59
  Florence 10+10 *see* under Italy
European Social Survey 124
European Trade Union Confederation (ETUC) 149, 234, 245
European Union (EU) protest-events analysis 6, 7, 13, 91–112, 280
  Arab Spring interpretation 92, 93, 99–112
  EU as ethical global actor 102, 103, 111
  liberal hegemonic frame 102, 103, 107, 111–12
  processualisation of 103, 107, 109–10, 111
  diffusion of 94, 102, 107–8, 109, 110
  progressive/regressive tension 96, 110
  frame-analytic reading of 94, 95, 102
  as global political actor 93, 94, 95, 97, 98, 100, 102, 103, 280
  neighbourhood/foreign policy and 94, 99–101, 102, 111
    Barcelona Process/ENP 99–100, 101, 104, 107
  political imagery, used in 98–100, 103, 110
  political legitimation 93, 94, 95, 98, 100, 101, 109
    'deep democracy' rhetoric 107
    democracy-promotion and 100–1, 105, 106, 111
    neo-liberal paradigm and 107
  self-image building 93, 95, 101, 106
European Union Strike Day (14th Nov. 2011) 160
eurozone 14, 137–8, 146, 147, 261
  crisis in 14, 123, 137–8, 141, 143, 146
  see also under Greece; Italy; Spain

event framing 93, 94–8, 102, 233
  anti-politics machine, concept of 94, 100, 104, 106
  attention capture, use for 96
  re-energisation of 96
  depoliticised speech and 97, 100 n.17, 101, 104, 106
  events/processes distinction 94, 97–8, 110
  frame analytic methodology 94–8, 102, 104
  interpretation in 95
  resonance and 95, 98
  moral ground provision of 95, 104
  see also case study, European Union; frames and framing

Facebook 76, 78, 125, 257, 259, 262, 270, 271
Ferguson, J. 94, 100
financial global crisis (2008-) 2, 3, 4, 37, 117, 122, 137–8, 139, 140, 237
  eurozone crisis 137–8, 141, 162
  neo-liberal restructuring and 138, 172
  protest waves/movements of 2, 3–4, 5, 122, 138, 171, 278, 279, 286
  anti-austerity discourse and 48
  corruption, attribution of 9
  as crisis of capitalism 172
  as 'thin' diffusion process *286*
  see also globalisation; neo-liberalism; transnational contention; under names of individual countries
frames and framing 95, 96–8, 232–3, 278
  cultural resonance in 96, 120–1
  Internet diffusion of 270–2
  issue framing, dynamics of 233–4
  local/global/national shifts in 233–4
  see also event framing
France, protest in 11, 278
French Revolution 92 n. 1, 96, 97, 99, 109

Gándara, F. 129
G8 meetings 6, 7, 15, 140, 201, 204, 209
  2001 Genoa 6, 7
Germany
  New Left, diffusion of 256
  protest in 11, 278, 289
Ghandi, M. 20, 256, 281
Global Justice Movement (GJM) 2, 4, 5, 6–7, 8–9, 16, 33, 44, 55, 128, 180, 193, 200–1, 227, 231
  consensual methods in 52, 53
  cross-time diffusion 47, 193, 194, 280
  legacies and 197, 210–12
  democracy within 61, 63, 64, 173
  direct models and 126
  development of 4, 6, 53, 58, 210–12, 231
  inspiration/influences in 120
  perceptions of change in 212–13
  discourses of 193–4
  democracy critique 194
  transnational anti-corporate 193–4
  frame-bridging activities of 9
  goals of 201, 212, 232
  neo-liberal globalisation and 212–13, 232
  localisation of 227, 231
  sectors of 201
  anti-capitalist 201, 216, 220
  anti-neoliberal 201, 212, 215, 220
  eco-pacifist 201, 215, 220
  social forums of 10–11, 12, 44, 49, 58, 215, 285, 286
  transnational diffusion of 6, 7, 9, 16, 128, 193–4, 214–15, 227, 231, 232, 235, 285, *286*, 287, 288
  counter-summits and 285
  global organisation change in 214–15, 232
  as 'thick' diffusion 285–6
  see also Italian GJM analysis; social forums; under Spain, protest activity in

globalisation 2, 117, 122, 139, 233
  financialisation and 122, 123
  market forces, dominance of 122
  neo-liberal critique and 5, 117, 138, 141, 201, 227, 233
  state power, loss of 122–3, 141
  see also financial global crisis (2008-)
Goffman, E. 95 n.8, n.9, 96, 102, 103 n.19
Greece 1, 137–63
  Aganaktismenoi (Indignados) 149, 150, *154*, 155, 173
  anarchist groups in 139, 150, 155
  European Monetary Union 140
  eurozone debt crisis 123, 127, 137–8, 142, 146, 147–8, 162, 278
  austerity laws/measures 146, 147–9, 150, 159, 160, 209, 287
  banks, role in 138, 139, 140, 146, 150, 162
    democracy, impact on 150
    IMF role in 138ff., 145ff., 150, 162
    Memorandum of Understanding (troika) 147–8
    neo-liberal policies, use of 141, 143, 149
    social effects of 150, 177
    troika' Memorandum's
    troika, pressures of 138, 146, 147, 149, 150, 159
  Golden Dawn 149, 160, 287
  Justice Groups 140, 150
  New Democracy 147
  PASOK 149
  Syntagma square occupation 119, 123, 126–7, 130, 131, 132, 155, 159, 160, 172, 259
    anarchist involvement in 126, 155
    direct democracy, call for *153, 156*
    People's Assembly 27th May 2011 *153*
    Spanish diffusion and 126, 130, 131, 132
  SYRIZA 149

  2008 uprising in 126
  2010–13 protests analysis 14, 138–63, 287
    anti-fascism in *160,* 287
    action forms/arrests in *156–7,* 159
    diffusion 141, 146–9, 162
    externalization 138, 141, 146, 159–61, 287
    inspirational sources for 130–1, 146, 149, 155
    international externalisation of *158*, 159–61, 287
    LPE dataset/coding 138, 142–3, 144–6
    Occupy movement 144, 155
    participating groups in 150, *151, 154*, 155, 162, 163
    protest campaign 138, 146–150
    protest phases of 147–9, 150, 161
    as representation crisis 123, 124
    social media/IT use in 143, 146, 155, 162
    targets/claims of protests 150, *152,* 162
    transnational contention 141–2, 161–2
    transnational features in 146–7, 149, 159–61, 162–3
    transnational solidarity 160–1, 162
    union involvement 142, 145, 147, 149, 155, 160
    violence/injury in 149, *156, 157,* 159, 163
  2012 elections 149, 150
  'piazza movement' 143, 149, 150, 155, 162
  Vio.Me Solidarity Initiative 131
Halbwachs, M. 197

Iceland 2, 129, 278
  as RDM inspiration 129
  2008 protests 3, 63, 129

Indignados/15-M movement 2, 3, 8, 10, 12, 21, 33, 35, 36, 50, 51, 53, 55, 102, 109, 110, 117, 122, 125, 129, 130, 140, 141, 227, 287
  diffusion of 146, 149, 162, 175, 255, 259, 271
  Greek protests synchronisation 159
  inspiration sources for 125, 129, 130, 173
  internalisation in 287
  organisation in 269
  public spaces, use of 51
  2011 Global Day of Action 8, 121, 122, 198, 203, 288
  see also under Spain, protest in
Indymedia 235, 283
International Atomic Energy Agency (IAEA) 79
International Monetary Fund (IMF) 6, 7, 138, 139, 141, 145, 201
  eurozone involvement 126, 127, 146, 147, 160, 162, 215, 229, 234, 236, 287, 288
Internet 1, 254, 257–9
  protest diffusion by 254, 257–8, 270–2
  usage by country 257 n.5, 270
  see also social media; social-networking
Invisible Committee 119
IT, protest use of 254, 257–9, 260, 270–2, 273, 282, 283–4, 284–5
  amplifier effect of 258
  'critical communities' in 254, 260
  direct/indirect ties of 257–8, 272
  language translation in 283–4
  see also Facebook; Internet; Twitter
Iran 13
  1979 Revolution 78, 79, 83, 105
    Rushdie *fatwa* 79
    US relations and 79
  human rights activism and 79–80
  nuclear weapons issue 79
  2009 protests 71, 72, 77–8, 85
    death of Neda Agha Soltan 71, 72, 77–8
    see also case study Agha Soltan, N.
Ireland, protest in 3, 11, 141
Israel 122
Italy
  ATTAC 200
  Disobbedienti 199, 200, 206
  economic crisis in 198, 278
    austerity measures, effect of 198, 202, 279
  FIOM 199, 202, 203
  Firenze 10+10 (2002–2012) 15, 195, 198, 199–200, 201, 202, 204, 217, 218, 219
    mnemonic project of 204
  neo-liberal sector in 199, 204, 206
  G7 counter-summit (1997) 201
  Genoa G8 summit (2001) 15, 195, 201–2
  Genoa 2001–2011 movement 195, 198, 203–5, 209–10, 214, 215, 217
    democracy as issue in 209
    event contextualisation in 205–6
    opinion vs material perception 212–13, 219
    police repression, effect of 205–6
    'We Were Right' mnemonic project 203–4
  Global Day of Action (2011) 198, 203
  GJM analysis 11, 15, 33, 49, 193, 195, 199, 200, 201–21, 279
    anniversary pessimism 216–18, 219, 220
    continuity/discontinuity perception 205–8, 210, 219
    crisis/austerity protests, effect on 198, 202–3, 212, 214, 216, 218, 219–20
    cross-temporal diffusion, concept use 195, 219, 279
    Eurocentrism and 214–16, 217
    group networks in 201, 209
    interviews/focus group methodology 195, 198, 199–201
    Iraq war, effect on 206, 207, 211

localisation of 210–11, 212, 214, 219
memory context in 197–8, 199, 204, 219, 220–1, 279
movement decline, perception of 205, 206–8, 210–11
neo-liberal globalisation action of 201, 204, 212, 219
Rete Lilliput 199
Rifondazione Comunista 199, 200, 207

Karyotis, T. 131
Klein, N. 55

Latin America 20, 23, 33, 34, 44, 45, 130, 138, 139
  see also acampadas; Argentina; Brazil; Chile
left activism 228–9
  Afghanistan/Iraq wars, effect of 229
  fall of communism, effect on 228
  financial crisis, effect on 229
  modes of 228
  see also study under Czech Republic
Libya 104, 255
Lorenz, E. N. 253

McAdam, S. 19, 20, 34, 118, 121, 131, 138, 172, 194, 195, 196, 201, 255, 256
media, mass 62, 197, 227
  diffusion processes, role in 20, 76, 193, 283
  injustice-symbol formation 75
  see also Internet; social media
Mediterranean, protests 45, 92, 93, 94, 98–101, 106–7, 117, 140, 161, 162
Mexico 122
  Zapatistas 33, 120, 130
    transnational diffusion of 130

neo-liberalism 5, 6, 101, 117, 122, 138, 139–40, 172, 183, 227
  global capital markets and 122, 139
  inequality, growth of 117, 124, 139
  protest activity against 212–13, 231, 232
  restructuring phases 139–40

Obama, B. 80, 124, 240 n.7, 243
Occupy London (2011) analysis 14, 171–89, 278, 279
  'Bank of Ideas' in 175, 176
  constitution of 181–2
  horizontal structure of 176, 188
  impact of 174, 188, 279
  inspiration for 173, 175, 179, 180–1, 187, 188–9
    Wall St. protests and 14, 171, 174, 175, 179, 188
  internal characteristics of 171
  interviews/survey data used in 171, 178, 182
  media attention to 174, 176, 181, 182, 183
  modest size of 177–8
  as movement of consciousness 185–7, 188
  narrative analysis 181–7
    anti-capitalist label 181, 183–4
    anti-materialism in 185–6
    economic and social inequality 178, 179, 180, 183, 188
    ideological character and 181–3
    protest, sustaining of 183
  participants in 171, 177, 178–9, 180
  political themes and activism in 178–9, 181–2, 185–6, 188, 279
  prefigurative ethos of 184–5, 188
  St. Paul's camp in 175–7, 179, 183
Occupy movement 8, 122, 123, 132, 140, 172
  diffusion of 146, 259 n.6, 268
  Greek protests synchronisation 159
  '99 Percent' frame of 120–1, 179, 209, 259
  representation crisis, response to 123
  social media use *271*
  2011 global protests of 132
  see also under United States

PAH (Platform of Mortgage Victims) 12, 20–36, 129–30
  assemblies in 130
  inspiration sources for 129–30
  organisation of 130
PAH protest analysis 12, 20–36
  criminalisation and 29, 32
  democratic deficit and 21, 25, 32, 35, 36
  discourse analysis, used in 22–3
  escrache frame, use of 12, 21, 25–37
    Argentinian diffusion and 21, 25, 26, 33, 36
    dictatorship comparison 26–7, 35
    ETA comparison and 28, 29, 35
    manual strategy and 30, 32
    as a moral frame 32, 34–5, 36
    provocative interviews strategy 31–2
    public statements strategy 30–1
  ILP proposals 24–5, 31
  media, role in 21, 27, 30, 36
  slogans, used in 25–6
  state/media counter-framing 27–9, 32–3, 35
Pakistan, Taliban activity in 71
People's Global Action (PGA) 235
Pew Research Global Attitudes Project 124
Pieterson, H. 86
Platform of Mortgage Victims *see* PAH
Platform for those Affected by Mortgages (PAH) 12, 21
  see also under Spain
  police 15, 29, 74, 86, 126, 131, 145, 146, 149, 159, 175, 177, 202, 203, 230, 282
  Greek killing by 143, 144, 147
  London Occupy tactics of 174ff., 178, 188
  Taksim protests 262, 263, 265ff., 270
Portugal, protest in 288

protest, concept of 45
protest camps 9–10, 11, 63, *286*
  participatory democracy in 10
  see also acampadas
  protest campaign *see* campaigns, protest
protest-event analysis 15, 142, 144, 229
  large (LPEs) use of 142
  protest event definition 229
  violent protest-event 75
  see also case studies Czech Republic; European Union
protest policing *see* police
Poland, Solidarity Movement 255
Portugal 11
  financial crisis in 138
  2011 demonstration 3, 142
  Facebook, role in 3
public spaces 48, 50
  protests in 48, 49, 55, 56
    democratic values of 49, 63
    emotional ties of 55–6
  reclaiming/occupying of 50, 51, 56, 125, 172
  as new social visions 57
  see also acampadas; protest camps; squares, occupation of

Quinatoa, A. 129–30

Rajoy, M. 31
Real Democracy Movement (RDM)
  analysis 118, 119
  direct democracy in 129
  frames used by 120, 121
  as global movement 121
    Global Day of Action (2011) 8, 121, 122, 198, 203
    representation crisis response 123–4
  as horizontal network 119, 121
  methodological framework 121–2
  state/party autonomy in 128
    anarchist activism 125, 126, 127–8

transnational diffusion of 119, 121, 129–34
  activist networks 125, 126, 128, 132, 133, 283
  cross-directional relationships 119
  as horizontal movement 125, 132
  inspiration, multiple sources of 128–32
  linear conception of 132–3, 283
  resonance, use of concept in 120–1, 132, 133
  rhizome concept and 119, 258, 283
  shared structural conditions 122–4, 128, 132, 133
  as wave of transmission/reception 130–1
Reclaim the Streets 235
representation, crisis of 117, 123–4, 128
  social inequality and 124
revolution(s)/uprisings 92, 96, 97, 99, 111, 273
  global revolution frame 97
  imagery of 97, 99, 104–5
  1989 revolutions 99, 105, 109, 110, 234, 255
ROAR Magazine 122–3
Rucht, D. 19, 20, 34, 118, 121, 138, 172, 196, 255, 256
media, mass
Ruiz, C. 130

Said, K. 73, 84
Singh, J. 71, 74
Slovenia 57
social forums 10–11, 12, 48–51, 54, 285
  consensus, emphasis of 48, 57, 58
  democracy critique within 58–60, 64
  vertical v. horizontal visions 59–60
  dimensions of democracy in *49*, 50
  inclusivity and *49*, 50
  downward diffusion of 228
  format of 49–50, 51
  frame-bridging in 54
  networking in 48, 50

see also Global Justice Movement; under Turkey, Gezi protests
social media 62, 270–2, 282–3
  cross-border diffusion 73, 76, 173, 254, 257–9, 270–2, 273, 282–3
  example/success story, use of 235, 273
  as 'thin' diffusion 286
  injustice-symbols formation 71, 86, 282
  protest participation, effect on 62, 170
  SmaPP data 270, 271
  see also Internet
social movement organisation 45, 46–7, 58–64, 280
  cultural changes and 47, 61–2, 280
  democratic structures in 58–60, 63
  innovations in 63
  vertical v. horizontal models 59–61, 63, 117
  diffusion and *see* diffusion processes
  environmental selection in 45–6
  learning processes/adaptation in 48, 49, 57, 61–4, 280, 281
  new technologies, effect on 46, 62, 283–4
  strategic action of 45, 47, 63
  prefigurative politics 46–7
social movement studies 2, 5, 45–6, 277–90
  diffusion, concept of *see* diffusion processes
  emotional/cultural turn in 72
  frame analysis 15, 93–8
    see also event framing; frames and framing
  localisation/nationalisation and 227–8
  organisational sociology and 46–7, 61
    cultural changes and 61–2
  resonance, concept of 119–121
    frame resonance and 120–1
  resource-mobilisation approach 45
  selective diffusion, research on 277–80

negative cases 279
opportunities v. crisis distinction 278–9
transnational *see* transnational contention
social-networking 1, 6, 8–9, 57, 62, 142, 162, 286
  acampadas, use in 48–9, 62
  focus groups and 208
  injustice-symbols promotion of 76, 86
  online 258, 260, 262, 267, 271, 282-
  social forums, use of 8, 48
  see also Facebook; social media; Twitter
solidarity protests 131, 144, 160, 176, 181–2, 261ff., 266, 267, 273, 287
Southern Europe 10, 45, 138, 141ff., 261, 282, 287
sovereignty 7, 14, 146, 150, 242
Soviet Union 256, 278
  East European revolutions (1989) 255, 256, 260, 278
Spain, protest activity in 1, 43, 142
  #AcampadaSol 125
  diffusion, role in 8, 21, 33, 130, 131
    Argentinian *escrache* tactic 12, 21, 33, 34, 280
    see also PAH protest analysis
  economic crisis, role in 3, 23–4, 37, 123, 287
    eurozone debt and 123
    housing, effect on 23–4, 129, 280
    unemployment and 23, 24, 123
    see also PAH protest analysis
  escrache feminista 37
  EU public confidence in 123–4
  Global Justice Movement in 33
  15-M/Indignados movement 2, 3, 8, 10, 12, 21, 33, 35, 36, 50, 51, 53, 55, 102, 109, 110, 125, 129, 172, 179, 198, 217, 218, 220, 267
    DRY platform 126, 129, 130
    2011 (May 15th) march 123
    see also Indignados/15-M

Okupa movement 125
Puerta del Sol camp 3, 10, 12, 43, 49, 50, 52, 55, 56, 119, 125, 127, 130, 132, 179, 259
representation crisis and 123
Right to Decent Housing Movement (2011–13) 19, 23, 34
squatter networks 33
squares, occupation of 3, 10, 11, 50, 52, 117, 172–3
  democracy in 53, 63
  collective identity in 55
  emotional reactions 55–6
  equality and democracy themes in 173
  as a political movement in 173, 181
  transmitter/adoption model and 173
  see also public spaces; Take the Square collective
strikes 126, 143, 147, 149, 238, 243, 278–9
  general 3, 14, 149
symbol, definition of 73–4
symbolism and protest 12–13, 71–86
  cross-border diffusion of 71, 72, 75, 85–6
  activist role in 76, 85
  dramatic process of 75, 76, 86
  global resonance generation 75, 76, 77, 84
  interpretive packages, use of 73, 77, 85
  meaning adaptation in 71, 73, 75, 76–7, 85
  dead activists, use of 12–13, 71
  injustice-symbols, formation 13, 71, 72, 73–5, 76, 86, 282
  agency in 74–5
  injustice frames, use of 74
  new technologies, role in 72–3, 86
  visibility creation in 75, 86
  see also case study Agha Soltan, N.; violent person events
Syria 73, 94, 255
  Hamza al-Khateeb, death of 73

Take the Square collective 122, 125, 129
Tarrow, S. 71, 75, 93, 118, 121, 123, 138, 139, 140, 141, 142, 161, 162, 163, 173, 194, 196, 228, 231, 232, 281ff.
Teivainen, T. 58
Tilly, C. 34, 93, 137, 138, 141, 142, 144, 161, 162, 163, 229, 232
Torreblanca, J. I. 124
transnational contention 138, 139–42, 161–3, 188, 230–1, 277, 285
   diffusion in *see* under diffusion processes
   downwards/upwards scale-shifts 227–9, 232
      scale-shift, concept of 228
   internal/external categories of change in 232, 286, 287
   international against capitalism 230–1
      national/local scale of 231
   issues and framing in 232–3
      basic directions of 233
   localisation of 231, 232, 233
   meganetworks in 141–2, 162
   organisation features of 140–1, 162
   phases of 139–42, 161
   post 2010 protests 141, 142
   see also diffusion processes; financial global crisis (2008-)
troika *see* under Greece
Tunisia, protests in 7, 8, 71, 104, 142, 255, 278
   death of Bouazizi 71, 73, 74, 255, 282
Turkey, Gezi protests (2013) analysis 2, 15–16, 132, 253–4, 259–73
   cultural legitimacy of 273
   data/interviews, use in 253
   diffusion in 15–16, 259–60, 264, 270–2
      emulation/similarity attribution in 254, 256, 260, 272, 273, 282
      innovators/adopters in 254, 255–6
      Internet/social media role in 270–2
      intra-national 15, 16, 265, 266, 269–70, 271, 273
      trans-national 265, 266–7, 269, 271, 273
      structural equivalence and 256–7, 260, 272, 282
   distinctive character of 260, 269–70, 272
      Gezi spirit template in 264, 267, 269
      pre-existing urban struggles 260, 261, 272
      street *iftars*, action of 269–70, 273
   economic/political background to 261
      shared Erdogan resentment in 264–5
   framing in 254, 266, 270–1, 273
      Occupy frame 265, 271
      'resistance' (*Diren!*) frame 15–16, 264, 265, 270–1, 273
   Gezi Park area demolition plans 261–2
   Internet/social media, role in 253, 259, 260, 269, 270–2, 273, 282
      hashtag, use of 270, 271
      police violence visuals 262–3, 270
      % informed through 270
      SmaPP report 270
   KONDA surveys 253, 263, 270
   participants in 263–4, 270
      networks of groups 264
   public forums of 266–9, 271
      co-ordination groups 268
      decision-making in 268–9
      global resonance of 272
      number of protests in 266
   state coercion, use of 263, 266, 267, 269, 273
      victims of 266
   Taksim Square, use of 119, 261, 262, 266, 269, 270
      commune spirit in 267
   Taksim Solidarity 261, 263, 267

Twitter 76, 125, 257, 259, 262, 270, 271, 284
  hashtag connections, use of 284
  Occupy Wall Street study 284

Ukraine, revolutions in 99, 103, 107, 278
unions, European 149, 150, 155, 162, 188, 201, 202, 203, 229, 230, 234–5, 238, 240, 243, 245, 247, 288
United Kingdom
  Anti-Roads Movement 33, 34
  Camps for Climate Action 180, 183, 189
  'Democracy Village' in 182
  direct action protests in 171
  financial crisis (2008-) 171, 177, 179, 180, 187
  Occupy London *see* Occupy London (2011) analysis 14, 171–89
  protests in 11, 14, 174, 188
  2011–12 expectations 174
  Suffrage Movement 256
  UK Uncut 174, 182
United States 1, 94, 101
  American New Left 256
  civil rights movement in 20, 196, 256
  financial crisis (2008-) 122, 124, 137
  hegemony of 109
  Occupy Boston 57
  Occupy Wall Street 2, 3, 14, 43, 53, 55, 56–7, 117, 120, 124, 127, 128, 174, 175, 178, 188, 193, 194, 198, 203, 209, 218, 227, 253, 254, 255, 259, 263, 267, 272
    anarchist inspiration in 127, 128, 129
    demands of 173
    global actions of 159–60, 288
    Internet usage, effect of 259, 271
    organisation in 269, 284
    transnational diffusion and 128, 129, 132, 175, 194, 253, 254
    Twitter study 284
  protest movements in 10, 53, 63, 122, 127
  anti-austerity actions 127
  student movements 256
  Wall Street crash (2008) 122, 124
  Zuccotti Park, use of 51, 119, 177, 259

Viejo, R. 128
violent person-events 71, 73, 74, 75
  activist promotion of 76, 86
  arrests 29, *157*, 159, 163
  chemicals used (tear gas, etc) 145, 147, 149
  injuries 71, 74, *157*, 159, 163
  moral shock arousal of 74, 75, 84
  North/South interchange of 73
  see also symbolism and protest

web-platforms, participatory 8
World Bank 6, 139, 210, 229
World Economic Forum, Davos 140
World Social Forums 7, 8, 49, 50, 58, 59, 140, 201, 203–4
  charter of 49
  Porto Alegre (2001) 201
  power relations and 58
World Trade Organization (WTO) 2, 140, 141, 201
  1999 summit demonstration 2, 4, 6, 140, 201, 231
Yemen 255
YouTube 76, 78, 83
Yousafzai, M. 71, 74

www.ingramcontent.com/pod-product-compliance
Lightning Source LLC
Chambersburg PA
CBHW071343290426
44108CB00014B/1429